Upward Mobility and the Common Good

Upward Mobility
and the Common Good

TOWARD A LITERARY HISTORY
OF THE WELFARE STATE

Bruce Robbins

PRINCETON UNIVERSITY PRESS

PRINCETON AND OXFORD

Copyright © 2007 by Princeton University Press
Published by Princeton University Press, 41 William Street, Princeton,
New Jersey 08540
In the United Kingdom: Princeton University Press, 3 Market Place,
Woodstock, Oxfordshire OX20 1SY

LIBRARY OF CONGRESS CATALOGING-IN-PUBLICATION DATA

Upward mobility and the common good : toward a literary history of
the welfare state / Bruce Robbins.
p. cm.
ISBN-13: 978-0-691-04987-8 (cloth : alk. paper)
ISBN-10: 0-691-04987-4 (cloth : alk. paper)
1. Sex in literature. 2. Mentoring in literature. 3. Welfare state in literature.
4. Fiction—20th century—History and criticism. 5. Fiction—19th century—
History and criticism. I. Robbins, Bruce.
PN3352.S48U69 2007
809'.93355—dc22 2006050255

British Library Cataloging-in-Publication Data is available

This book has been composed in Sabon

Printed on acid-free paper. ∞

press.princeton.edu

Printed in the United States of America

10 9 8 7 6 5 4 3 2 1

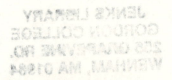

My father stood outside the bus that day, his hat—a gray fedora—in his hands; helpless as I left the only world he would ever know. . . . there was no metamorphosis possible for him. So we never spoke of this parting, or of the pain in his beautiful eyes as the bus left him there by that lonely Georgia highway, and I moved—blinded by tears of guilt and relief—ever farther and farther away.
    —*Alice Walker, "My Father's Country Is the Poor"*

The welfare state does not seem able to arouse strong loyalties. . . . it seems easier, if not more intelligent, to die for the Stars and Stripes, or the Proletarian Fatherland, than for unemployment insurance and social security. There are fewer subrational loyalties, and perhaps no encompassing mystique, for the welfare state to exploit.
                    —*Irving Howe,* Beyond the Welfare State

The idea of a benefactor captured her—and she wondered who her benefactor would be. The convict or the unmarried woman. The Black or the white. Both perhaps. . . . Who would she choose were she given the choice: Miss Havisham or Abel Magwitch?
                    —*Michelle Cliff,* Abeng

Contents

Someone Else's Life

Woody Allen tells the story of being a civil rights worker about to be lynched by the Ku Klux Klan. His whole life flashes before his eyes. He sees images of himself buying some gingham for Emmy Lou, swimming in the old swimming hole, and cooking up a mess o' catfish (the o' is accented). Suddenly he realizes—it's not his own life he's seeing. It's someone else's.

I considered giving this book the title "Someone Else's Life." The tribute would have been in part to Woody Allen, who grew up on the same Brooklyn street as my father and, as local boy made good, became a source of pride as well as entertainment and philosophical instruction for me, my parents, and my siblings. Pride of this sort was not to be counted on in my family. My grandfather, running into Woody Allen's father one day in Florida, where they had both retired, bragged that his son, my father, was in textiles and doing very well. "And your boy?" he asked. "Still writing jokes?"

The other lives to which I would have paid tribute by means of that title, and to which (having opted for a more pedestrian and informative title) I am now attempting to pay tribute without it, belong to my parents. The first upward mobility stories I heard, the ones I have never managed to stop thinking about, were theirs. As I was growing up, much was said about what they had gone through during the Depression. When they were barely teenagers, one in Brooklyn, one in the Bronx, each was already the main source of income for their struggling families. They had stories about evictions, stories about being humiliated in front of the butcher and the grocer. Poverty was not always ennobling. My father's family was not always on the right side of the law. My mother's family sometimes relied on assistance from unnamed institutions. My grandmother was ashamed to be seen taking handouts, so my mother and her sister were sent with a wagon to bring home the free flour, rice, and beans. Even as my parents hauled themselves into respectability in the boom years of the 1950s, damaged lives surrounded them, demanding their help. When Uncle Willie had to skip town, he hid in a doorway across the street from the bank while my father withdrew all but $100 of his skimpy savings. The effort to keep the extended family's heads above water never seemed to end. By comparison, my brother and sister and I were coddled, and we knew it. Making this known to us was one of the standard evasive measures our parents took to ward off the worst of the inevitable spoiling—assigning chores, encouraging jobs, offering little lectures against conspicuous consumption. They were never obnoxious about contrasting how hard their childhoods had been and how soft ours were. On the contrary, they were grateful that things had worked out so well. But the contrast was there.

Obnoxiousness isn't easy to avoid. In a sense, this book does nothing more than try to understand the surprising human magnanimity and narrative grace by which upward mobility stories somehow manage *not* to be obnoxious.

Upward mobility stories are routinely described as "inspiring." But is "inspiring" the right word for how readers feel if and when they worry, as most have reason to, that they themselves may fall short of the success they are asked to contemplate? What if there is no way you can qualify, having benefited from an otherwise enviable degree of comfort at an early age? What if, wherever you set out from, you do not seem to be on your way to becoming a star in your chosen field of endeavor, and this despite your best efforts? What if you are now looking back on missing efforts, efforts that at the time you didn't think to make? Under all sorts of circumstances, being on the receiving end of a rags-to-riches, star-is-born story would seem most likely to result not in inspiration, but in a sense of personal deficiency. If you have been too fortunate, you may feel a paradoxical sense of personal misfortune. Anyone who has ever heard an upward mobility story without having one to tell in return may well suspect that these stories are rhetorical weapons designed for the ruthless seizure of moral advantage.

This is one profound lesson of Monty Python's "Four Yorkshiremen" sketch, a series of reminiscences about childhood poverty exchanged over a bottle of expensive wine at a Hawaiian resort. Eric Idle says his family used to live in a tiny house with holes in the roof. "Ee, tha were lucky," Graham Chapman replies. *His* family—a family of a hundred and twenty six—lived in one room. Terry Gilliam says they were lucky to *have* a room. *His* family lived in a corridor. Michael Palin says a corridor would have been a palace to him. He and his family lived in a water tank in a garbage dump surrounded by rotting fish. Idle backtracks—by "house" he only meant a hole in the ground. Chapman says his family was evicted from their hole in the ground. They went to live in a lake. The lake seems like a sure winner. But it is trumped by a shoe box. The shoe box does not end the conversation.[1]

This race to the bottom is of course still very much a race. It's not just that the claim to low social origins, like the child-crushing fable of the parent's expandable three- or five- or ten-mile walk to school through a perennial snowstorm, is not always gospel truth. The point here is that reverse snobbery is still snobbery, a way of scoring points. This is one sense in which the present book would have to be described as "literary," though it deals with a sociological topic and with nonliterary narratives as well as novels. I have allowed myself to be guided by the Pythons' insight. I assume that whatever it may be to the sociologists, upward mobility is also a story. And I assume that in this story, the initial state of economic deprivation represents a perverse sort of capital, capital that can only be realized by being shown off to others. Rather than asking how many people really have upward mobility stories to boast of and how representative they are of the population at large (the answer is: not very), I skip straight to the act of boasting. Reverse snobbery is more mysterious than it may first appear. If ostentatious poverty is a move in a narrative game, one suddenly wants very much to know what sort of game this is. Why is it, after all, that one-upmanship like this ("one-down-manship" has been suggested as an alternative) is considered to *work*? Why does the listener feel obliged to admit that points have successfully been scored? Is it just that the greater the distance climbed, the larger the bragging rights for the achievement? If so, upward mobility stories would probably be greeted with more overt and unmixed hostility. It seems probable, then, that something less obvious is at work here, some hidden principle of sociability that rewards self-narrating social climbers for *not* hiding or forgetting their humble origins, some pride that can be shared, some trick of the imagination by which the reader can be included in those humble origins. In one way or another, every successful storyteller must always be factoring in the likely effects of his or her story on someone whose life has been different. Isn't there a sense, then, in which "someone else's life," assumed to be a very different life, would have to be built into the upward mobility story's structure and tone?

The rediscovery of class, which got a brief boost from Hurricane Katrina and the flooding of New Orleans in 2005, has in fact been going on for some years, both in the culture at large (for example, in the recent *New York Times* series "Class Matters") and in academic conferences and journals.[2] We may think we know why class is usually ignored. It's worth speculating about why class is remembered when it *is* remembered. The answer may have something to do with the pleasure taken in upward mobility stories.

One of the benefits of this recent remembering has been to encourage fresh questions about where upward mobility stories are to be found and what actually happens when they are told, whether in literature or in life. Accustomed to categories like "coming-of-age" or "coming-to-America," we may need to reacquire the habit of thinking that these even *are* upward mobility stories. But when that label is polemically thrust upon them, we are likely to be pleasantly surprised at how much richer and less predictable these stories become. For instance, contemporary nonfiction classics like Carolyn Steedman's *Landscape for a Good Woman* and Richard Rodriguez's *Hunger of Memory*, which have won their place in the undergraduate classroom for their insightful treatment of gender and ethnicity respectively, now look more like upward mobility stories, and indeed stories in which disadvantages like gender and ethnicity become (among other things) a kind of resource, a means by which the protagonist's social status can be renegotiated upward.

Since by definition they follow selected individuals up and out, leaving the majority behind, upward mobility stories are not an ideal way of talking about class struggle or class solidarity. But they are a way in which class is frequently discussed, and that alone would make them interesting. The working premise of this book, unsurprisingly, is that they are quite a useful way. This is not so much because they get any given class identity right; that rarely seems to be their object. (In any case, class does not lend itself to distinct identity any more than to opaque otherness.) And it's not because they encourage revolutionary demands. They don't. It's because, by focusing on the passage *between* identities and how one gets from here to there, they reveal something important about power, which can never be located within one identity alone. In a sense, then, while falling short of both sociological accuracy and revolutionary transcendence, they might be described as speaking to class as a specifically *political* concept. Politics, as Antonio Gramsci observed, brings out what is common to different classes, forced upon them by the common obstacles they confront, the historical compromises they accept, the shared goals they strive for. It is not to be expected that the identity of any class can emerge from these common struggles unchanged.

Politics offers one line of approach to the question of what exactly we are supposed to *do* with class once we've rediscovered it. Fortunately it is now possible to admit to some productive confusion on this issue. In a 2005 essay in the journal *N+1*, Walter Benn Michaels suggests that in some recent fiction, the "solution" proposed for "class privilege" is that "poor people shouldn't be made to feel inferior, in novels or in life" (71). It's as if the problem were not poverty and what to do about it, but only the feelings that accompany poverty, feelings that can presumably be assuaged, Michaels notes, without any drastic changes to the structures of the social world.[3] Of course, feelings do matter, and precisely because they prepare people to try to change (or on the contrary resign themselves to accepting) the structures of the world. Michaels's point seems to be that even at the level of feelings, there are more various and significant options than respect or disrespect. I agree. This book will therefore focus on an alternative gamut of class-related feelings, political or politicizable. Some of these are obvious, like anger. Some are less obvious, like boredom, an "aristocratic" sentiment that seems interestingly out of place in Balzac's and Stendhal's nineteenth-century classics of upward mobility. Also less obvious is the set of feelings, not always as decorous as they may seem, that are associated with caring for others, whether officially or unofficially.

Somewhere between the extremes of caring and boredom lie what are probably the most important feelings for the purpose of my argument: erotic ones. "Erotic" may not always be the most precise word. This will be clear from my starting point: the relationship between Hannibal Lecter and Clarice Starling in *The Silence of the Lambs*. I don't claim to know the proper word for this inconclusive though highly charged not-quite-alliance. Yet there is nothing terribly unfamiliar about it. We have all seen many versions and degrees of the intimacy that, as in *The Silence of the Lambs*, brings together a younger person on the way up with another who is socially established, more powerful, perhaps inclined to help, perhaps inclined to help only for a price. We have probably all vacillated between cynical and less cynical readings of such intimacy. We know that social climbing seeks shelter in love stories, where it can hide its true colors. What better camouflage for the pursuit of social advantages than to make them seem the unintended result of pairing up with the boss or the boss's daughter, hence as natural and innocent as falling in love? This is just a love story, isn't it? Do we really have to look under the hood? On the other hand, who can keep from entertaining the mean-spirited hypothesis that the drive toward the final tender embrace is fueled by high-octane ambition?

Where relationships like this are concerned, cynicism and sentimental self-forgetfulness seem equally unavoidable. Yet neither can satisfactorily account for the erotic component in upward mobility. What is needed is a willingness to be a bit unconventional about both erotics and politics. Like the unnameable relation of Lecter and Starling, the peculiar varieties of attachment that gravitate to upward mobility seem engineered, on the one hand, to keep us from seeing in such relations nothing but love. On the other hand, they also seem intended to keep us from identifying the ambition we see there with nothing but self-interest. To put this in another vocabulary, upward mobility stories might be said to specialize in "unnatural" love—provisional, frustrating, often unconsummated matchups that do not aim at or end in marriage, reproduction, or heterosexual union of any sanctioned or enduring sort. If ordinary heterosexual unions can be said to make upward mobility seem natural, and thus to naturalize as well the value of the society toward which upward mobility tends, then anything that rules out natural or normal coupling would seem to *de*naturalize both. Politically speaking, the denaturalizing of upward mobility's society of destination is a narrative twist of some importance.

From this perspective, the nineteenth-century novel's tendency to pair older women with younger men, or younger men with older men of uncertain sexual inclination, comes to seem intriguingly continuous with recent attention to illicit erotic involvements that link coaches, bosses, ministers, teachers, therapists, and other trusted representatives of society with those placed under their authority—in other words, with what has come to be classified as sexual abuse and sexual harassment. Taking the liberty of putting the moral and legal urgencies of such cases on hold, this juxtaposition is intended to launch a larger historical narrative that can shed light on our considerable current interest in sexualized abuses of authority.[4] I will be telling a story about the "unnatural" emergence of the institutions of modern social democracy, institutions that could come into existence only by taking over some of the functions and responsibilities that used to be seen as natural to the individual and the family. So-called welfare institutions, however imperfectly they have delivered on their promises, offer the version of the common good within which, I argue, most of the upward mobility genre makes the most sense.

My analysis of the genre's erotic mechanism will suggest that the new society the protagonist seeks to enter is not merely a featureless and uninteresting "status quo," as so many readings seem to assume it must be. It will suggest that the social destination is as unnatural as the bizarre social bonding that facilitates the transition upward, and unnatural in some of the same ways.[5] In this interpretation, the motives of the protector and protégé, however ambiguous, are freed up from the prevailing cynicism and thus allowed to become allegorical of social hypotheses. If what exists between them may be love, for example, and if the motives of love are at least conceivably disinterested, then the hypothesis emerges that, despite the protagonist's apparent self-interest, the society the upward mobility story aims at may also involve some degree of disinterestedness. In other words, reading upward mobility stories may be deviously teaching us not to be self-reliant and self-interested, as is usually taken for granted. It may be teaching us to think about the common good.

If so, then the upward mobility genre may be thought of as accomplishing an unexpected sort of cultural-political labor. Modern social democracy could not have come into existence, even to the limited extent that it has, unless it was first desired, unless it could become the personally wished-for project of a multitude of protocitizens. Even today, it must be desired (again within those limits) in order to be sustained. Desire does not require idealizing; social democracy's flaws, failings, residual hierarchies, and spineless compromises can and must remain in the picture. Still, the desire *for* upward mobility stories, I argue, has much to do with the desire *in* upward mobility stories, and both have to do with social democracy. Beginning with the young Jean-Jacques's relations with Mme de Warens in Rousseau's *Confessions*, I will draw a line from what might be called "bad sex," which the father of democratic theory describes with strange zest, to something that might be called good citizenship. Thickening this narrative with commentaries on various novels and memoirs of the nineteenth and twentieth centuries, I will follow it to the more responsible version of good citizenship that T. H. Marshall called "social citizenship." Thus, after a long detour, I will try to bring the argument circuitously back from class as a domain of actually existing feeling to class as a domain of potential and urgently needed legislation.

Though it plays a bit fast and loose with the concept of the erotic, this narrative should not sound entirely perverse. One article in the *New York Times'* "Class Matters" series presents the story of an African American single mother of five who is saved from welfare and poverty thanks to the love of a good man.[6] But another *Times* article, one year earlier, had offered the story of a Mexican American who rose out of poverty thanks to the help of a good union.[7] From the viewpoint of the narrative, a man's love and a trade union's help occupy the same structural slot. It's the slot itself, the function of the patron or benefactor, that is eroticized. One can therefore expect to find strong and complex emotions attached to objects other than eligible erotic partners, objects that include collectivities and institutions as well as apparently ineligible people. The somewhat forceful phrase "erotic patronage," which serves as the title to chapter 1, in fact covers the formal argument of the book as a whole. On the formal level, this book argues that the emotional center of an upward mobility story lies not in its protagonist but in the protagonist's relation with a patron, mentor, or benefactor, a figure who stands between two worlds, who can both help and obstruct the passage between them, and who therefore elicits an emotional complexity, somewhere in the middle of the story, at least equivalent to the passion associated with trophy wives and husbands at the end.

If a display of modest origins can be a form of immodesty, a display of patrons, mentors, and benefactors can be a form of humility. This reverse ostentation insists that, whatever the official ideology of individualism may say, this has not been a story of heroic self-reliance alone. In still another sense, it says that one person's upward mobility is really someone else's story.

That is what I was taught at home. My father spoke with a special reverence about the boss who gave him his first real break. The boss, Louis Hand, had moved up from a pushcart on the Lower East Side to found the business for which my father sold curtains. When I was taken to see Mr. Hand, long after his retirement, he seemed to me very small and shriveled-looking, an old man out of place in a very, very large house. I didn't see the glamor that had emboldened my father. But there was some of the same glamor and some of the same gratitude in my father's stories about the Army Air Corps, and before that about Brooklyn Tech. My mother expressed her indebtedness to the incipient institutions of welfare that got her family through the hard times both before and after her father fell off a scaffold while on a construction job. Nothing in their lives suggested that these diverse individual and institutional objects of gratitude, private and public, could be boiled down to any one principle of goodness.

The texts, however, are more coherent. If this book has a real surprise in it, it's the connection that the canon displays between upward mobility and the historically particular version of the common good embodied in the welfare state. This is an unexpected fact about both the canon and the welfare state. We are accustomed to thinking of the welfare state and upward mobility as almost antithetical. For people of my generation, the phrase "upward mobility story" is likely to recall, for example, Justice Clarence Thomas's notorious contrast between his own hardy independence and the parasitism of his "welfare queen" sister, who supposedly sat home all day waiting for the postman to deliver her check from the government. The large and counterintuitive thing I have discovered in my study of recognized narrative claims to hardy independence is how much they, too, turn out to be stories of reliance on others, stories that reach out to others, and thus an unexpected part of our society's unfinished education in how to pay heed to the common good.

Of course, the common good cannot be restricted to the citizens of a single state. If the Pythons' comically insistent discrimination of initial poverties has become inescapable analytic business, if the rules of the game of upward mobility have never seemed so resistant to the understanding, it's also because of the inescapably global situation in which upward mobility, like everything else, must now be situated. "We were poor," the Dominican narrator of Junot Diaz's *Drown* tells us. "The only way we could have been poorer was to have lived in the campo or to have been Haitian immigrants." It's as if his family were playing a Pythonesque game: how poor were we? "At least you're not in the campo," he is told by his grandmother. "You'd eat rocks there." Well, the narrator says, "We didn't eat rocks but we didn't eat meat or beans, either" (70).[8] One reason why it has become so hard to talk about class without getting caught up in this tragi-comic game of comparisons is the Haitian immigrants to the Dominican Republic, or rather what they stand for: a global economic system in which everyone knows that no matter how badly off they are, there are others, here or elsewhere, who may be still worse off. As we learn from Immanuel Wallerstein, among others, the existence of capitalism as a world system prevents us from thinking of class as if it ever possessed a fully transparent meaning in any given locality. It is worth speculating that the literary shape of *Drown*, which rejects chronological order so as to put the son's bitter disillusionment-with-America story first, and the father's triumphant coming-to-America story last, is a way of rewriting upward mobility so as both to refuse it and embrace it. I suspect I may have done something similar myself.

As I've said, this is a "literary" book, a book written by a literary critic. It is not so much about upward mobility as about upward mobility stories. Many of these stories are literary in the strong sense—canonical works of fiction. Others are works of nonfiction, which is to say literary in a weaker sense. The works of nonfiction, too, are more or less aware of the threat of obnoxiousness. They too are buffeted by other impulses. They too experiment with appropriate or less appropriate tones, shape and perhaps exaggerate experience, fall into rhetorical and narrative structures that will sometimes recall the bragging and joking that takes place in ordinary conversation. The people I've most often had in mind when I wrote have been people who study and care about literature. But I hope others who are interested in making sense of upward mobility, like my family, will find something here as well. This is not a "how to" book, but the book does contain an answer to the question of "how to succeed." It's an answer first of all about how people succeed in stories, but it's not irrelevant to life in general.

This book has been a long time in the writing, and that means I have probably forgotten a considerable number of people to whom I owe varieties of intellectual debt. I hope both that they will forgive me and that they will not be too upset at the final product they helped bring into existence. So far as I recall, the book began as a distinct project with kind invitations from Peter De Bolla and Meaghan Morris to speak at their respective institutions. Before that, I had an inkling of the argument to come when students at Rutgers University responded with surprising generosity to the suggestion that *Père Goriot* and *The Silence of the Lambs* had something important in common. I am grateful to them, and to the intelligence and enthusiasm of students in several later seminars on films and novels of upward mobility, both at Rutgers and at Columbia. Casey Hankey, Dennis O'Brien, Mark Schmidt, and Paige Washington will have to stand for them all. Long before that, there was an undergraduate honors essay on how James Joyce and Louis-Ferdinand Céline rewrote the nineteenth-century's Young Man from the Provinces story. Jonathan Arac and Anne Gillain, being very clever about the shaping of lives as well as about texts of all sorts, will know how very much I owe them for their help at that interesting time of my life and for a great deal more.

Among the many friends and colleagues who have taken time out that they didn't have and given extraordinary insight and encouragement on this project, I would like to offer thanks to the following: Etienne Balibar, Robert Caserio, Leonard Cassuto, Margaret Cohen, Brenda Coughlin, Jenny Davidson, Lisa Fluet, Jane Gallop, Dehn Gilmore, Lauren Goodlad, Gerald Graff, Bonnie Honig, Laura Kipnis, George Levine, Jim Livingston, Tina Lupton, John McClure, John McGowan, Scott Malcomson, Edward Mendelson, Franco Moretti, Andrew Parker, Donald Pease, Caryl Phillips, Adela Pinch, Dana Polan, Andrew Ross, Michael Rothberg, Helen Small, Hap Veeser, Priscilla Wald, Cheryl Wall, Ken Warren, and Jeffrey Williams. Mary Murrell and her successor Hanne Winarsky have been everything an author could wish for.

As I was finishing revisions on the manuscript, I attended the funeral of Fred Pfeil in Port Allegany, Pennsylvania and realized, not for the first time, how many instructive enigmas have always hidden out in Fred's world-class stories about leaving and loving a small town.

My mother, Lynne Robbins, will discover the imprint of her wise stories and magnanimous commentaries throughout. But for this she'll have to get past the preface. My son Andreas claims "large philosophical input." It's true, and it's true for his sister Sophia as well. Still, I know they'd both prefer something livelier and made up.

This book is for Elsa.

Upward Mobility and the Common Good

The Fairy Godmother

Early in Thomas Harris's novel *Silence of the Lambs* (1988), Dr. Hannibal Lecter, psychiatrist, serial killer, and cannibal, makes a proposal to Clarice Starling, FBI trainee, through the bars of his cell.

"I'll give you what you love most, Clarice Starling."
"What's that, Dr. Lecter?"
"Advancement, of course."[1]

As usual, Lecter is right. *Silence of the Lambs* could be described in various ways—as a Gothic horror story, a detective thriller, or an oblique argument for vegetarianism. But if what matters is what Starling wants most (which is also what she gets), then the novel should be classified as a story of advancement, a modern-day Cinderella fable.

The fairy godmother of this Cinderella story is of course Lecter himself. Approached for advice in solving a fresh series of murders, he describes Starling to her face as "white trash," then goes on to reward her for glimpses into her inner life by supplying riddlelike clues. Deciphering the clues, she will track down the killer, rescue the prospective victim, and finish her training in a blaze of professional glory. However diabolical his character may be, Lecter's narrative function is thus indisputably benevolent: he bestows on the virtuous but disadvantaged protagonist the magical help that makes possible her advancement.

In the pages that follow, I will be working from the premise that a broad range of narratives, fictional and nonfictional, can be described more or less as Lecter describes Starling's. Whatever else these stories appear to be about, they are also about advancement. This book assembles an archive (perhaps less consistent than a genre, though I will use that term as well) composed of stories that can be shown to display a common problematic of upward mobility. Having chosen to discuss very few texts out of an almost infinite field of possibilities, I offer my choices up in the hope that, analyzed in my somewhat obsessive terms, they will also resonate interestingly in the much wider circle of texts around them. This pushy procedure will seem worth carrying out only if it can be established at the outset that these stories are doing cultural work of an unpredictable and significant sort—doing something other, that is, than peddling simple wish-fulfill-ment fantasies or the shopworn ideology of individual self-reliance we have come to associate with them. This is what I want to suggest by pro-posing *Silence of the Lambs* as a characteristic upward mobility story of our time and Hannibal Lecter as its unlikely fairy godmother.

What could be more characteristic of our time than a Cinderella story without a Prince Charming? Starling seems to seek only what she finds: the satisfaction of solving the case, getting the respect that goes with a job well done. What she loves most is professional success, sweetened only by the admiration of her colleagues and superiors. Even as late as 1991, when Jonathan Demme's enormously successful film version ap-peared, viewers expressed surprise and elation that the Jodie Foster char-acter seemed so uninterested in finding a suitable mate. As Elizabeth Young observed, "It is not that she is waiting for the right man to come along; rather, she seems utterly indifferent to any suggestion of romance as the film proposes it, in heterosexual terms."[2] Was it possible that a Hollywood blockbuster was really offering up a beautiful female star and yet eliminating from her ambitions any romantic interest, leaving only the striving to succeed? No, it wasn't. But the moment did seem to mark a turning point in the erotic economy of spectatorship. The audience was not asked to forsake entirely its usual vicarious pleasures. Instead, it was invited to take those pleasures in a displaced and diluted form: as a series of hints, threats, and promises surrounding two older men, Lecter and Crawford, Starling's boss at the FBI. Each is established in a position of superiority over her, with effects both vexatious and flirtatious. With each, Starling has intense and somewhat ambiguous if only intermittent and finally inconclusive relations. These not-quite-relations seem to re-place the dynamics of romantic coupling that, from novels like Richard-son's *Pamela* to films like Mike Nichols's *Working Girl*, had merged the protagonist's advancement in her erotic bonding with a social superior and the promise of a new, socially elevated family to come. Rather than being wooed and wedded by her prince, one might say—taking the itali-cized term in a slightly more neutral sense than is customary—that Star-ling is *patronized* by her mentors. The activity of patronizing does not result in reproduction. Still, however disagreeable it may sound, it does not rule out some degree of seduction.

The historical shift from marriageable masters to unmarriageable men-tors, a shift that could only happen once paid employment for women outside the home had become the rule rather than the exception, marks a shift toward greater gender equality. A prince, once wedded, would remain a superior. A patron or mentor, however intent he may be on preserving his putative superiority, is structurally obliged to allow the possibility of final freedom and equality. If for no other reason, this is true because, having helped raise the protagonist up, he will then disengage from the protagonist's life and very likely disappear from the plot. This means that, though the mentor may engage less of the protagonist's desire, and thus less of the accompanying desire of the reader, what desire there is is rerouted in a more democratic direction.

Appearances to the contrary, then, the mentor is a figure of (relative) democratization. This paradox accounts for why, though he is no prince, Hannibal Lecter is charming. His charm does not stand solely for the sexiness of power, a psychological fact that can never be safely neglected. Nor does it merely register a residual charisma that cannot be banished from the dominant bureaucratic rationality, though the Weberian vocabulary seems pertinent. His charm emerges at the exact point of power's *susceptibility*, its mysterious but narratively necessary willingness to break its own rules so as to open up, however slightly, to aspiration from below. Without it, there could be no story. Since Starling needs the scientific expertise that Lecter possesses, the extracurricular murders that accompany his rule breaking show another, more sinister face of the world of experts she is so eager to enter. But Lecter does not block the entrance or in any way discourage her efforts. No matter how murderous he is, on the level of narrative function he remains first and foremost the fairy godmother, the one who enables and approves Starling's accomplishment, even if that accomplishment trains and accredits her to come in search of criminals like himself. This is the source of his charm. And his charm pulls the story away from what might otherwise seem its proper destination.

I am not suggesting that Starling's rise is all pull and no push, dependent on Lecter's intervention alone and owing nothing to her own demonstrations of merit. That merit is much in evidence. But the true logic of her rise only appears when her merit suddenly coincides with Lecter's susceptibility to it. One has to ask, therefore, what Starling offers that Lecter wants or needs.

An initial hypothesis might be that power is acquired, in *Silence of the Lambs*, by mastery over sex—in other words, that Starling acts out something like the Protestant work ethic, indefinitely sacrificing present sexual gratification in a quest for the higher if delayed good of social advancement. This hypothesis is supported by the manner in which Starling acquires her benefactor's support: Lecter decides to offer his assistance, having initially refused, only after she is sexually assaulted or insulted by his sperm-throwing fellow inmate Miggs. As we shall see, this is a crucial type of scene for the genre as a whole. That is, it responds to the same causal logic as the benefactor. If the benefactor's support is the cause of the protagonist's rise, then one needs to know how and why the support itself was obtained. What was the cause of the cause?

Evidence for this hypothesis is also to be found in the narrative's deep structure. Starling's upward mobility is accompanied by the symbolic elimination of those two contrasting characters whose ambitions *are* expressed sexually, that is, the film's two genuine villains, Buffalo Bill and Dr. Chilton. Chilton, the head of the asylum where Lecter is incarcerated, tries to take advantage of his position by grossly and gracelessly coming on to Starling. Professionally speaking, he is also Crawford's ambitious and unscrupulous antagonist.[3] This sexualized ambition, or ambitious sexuality, seems largely responsible for the fact that, as the credits scroll, audiences find themselves unexpectedly cheering the prospect that Hannibal the Cannibal is about to "have" the bureaucrat for dinner—a serious measure of the film's achievement, and a hint, though finally a misleading one, about its politics.

But what about the sublimated or not-so-sublimated sexuality in the relationship between protagonist and mentor? Critics have disagreed about the presence or absence of an erotic subtext between Starling and Lecter. For Elizabeth Young, "Lecter sexualizes all discussions with Clarice in the guise of exposing her emotional interior. . . . Clarice, while clearly attracted to Lecter's eroticized advances, just as clearly resists them" (Young, 9,12). Adrienne Donald, on the other hand, sees Lecter as an ideal mentor for Starling because of "his sexual indifference to her as a woman" (358). This erotic uncertainty again seems characteristic of upward mobility in our time. It reflects a narrative in which the goal of advancement has broken free from customary heterosexual bondings that refer explicitly or implicitly to marriage and the reproduction of the patriarchal family and for better or worse has come to reside increasingly in looser, half-formed relationships, neither biologically reproductive nor necessarily heterosexual, that seem to fit social units other than the family. Like the reproduction of the family, the reproduction of institutions, disciplines, teams, professions, and even corporations involves the eliciting and channeling of erotic energy, if not in the direct and literal way demanded by procreation. This is one reason why the fairy godmother can also be perceived as a "fairy" in the somewhat (but not entirely) modern sense of the word. Indifferent to the usual destinations of heterosexual desire, Starling aims the narrative of upward mobility at something less familial than collegial. Borrowing from Eve Kosofsky Sedgwick, we might think of this collegial alternative as "a vision of 'family' elastic enough to do justice to the depth and sometimes durability of nonmarital and/or nonprocreative bonds, same-sex bonds, nondyadic bonds, adult sibling bonds, nonbiological bonds, bonds not defined by genitality"(71).[4] "Fairy godmother" is one of the items on the list of roles that Sedgwick associates with "queer tutelage": "patron, friend, literal uncle, godfather, adoptive father, sugar daddy" (59). As a patron, Lecter is also something of a queer tutor. His indeterminate sexuality, which hints at an erotics of male-female mentorship while also drawing Starling into an atmosphere of campy homosexual performance, urges her toward a nonmarital, nonprocreative endpoint which seems to have more in common with a workplace or some other nondomestic grouping.

The central moment in the film, I would argue, is the one that reveals this rechanneling of desire away from reproduction and into the workplace. This is the "silence of the lambs" story alluded to in the title, a story that emerges in Starling's final therapy-like session with Lecter. As Judith Halberstam writes, "The secret of her past that threatened all along to be some nasty story of incest or rape is precisely not sexual. Clarice Starling is the girl who wanted to save the lambs from the slaughter, who could only carry one at a time and who finally could not support the weight" (44). Making much the same point, Elizabeth Young credits Starling with a "refusal to give Dr. Lecter what he wants: the narration of a childhood experience explicitly involving sexuality (that is, the primal scene)" (12). The film's titular secret is thus not a sexual but a professional secret: a secret about why Starling wants to practice her profession.[5] In other words, it is something that need not have been a secret at all. Instead of the shameful memory of sexual abuse or Oedipal hatred that one might have expected from the narrative's lurid atmospherics, we are given a story that Starling might tell voluntarily and even with pride. For it merely explains why she wants to do the work of rescuing the helpless for which she is in training. Indeed, it is a sort of myth of professional legitimation. By going through the University of Virginia and the FBI Academy, this myth tells us, Starling is not just climbing the social ladder. She is trying to alleviate the suffering of women like herself. Her efforts fuse the two motives together.

There is no reason to credit this revelation, as Young does, to Starling's "refusal to give Dr. Lecter what he wants." It makes more sense to give at least some of the credit to Lecter himself.[6] Faced with this evidence of what Starling really loves, he neglects to be ironic. He does not suggest that her advancement in the FBI will be an unhappy ending, a consummation unworthy of her efforts. He is speechless. The film's close-up of his expression when he elicits this avowal suggests that Lecter is deeply and strangely satisfied by discovering a nonerotic key to Starling's character. It is the suggestion, in both film and novel, that he embraces this asexual, ethically generous interpretation of Starling's deepest motives, and indeed derives from it something equivalent to erotic pleasure, that most clearly marks him, in spite of his bad habits with everyone else, as a good mentor to Starling.[7]

In short, the common ground on which Starling's merit and Lecter's susceptibility to that merit coincide, thus enabling and affirming her rise, is her sense of vocation. Perhaps unsurprisingly, a professional therapist (though no longer licensed to practice) approves the commitment of another would-be professional, her commitment to tend to those who are in need. What Lecter reassures Starling of by his interpretation of her story is that the "cool professionalism" she seeks is not, as Adrienne Donald thinks, "a vain flight from her white trash origins" (352), but rather a reconnection of sorts with those origins, an identification that is also a rescue, a rescue that is also an identification. "The corpse laid out on the table," Judith Halberstam writes, ". . . is a double for Starling, the image of what she might have become had she not left home, as Lecter points out, and aspired to greater things" (42). According to Lecter, the corpse would also be proof that her aspiration to greater things is not an abandonment of those left behind or below, a proof that she advances, forward or upward, precisely so as to do something for them, and precisely because they are versions of herself, because she is what she must take care of. This professional creation myth demonstrates to anyone who might doubt it—and we have every reason to believe that readers and spectators will indeed be skeptical on this point—that her individual advancement will be in the interest of society as a whole.

References to the interest of society as a whole, like references to the common good, are most often made these days in a more or less cynical mode, as if we assumed that such claims could only be ideological, hence self-aggrandizing and self-incriminating. I'm not convinced that a post-Gramscian or post-Althusserian understanding of ideology should permit this assumption.[8] If there is no privileged (that is, theological) position completely outside ideology, attempting to reconcile versions of self-interest with versions of the general welfare becomes something all social players are obliged to do. Making and defending claims like this is simply what we mean by political discourse. In this case, politics would have to be understood as involving the tricky, unending task of discriminating less desirable from more desirable claims—in large part a matter of timing and context.

The local context in which Lecter approves Starling's claim, and thus some of the force behind his approval, can be gauged by a scene in which what we observe is a failure in this reconciliation between self-interest and the common good. As Young notes, when Starling finally enters Buffalo Bill's cellar and finds the young woman he has kidnapped, Catherine Martin, the moment can be compared to "the terrified encounter between Jane Eyre and Bertha Rochester" (17). "As she enters the room, Clarice calls out, 'FBI, you're safe,' a line so obviously incongruous—given the precariousness of her own situation at this moment—as to provoke laughter, while Catherine, hearing her leave, yells, 'You fucking bitch!' " (17). I would like to draw a little circle around this fleeting moment and its allusion to the upward mobility problematic of *Jane Eyre*, to which I will return below. The basement encounter with Buffalo Bill's intended victim, a kind of madwoman in the basement, can be seen as a beautifully miniaturized allegory of professional discourse in the moment of its failure to legitimize itself. It is an allegory, one might say, of the Reagan/Thatcher years, years that saw a frenzy of delegitimation aimed at "official" or credentialed, professional or state efforts to "rescue" private citizens. The grassroots structure of feeling that grew into a sense of its power in those years has of course continued, under different administrations, giving us among other things the Oklahoma City bombing and so-called welfare reform.[9] As a result, we are still living with the powerful populist antifeminism, antiprofessionalism, and antistatism that are neatly joined in the misguided animosity of "you fucking bitch!"

A justifiably desperate Catherine Martin pronounces those words because she takes Starling's apparent indifference to her as aggressive. This is an error, but in a larger sense, she has a point. Performing the rescue as her professional training dictates, Starling can also be seen as attacking the resistant, antistatist subject as such, the one who doubts the suitability or competence of official rescuers—especially when they are women, or presumed beneficiaries of federal legislation. The antistatist subject is ready in an instant to tear off the facade of impersonal officialdom and reveal a reality that is always finally personal. *You* can't be a proper representative of the authorities, the logic would go. You're just a woman like me. But if this is the logic, then Starling too is right. For by her impersonally aggressive rescue she is breaking down a resistance that not only stands in the way of professional advancement for herself, but also stands in the way of any progressive politics, any demand that the social welfare state fulfill and extend its long unkept and now ever more retracted promises—in short, any collective social advancement in the United States under our present unpropitious conditions.[10] What the scene offers is another way of measuring the political achievement of *Silence of the Lambs*: its force as relatively successful propaganda, against a background of free-market antistatism, in favor of welfare-state institutions and at the same time in favor of the enlarged market for professional service and expertise that the welfare state has always implied—in favor, in other words, of the welfare state as a social space in which an individual can rise while doing good for others.

I am claiming that the paradoxical key to Clarice Starling's upward mobility story is the welfare state, here understood very loosely as including all the state's caring and rescue functions, even when these functions are carried out by the FBI.[11] Here and throughout this book I will be asking the reader to see the welfare state as a personal matter. It would be absurd if Starling's gender and sexuality were *not* implicated in the story of her advancement, for nothing could be more representative of the larger social changes in which that advancement participates. "At a moment in time when the federal government assumed greater authority over the distribution of resources," Alice Kessler-Harris shows in her study of economic citizenship in and after the New Deal, "gender constituted a crucial measure of fairness" (6).[12] Only the mutual dependence of these two shifting concepts—of fairness on gender, and of gender on fairness—can explain how deep into personal identity these changes go. To make sense of the policy shift "from staunch opposition to federal government intervention in the lives of most men (but not women) to eager experiments with government mediation of all sorts," one has to see "how profoundly the expectations of ordinary people altered" (64). This alteration would have had to be profound—certainly profound enough to work its way into novels. It would have had to affect both the going sense of who, what, and where the mediators of power are and where, so to speak, one's own story is located. What could be more personal?

In following Starling's hunt for the killer and the self-searching conversations with Lecter that make the hunt successful, I'm suggesting, what audiences experience is a reworking of desire, an apprenticeship in the ambiguities and affective transformations that advancement within a bureaucratic frame has come to require. I am not suggesting that adjusting individual ambitions to the obliqueness of an emergent welfare state means learning to live without inequality. In many and perhaps most cases (though not in *Silence of the Lambs*, as it happens), the credentialed carer or rescuer thereby preserves and legitimates a social advantage over the one who is rescued—an allegory of the distance between welfare-state capitalism and any socialism that would deserve the name. I would argue that this new set of lessons about responsibility, social interdependence, and desire brings a net ethical gain even though, as is obvious enough, some of these lessons were equally necessary to capitalism's emerging corporate form and to the civil/bureaucratic institutions emerging to constrain and contain it, or to save it from its own self-destructive drive to achieve short-term profit at all cost. It should not be shocking, given the fragility of welfare-state institutions in the era of globalization and privatization, that we are still in the process of learning, forgetting, resisting, and relearning these lessons.

This book will try to expand this counterintuitive linkage of fiction and the welfare state so as to cover a number of otherwise diverse upward mobility stories of the past two centuries. It will suggest that *Silence of the Lambs* is a recent addition to a long and largely hidden tradition of narratives that fill in the missing emotional landscape of life among welfare-state institutions, and that the apparent bleakness of this institutional landscape represents the imperfect historical form that we should expect even the most genuine progress toward social equality to take. Unsatisfying as it may be, this is the collective progress, I will argue, against which individual narratives of progress must be plotted.

Let me spell out a few further assumptions that underlie this argument. I understand the welfare state as a set of imperfect institutions, produced in part by management from above and in part by pressure from below, which also enters into the unfinished project of "social citizenship," a phrase that Étienne Balibar has recently sought to revive.[13] I see no need to disguise the fact that, alongside the sheer scholarly delight of discovering so unlikely a historical context for so pervasive a set of literary texts, I took some of the motivation for this argument from disgust at the partial dismantling and further endangering of the welfare state, as alluded to above, as well as from incipient attempts to extend social citizenship on an international scale, an effort to which Balibar is a useful guide. I will be assuming that upward mobility under capitalism is not restricted to the single option of playing and winning at the game of profit-and-loss and affirming the eternal fitness of the rules capitalism has laid down. History knows no such thing as a "free" capitalist market. Actual capitalist markets have always required immense infrastructural investment and the continuing support of various institutions, some of them classified as "welfare" institutions, like Lecter's asylum, and others not, like Starling's FBI. Yet in the broadest sense all of these institutions, even one as blatantly tarnished as the FBI, can be said to belong to the welfare state. All of them, while supporting capitalism, also interfere with it.[14] The reality of the interference can be measured by the wrathful corporate will to dismantle and defund that such interference incites. In this context of dismantling and defunding, the persistence of the Foucaultian school in interpreting the welfare state as an apparatus of domination based on hypocritically benevolent surveillance seems to me open to new and sharp questioning.

Since the hypocrisy is often real, the benevolence is always limited, and the opportunities for misunderstanding are endless, let me repeat: I am aware that the welfare state is not the sort of ideal that deserves to dictate all of one's political commitments and aspirations. This is a point that is well marked within *Silence of the Lambs* itself. The film ends in the Caribbean, where Hannibal Lecter, after congratulating Starling on her success by telephone, is in hungry pursuit of the asylum director, the film's unpalatable and therefore eminently edible bureaucrat. The Caribbean or Third World or global south, one might say, is where one finds oneself when one gets off the phone with the FBI, where there is neither FBI nor welfare state. There the contradictions of the welfare state can be exported, and the inevitable collision of values between Starling and Lecter can be evaded or at least postponed. It is the place where Lecter and Starling would not need to be separated by bars, where Lecter would only eat those who richly deserve to be eaten, where "bad" professionals would be eliminated and only the "good" ones would remain. All of which is of course once again to use neoimperialism's familiar double standard so as to make a space elsewhere for what cannot happen at home.

I will have more to say at the end of this book about the line drawn by the international division of labor between countries that can and cannot afford some semblance of a welfare state. It is arguable that this line traces some of the most urgent and delicate political tasks of the coming decades, including the challenge of negotiating critically with a new American nationalism. The best arguments for nationalism are those that appeal to the solidarity embodied, at its best, in the welfare state. This book was written in part because I am so concerned that the political project of the welfare state, as a set of real historical accomplishments as well as still energetic impulses begging to be extended further, seems to have been prematurely given up for dead by everyone *but* the new nationalists. I have sought to respond, after my fashion, to Fredric Jameson's somewhat reluctant imperative in his "Five Theses on Actually Existing Marxism": "the Left is . . . today placed in the position of having to defend big government and the welfare state, something its elaborate and sophisticated traditions of the critique of social democracy make it embarrassing to do" (4).[15]

This task is especially pressing for American intellectuals, and especially embarrassing, for two additional reasons. First, because we ourselves depend so heavily on the legitimacy and the financial support of the welfare state. And second, because the welfare state is a cross-class project, the historical result of popular demands for protection combined with the rising influence of technocratic expertise. Thus it is the closest thing we have had to an ideological synthesis, a defensible common program in which the glaringly different interests of the poor and needy, on the one hand, and elite experts, on the other, can even appear to be resolved. I look forward to the day when a better one will have replaced it.

"I DON'T WANT TO BE PATRONISED"

Focused as it is on a professional career woman, *The Silence of the Lambs* is very much a text of its times. It hardly seems coincidental, given its attention to the potentially abusive power and the sexual ambiguity of older, institutionally powerful men, that the film version came out in the same year as the Clarence Thomas/Anita Hill hearings, with their sensational testing of society's recent and still fragile will to resist sexual harassment. For me, as for Rosemary Bray, whose memoir *Unafraid of the Dark* is discussed in a later chapter, it was a scandal that public opinion permitted Thomas to set his story of self-reliance against the dependence of his "welfare queen" sister, and this scandal provided another topical motive to rethink the ubiquitous opposition between upward mobility and the welfare state.[16] And yet how topical is a figure like Hannibal Lecter? No one who has ever encountered the female Gothic, from Ann Radcliffe to *Rebecca*, will imagine that Lecter's show-stealing, attractive-repulsive prominence is entirely unprecedented. Though stories closely resembling *The Silence of the Lambs* remain rare, though we do not often see the husband/master entirely replaced by the mentor, though this shift from master to mentor is both incomplete and likely to remain so, figures like Hannibal Lecter are not a recent literary phenomenon. Nor is their entanglement in narratives of advancement. Consider, for example, Lecter's resemblance to the older male criminals who oversee the protagonist's rise in such masterpieces of the realist bildungsroman as Balzac's *Père Goriot* and Dickens's *Great Expectations*. In the first, there is the gay and charismatic master criminal Vautrin. Like Lecter, Vautrin is a man of almost superhuman knowledge and ability. Like Lecter, he offers his services to the ambitious (male) protagonist for reasons that seem obscure but hint strongly of sexual attraction. This is an attraction for which the novel, like *The Silence of the Lambs*, will find no outlet. Yet it is Vautrin who explains to Rastignac his eventual ascent in the Parisian world and in a sense presides over it even after he has been arrested and banished from the plot. In *Great Expectations*, there is another patron who is also a criminal. The moral center of the plot is generally agreed to be the passionate bond between Pip and Magwitch, the secret source of the funds that make Pip a gentleman. Once again, a taint of criminality hangs over the hero's upward mobility. Why should these patrons be criminals? Why is it that in both cases the hero's emotional entanglement with these criminal patrons upstages their somewhat pro forma passions for trophy women? If we cannot call it love, what *can* we call the bond between them?

A bond that is not quite hot enough for love is also characteristic of another set of patrons, again represented in both *Père Goriot* and *Great Expectations*. Balzac's Mme de Beauséant inexplicably invites Rastignac into her exclusive and much-coveted circle, providing him with a stock of social capital he can trade for further advancement and thus accomplishing much of what Vautrin had planned for him. They do not sleep together, but thanks to her he will have the choice of a mistress who resembles her. Dickens's Miss Havisham merely pretends to be Pip's patron, concealing from him the criminality of his true patron. In both cases, the Older Woman is a kind of front for the Male Criminal. But she also helps account for the power the two categories of patron share. Like the homosocial bond between older and younger man, the bond between younger man and older woman stands apart from the cycle of biological reproduction that has traditionally channeled and legitimated desire.[17] Her age and position make her unmarriageable. Unavailable for the production of offspring, she cannot be the object of a desire that aims at constituting a new family unit, which is to say a unit that would put her at a disadvantage. The ambition that passes through her will look criminal, for it cannot be an ambition that aims at reproducing society as it is. The desire for her and the desire for her patronage, two desires that frequently meld into one, define the protagonist's upward mobility as a paradoxical project, one that leads both into and away from the status quo.

These two desires are more likely to be indistinguishable in the novels of Balzac and Stendhal. Miss Havisham, who in a French novel would have been a bit younger and Pip's lover, in England must spin off a younger and more acceptable appendage as a receptacle for romantic desire. (Woody Allen's *Bullets over Broadway*, which rewrites *Great Expectations* as well as *Sunset Boulevard*, foregrounds both categories of patron, the gangster-who-supplies-what-the-protagonist-lacks and the diva-of-a-certain-age, and comes closer to the French model in its treatment of the latter.) But Estella's much-emphasized coldness is a sure sign that, structurally speaking, her identity remains that of her adoptive mother, the woman traumatized by unconsummated marriage who turns therefore against marriage itself and the society of which it is paradigmatic. To reject the option of joining with the hero to found a family is not to rule out love. But it means that love will look different, and will prefigure a different sort of society. The coldness of the unmarriageable female— what René Girard calls, apropos of the love between older woman and younger man in Rousseau and Stendhal, "cerebral love"—is a figure for ambition that is not merely illegitimate in the eyes of the social order. It is a figure for ambition in pursuit of a different legitimacy.[18]

As I have suggested, the ambition of the lowly can be imagined as legitimate only if power is imagined to be something other than a united and impenetrable front, a sovereignty that is both inviolable and homogeneous. The outlandish and sensational bursts of imagination that go into shaping the figure of the patron seem intended to solve this problem, to present power as contradictory and thus permeable. The patron must, by definition, possess the power to raise the protagonist up. By definition, possessors of power are defenders of the social order from which they benefit. But by raising the protagonist up, the social order would seem to be violating itself. Why would it ever do such a thing? Older Women and Male Criminals are imaginary solutions to the paradox. They are ways of imagining a hierarchical social order as simultaneously resistant to democratic transgression and deviously willing to permit or even invite it. Logically speaking, they are at the very center of the upward mobility story, for they and only they attempt to explain how it is possible for upward mobility to happen, or to go unpunished.[19] Factoring in again the social interdependence on which all supposedly independent effort depends, they make the upward mobility story more believable and more interesting.

It is the intersection of my formal interest in the mentor/mediator, as a sort of catalyst inciting or supervising the passage from origin to destination without entering into the end product, and my historical interest in the gradual emergence of the welfare state, as a context that makes some sense of these figures and their narrative effect, that narrows the otherwise unmanageable field of texts that must be consulted. There are of course upward mobility stories, in the broadest sense of the word, as early and as far abroad as one cares to look. In his quest for the origins of the English novel, Michael McKeon offers an upward mobility narrative from 1701 (from a dialogue by Charles Davenant), then trumps it with another (Thomas Deloney's *Jack of Newbery*) from 1597.[20] Even the unstable balance between indulging and chastising the desire for mobility (for McKeon, "progressive" and "conservative" readings) goes back at least that far. The overcoming of obstacles and the satisfaction of desires for greater prosperity, security, and so on are most likely cultural invariants to be found wherever there is storytelling. Why not include in the same category freed slaves in classical antiquity, folktale variants of the Cinderella motif, younger sons under primogeniture, and a wealthy nineteenth-century German-Jewish parvenu like Rahel Varnhagen as described by Hannah Arendt?[21] A rigorously comparative study that would have something to say about all of the world's literary traditions would of course have to specify with precision the social context in each case, including the nature of the social obstacles overcome (class, caste, slavery, or whatever) and the forces and vulnerabilities that allow for their overcoming. This is beyond my own capacities. I also have some suspicion as to whether, at that planetary level of historical and geographical abstraction, a coherent object called upward mobility can even be said to exist.

The present book concerns itself mainly with the United Kingdom and the United States, and to a lesser degree France, in the period since 1800, and even within those limits (in some respects no doubt too loose) it is obliged to be impressionistic. The year 1800 marks not an absolute origin but a relative point of departure, much as it does for Raymond Williams in *Culture and Society*. The Industrial Revolution and the French Revolution, dramatic stages in the respective development of capitalism and democracy, generated objects of culture in which anti*capitalist* responses are often difficult to tell apart from anti*democratic* responses, and impulses to achieve more democratic representation may easily be confused with impulses to liberate the market. These cultural confusions extend to the development of the state. Like culture, the state arguably assumes its modern form in the years following 1800. In his history of the eighteenth-century English novel, John Richetti argues that the state in the modern sense could not exist in the eighteenth century because "society" in the current (that is, nineteenth-century) sense did not exist. Instead, there was "a constellation of distinct spheres of influence, a loosely federated collection of interests and smaller social units" (5–6).[22] The same would have to be said about the state. Richetti cites Anthony Giddens to the effect that "Britain in the eighteenth century is not yet a modern nation-state but rather what Giddens calls a 'class-divided' society in which large spheres 'retain their independent character in spite of the rise of the state apparatus'" (6). After 1800, the rise of the state apparatus accelerates (again like culture) because that apparatus is asked both to serve capitalism and to manage its contradictions, among them its contradictory effect on democracy. Again, this is not a process that calls out for unconditional approval. David Lloyd and Paul Thomas make an eloquent case that the theory and practice of culture since the early-nineteenth century should largely be understood as a "supplement" to the state, concerned with breaking down popular desire for autonomy and resistance to representative government.[23] Unlike Lloyd and Thomas, I do not read the Reform Bills of 1832 and 1867 primarily as contributions to "the considerable work of disciplining and pedagogy, such that the emergence of the citizen may seem inseparable from the efficacy of another kind of reform and another mode of pedagogy, that of the reformatory" (58). Resisting the metaphorical slide that begins by identifying the state with the school and ends by identifying it with the prison, I hold that prisons are part of the story (indeed, quite a large part, to judge from narratives of upward mobility), but they are not its definitive point. But I too see culture as working along with and on behalf of state formation. I will try to show much the same linkage to the state in a number of nineteenth-century works of fiction.

If apologies are not in order for taking on too little material, perhaps I should apologize for taking on too much. The phrase "welfare state" does not seem to have been used before the 1930s. Those few books that have made the risky link between the welfare state and literature, like Sean McCann's *Gumshoe America* and Michael Szalay's *New Deal Modernism*, both published in 2000, have solidified their case—to me, both brilliant and utterly convincing—by restricting it to a decade or so.[24] Yet there is also something to be said for a moderately more expansive historical scale. As Daniel T. Rodgers shows in *Atlantic Crossings: Social Politics in a Progressive Age* (1998), the great break with laissez-faire policy began in Germany in the 1870s, then crossed the Rhein, the Channel, and the Atlantic in a fascinating pattern of back-and-forth exchange. The national trajectories are distinct. Yet Rodgers's experiment in transnational history works: a common object emerges into view across a geographical space that has been stretched and a *durée* (seventy or eighty years) that is longer than is usually claimed for Progressivism. Without pretending to the same richness of historical detail, I too am interested in stretching the dimensions of the welfare state. If the nineteenth century largely believed, as Norman Barry notes, that the market itself could not possibly be a *cause* of so-called social problems (29), and thus differed dramatically with the twentieth-century opinion that produced the New Deal and the Beveridge Plan, it is also true that under close inspection the earlier period reveals the slow, diffuse cultural preparation that eventually made it possible to break with this dogma. Hence the two centuries can fit gracefully enough into the same temporal frame. Instead of a sequence of relatively discrete developmental stages, then, as would be appropriate to a fine-grained treatment of social policy, this work of cultural criticism offers a sort of moral X ray, capturing a hidden skeletal configuration that helps explain long-term symptoms. Though my subtitle lays claim to history, that term is meant to be seriously qualified by its modest preposition. Perhaps a more accurate word would be *anatomy*.[25]

If the modern state did not exist before 1800, neither did the modern patron. It is only the rise of individualism that gives people a vocabulary in which patronizing registers as a violation. And it is only when enough people register that sense of violation that the patron's ambivalence-producing interference in the upward mobility story becomes possible. Consider the history of the word *patronizing*. "To patronize" originally meant simply to act as a patron toward, to protect, support, favor, encourage. There was no suggestion of any affront to the dignity of the one patronized. The more familiar adjectival form *patronizing* gets a new lease on life only at the point, around 1800, when the word acquires its present pejorative meaning: displaying an air or manner of superiority and condescension. The OED gives an example from Disraeli: "Spruce ... had a weakness for the aristocracy, who ... patronised him with condescending dexterity." And a still more paradigmatic one from Dickens: "I don't want to be patronised." The word acquires this pejorative meaning when the rise of democracy opens up possibilities for upward mobility and, with them, an uncertainty as to whether the distance between superior and inferior is indeed being disregarded or erased. Something similar happens to the near synonym *condescension*. Originally understood, without prejudice, as a voluntary abnegation of a superior's privileges, an affable disregard of differences of rank or position (OED), *condescension* has come to mean making a display of one's affability that, whether intentionally or not, reminds the recipient of one's superiority by and while appearing to forget it. It too could seem neutral only while the distance between superior and inferior remained absolute and unbridgeable. Both terms have come to refer to an undesired and annoying *appearance* of democracy only since democratic leveling entered the realm of realistic possibility.

On the other hand, the modern relationship with the patron is not all annoyance. Nor is it adequately characterized as self-abasing love. Arendt quotes Rahel Varnhagen's parvenu husband, who tries to "'honor myself in my superiors, so as to track down their good qualities in order to love them'" (237). "Making a strenuous effort to love," Arendt comments drily, "where there is no alternative but obedience, is more productive of good results than simple and undisguised servility" (237). One would prefer not to obey at all. But if one has to obey, then better to disguise the servility (even to oneself) as love. Better, that is, to transform it into love. This is the logic of a social world (the Prussian nobility around 1814) whose hierarchy is still relatively stable. In England, France, and the United States, though each was on a somewhat different timetable, having come through different revolutions, the alignments of power were shifting more rapidly, the transitivity of roles was at least a theoretical possibility, and the sort of emotional bond one finds between protagonist and patron—love is not the right word, but there may not be one—is correspondingly unstable, unpredictable, creative. That bond begins in a mixture of annoyance (that one must obey at all) and seduction (by a role one may not merely benefit from, but perhaps come in one's turn to occupy), and it goes on from there.

In elaborating on this correspondence between power and emotion, I do not claim to detect a consistent and full-scale allegory linking the novel's love stories to political theory. The sorts of literary effects I am talking about are too partial and fragmentary. Focusing on characters, functions, and relationships that occupy the somewhat neglected middle ground of these texts, texts more frequently and more readily grasped in terms of protagonists and final destinations, I am content to solicit respectful attention for what might be described as fiction's figurative dimension, its ability to transcend its own social horizon and to do so not in the interest of an ahistorical utopia, but as a further imaginative development of desires and energies that are already at work within that horizon.

One final qualification. In making the case that there exists something like a genre of upward mobility stories, I will be insisting that a certain number of texts that are not usually seen in terms of class (like *The Silence of the Lambs*) make better or richer or more urgent sense if class is factored back in. This insistence is all the more necessary when these texts give a prominent place to gender, as in *The Silence of the Lambs*, and if the difficulties of gender are accompanied by racial, ethnic, or postcolonial issues, as in the writing of Jamaica Kincaid. But my point here is not to argue that class trumps all other considerations.[26] It is by no means clear that the concept of class should have such interpretive authority, even over upward mobility stories. It is the *weakness* of the concept of class, its historical inability to structure from within the daily experience of the people to whom it is supposed to apply most urgently, that in large part leads me to this project. Stuart Hall's description of race as the mode in which class is lived is also true, if less universally, for upward mobility stories. These stories provide a narrative vocabulary, theoretically tainted and imperfect but extremely widespread, in which class has been and continues to be experienced. If there is authority in experience—even an authority shared with professional interpreters—then the discourse of class has as much to learn from these persistent commonsense narratives as it has to teach them. One thing it has to learn from them, at least as they are interpreted here, is its own dependence on the state, which cannot be seen as constituted *by* class identities and interests without also being seen as *constituting* class identities and interests.

DESCRIPTION OF THE CHAPTERS

In Stendhal's *The Red and the Black*, as in Balzac's *Père Goriot* and elsewhere, the social superior who "recognizes" the protagonist and becomes his benefactor is an Older Woman. With help from Margaret Cohen's *Sentimental Education of the Novel*, chapter 1, "Erotic Patronage," asks why the sentimental language of female self-sacrifice is not only admitted into the domain of male realism, where upward mobility takes flight, but is assigned to the commanding position of the mentor. Taking off from Rousseau's account in the *Confessions* of his youthful relations with his patron and lover Mme de Warens, I connect the Older Woman as transitional love object in a male upward mobility story, on the one hand, and the early theory of democratic citizenship, on the other. If the disinterestedness of the Older Woman is the site of an unacceptable renunciation of interest and agency on the part of women, for Rousseau it is also, and simultaneously, a model of the ideal and necessary alienation and rediscovery of the self in the general will. Despite its apparent fidelity to a residual aristocratic model of patronage, therefore, the upward mobility story can be seen as integral to the development of a "thick" discourse of democratic citizenship. Julien Sorel's boredom, which Erich Auerbach diagnosed as "aristocratic loftiness," becomes more interesting when assimilated to Cohen's tradition of sacrificial disinterestedness. And it is the hold of this politicized sentimentality over male nineteenth-century fiction that explains why, like the Pythons' childhood poverty game, the game of female self-sacrifice continues to work, dictating the course of upward mobility within a social world supposedly given over to brutal self-interest. Borrowing Fredric Jameson's analysis of donor-acquisition scenes as a key to what happens between protagonists and their mentor/benefactors, this chapter traces an unlikely commitment to democratic theory through works of nineteenth-century French fiction by Constant, Stendhal, Balzac, and Flaubert, with side glances at Dickens and Dreiser. It ends with Nuala O'Faolain's reflections on erotic patronage, careers, and age for women.

Chapter 2, "How to Be a Benefactor without Any Money," juxtaposes the theme of mentorship in two nineteenth-century classics of the genre, one British and one American. Dickens's *Great Expectations* is the very epitome of moral seriousness; Horatio Alger's *Ragged Dick* is its apparent antithesis. A reading of *Ragged Dick* attempts to display the centrality of the patron or benefactor figure even at the unrepentant heart of the ideology of self-reliance. Borrowing from Michael Moon's brilliant essay connecting Alger's benefactor figures to his pedophilia, I argue that these benign benefactors, who seem to contrast starkly with the sinister Hannibal Lecter, in fact share with him both a suspicion of unspeakable self-interest and a bond with their protégés that undercuts, socializes, and enriches the supposed rags-to-riches story for which Alger is notorious. The continuity between Alger's work with homeless children in New York City and the "no fault" or "therapeutic" ethic of the modern welfare state is explored in a brief commentary on the film *Good Will Hunting*. The chapter's third section extends the upward mobility story's emphatic entanglement with the issue of homelessness into a reading of *Great Expectations*. Homelessness, which marks the breakdown of the family, calls into being the agencies of the (just emergent) Victorian state bureaucracy. The effort to rescue the homeless, I argue, underlies and explains the genuine upward mobility that persists beyond the moral chastisement and failure of Pip's self-centered "great expectations": the more muted success of his not-quite-disinterested actions as a benefactor-without-any-money, a bizarre figure of administrative expertise who stands prophetically for the welfare state that would aim at not-quite-disinterested care for Magwitch and those like him.

Chapter 3, "It's Not Your Fault," takes its title from the film *Good Will Hunting*, which like *The Silence of the Lambs* organizes its upward mobility story around a mentor/ benefactor who is also a therapist. The therapeutic or "no fault" ethic, which outraged critics of the welfare state like Christopher Lasch for its neglect of individual moral responsibility, becomes the thread tying together three classic American upward mobility stories running the length of the twentieth century: Theodore Dreiser's

The Financier (1912), Budd Schulberg's *What Makes Sammy Run?* (1941), and E. L. Doctorow's *Billy Bathgate* (1989). In each, I argue, the refusal of individual responsibility is real and central, but it is not the moral disaster that antistatists like Lasch saw in it. On the one hand, this refusal makes the moral space required for upward mobility, which is incompatible with the strict moral accounting that is its ideological face. On the other hand, however, it obliges the upwardly mobile protagonist to bend to a new sort of responsibility, this time public and collective. The "no fault" motto is so potent, I suggest, because it stands in for the rechanneling of responsibility in the direction of emergent public collectivities like the trade union, the profession, and the municipality, which is in the course of becoming an increasingly self-conscious moral agent. In their different ways, these institutions embody a principle of loyalty set against the chaotic, self-destructive working of self-interest that we see in self-reliant criminal protagonists like Dreiser's Cowperwood, Schulberg's Sammy Glick, and Doctorow's Dutch Schultz. The therapist, like the social worker and the municipal inspector, is thus a representative of what the previous chapter had called the benefactor without any money. Yet here as elsewhere the therapist must share the spotlight with the gangster, an alternative figure (again descended from Vautrin and Magwitch) for this ethical turn, which is of course as characteristic of corporate capitalism as it is of the welfare state.

Chapter 4, "A Portrait of the Artist as a Rentier," centers on a subgenre of British upward mobility stories from the late-nineteenth and early-twentieth centuries that deal with figures of the writer, artist, or intellectual. In readings of George Gissing's *New Grub Street* (1891) and *Born in Exile* (1892), George Du Maurier's *Trilby* (1894), H. G. Wells's *Kipps* (1905), and George Bernard Shaw's *Pygmalion* (1914), I argue that the writer's rejection of social climbing implies an unconscious alignment with the old aristocracy, which of course did not have to climb. But this alignment also *enables* social climbing, as we see in the period's brilliant and enduringly popular array of Lecter-like sinister-but-seductive mentors, from Du Maurier's Svengali to Leroux's Phantom of the Opera. Why the repeated mixture of extreme power with extreme marginality or disability? In an attempt to explain this paradox, I pursue the idea that this alignment with old landed money overlaps significantly with the new, still fragile ethic of the welfare state. The rentier, or person living off rent on property, is a visible ancestor of the "no fault" sense of entitlement, disconnected from individual effort, achievement, or responsibility. And if, as Pierre Bourdieu suggests, it was independent incomes that funded the artistic Bohemias where figures like Svengali and the Phantom flourish, then it becomes interesting not only that so many upward mobility stories are set in Bohemia, but that upward mobility should be so identified with the activities of writing and art. The answer to how one can rise in the world without identifying with the dominant new-money ethic of commercial self-interest is an identification that is at once residual and emergent, a sense of entitlement that, like the Fabian paternalism that jump-started the welfare state, owes something both to the rentier and to the state bureaucrat. The life of the writer or artist serves the genre of upward mobility because it is itself a metaphorical compromise between individual social climbing and commitment to some version of the common good.

Chapter 5, "The Health Visitor," treats a series of British and American upward mobility stories of the mid-twentieth century that share two common features. First, they are all taught frequently to undergraduates, and thus indicate something of importance about the overlap between upward mobility and the self-appointed role of higher education in providing and commenting upon it. Second, they all include and indeed revolve around a traumatic visit to the child-protagonist's family by an authorized representative of the state. (Or the public authorities—it's in this chapter that I declare and explain my support for Daniel Rodgers's position in *Atlantic Crossings* that in spite of real differences in the weighing of private and public, welfare-state discourse works to unite Europe and the United States.)[27] This traumatic invasion of private space, which seems to lend itself to a justifiably paranoid view of the activist state, in fact becomes constitutive, I argue, of the upward mobility that follows from it, an upward mobility that can be justified only by means of a justification of the welfare state. The texts discussed include Carolyn Steedman's *Landscape for a Good Woman*, Richard Rodriguez's *Hunger of Memory*, Tillie Olsen's "I Stand Here Ironing," Alan Sillitoe's "The Loneliness of the Long-Distance Runner," and—as a noncurricular coda—Steven Soderbergh's film *Erin Brockovich*.

Chapter 6, "On the Persistence of Anger in the Institutions of Caring," begins by examining a number of British novels that participate with more or less enthusiasm in the extreme distrust of state intervention characteristic of the last two decades of the twentieth century. After glances at two "social" novels by Pat Barker and an "academic" novel by Malcolm Bradbury, I discuss at length Kazuo Ishiguro's *Never Let Me Go* (2005), which features a futuristic version of the "health visitor." Ishiguro's novel sums up the meaning of caring for another by repeating and interrogating a line of some importance to my argument: "it's not your fault." Does this refusal of individual responsibility point a hostile finger at where the welfare state goes wrong? Has this motto become a hindrance to upward mobility, evidence of its decline? Does it abandon all commitment to a properly political anger, anger against injustice? Or is caring, the constitutive action of the welfare state, itself a vehicle for anger? The anger of sociologist Pierre Bourdieu, a representative as well as an analyst of the institutions of social welfare, offers a segue to a section on the autobiographical writings of three sociologists (the other two are Richard Sennett and Paul Willis). All three can be seen as telling, if only in fragments, the story of their own rise from the working class. Both in their lives and in their work as sociologists, all three are profoundly concerned with the question of whether this rise must be thought of as a betrayal of those left behind and the necessary anger that flows from the class system. In academic versions of the paradigmatic "writer" story discussed in chapter 4, these sociologists can be seen as proposing that being a sociologist, or being a sociologist of the sort they themselves have become, represents a kind of answer to the threat of betrayal, a mode of mixed but tangible loyalty to their working-class origins. Pushing on the differences between their accounts, I also underline their common turn to the state. As guarantor of the discipline of sociology as well as employer of the social workers who apply it, the state is the site where their conflicting loyalties can partially and potentially be resolved. In making this turn, I argue, the sociologists are obliged, like Ishiguro's novel, to imagine the state and its employees as bearers of anger. The chapter ends with a brief further discussion of two works already mentioned: in *Parallel Time*, Brent Staples's account of his upward mobility and the role of anger in it, and in *Brothers and Keepers*, John Edgar Wideman's account of what federal funding means to the brother left behind.

The conclusion, "The Luck of Birth and the International Division of Labor," takes Debra Dickerson's *An American Story* as an illustration of the national boundaries that confine the book's argument. Aside from the welfare system's exclusion of distant foreigners, state policy in the metropolis is at best indifferent to them, and at worst seeks them out for more active sorts of injury. The form in which the state offers to play mentor/benefactor to the upwardly mobile Dickerson, for example, is the United States Air Force. If the price of Dickerson's newly credentialed post in military intelligence is paid by those on whom the bombs fall, how strong can the case ultimately be for her upward mobility, when that mobility is seen from a global perspective? The borders of the nation would seem to set severe limits to the defense of upward mobility offered here. How severe? I pursue this question through discussions of two refugee novels, Caryl Phillips's *A Distant Shore* and Lorraine Adams's *Harbor*, before turning in conclusion to Gayatri Chakravorty Spivak as a reader of Jamaica Kincaid and as a reluctant but compelling theorist of upward mobility across the international division of labor.

Erotic Patronage: Rousseau, Constant, Balzac, Stendhal

> Another boy (in this case a highly gifted student),
> fifteen years old, having an affair with a twenty-year-
> old girl, did a legendary paper not mentioned in the
> catalogue on the Older Woman in Stendhal and
> Benjamin Constant.
> —*Mary McCarthy*, The Groves of Academe[1]

OLDER WOMEN

The early books of Rousseau's *Confessions* devote some of their most famous pages to the young Jean-Jacques's singular relationship with Madame de Warens, a Swiss convert to Catholicism who had separated from her husband and moved to Annecy.[2] Some thirteen years older than Rousseau, Madame de Warens picks the fifteen-year-old runaway off the streets, gives him a home and a start in the world, and after some time makes him her lover.[3] In the last of his *Reveries of a Solitary Walker*, Rousseau recalls that the happiest days of his life were those he spent with the woman who he felt understood him perfectly and whom he never stopped calling "Maman." His description of life with Madame de Warens is "liltingly reminiscent," Nicole Fermon comments, "of the best state man can aspire to, the social contract lived in its full dimensions"(27).[4]

The social contract in an idealized two-person version is probably not what most readers will take away from the story as it is narrated in the *Confessions*. On the contrary, Rousseau's autobiography seems to anticipate the wonderfully and distressingly ironic analyses of sexual entanglements that readers have come to expect from novelists like Constant, Stendhal, Balzac, and Flaubert. One unremarkable morning, walking in the garden with her "petit," Madame de Warens proposes that they become lovers. Rousseau is a bit disconcerted, he says, by the formal, dispassionate style of this proposal. Given a full week to reflect on it, he is also bewildered by his own sudden lack of eagerness for the culmination he says he has long fantasized about. He has adored Madame de Warens, body and soul, since the first moment he saw her, he declares. But he wishes the week of delay would somehow last longer. The day comes, the yes is said, and the deed is done. But the experience falls short of his expectations. Trying to make sense of his disappointment, he reinspects Madame de Warens with a somewhat uncharitable eye. Her speeches to him, he says, had been anything but "cold and sad." But the adjectives he goes on to use about her are not warm or joyful. She is "not very sensual." She has a warm sensibility, he observes, but "an icy temperament." If this is love, it is love of a chilly sort. His own coolness might result, Rousseau speculates, from the fact that she is already "possessed by another man," which means that the present arrangement will involve "sharing."[5] Or perhaps he has sensed that she was never erotically "interested" in him at all, but inspired rather by motives that are generously pedagogical and altruistic. After all, Rousseau says, she was more concerned with instructing him than with seducing him. He concludes: "She knew only one real pleasure in the world, and that was giving pleasure to those she loved."[6] He doesn't dwell on whether "pleasure" can still be the proper word, whether for what "those she loved" (a painful plural) take from this self-abnegating gesture or for the feeling thereby enjoyed by the selfless giver.[7]

This lowering of the emotional thermostat could be accounted for in any number of ways. One suggestion has been Rousseau's misogyny. He is making homeopathic use of Madame de Warens, Fermon notes: "without desiring to possess her," he says, "I was very glad that she removed my desire to possess others" (32). Linda Zerilli adds that Rousseau is using "the image of the mother substitute (Madame de Warens)" (45) to safeguard himself in particular against those he calls "big-city women, who practice a false species of dissimulation and never love anything but themselves" (50).[8]

Joan Landes's *Women and the Public Sphere in the Age of the French Revolution* develops some of the same themes, but it also suggests that Rousseau is "far from a pedestrian misogynist"(67).[9] Landes describes "the beneficent mother or desexualized bestower of Good" who is "Rousseau's preferred female figure" as "the *utopian* Maman" (86—my italics). Why utopian rather than, say, regressive? In his programmatic political writings, Landes observes, Rousseau "insists over and over again on the importance of woman's reproductive role" (86). But this is not the role Madame de Warens plays. What is so striking about Rousseau's idealization of "Maman" is that she is *not* literally speaking a mother. Indeed, the peculiar love between the two departs from the norm both in its gesture toward the leveling of conventional gender hierarchy and in that it does not end in, aim at, or imitate the realm of biological reproduction. The lovers' disparity in age may not be a dependable contraceptive, but it does deflect and distance them from the reproductive cycle. And distance from reproduction is essential to Rousseau's political project. Despite his uninspired views on the proper place of women, Rousseau argues not merely that the family cannot be a model for the state, but that the self-alienation required in order for individuals to rediscover themselves in the general will means going "against nature," at least in the sense that the natural is the familial. As Fermon puts it, "democracy becomes possible" only because of an "extensive denaturing process" (11). This denaturing process seems a suspiciously apt characterization of what we glimpse when the young man's fantasy about the older woman is translated into this awkward, self-conscious, and yet somehow gratifying union.[10]

To put this another way, one might say that this episode of seduction or instruction is called into being by Rousseau's political theory. In order for democracy to be chosen, Rousseau suggests, it must be desired. In order for it to be desired, it must be eroticized, must come to permeate everyday affective impulses. Yet how is a general will to emerge if desire continues to flow along conventional channels, aiming by whatever detours at the eventual reproduction of the family? Where is a new, distanced, democracy-building desire to come from, and how will anything so new come to be felt as a genuine visceral desire? By contrast with more familiar and instinctive versions, the nonreproductive, suprafamilial desire necessary for the founding or sustaining of a democratic state would almost have to seem, at least initially, somewhat pale, eccentric, or ambiguous. There might be reason to doubt whether it is genuinely erotic at all. Such doubts and ambiguities are the traditional subject matter of the realist novel, which sometimes looks like a sophisticated machine churning out endlessly varied exhibits of Stendhal's ironic principle: "N'est-ce que cela?" But the novel performs more than one kind of cultural work. And it seems plausible to speculate that, despite its gift for ironic estrangement, it is also capable of working with rather than against the aims of Rousseau's political theory. In other words, one thing we see the novelistic mode representing is what that political theory demands: passion in the process of being subdued and disciplined, yet also nourished and redirected. With a blink and a shake of the head, the novel's all-too-familiar disillusionment can be thus seen as simultaneously something quite different: the mode of citizenly desire necessary to the emergence of a democratic state.

The classic problem of Rousseau's political theory is that his ideal state presumes the prior existence of the subjects it would logically have to produce, and vice versa. As Bonnie Honig puts it, "You cannot have good laws without good people and you cannot have good people without good laws."[11] In order to break the vicious circle, Honig argues, Rousseau needs a deus ex machina: "the figure of the founder, a good person prior to good law, a miraculous lawgiver" (20). In *On the Social Contract* Rousseau writes: "The discovery of the best rules of society would require a superior intelligence, who saw all of men's passions yet experienced none of them; who had no relationship at all to our nature yet knew it thoroughly; whose happiness was independent of us, yet who was nevertheless willing to attend to ours."[12] A miraculous, unnatural lawgiver who experienced none of our passions, whose happiness was independent of ours: in other words, a kind of beloved and beneficent monster. For Honig, this figure is the foreign founder. But the description might also apply to altruistically inclined nonmothers with icy temperaments, such as Rousseau's Maman. Or for that matter Hannibal Lecter, a "superior intelligence" whose independence of the happiness of others makes him a cannibalistic serial killer as well as, more shockingly, a good mentor.

This juxtaposition of Hannibal Lecter with Madame de Warens is intended to suggest that there exists a significant historical continuity running from the "bad sex" of the *Confessions* to the lapses from passion, the frustration or evasion of conventional erotic commitment and resolution that we have just seen in *The Silence of the Lambs*. And since this line of libidinal blockages is also a series of libidinal rechannelings, I'm also suggesting that in the two centuries of fiction between these two upward mobility stories, the ambiguous erotics between protagonist and mentor continues to be caught up in the historical movement toward the goal of Rousseau's political theory: the ever-postponed, ever-incomplete rise of what Robert Castel calls "the social state."[13] In other words, character types like the maternal older woman and the male criminal of ambiguous sexuality serve as something like fiction's own "miraculous lawgivers," casting the cool light of their characteristic affect over the individual's desire for upward mobility in order to direct it toward a seemingly less attractive, more generously democratic version of the general welfare.

It is a bit of a stretch, of course, to think of the scrupulously benevolent Madame de Warens as a direct ancestor of Hannibal Lecter. Yet I hope the reader will at least grant the initial premise that her role in the *Confessions* and the many pairings between younger men and older women that follow in the nineteenth-century novel represent something other than a mass outbreak of male Oedipal regression. The prevalence in this period of the character Balzac named "la femme de trente ans" (the woman of thirty—did any act of naming ever reveal more graphically the historical malleability of age?) has always seemed to invite the comment that John Osborne's play *Look Back in Anger* offers about its protagonist's former lover: "She was nearly old enough to be his mother. I expect that's something to do with it!"[14] Like Rousseau, both Constant and Stendhal lost their mothers early in life, and their biographers have made much of the fact in interpretations of their fiction as well as their love lives. Yet Balzac and Flaubert suffered no such loss. And one must therefore look elsewhere to explain the shared narrative patterns—and for that matter the shared patterns in life. Each of them had at least one early and hugely significant relationship with a woman considerably older than himself. Flaubert's relationship with Elise Schlesinger, the model for Madame Arnoux in *Sentimental Education*, has been amply documented, as has Balzac's with Laure de Berny, an aristocratic woman twenty-three years older than Balzac and one year older than his mother. Examples from other authors might be adduced, including some who are not French. But the more biographical details are brought forward, the less plausible is any merely biographical reading. Individual psychology might have seemed the likeliest candidate to interpret any one of these relationships, but faced with a number of quite different personalities and life trajectories, it can hardly expect its opinion on the collective phenomenon to be taken as decisive.

As might be expected, French novelists of the early- and mid-nineteenth century are less than perfectly consistent in their treatment of older women, whether in life or in fiction. Balzac wrote to Madame de Berny that she was his "fixed star": "Amid these illusions, elegant daughters of a too lively imagination, there will always be a fixed star, always brightly shining, which will serve me as a compass. It will be you, my dearest friend."[15] Unlike Balzac's mother, who thought Madame de Berny "was trying to *get him*" (99), his biographer André Maurois seems convinced by the star metaphor: "She was lover and passionate mistress, counselor, companion, protectress and confidant. She lighted the world for him."[16] As she was dying, Madame de Berny kept a copy of Balzac's *Le Lys dans la vallée*, one of his "older woman" novels, next to her bed.[17] Yet consider another, more famous older woman, this time from Balzac's fiction: Madame de Bargeton in *Les Illusions Perdues*. Balzac shamelessly uses Madame de Bargeton to point the contrary moral: no stars are fixed. Having fallen in love with the young poet and commoner Lucien de Rubempré in the provinces and to his delight taken him off to Paris with her, she suddenly regrets her choice. In Paris she finds herself "humiliated in her love" (171), for "Lucien counted for nothing here" (174).[18] When she drops him, she is following the advice of Madame d'Espard, who has "the occult power which a great lady with ambition wields . . . she had promised herself success if she became the satellite of this star" (170). There is now a new and brighter star, and Madame de Bargeton wants to revolve around it. As does Lucien, who is equally smitten with Madame d'Espard. This "queenly person" makes "the same impression on the poet as Madame de Bargeton had made on him in Angoulême. His volatile character promptly impelled a desire in him for the protection of so lofty a person, and the surest means for this was to win her as a woman—all the rest would follow!" (178–79). Observing Madame de Bargeton and Madame d'Espard together, Lucien sees his lover transformed into "a tall, desiccated woman with freckled skin, faded complexion and strikingly red hair; angular, affected, pretentious, provincial of speech and above all badly dressed!" (169). Though Madame de Bargeton will be permitted a further and more gracious makeover, her raising up as a celestial paragon seems largely an excuse for the enthusiastic defilement that follows.

Some such pedestal effect, with its overtones of aggressive misogyny, is no doubt at work elsewhere as well. But it's not all that's at work. It's not all that's at work even in Benjamin Constant's bitterly disabused novel *Adolphe* (1816), which makes use of Constant's youthful relationships with the writers and pioneer feminists Madame de Staël (the original of Madame de Bargeton) and Isabelle de Charrière.[19] The young protagonist's love affair with Ellénore, who is ten years older, rapidly becomes a nightmare.[20] In trying to woo her away from the nobleman to whom she has long been the publicly respected mistress, Adolphe has presented himself to Ellénore as possessing "un coeur étranger à tous les intérêts du monde," someone who neither hopes for nor demands anything (53). But even before she generously "gives herself" (59) to him, Ellénore makes a still better case for her own obliviousness to worldly interest, her "amour pur de tout calcul, de tout intérêt" (62) ("love devoid of calculation and self-interest" [85]). "Elle m'avait tout sacrifié, fortune, enfants, réputation; elle n'éxigeait d'autre prix de ses sacrifices que de m'attendrir comme une humble esclave, de passer chaque jour avec moi quelques minutes, de jouir des moments que je pourrais lui donner" (75) ("She had sacrificed everything on my account: her fortune, her children, her reputation; the only reward she wanted for these sacrifices was to wait for me like a humble slave, to spend a few minutes with me each day, to enjoy the few moments I could give her" [102]).[21] It soon becomes clear to Adolphe that this sacrifice of all self-interest is a form of moral combat in which the larger the sacrifice, the greater the leverage over the one who receives it. (The reader will perhaps be reminded of the Pythons' "Four Yorkshiremen.") When Ellénore refuses half the fortune of her former lover in order to stay with Adolphe, the latter is plunged into "désespoir" (despair) by this "nouveau sacrifice" (new sacrifice [109]) (80). Two pages later, Ellénore tops this renunciation with a still more crushing move: she refuses an invitation from her exiled father, now restored to enormous wealth, to come to Poland, share in his prosperity and high rank, and thereby assure "une grande fortune" (a considerable fortune [113]) (82) to her children. She is playing the game of sacrifice, and she is winning big. Adolphe decides that self-sacrificing love of this sort is "de tous les sentiments le plus

égoïste, et, par conséquent, le moins généreux" (83). But this consciousness doesn't help him. The ultimate sacrifice, her death, will leave him a
broken man, not a liberated one.

Feminist critics working within the tradition of psychoanalysis have
tended to be skeptical about the idealization of mother figures in male
fiction. They have objected, reasonably enough, that such figures serve
a system of values that does not go out of its way to do justice to women.
This is the brunt of Laurie Langbauer's argument, for example, that
motherhood cannot be allowed to serve as a selfless antidote to male
egotism (56–60). Her critique targets Fredric Jameson's reliance "on the
fantasy of the pre-Oedipal mother" who both "exists to reflect back the
self, convincing the infant that the outside world is actually a sustaining
part of him," and also "supplies a wishful figure for the critic's harmoni-
ous coexistence with the dominant system in which he works" (15).[22]
Whatever the rights or wrongs of these wishes, Langbauer's critique
helps underline one role that mother substitutes are indeed asked to play
in male stories of upward mobility: representing a version of society,
whether existent or utopian, that would be "sustaining" both for the
protagonist and in general. And it highlights the interesting fact that, if
only because they are erotically active and indeed (like Madame de Warens) proactive, these women cannot be characterized as unambiguously
"selfless." To see them as both self-interested *and* sustaining, however
unequally, is to make them much more interesting, and with them the
logic of upward mobility as well.

In *The Sentimental Education of the Novel*, Margaret Cohen offers
another feminist interpretation of this mother-substitute role, but one
that is more compelling because more strenuously and comprehensively
historical. According to Cohen, what early-nineteenth-century male realists were criticizing by means of characters like Constant's Ellénore
was a well-established eighteenth-century tradition of female sentimental writing, a tradition whose primary theme was democratic citizenship.
"Sacrifice is a privileged term in the sentimental vocabulary to describe
an individual's abnegation of individual freedom out of respect for collective welfare."[23] Adolphe's interpretation of Ellénore's self-sacrifice as
disguised egotism is natural enough, Cohen argues, in that "collective
welfare" pointedly included the interests of women. (Then as now, the
concept of welfare is visibly gender-weighted in its effects.) In Cohen's
view, "collective welfare" aims at a democratic inclusiveness that crosses
both gender and class lines. She takes issue with Peter Szondi's characterization of sentimentality as "the consolation of a class blocked from
political power" (70), in other words a model for the bourgeois citizen
who under absolute monarchy is forced into a merely domestic exercise
of virtue. She attaches it instead to a larger object, a "hybrid class" (71)

or broad cross-class coalition that "already has substantial political, cultural, and economic importance in the second half of the eighteenth century and will emerge to hegemony with the Revolution" (71). For this hybrid class, "made up of the *noblesse de robe* and some members of the *noblesse d'épée* as well as professional, financial, and protoindustrial bourgeois" (43), sentimentality offered a sort of apprenticeship in what it would mean to be a citizen.

The male rejection of female sentimentality, Cohen concludes, must therefore be counted as a serious political loss. For it marks a narrowing of political vision. Indeed, that narrowing is one thing that makes realism seem realistic. Whereas sentimentalism asserted a boldly forward-looking and effectively transgendered claim to citizenship, realism quietly submits to the given reality of gender inequality, differentiating "women's careers within the family from men's access to political and professional self-realization" (107). In inventing or reinventing the upward mobility story, it gives that story to men alone, assuming that women want only the gratifications of love and thus fixing and naturalizing the gender facts of one historical moment. It is solely as a figure of love, without reference to the sentimental claim to citizenship, that these male realists present the composite figure Cohen refers to as "the older woman" or the "femme de trente ans." This figure, whom Balzac and later critics have agreed in judging "one of his great literary creations" (107), represents in fact a step backward from the sentimental heroine who was Balzac's immediate source: "the older woman is the sentimental heroine stripped of her ethical grandeur. She does particularize sentimental universalism, but her specifically female conception of happiness is just as distanced from women's historical experience as sentimentality's use of women to embody the impasses of liberal subjecthood" (108).

This is a powerful argument, and for my purposes here an indispensable one. I depart from it only in emphasis. When the masculine novelists borrow the older, self-sacrificing woman character from sentimentalism, don't they also borrow and thus sustain, despite their irony, some of that character's "ethical grandeur"? To Cohen, their relation to the female discourse of citizenship seems simply and unambiguously critical. But is that necessarily the effect of, say, raising the possibility that self-interest might be one element among others in the makeup of such a female character? Even in the extreme case of *Adolphe*, can we say that the sentimental tradition is taken on only in order to be pointedly and categorically rejected?

A self-described disciple of Helvétius in his youth, Constant clearly continues to value self-interest much more highly than the sentimental writers do, or for that matter than Rousseau does. In the liberal tradition of Montesquieu, Constant demands more autonomy for a private sphere in which self-interest will be protected from the state or the general will.[24] Yet in his political writings Constant continues to pay homage to Rousseau, and he is by no means an unconditional supporter of self-interest.[25] On the contrary, as Biancamaria Fontana puts it, "The only relatively clear image of a possible historical future to be conjured up in Constant's writings appeared in the form of a nightmare: a society of isolated individuals, without faith, without culture, without local ties, uninterested in their own political destiny, mere machines bent to the reproduction of their own material interest."[26] Constant's commitment to something other than "isolated individuals" and their "material interest" also resonates in the ending of *Adolphe*. After all, the question of the ending is not whether Constant approves of Ellénore's game of incremental sacrifice. The more pressing and pertinent question is why, despite the cold-eyed scrutiny to which Adolphe subjects it, this game still *works* on him—why disinterestedness possesses so decisive a power, why self-sacrifice is so crushingly efficient a weapon. If Adolphe can recognize Ellénore's gestures as displaced egotism, why can't he just shrug them off? I see only one explanation: among the other things she represents, Ellénore also remains a figure for the democratic imperative, for the popular or general will. Constant is of course imagining, with liberalism's characteristic anxiety, that the general will might become a disguised, unofficial despotism over the individual. But this does not mean he can say no to it. He remains a democrat as well as a liberal, and a democrat in a strong, demanding sense. He cannot refuse Ellénore's sacrifices because he cannot refuse the democratic project.[27]

The productiveness of ambivalence like this may not be obvious; I will try to explain it further in a minute. But first let us pause to note how much of it there is. The ending of *Adolphe* is echoed by many other endings in which upward mobility either fails or is renounced, and in which the failure or renunciation is again presided over in some sense by an older woman. To take only a handful of unquestioned classics, examples would include Stendhal's *The Red and the Black*, Dickens's *Great Expectations*, and Flaubert's *Sentimental Education*. The protagonist of *Sentimental Education*, Frédéric Moreau is not an obvious hero of upward mobility; he comes into an inheritance early in the novel and from that time forth is largely passive, spending his money more or less unwisely rather than scheming to make a name for himself in some area of endeavor or effecting any fundamental change in his status. But he does scheme to obtain a higher position as the lover of Madame Dambreuse, wife of an aristocratic financier. To the limited extent that this challenge ever commands Flaubert's attention, it takes its decisive turning with another renunciation, late in the novel. In a desire to humiliate her already defeated rival, Madame Dambreuse buys up one of Madame Arnoux's possessions at an auction. Frédéric immediately walks out on her: "He was proud of having avenged Madame Arnoux, by sacrificing a fortune to her" (409). As in *The Red and the Black*, the protagonist's decision that he is bored with the project of upward mobility and ready to withdraw from it is enacted in the name of faithfulness to an older woman who has been the first great love of his life. There is a certain paradox here: it is Madame Arnoux who inspires Frédéric's final rejection of the very idea of accomplishment, but it was also Madame Arnoux who inspired such efforts as he ever made to accomplish something. So whatever she stands for, it is not simple renunciation. Moreover, in a novel that seems to leave no square inch of social space that is not saturated with irony—Frédéric's gesture is certainly not exempt from it—Madame Arnoux is the only character who emerges more or less unscathed. Thus we are again presented with the mystery of a younger man/older woman bond that seems to break the rules otherwise in force—yet a bond that has its own force and seems to define its own rules.[28]

In a final renunciation of upward mobility like this, it is hard not to see the persistence of sentimentalism, though not perhaps with its full democratic energy intact. Some of the novel's trickiest and most interesting evidence for this continuity, however, comes not from endings but from middles. Consider for example Cohen's reading of Balzac's *Père Goriot*. In order to win the considerable fortune of Mademoiselle de Taillefer, Cohen astutely points out, Rastignac is advised by Vautrin to feign sentimentalism's signature gesture: self-sacrifice. If he pretends to "sacrifice his social ambitions for her love," she will throw her riches at his feet. In other words, the episode offers a further critique of the sentimental novel, for it transforms sacrifice "from a sublime affirmation of community to a calculated strategy of self-interest unfolding with the banality of everyday life. . . . sentimental sacrifice is a ruse" (111). True enough. And yet if Balzac's view of sacrifice runs up against the limits of his "misogyny" (107), one might say that Cohen's view runs up against the limits of a certain heteronormativity. For how can we ignore the element of "sentimental sacrifice" in Vautrin's own relation to Rastignac? In laying out his scheme to his handsome young fellow lodger, Vautrin attempts to keep up the appearances of cynical self-interest, and many critics have been willing to cooperate. One can always conclude that he wants to get his revenge on society through Rastignac, or simply wants to get Rastignac into bed. Self-interest can never be safely ruled out. Yet Vautrin's attempt to appear cold-blooded is as utterly unconvincing as his declared aim of using his share of the profits in order to become a slaveholder on the American frontier. He cannot hide either his erotic investment in Rastignac or his willingness to sacrifice for his love. Since Vautrin is removed from the novel (by the police) before the plot can go any further, the ingredients of self-sacrifice and self-interest mixed to-gether in passion's heady compound are given no time to precipitate out. We are not permitted to know exactly how high love has raised Vautrin, as his speech suggests, toward a genuine imitation of the sentimental ideal. What is sure is that, even trailing this ambiguity after it, Vautrin's bond to Rastignac remains the vehicle for something like an "affirmation of community." *Père Goriot* contains no more magnificent contradiction than that between what Vautrin says *to* Rastignac—his cynical vision of a society controlled by ruthless self-interest—and how Vautrin seems to behave *toward* Rastignac: with the sort of solidarity, selflessness, and generosity for which there appears to be no room in the universally rapa-cious society he himself has described.[29] On this evidence, the democratic, community-building virtues and vision that Cohen prizes in the sentimen-tal novel do not in fact disappear from realism, tricky as it is to identify and evaluate them there.[30]

INTEREST, DISINTEREST, AND BOREDOM

It is tempting to think of self-sacrifice as a virtue preeminently belonging to women—that is to say, a virtue forced upon women. In female versions of the upward mobility story, the virtue picked out for reward is most often the paradoxical one of not seeking to be rewarded. In *Jane Eyre*, for example, Jane is granted a class-transgressive marriage with her (older) master, and is seen to deserve that prize, in large part because she refuses to deploy any of the self-serving contrivances that might be ex-pected of her and instead behaves toward Rochester in an ostentatiously disinterested manner. Women could be allowed upward mobility if and only if they didn't strive for it. (Ten years before *Jane Eyre* was published, its author received this explicit advice in a letter from poet laureate Robert Southey: "the less you aim at celebrity, the more likely you will be to deserve and finally to obtain it.")[31] Still, when Leo Braudy describes "the secret of selling a self whose value was that it was ultimately not for sale," he is talking not about the usual double standard, but about a principle that extends to men as well.[32] As is Kant when, in Alasdair MacIntyre's paraphrase, he allows happiness to be "the reward of virtue only if it [happiness] is unsought."[33]

No further explanation of this broad cross-gender phenomenon is needed than Margaret Cohen's, already cited above. Why do so many elements of sentimentalism persist into realism? Why does the genre of the upward mobility story, which seems the very epitome of self-interest, allude so often and so creatively to disinterestedness and self-sacrifice? Self-sacrifice, Cohen reminds us, belonged to the ideology of the rising cross-class coalition that becomes hegemonic after the French Revolution. Bourgeois revolution might seem in theory to lead toward a shameless celebration of self-interest. But the lonely moment of predicted ideological purity did not come in 1815, or 1830, or 1848, or indeed at any point in the nineteenth century. As Stefan Collini argues, the sensibility of the most prominent Victorian intellectuals "was marked at least as much by an obsession with the role of altruism and a concern for the cultivation of feelings as it was by any commitment to the premises of self-interest and rational calculation" (62).[34] And despite the propaganda of Thatcher, Reagan, and the more recent generation of free-marketeers, a commitment to no-holds-barred self-interest has still not had its moment alone in the ideological spotlight. If it had, capitalism would arguably have shaken itself to pieces.

For more than two centuries, two conflicting factors have made disinterestedness internal to the ideology of capitalism: the need to *disguise* self-interest and the need to *constrain* self-interest. Both are characteristic functions of the state. And both inhere in characters like Madame de Warens and Hannibal Lecter. The difficulty of distinguishing one function from the other accounts for some of the obscurity we confront when we try to make ethical sense of such characters. They oscillate between the two, and the ambiguity seems irreducible. As I have been trying to suggest, this ambiguity is a crucial hinge between the formal operations of the upward mobility story and the ideological work of democratic theory under capitalism—a democratic theory that both expresses and obstructs capitalism.

It follows that disinterestedness cannot simply be set against capitalism. And from this one may also deduce, more tentatively, that interest or self-interest, which is so strong a motive in the upward mobility story, cannot simply be aligned *with* capitalism. When the meaning of the word *interest* narrows in the direction of "economic advantage," as Albert O. Hirschman argues about an earlier period, the value of disinterestedness enlarges.[35] But the broader, eighteenth-century sense of "interest" does not fade away. In seeking to engage the reader's "interest," Margaret Cohen writes, sentimentalism is looking for the reader's *sympathy* (62). This sense of the word—not egotism, but force of attraction, ability to command attention or sympathy, that which makes someone interesting— helps explain why older women could stand for as well as against interest. And this sense remains visibly active in Constant and his male successors. When Constant replays the question of the Ancients and the Moderns, he takes the side of the Moderns on almost everything. Better to have fewer poets and no slaves, as he puts it somewhere. But he also sees that the likely result of the retreat from ancient-style democratic participation into modern privacy and leisure will be "boredom" (ennui). According to Todorov, the fear of boredom is a theme that Constant shares with Madame de Staël and articulates in his first political pamphlet: the "lack of goals, interests, and hopes other than narrow, personal ones" (49) ("privation de but, d'intérêts et d'espérances autres qu'étroites et personnelles") makes life seem futile and empty. Restored here to its origins in privation, privacy is the unfortunate result when "domestic affection replaces great public interests."[36] Here self-interest signifies a *loss* of interest. Even while generating an extremely unsentimental analysis—for example, how a love affair needs obstacles, or "the interest of difficulty," in order not to become boring and burdensome—this other sense of interest sustains something of the expansive democratic vision of Cohen's sentimental writers.[37] One again sees both at work when Constant says that in order to stave off boredom, what we need is to be "electrified by the recognition of our equals" ("électrisé par la reconnaissance de ses égaux"). One would not have suspected such potential compatibility between love and democracy.

In terms of upward mobility, this compatibility suggests a hypothesis: that the protagonist can be interested without being merely self-interested. It is theoretically possible, that is, to reconcile the desire for individual success and achievement with sympathy for and from others, with an achievement that somehow touches their welfare as well as one's own. Stendhal is being gently ironic with Julien Sorel when the latter expresses his dream of "distinction for himself and liberty for all ("distinctions pour lui et la liberté pour tous) (302). But it is arguably just this dream, with its imperfect but palpable effort at synthesis, that informs *The Red and the Black*. Including its equivocal use of "boredom" as the term that opposes both senses of "interest."

Boredom is the mystery that Erich Auerbach sets out to solve in chapter 18 of *Mimesis*, which deals with nineteenth-century French realism. The chapter begins with a passage from *The Red and the Black*.[38] In this passage Mademoiselle de la Mole overhears Julien, her father's low-born secretary, as he tells the Abbé Pirard how bored he is at the family dinner table. The Abbé reminds Julien of the obvious: that his presence at dinner is an honor and a privilege. Since Julien is engaged in self-conscious social climbing, he knows that the chance to dine with his aristocratic employer is also in his interest as he himself conceives it. And yet he finds the dinners tedious, and he wishes if possible to be excused.

Addressing himself to this conundrum, Auerbach offers possible explanations: the stifling conventionality of the Restoration salon and Julien's politically motivated "loathing and scorn" for the classes in power. But the real solution to the mystery, he says, lies in Julien's "sense of inner superiority" (457), and this sense of superiority is grounded in Stendhal's identification with those who governed France under the ancien régime. In spite of his nonaristocratic background and democratic-republican politics, Auerbach says, Stendhal looks down on all classes of nineteenth-century society, those above as well as those below him on the social scale, with a contempt that can only be described as aristocratic: "Stendhal is an aristocratic son of the *ancien régime grande bourgeoisie,* he will and can be no nineteenth-century bourgeois" (464). In his eyes, the bourgeoisie of his day is degraded, and the aristocracy has lowered itself both by reaction to and by imitation of its inferiors. His contempt is possible, and with it his "sometimes almost morbid aversion to entering into contemporary life" (467), because of what Stendhal himself terms his "aristocratic instincts" (464).

In Auerbach's judgment, these "aristocratic instincts" place severe restrictions on Stendhal's brand of realism. Contrasting it with the realism of Balzac, he proposes that Stendhal's aristocratic self-assurance and the boredom it encouraged prevented him from achieving the "Historicism" that is Balzac's claim to greatness.[39] In the well-known analysis of *Le Père Goriot* that immediately follows the section on Julien's boredom, Auerbach argues that Balzac's anthropologically thick description of the Maison Vauquer creates a sense of historical "milieu" so powerful and pervasive that no character, and no criteria of social judgment, can escape it. "The spirit of Historicism" that is also "the spirit of [Balzac's] entire work" (477) effectively disables any moral critique that is more than momentary. Stendhal's heroes, he concludes, "think and feel in opposition to their time, only with contempt do they descend to the intrigues and machinations of the post-Napoleonic present. . . . In Stendhal the freedom of the great heart, the freedom of passion, still has much of the aristocratic loftiness . . . more characteristic of the *ancien régime* than of the nineteenth-century bourgeoisie." Balzac, on the contrary, "plunges his heroes far more deeply into time-conditioned dependency; he thereby loses the standards and limits" by which the present could be judged (482). The boundaries of Stendhal's realism are the "standards and limits" by which he judges society, which is to say his "aristocratic loftiness."

This contrast between Stendhal and Balzac is plausible enough, but it sends us back to Auerbach's opening passage with a certain puzzlement. From the perspective of our argument, what we glimpse in this passage (though this is not Auerbach's own focus) is a crucial step in Julien's upward mobility. Unaware that he is being overheard, Julien makes his declaration of boredom. Overhearing it, Mademoiselle de la Mole suddenly forgets their respective places in the social hierarchy and begins to be intrigued by him. The scene Auerbach has picked out is thus uncannily central to the plot. More than any other single moment, it could be said to "cause" the love affair between Julien and Mathilde, hence also to explain the upward mobility itself. Eventually Julien will renounce the considerable advantages bestowed upon him by this liaison. But for now the paradox seems unavoidable: his boredom, which announces his indifference to rising, has facilitated his rise. As far as upward mobility is concerned, therefore, Auerbach would seem to be implying something counterintuitive. If Julien's boredom is a secret cause of his upward mobility, and if the secret cause of Julien's boredom is an "aristocratic loftiness" he shares with his author, then the force behind upward mobility in *The Red and the Black* would seem to be the protagonist's espousal of a worldview that looks down upon society from above, not up at it from below.

By definition, upward mobility is about moving up in a social hierarchy. So what is boredom, sign of an anachronistic "loftiness," doing at the heart of the upward mobility plot in one of the genre's seminal and unquestioned classics? One way to cast some light upon the now compounded mystery of Julien's boredom would be to consider it as a late, psychologized variant of the motif of the noble foundling. Lower-class characters in Fielding and Smollett, for example, are occasionally permitted to transgress class boundaries, but at least some of their threat to social order is dissipated when the plot reveals, in a formulaic flourish of tokens and recognitions, that these figures were of noble birth all along. Stendhal could be seen as taking the tokens and the ancestry and internalizing them, substituting subjective nobility of character for objective nobility of birth.[40] From this perspective, Auerbach's passage would turn into a sort of precocious, middle-of-the-plot recognition scene in which Mathilde, who shares Stendhal's contempt for the debased aristocrats of her own day, discovers in Julien the genuine aristocratic qualities she has hitherto found only in history books.[41] This seems reasonable enough. But if so, what follows? To the extent that Stendhal is encouraging us to see these qualities as natural, universal ones, representative of no social class but only of exceptional individuals, he would seem to be implying that the existing class hierarchy itself is unnatural. But he would also be renaturalizing social hierarchy according to the new criterion of whether or not one possesses these qualities. And if Stendhal is suggesting that these qualities are indeed aristocratic, as Mademoiselle de la Mole believes, he would seem to be proposing that there already exists an ethical common ground *within* the existing class hierarchy where aristocrats and talented commoners can come together. This overlaps with Margaret Cohen's historical analysis, which draws on Guy Chaussinaud-Nogaret's *The French Nobility in the Eighteenth Century*.[42] René Girard makes the same point from the other side when he discusses the marquis de la Mole, whom he sees appreciating in Julien virtues that are here identified as plebeian—an appreciation equally crucial to Julien's rise. "M. de la Mole is still capable of approving the rise of a talented commoner. He proves it with Julien Sorel. . . . Julien owes his success to that element under the new regime which has most truly survived from the ancien régime. This is a strange way of Stendhal to campaign against a return to the past."[43] Indeed, this praise of the *ancien régime* could also be extracted from the description of Madame de Rênal, the aristocratic older woman whose love for Julien initiates his social ascent and to whom he ultimately returns. But whether we see Julien's qualities as embraced because they are natural or because they are aristocratic, we lose any strong sense of his rise as rebellious or disruptive. Either he already takes after his aristocratic superiors, or, just as strangely, the aristocracy is already predisposed to make room for him. In either case, there is less mobility here than meets the eye.

If Julien rises because he is recognized by virtue of his ethical character alone, in spite of his status as a commoner, then one of two conclusions would seem to follow, each of them apparently discouraging for a book about upward mobility. On the one hand, we might decide, generalizing from Stendhal's example, that the very concept of an upward mobility story is misleading and misguided, for no one rises who does not already belong to the higher class. Ethics and psychology would thus be more relevant than class identity to what is most variable and interesting about the genre, a genre that would thus be ripe for hostile takeover by some other, less class-inflected category, for example the bildungsroman. Boredom would seem to be the legitimate response both for Julien and for the reader, who would have every reason to throw up his or her hands at the whole idea of upward mobility as a unit of literary analysis. Given the sloppy approximativeness of class terms like "aristocratic" and "bourgeois" and the notorious historical difficulty of disentangling a rising class from antagonists it fought only by joining, or which surrendered to it but in surrendering also shaped the identity of their conquerors, this option may strike the reader as a welcome exit strategy from a failing enterprise.

On the other hand, there is also the option of rescuing the concept and tradition of upward mobility, but doing so only by excising Stendhal from it. If we decide that Stendhal did not really do upward mobility, the genre's nineteenth-century history could be rewritten in tandem with Auerbach's history of nineteenth-century realism. Just as Auerbach's ancien régime Stendhal does not achieve genuine realism, which had to await the post-Revolutionary sensibility of Balzac, so we would conclude that Stendhal's treatment of upward mobility remains faithful to a conservative eighteenth-century view of class and cannot represent the genuine transgressiveness of the upward mobility narrative, which comes into its own only afterward.

There is clearly some truth in both of these options, but neither seems quite right. The trouble with the second hypothesis is that, as we shall see, it misrepresents what comes afterwards. If we think of Julien's aristocratic self-confidence as a vestige of earlier class society that the novel later outgrows, then we will be surprised to find that the novel does *not* in fact outgrow it. Stendhal turns out to be not the exception but the rule. Julien's sense of bored superiority to his own opportunistic career-making is not an infantile disorder or anachronistic residuum that the upward mobility genre eventually overcomes. Again and again those characters who seem most eager to rise in the world are also those who are most capable of forgetting or transcending their self-interested desire. In *Great Expectations*, Pip assures Miss Havisham that no, he wants no money for himself, only for his friend Herbert. With a Dickensian insouciance, Alger's Ragged Dick tells his benefactor-to-be, "All my money's invested in the Erie Railroad." In her big moment onstage, Dreiser's Carrie distinguishes herself by introducing herself with a self-effacing "I am yours truly."[44] In a bar with the wealthy man who is about to send him off to Europe, all expenses paid, Patricia Highsmith's Tom Ripley says to himself, "He was bored, God-damned bloody bored, bored, bored!"[45] The genre of course contains plenty of the self-interested activity that is vulgarly called "sucking up." But boredom is also there from the beginning, and it remains. Indeed, nothing could be more persistently central than the play between being bored and being "interested," or the identification of being bored with being interest*ing*. Nothing could be more characteristic of the genre than a recognition scene, or something like a recognition scene, in which a superior looks at an ambitious inferior and contrives to see what Mathilde de la Mole sees in Julien's boredom: the mysterious marker of an inexplicable disinterestedness, a disinterestedness that affirms something in herself. The rapprochement that happens in such scenes is the ideological heart of the upward mobility story.

And yet I will also argue—this is perhaps where my argument diverges most perilously from received wisdom—that focusing on the successful recognition between protagonist and benefactor does not send us back to the hypothesis that the upwardly mobile protagonist is merely a rich man in disguise. It can be shown that all class identities are not fixed in advance, and neither is the game of upward mobility. Thus the genre can be shown to furnish some pleasant political surprises.[46]

The Acquisition of the Donor

Had Auerbach sought a closer, structural parallel with his passage from *The Red and the Black*, he might have found it in another early scene from *Père Goriot*—again, something like a recognition scene. This is the moment when Rastignac, penniless and friendless in a Paris in which he desperately wishes to rise, wins what will turn out to be the decisive support of his distant cousin, the vicomtesse de Beauséant. This is not accomplished by means of the "distant family connection" (64) ("bout de parenté" [109]) which Rastignac finds can easily be ignored. His initial attempt to call her "cousin" is coldly and instantaneously rebuffed (63). How then does Rastignac succeed? He comes upon Madame de Beauséant at a moment when she is extremely vulnerable; she has just received the news that her lover is about to marry a wealthy heiress. Among the elements that work toward her about-face are Rastignac's willingness to defend her against the malice of the friend who has delivered this news; his unrehearsed, scandalized outburst of emotion when he hears how Père Goriot is treated by his daughters; and his pretense of acting with the emotional directness of a child clinging to her skirt. He asks her to play "fairy godmother" (64) to him ("une de ces fées fabuleuses" [109]). She seems to translate all this as proof that he, unlike her lover, would be "sincere in [his] love" (64) ("vous aimeriez sincèrement, vous!" [110])[47] And she goes on to promise him her assistance. Yet Balzac does not quite permit us to think that the trick is turned merely by Rastignac's demonstration of natural inner goodness.

The two sentences that follow get to the heart of the logic by which Rastignac manages, as he has intended, to "secure her goodwill" (67) ("capter la bienveillance" [112]). "La vicomtesse s'intéressa vivement à l'étudiant pour une réponse d'ambitieux. Le Méridional en était à son premier calcul" (110). Here the World's Classics translation has: "The vicomtesse found the student's bold answer extremely interesting. For the first time the Southerner had become calculating" (64). This seems to get the emphasis slightly wrong. The point in the first sentence is not that she finds him interesting, but that she finds him interesting specifically because he gives the answer of an ambitious man (not a "bold" one). In other words, we are told that Madame de Beauséant sees through what she herself has just called sincerity to the ambition that has motivated Rastignac's kind words to her. But instead of disapproving his hypocrisy, she becomes actively interested or attracted.[48] In the second sentence, however, the emphasis falls less on the fact that he has become calculating than on the innocence that he is just at this moment at the point of losing. He still so *new* at calculation—the calculation that an ambitious man has no choice but to become competent at, as Madame de Beauséant herself will now go on to tell him. In effect, what we behold in these few lines is the whitewashing of Rastignac's ambition, which comes forth from Madame de Beauséant's tender translation looking like the very innocence that might at first have seemed its antithesis. This is a magical resolution worthy of a "fairy godmother."[49]

" 'The world is loathsome and wicked,' " Madame de Beauséant remarks. And then a couple of sentences later, " 'Well, Monsieur de Rastignac, treat the world as it deserves. You want to get on, I will help you. You will plumb the depths of women's corruption, you will measure the extent of men's miserable vanity. . . . The more coldly calculating you are, the further you will go. Strike without pity and people will fear you. Accept men and women as mere post horses to be left worn out at every stage and you will reach the summit of your ambitions" (71–72). The speech is one long self-contradiction. Why is present company excluded from Madame de Beauséant's speech? Why doesn't she treat Rastignac like a post horse to be worn out and then left, or realize that he is treating her like a post horse? Why does she take pity in the very act of saying that he must be pitiless? If the world is as she says it is, why should she help him? No grounds are given to think that Rastignac is less a creature of "miserable vanity" than other men. On the contrary, he has just confessed to that vanity. Given a world as coldly and self-interestedly calculating as she says, she should consult her own self-interest and choose to help only someone who has the power to help her in return.[50] If she is right, therefore, then she is also wrong.

The bond between them remains nameless as well as anomalous. Yet Balzac clearly has a strong investment in this not quite lovelike form of adhesion. The contradiction between Madame de Beauséant's harsh vision of society and her strange sociability toward Rastignac reappears later in the novel, as I remarked above, in Rastignac's relations with Vautrin. Paris, he tells Rastignac, "is like some forest in the New World" (100), a place of savage competition of all against all. Yet he himself is not competing savagely with Rastignac. This vision fails to allow for the sort of real if partial disinterestedness with which he himself is presently behaving. "I'll bequeath you my fortune. Isn't that the act of a friend? But I am fond of you, and my passion is sacrificing myself for others. I have already done so. You see, my boy, I live on a loftier plane than other men." (148). This "loftier plane" echoes the "aristocratic loftiness" that distinguishes Julien's strange intimacy with the aristocrats.[51] The sort of loyalty Vautrin offers finds no interpretively satisfying place in the ending. And yet without this unlabeled, perhaps unclassifiable connection or covenant the plot could not proceed. Thus the principle that allows the two to adhere ought to have at least as much impact on our interpretation of what is happening as the social vision it stands apart from. In forcing us to acknowledge, *pace* Auerbach, the existence in Balzac as well of a zone of "aristocratic loftiness," this scene also suggests that "loftiness" may be newer, more pervasive, and more mysterious than any mere "aristocratic" vestige.

It is a noteworthy coincidence that, formally speaking, this unarticulated sociability is located at the same point in the plot where Auerbach exposes the loftiness in Stendhal. In the vocabulary of narratology, this point might be described as "the acquisition of the donor." Paraphrasing Vladimir Propp's *Morphology of the Folktale*, Fredric Jameson describes the donor as a figure "who after testing [the hero] for the appropriate reaction (for some courtesy, for instance) supplies him with a magical agent . . . which enables him to pass victoriously through his ordeal" (65). This figure is of more than instrumental importance, Jameson goes on, because "wish-fulfillment" alone (66) is insufficient to turn a mere string of episodes into a genuine narrative. Using Arthur C. Danto's account of historical narrative as any " 'causal' explanation of how a given state of affairs A turned into a given state of affairs B" (66–67), Jameson argues that it is in the donor, and not the hero or villain, that the "explanation of the change" resides—the logic that enables wishes to be fulfilled and a new state of affairs to result. Surprising as it may seem, then, the donor is the real heart of the narrative. "The donor is . . . the element which explains the change described in the story, that which supplies a sufficiently asymmetrical force to make it interesting to tell, and which is therefore somehow responsible for the 'storiness' of the story in the first place" (67).[52]

If the scene in which a social inferior "secures the goodwill" and assistance of a social superior occupies the pivotal slot that explains the narrative's trajectory and thus represents its "storiness," and if this scene repeatedly and prominently displays some version of disinterestedness, then disinterestedness would seem to be a sort of magical key to the meaning of the upward mobility story. But what doors does it actually open? How different do these novels look if one inspects them from the perspective of the momentary but well-located disinterestedness on which they pivot? And how far can this intriguing nexus of form and ideology take us toward understanding the effect of democracy in some usefully specifiable sense of that overused word?

I have already mentioned one example of a scene in which the donor is acquired. In *Silence of the Lambs*, Clarice Starling secures the goodwill of the imprisoned Hannibal Lecter, who has begun by refusing all cooperation, when she starts to leave and is suddenly assaulted by the prisoner in the next cell, one Miggs, who ejaculates into his hand and, cursing her, flings his sperm at her through the bars. Lecter's horror at this gross insult abruptly weakens his resolve, and he changes his mind. Why? What can horrify a cannibal? One might speculate that the sperm-throwing acts out a version of his own messy mixture of hostility and erotic ambivalence. But whether it does or not, Miggs's gesture provides Lecter with an opportunity to display his fastidious superiority to that sort of naked aggression and predatory desire, his ability to keep such impulses under control—an ability that for obvious reasons is open to doubt. Simple self-interest does not work on him. What he responds to is not the usual sticks and carrots, but an implicit appeal to his generosity. One might describe his change of heart, then, as a display of both socialization and disinterestedness. And though neither goes quite far enough, one must note that Lecter's response acts out the precise behavior modification that the state asylum in which he is incarcerated was supposed to produce, but has manifestly failed to. Toward Starling, at least, Lecter acts like a rehabilitated citizen. Indeed, as I argued above, when he solicits and supports the "silence of the lambs" story, which expresses Starling's deep commitment to the work of the FBI, Lecter is doing the bidding of the state that has taken him in charge. In this sense he can even be considered the state's unlikely representative.

Now consider the scene in *Great Expectations* when a bond is again cemented between donor and protagonist that will again be the direct cause of the latter's upward mobility. I am referring of course to the novel's first and most famous scene: Pip's meeting with Magwitch in the churchyard and the delivery of the stolen food and file. There is much in this astonishingly rich sequence that resists the gross and reductive label of donor-acquisition. For one thing, the roles appear to be reversed: it is Pip who is acting the part of Madame de Warens, offering assistance to a homeless man. The homeless man, who like Rousseau will go on to idealize this moment and organize his worldview around it, is older and more powerful. For most of the novel the relationship thus formed also remains invisible. Still, putting this scene in comparative structural perspective has its uses. It reveals, for example, how by making us wait so long to discover a social tie that is elsewhere almost always peripheral and obscure, *Great Expectations* throws it into relief, making its nature and meaning central to the interpretation of the text as a whole. And by creating a prolonged confusion as to who has helped or rescued whom, *Great Expectations* might also be said to level the two roles and make them interchangeable or at least communicable.[53] The possibility is thus raised that the role of benefactor might be an endpoint of upward mobility as well as its proximate cause. This is a possibility about which I will have more to say below.

Equally important is the fact that, in *Great Expectations* as in *Silence of the Lambs*, the donor is a prisoner. In both texts, that is, the protagonists acquire a donor and thus "earn" their upward mobility by offering something needed or wanted by a convicted criminal. (Pushing this argument to its limit, one might say that in both cases, though in different ways and to unequal degrees, loyalty between protagonist and donor entails complicity in the prisoner's escape.) This loyalty therefore seems set against loyalty to the state, which has done the imprisoning. And the same would hold for the upward mobility the donor makes possible. It is in this spirit that, with Orwell, one might define the value in whose name Pip helps the escaped convict as simple human decency, a universal presumably contrasted with any particular political arrangements or ideologies. As I will argue in the next chapter, however, this is only partially accurate. For one thing because, like the state, Pip is trying to protect himself. He is too frightened of the convict to behave in a entirely decent, which is to say an entirely disinterested manner. Yet Pip successfully resists the temptation to see Magwitch as *nothing but* a dangerous criminal, and in this sense one might say that he is acting as the state *should* act toward Magwitch, but does not—that is, with a certain confidence that he is not at risk, with a (sometimes comic) impersonality. We will learn only later, when Magwitch comes back and tells his story, that criminality was the more or less inevitable result of the homelessness and defenselessness into which he was born and from which it was not yet anyone's official business to rescue him or those like him. In treating this escaped prisoner as a homeless man in need of rescue, Pip is taking on the role the state ought to play toward the homeless, the role it ought to have played in order to prevent lives like Magwitch's from falling into crime and misery in the first place. It is this role that the state will slowly and inadequately come to play in the course of the nineteenth and twentieth centuries. At this level of (perhaps utopian) abstraction, then, Pip could be said to identify with the state. And in this sense, the *cause* of his upward mobility is also a possible *destination* for his upward mobility, a social position he might come to occupy that would both represent and legitimate his rise in the world.

Critics have often noticed a connection between upward mobility and prisons. Pip's haunting by penal institutions has tended to be classified along with other evidence of his psychological guilt, in other words his unconscious sense that, by standards that remain unspecified, his desire for upward mobility is illegitimate. The oft-noted happiness that Stendhal heroes like Fabrice and Julien enjoy in prison has been explained in terms of their release from the burden of upward mobility: as Victor Brombert puts it apropos of Julien, a "retreat from ambition" (73).[54] Brombert continues: "He no longer feels judged by the eyes of others. Out of time, yet in full possession of his being—that is the enviable prisoner fate" (74). In other words, the prison carries the same message that seems to be articulated by the Older Woman: if you can renounce upward mobility, you can be loved for who you really are. From the standpoint of the present argument, this interpretation falls short in at least three ways, ways that turn out to be related. First, it imagines that individual identity can and should be detached from "the eyes of others," or what others think. Second, it associates the Older Woman wholly and unambiguously with the renunciation of upward mobility. And third, it underestimates the extent to which upward mobility is *not* fully renounced.

Consider the early scene in *The Red and the Black* in which Monsieur de Rênal decides to take Julien Sorel into his house as the *précepteur* for his children. This is not quite a donor-acquisition scene, but it is a link in the same chain; in a sense, it explains how he is handed off from his spiritual mentor, Father Chélan, to his erotic mentor, Madame de Rênal. The decision to hire Julien is made in a chapter (the novel's third) entitled, strangely, "Care of the Poor" ("Le Bien des Pauvres"). The obvious reason for this title is what M. de Rênal has on his mind. He is worried about a man who has come from Paris to check on the proper functioning of the prison, the hospital, and the workhouse, which fall under Monsieur de Rênal's responsibility. The authorities of the town, himself included, have tried to keep the visitor from snooping on these institutions. But Father Chélan, who has permission to visit prison, hospital, and workhouse whenever he pleases, has deliberately shown the visitor around, and for this offence has just been stripped of his office. As Monsieur de Rênal and his family are strolling and chatting, Monsieur de Rênal is thinking about Father Chélan's response when accused of aiding the inspector: "what harm can he do our paupers and our prisoners?" (13) ("quel mal peut-il faire à nos pauvres et à nos prisonniers?" [18]—translation altered). Stendhal leaves out the conversation Monsieur de Rênal has on this subject with his wife, thus adroitly creating a sort of prose rhyme. Without us hearing that she has heard it, Madame de Rênal repeats the same question. "What harm can this gentleman from Paris do to our prisoners?" ("Quel mal ce Monsieur de Paris peut-il faire aux prisonniers?" [18]). Put on the spot—it is he himself who stands to lose by the inspection, not the prisoners—her husband is about to lose his temper. Then "a small event" occurs. His wife cries out; their son has climbed up on a high wall with a large drop on the other side. Seeing his mother's sudden paleness, the child jumps down, runs to her, and is scolded. Stendhal then comments: "This little incident gave a new turn to the conversation" (13) ("Ce petit événement changea le cours de la conversation" [18]).[55] It's at this point that Monsieur de Rênal suddenly announces his decision to hire "Sorel, the sawyer's son," who will "keep an eye on the children" (the French is "surveillera") and be their instructor.

The event receives no further elaboration, and it can no doubt be read as no more than an artfully oblique way of introducing Julien and emphasizing how very small a thing this momentous change in his existence is in the world of his employers. But there is a kind of supplementary logic here. It is only because Paris interferes in the provincial life of Verrières, sending out its new and fearsome inspectors, that a new and higher place is made for the son of a peasant. And Julien's new position is linked to that of the Parisian inspector in another sense as well. In his surveillance of the children, Julien will do what the "Monsieur de Paris" is trying to ensure that the town is doing with its poor and its prisoners: he will be taking care of those who cannot take care of themselves.[56] Of whom he is of course one. Julien himself makes the link between the chapter title "le bien des pauvres" (the French emphasizes what the poor rightfully have coming to them) and his own status. Monsieur de Rênal has doubled or tripled his fortune by his rapacious and corrupt manner of administering "le bien des pauvres," Julien thinks, adding: "I'm ready to bet he even makes a profit on the funds set aside for the foundlings. . . . I too am a sort of foundling" (37) ("Je parierais qu'il gagne même sur le fonds déstinés aux enfants trouvés. . . . Et moi aussi, je suis une sorte d'enfant trouvé" [41]). Later, at a rich dinner given by another wealthy local administrator, Julien hears that the debtors on the other side of the wall (his host is running a sort of prison sweatshop under his roof) have been told to stop singing. A tear runs down his cheek. He reflects on the prosperity he is supposedly striving to achieve: "You may well get a post worth twenty thousand francs, but you will be obliged, while gorging yourself on meat, to prevent the poor prisoner from singing" (147) ("Tu auras peut-être une place de vingt-mille francs, mais il faudra que, pendant que tu te gorges de viande, tu empêches de chanter le pauvre prisonnier" [146]).[57]

I will speak more below about the strange importance to the upward mobility story of the visiting inspector or health visitor, representative of the state bureaucracy. But the first French social protection law was not passed until 1841.[58] And even after that date, real movement toward what came to be called "l'état maternel" was slow in coming. In the decade of the 1830s, Robert Tombs writes, the French state was still so "helpless," so beset with "unshakeable institutional inertia," that "even the harshness of the English Poor Law was often praised by comparison" (178). The state's "ambitious reforms, minute regulations and constant reorganization of Byzantine but inoperative bureaucratic structures contrasted absurdly with the facts: provision was left increasingly to the voluntary initiative of local authorities, *notables* and charities" (178). In short, Monsieur de Rênal and company were still in charge. In the era of Stendhal, therefore, it remains much easier to imagine a protagonist like Julien rising in order to betray these prisoners than rising in order to do something for their welfare. Yet it is not too soon to detect the social forces that would gradually lead to the new laws and institutions of "l'état maternel" or "l'état providence." There are signs in Stendhal himself.

There are not many of them, it must be admitted, in the ending of *The Red and the Black*. That ending strongly suggests that Julien could not be happy until, a prisoner himself and awaiting execution, he renounces upward mobility and is reunited with Madame de Rênal.[59] Yet that renunciation can never be complete. Madame de Rênal cannot stand for the renunciation of upward mobility, for their relationship has been achieved by deliberate conquest; her love is a product of Julien's upward mobility and is indeed inconceivable without it. What Julien returns to is not the premobility state from which he started out. He returns to a woman who has cried when she thought of his poverty (45), has been awestruck by his genius, and has dreamed of one day seeing him pope or prime minister (102–3). Embarrassing as it may be, her seconding of his self-interest cannot be expurgated. Like Madame de Warens, Madame de Rênal has the charm of disinterestedness: "the expression of deep serenity, seemingly above all the vulgar concerns [the French is "intérêts"] of life" (73).[60] Yet one page later, we are informed of her "expression of interest" (74) ("expression de l'intérêt") [76]) for Julien. We can take this as disinterested sympathy, or we can take it as sexual attraction, or we can take it as an inscrutable combination of the two. The ambiguity leaves the disinterestedness celebrated at the end similarly impure and unstable: it too tries to combine "liberty for all" with the self-enclosed "distinction" of the lovers. And as with interest, so with "the eyes of others." The novel offers a more politically generous option for understanding the phrase. How far is it from "what others think" to a politically indispensable concern for others? Until quite late in the novel, Julien continues to worry that he is being mocked.[61] And the novel continues to insist that it's *good* to think about what others think. The natural and unselfconscious passion of Madame de Rênal is of course contrasted with Mathilde de la Mole's theatrical side glances at her noble ancestors. But Madame de Rênal casts side glances of her own, however untheatrical, at the well-being of others. She is not bookish, but how distant is interest in what others have written from interest in what others have suffered? The values that are affirmed in the idyll of imprisoned love include Julien's glances at the earlier prisoners and the Paris inspector's glances at the inmates of the prison, the hospital, and the workhouse. Conceived as an extension of surveillance, as a network of circulating glances, the common welfare becomes interesting. And it becomes part of the meaning of Julien's self-interested upward mobility.

In his last, unfinished novel, *Lucien Leuwen*, Stendhal offers an apparent formula for upward mobility that directly recalls Julien's prisoners.[62] The "desire for advancement" (96) ("envie de s'avancer") can only be satisfied, he has his hero remark, if one is prepared for "drawing your sword on workingmen" ("tirer le sabre contre les ouvriers" [89]). A lieutenant struggling to make a career for himself in the army, Lucien is also the only son of a Parisian banker who is rich, generous, and—though he has an extravagant taste for irony—tolerant of his son's foibles. Lucien thus has considerable grounds for self-assurance, enough perhaps so as to disqualify this as a story of upward mobility. Still, his psychology resembles Julien's, as does his relation to his first great love, Madame de Chasteller, a widow somewhat older than himself. His case against ambition, here too anchored in this first love, is again much the same. Indeed, it makes reference once again to prisoners.

Once its hero has been chased away, his passion still unconsummated, *Lucien Leuwen* never returns to Madame de Chasteller. The love affair that occupies the novel's final sections, between Lucien and one of Paris's most celebrated beauties, is stage-managed by Lucien's father. It is undertaken as a matter of ambition and filial duty on Lucien's part, and as a matter of pure ambition (her husband has been promised a ministry) on the part of Madame Grandet. Still, she falls genuinely in love with him. In doing so, this supremely ambitious woman also puts herself into Lucien's own self-declared role vis-à-vis Madame de Chasteller: in the interest of love, she is ready to sacrifice everything, "even the interests of her ambition" (part II.356) ("même les intérêts de son ambition" [595]). Thus the novel extends a slight but intriguing possibility that, though he has never been truly captivated by her and indeed up to now has found her somewhat tedious and superficial, Lucien too will fall in love with her.[63] Yet his impulse to tenderness is blocked. Consider how. In the midst of a passionate scene, Madame Grandet has thrown herself at his feet in tears, then fainted. We follow Lucien's thoughts: "a recollection, utterly ridiculous at such a moment, suddenly drove away all idea of compassion" (II.358) ("Il lui vint une idée, bien ridicule en cet instant, qui coupa court à tout attendrissement" [596]). What suddenly fills his mind is the memory of a group that had come to Madame Grandet's door, seeking warm clothing for prisoners about to be transferred to Paris in the dead of winter and who had been issued no blankets. His mistress had refused them, then told the story for the amusement of her salon. When she faints, what Lucien sees is "the same impassive look on her face when he had spoken of the prisoners dying of cold on the road" (II.358) ("l'image des prisonniers mourant de froid et de misère sur leurs charrettes" [596]). These prisoners intruding on a love scene are the same whose fate—the responsibility of the ministry they serve—has come up much earlier when his colleague Coffe explains to Lucien how little he wants to serve the ministry and how much he would like to be independent of it.[64]

This love scene takes place in Lucien's office at the ministry of the Interior. When Madame Grandet shows up there, unable to bear his absence, we are told that Lucien sat motionless "in a position more bureaucratic than gallant" (II.351) ("immobile, dans une position plus bureaucratique que galante" [590]). The bureaucratic position or posture might seem pure farce. But on second thought it also seems part of the rebuke to Madame Grandet. Though there have been references to "this stupid bureaucratic work" (II.340) ("ce stupide travail de bureau" [581]), Lucien has also considered that, however stupid, bureaucratic work "has at least proved that I am capable, if necessary, of supporting myself" (II.340) ("me prouve au moins que je suis capable de gagner au besoin ma vie" [581]). In other words, it makes possible a sort of independence from his father's money. And indeed this is more or less where the novel deposits him at the end. Refusing to decide between the two unequal love interests—to return to Madame de Chasteller or, much less likely, to make something new and interesting happen with Madame Grandet—Stendhal kills off the rich and talented father, makes his fortune vanish with a wave of the novelist's wand, and leaves Lucien with much diminished resources. He will now work in the government, but on terms more like those of others, terms influenced less by his father's former position and more by his own talents and achievements.

The novel's official position is against ambition, as it is against bureaucracy. Unofficially, it makes a place for ambition, at least in this chastened form, and that place is officialdom: in the bureaucracy. Julien knows that the justice of his government mission to Caen is "somewhat dubious" (II.225) ("fort disputable" [476]). After his almost superhuman efforts to get the government representative elected (over a man he himself sees as far superior), he asks himself what Madame de Chasteller would say if she knew ("Que dirait Madame de Chasteller si je lui racontais ma conduite?" [489]). This is a question he need not ask of Coffe, the colleague and fellow republican with whom he has shared every step of the electoral campaign. Coffe, a lower-class surrogate for Lucien whose rise in the state machinery is genuine, is even allowed the privilege of replacing Lucien for short periods as the center of narrative perspective. Coffe has seen him in great weakness, indeed in tears, Lucien tells him. Coffe says, "A good reason for your hating me and having me removed from the Ministry" (II, 226) ("Vous devriez me haïr et m'éloigner du ministère"). To which Lucien replies that instead, he now enjoys the "great comfort"— the literal translation would be "sweetness"—of being "able to tell you everything" (II.226) ("la douceur de pouvoir tout vous dire" [477]). Even the wording recalls the sweetness of freely confessed vulnerability that distinguishes both Julien's relations with Madame de Rênal and Lucien's relations with Madame Chasteller.

Indeed, this is how the intimacy with Madame de Chasteller is sealed. In his campaign to seduce an aristocratic lady, a campaign that all but succeeds—succeeds far enough at any rate so as to achieve some moments of happiness, if not the permanent satisfaction of his vanity—Lucien advances under cover of hypocrisy, hiding his republicanism and miming religious attitudes that he finds repulsive. But like Julien he is most successful when he is least strategic, least under his own control: when he inadvertently displays to his would-be beloved his vulnerability and generously noble nature. In a crucial scene, Madame de Chasteller tells Lucien she is worried about what people are saying; she has resolved that he must visit her less often. Lucien is devastated and cannot hide it. He responds, "And so . . ." (I.306) ("Eh bien?" [264]). And she draws back from her resolution, disarmed. Stendhal comments: "The tone of voice in which he pronounced the words *and so* . . . might well have been beyond the powers of an accomplished Don Juan; with Lucien it was no trick of artifice but the impulse of his nature—it was natural. That simple exclamation changed everything" (I.306) ("Le son de voix avec lequel il pronoça ce mot: *eh bien*, eût manqué peut-être au Don Juan le plus accompli; chez Leuwen il n'y avait aucun talent, c'était l'impulsion de la nature, le naturel. Ce simple mot de Leuwen changea tout" [264]).

It seems bizarre that a bureaucracy, of all places, should make possible a similar expression of vulnerability and the trust that is earned thereby. But something like a mode of bureaucratic or professional intimacy, analogous to the bonds linking the protagonist to the Older Woman, seems precisely what Stendhal has in mind. Speaking of the mud with which Lucien is spattered when caught by a crowd in the midst of his attempt at election-stealing, D. A. Miller asks a very pertinent question. The imagery of mud, he says, "always threatens to reduce the electoral intrigue to the primal slime from which, in moral terms, it has emerged. Why, then, does it never do so? Why does Lucien continue to spin out the plot, elaborating it far beyond the bureaucratic requirements of the situation?" (133).[65] Stendhal gave enormous value, Miller answers, to "the possibility of aesthetic performance, retrieving 'the highly dubious justice' of Lucien's enterprise in a game compelling on its own terms" (133). In its dangerous but enticing protection from the urgencies of the ethical and the personal, bureaucratic or professional work parallels aesthetic disinterest (134). Yet this work is not ethically neutral or indifferent. We see Lucien use a number of bureaucratic devices to save one Monsieur Tourte, a hapless clerk in the provinces, from the deputy who wants him thrown out of his post. It is like something out of the film *Brazil*, but in reverse: the government clerk or minor functionary plays the godlike role of anonymous friend to someone he has never met, merely in order to stop a piece of ordinary corruption in which he has no personal interest whatsoever. This is disinterestedness in action, disinterestedness plus power. The logic of the narrative implies, though the point is not made explicitly, that since Lucien works in the Ministry of the Interior, which is responsible for them, he might now be capable of doing something for the very prisoners about whom he has had such untimely thoughts.

There is no need to insist further on the moral impurity of state employment. It is obvious enough. What must be underlined is how far the parallel extends to the embrace of the Older Woman. Like other such characters, Madame de Chasteller seems above all self-interest. Stendhal's vocabulary for her suggests that she is a being so elevated above the ways of her world as to be almost unnatural: she is "a soul aloof from . . . petty vanities"

(I.177) ("une âme trop haut placée pour être troublée par les minities vaniteuses" [153]), and "the purest, the most celestial being, and the far-thest removed from all considerations of vanity and money" (I.215) ("l'être le plus pûr, le plus céleste, le plus au-dessus des considérations de vanité et d'argent" [187]). Thus Lucien can use his love for her as a stan-dard by which to judge his desire for upward mobility. "These absurdities of ambition prevent me from thinking of the only thing in the world that has any reality for me. I sacrifice my heart to my ambition and I have no ambition" (II.251) ("Ces sottises d'ambition me distraient de la seule chose au monde qui ait de la réalité pour moi. Il est drôle de sacrifier son coeur à l'ambition, et pourtant de n'être pas ambitieux" [496]). To the extent that he has given his heart to Madame de Chasteller, however, Lucien cannot claim not to be ambitious any more than he could make such a claim about the government bureaucracy. Before becoming the standard by which ambition is judged, Madame de Chasteller, like Ma-dame de Rênal, has first represented an object of the protagonist's ambi-tion. Lucien has defined his success with her as a test of his merit. And though there is a difference in degree (the degree of disinterestedness), it would be hard to say that there is an absolute difference in kind between this success and his other, nonerotic successes—in particular, his success as an emissary of the government. One might decide that this diminishes the value of her love. Or one might conclude on the contrary that it in-creases the value of those other successes: the value, that is, of his upward mobility.

". . . SOMETHING A BIT LIKE LOVE"

On the last page of *Lucien Leuwen*, as Lucien is on his way to take up a post in Italy, the last act we see him perform is a visit to the haunts of Rousseau, where he inspects a bed that is said to have belonged to Ma-dame de Warens. I have been suggesting that, though he is not enthusiastic about the government he serves, there is a strange and unexpected conti-nuity between his service to the state and the idealistic adoration of women like Madame de Warens.

Outside French realism, there are fewer direct descendants of Madame de Warens. And the constellation of linkages between the Older Woman, upward mobility, and the state is of course more sexually oblique as well as more obscure in other ways. But it is no less compelling. Though Dick-ens's Miss Havisham is no longer the erotic object of a young man's ambi-tion, her absolute desexualization only amplifies a tendency that, we re-call, has been intrinsic to the character type since Rousseau. Miss Havisham also brings into the open the possibility (mostly underdeveloped, though never entirely absent, in the French line of characters) of the woman as an active desiring subject, ambitious in her own right. She expresses her ambition in a displaced form, through her adopted daughter, but Miss Havisham does so precisely in order to take revenge for having been an unwitting object of male ambition. In that sense she offers an extremely direct and welcome commentary on the conventions of the upward mobility story. Like other inheritors of the politically mobilized sentimentalism discussed above, she is also curiously "immune," as Helen Small puts it, from the sort of wholeheartedly ironic or satiric treatment that might have been expected.[66]

With a little effort, one can also begin to unearth buried or latent connections between such a character and the state, connections that our usual habits of novel reading have not taught us to register or treat as significant. Like so many other nineteenth-century characters, including Magwitch, the male criminal and true donor with whom she is structurally paired, Miss Havisham inhabits an intermediate zone between responsibilities to which the family is now inadequate and responsibilities that the state has not yet taken up. For Miss Havisham, her identity self-defined around the traumatic moment of nonmarriage, it is exteriority to the family that is most obvious. Yet the novel's gestures toward hypothetical state-affiliated identities are also worth mentioning. She *almost* solicits the state's attention both as the victim of a crime—the broken promise of marriage—and again as the perpetrator of one: the loveless raising of Estella as an instrument of revenge, in other words dereliction of her duty as an adoptive parent. And but for her riches, she would be a potential object of the state's therapeutic agency: a madwoman. Sinister as the thought may appear in this context, it is only by caring about the course of the state beyond the nineteenth century that we can know how to care about this false benefactor and her not entirely ironic hold over Pip's expectations.

It is not odd that there has been so little effort to measure the impact of fairy godmothers or "fées fabuleuses" upon the social meaning of realism or upon the narratives of upward mobility that take up so much space within the realist canon. Such figures work not below realism's surface but in plain view, and their tasks include the heavy lifting that moves the plot along. But they are not especially realistic themselves. Indeed, they are often an embarrassment to realism. Contemporary reviewers described Miss Havisham as evidence of "fancy run mad" (*Blackwood's Magazine*), a "galvanized puppet" (*Westminster Review*), and "too exceptional, too nearly bordering on the monstrous and loathsome, to be appropriately introduced into in the midst of a story of ordinary English life" (*Saturday Review*).[67] These objections translate directly into a retrospective critique of the English novel's unrealistic treatment of upward mobility. "So many 'monsters' in English fiction," Franco Moretti exclaims.[68] According to Moretti, English society was too conservative to acknowledge the upward mobility in its midst. Its fiction solves this problem by projecting mobility's disruptive dynamic onto monstrous figures at the narrative's margins who, for good or evil, will serve as exterior, unknowable causes. Monsters need not be villains. Moretti's reading overlaps with George Orwell's observations on "the Good Rich Man" in the early Dickens, "a superhumanly kind-hearted old gentleman who 'trots' to and fro, raising his employees' wages, patting children on the head, getting debtors out of jail and, in general, acting the fairy godmother. Of course he is a pure dream figure. . . . Even Dickens must have reflected occasionally that anyone who was so anxious to give his money away would never have acquired it in the first place" (52).[69] From this perspective Miss Havisham would be an early-Dickens fairy godmother displaced into a late novel that has lost its faith in whatever vision of power these providential patrons had once embodied. Thus she, like Magwitch, could be read as a subversive parody of the benefactor device and evidence for Orwell's case that *Great Expectations* is "definitely an attack on patronage" (53).

By the standards of realism, the treatment of older women I am discussing does not measure up well. How life might look from the older woman's point of view is not much on the agenda in the nineteenth-century novel. For an alternative, one might have to turn to novels like John Braine's *Room At the Top*, films like *Sunset Boulevard* and *All About Eve*, works of nonfiction like Hannah Arendt's *Rahel Varnhagen* or Nuala O'Faolain's *Are You Somebody?* Both of the latter books focus on the older woman both as a benefactor and as a recipient or former recipient of benefaction. O'Faolain is eloquent on the more conventional relation of the younger woman to older men in power, or as she neatly puts it, "acquaintances mistaken for uncles" (101).[70] Finding herself partnerless and no longer young, O'Faolain bravely begins to imagine a normative life trajectory that will leave her in the end without a partner, at least in the strong sense of the word. She will have to make do with something less, "something a bit like love" (217) rather than the thing itself. Women like herself, who have put their careers first, are perhaps obliged "to become benign witches" (206).

Clearly there is much here that could not be said, or at any rate wasn't, in the novels of the male realists. And yet one cannot help noticing some uncanny parallels. The benign witch is after all a recognizable version of the mentor or benefactor role that older women play in male upward mobility stories. As I have already suggested, the replacement of full reproductive partnership with "something a bit like love" but weaker, more generalized, and more promiscuous in its objects has much to do with the teleology of the upward mobility story even in its classic and restrictively male version.[71] Consider too O'Faolain's extended commentary on those multiple moments in her career when she received career assistance from older men who were sexually interested in her:

> I was soon commissioned to edit an anthology of Beckett criticism. This came about through being taken up by a very well-known English academic, who came to Dublin to give a lecture. I lived high up above Merrion Square, in a old flat where the servants had once lived, underneath the roof. He came back there, after an increasingly breathless day wandering Dublin, but left dramatically because my bedspread was the same as the one on his son's bed at home. . . . He was one of three or four established academics who took an interest in me in those years. That was how it was, and perhaps is, when you are a young woman in a male-dominated field. The men dispensed patronage. They could tell you where the jobs were, and get you invited to conferences, and endorse you for grants, and mention your name to publishers. This wasn't exactly corrupt, but it wasn't fair, either; they wouldn't do it for you if they didn't like you, or if they didn't feel you were personally grateful. I didn't see any general truths such as that, of course. I was blinded by the habit of translating everything into personal terms. I saw the academic world around me as being comprised of such-and-such a nice man and such-and-such a nasty man and so on—I didn't notice that it was ninety-nine per cent comprised of men. I didn't ask any of them for help. I wanted to be liked, not helped. I had no sense of being at the start of a career. (107–8)

Looking back, O'Faolain judges herself not guilty. The help could be taken because it was not what she wanted. The career could advance because the career making is considered an accident, not something self-consciously schemed for or even considered. This is indeed "blindness," but not of a uniquely gendered or indeed a historically delimited sort. The "habit of translating everything into personal terms" is not a peculiarity of young women starting out in the days before feminism; it is a common denominator of the upward mobility story. Taking refuge behind her refusal to be calculating, O'Faolain does retrospectively with her own ambition more or less the same whitewashing job that Madame de Beauséant does with Rastignac's ambition. The protagonist's self-interest may be a bit more freely acknowledged in Balzac.

There are excellent reasons for showing moral generosity toward O'Faolain's younger self, who was doing nothing that is not traditionally done by the male leads of classic upward mobility stories. My point is that this moral generosity is offered by the literary convention in which she is here participating. Telling us what it feels like from a woman's perspective, O'Faolain does not repudiate the benefactor role, but rather offers a renewed vision of it on the part of one who has been on the receiving end but is now, later in life, consciously trying it on for size, exploring its subjectivity rather than its instrumentality, tentatively inquiring as to whether it might not after all be fitting and suitable. The proposition O'Faolain asks us to consider is whether older women like herself might also stand to benefit if the witchery operated by fairy godmothers can indeed be seen, in a sense that has yet to be elaborated, as mysteriously benign.

CHAPTER TWO

How to Be a Benefactor without Any Money

"My brother's body lies dead and naked . . ."

On the first page of Gissing's *New Grub Street* (1891), the early and upwardly rising Jasper Milvain announces to his mother and sister over breakfast: "There's a man being hanged in London at this moment."[1] Looking back at this scene from the last page, when Milvain has realized his ambitions, his friend and fellow writer Reardon has fallen into poverty and died, and Milvain has married Reardon's beautiful upper-class widow, the logic seems clear and zero-sum. Someone has to die in order for someone else to rise.

This logic fills the upward mobility story with deaths just as it fills the upward mobility story with prisoners. The genre's signature effects include immobile bodies, bodies mentioned casually in passing or stepped over, hovered over, brooded over, and even knocked over by an upwardly mobile protagonist. John Edgar Wideman's autobiographical *Brothers and Keepers* (1984) opens with a fresh murder: "I heard the news first in a phone call from my mother. My youngest brother, Robby, and two of his friends had killed a man during a holdup. . . . The police were hunting him, and his crime had given the cops license to kill. The distance I'd put between my brother's world and mine suddenly collapsed."[2] The brother who did not rise will spend the book in prison. In *Parallel Time* (1994), Brent Staples sets his own rise as a writer against the drug-dealing life and violent death of his brother Blake. The first sentences look down on Blake's body from a distance, a distance that is again threatened with collapse: "My brother's body lies dead and naked on a stainless steel slab. At his head stands a tall arched spigot that, with tap handles mimicking wings, easily suggests a swan in mourning."[3]

Both the horizontal corpse and the artfully detached swan simile recall the opening scene of *Great Expectations*, which presents Pip in the village churchyard, tearfully but wittily contemplating the tombstones of his brothers:

> To five little stone lozenges, each about a foot and a half long, which were arranged in a neat row beside [my parents'] grave, and were sacred to the memory of five little brothers of mine—who gave up trying to

get a living, exceedingly early in that universal struggle—I am indebted for a belief I religiously entertained that they had all been born on their backs with their hands in their trousers-pockets, and had never taken them out in this state of existence.[4]

The swan in mourning and the brothers born with their hands in their pockets are accomplished images. Signs of the imagination hard at work, they make no effort to hide the meritorious expenditure of effort that, more than merely being alive, sets apart the brothers writing from the brothers written about. To this Dickens adds an extra insistence on Pip's brothers' *lack* of accomplishment. Flat on their backs, their horizontality offering a brisk contrast to the vertical ascent that Pip anticipates for himself, their hands comfortably pocketed rather than busy and active, they, unlike Pip, are not going anywhere. The cemetery scene enacts a social distance that Pip, in order to follow his "great expectations," would in any case have had to put between himself and his family if fate had not already done so. Had his brothers lived, he would have had to bury them anyway, metaphorically speaking, and that is more or less what his language does when it identifies the dead, however jokingly, with the lazy and undeserving poor, those who "gave up trying to get a living exceedingly early." As Julian Moynahan has pointed out, Pip's own determination to push farther than his brothers in the struggle for existence helps explain why his story is saturated with "the equivalent of a murderer's guilt" (662).[5]

It is not hard to imagine why the upward mobility story should seek equivalents for a murderer's guilt. Along with the patron or fairy godmother, the most visible thing these narratives have in common is ambivalence about their protagonists' rise, recognition of conflict between loyalties to the family and friends left behind and a desire for the options and rewards of a life elsewhere. This conflict between origin and destination is never absolute, since family and friends will often wish the protagonist well despite the fear that success may separate them. But some conflict seems unavoidable. The families of Wideman and Staples, broken apart along the line separating literary legitimacy from manhunts and gunshot wounds, display dramatically a division to which other nonfiction writers also repeatedly testify. In *Making It* (1967), Norman Podhoretz explains his "guilt" as follows: "My mother wanted nothing so much as for me to be a success, to be respected and admired. But she did not imagine, I think, that she would only purchase the realization of her ambition at the price of my progressive estrangement from her and her ways."[6] Richard Rodriguez, who as a child responded to the clash of Mexican home with American school by refusing to speak Spanish, writes in *Hunger of Memory* (1982):

Perhaps because I am marked by indelible color they easily suppose that I am unchanged by social mobility, that I can claim unbroken ties with my past. The possibility! . . . I retain certain features of gesture and mood derived from buried lives. I also speak Spanish today. And read García Lorca and García Marquez at my leisure. But what consolation can that fact bring against the knowledge that my mother and father have never heard of García Lorca or García Marquez? . . . This is what matters to me: the story of the scholarship boy who returns home one summer from college to discover bewildering silence, facing his parents. This is my story. An American story.[7]

Rodriguez establishes that this is not merely an American story by alluding at length (46ff) to Richard Hoggart's classic narrative of the "uprooting" of the working-class British "scholarship boy" in *The Uses of Literacy* (1957).[8] Hoggart's account is less personal, more earnest and restrained. He does not say, as Rodriguez does, "I intended to hurt my mother and father" (50). There are no hangings or murders. Yet when Hoggart describes how it feels to be "at the friction-point of two cultures," laying out the scholarship boy's ordeal in trying to negotiate between school and family, one can feel behind his words an explosive shame and rage that could well take more violent or melodramatic shape: "the test of his real education," Hoggart writes, "lies in his ability, by about the age of twenty-five, to smile at his father with his whole face and to respect his flighty sister and his slower brother" (242).

One ideological crux of the upward mobility genre over the past two centuries has been the question of the flighty sisters and slower brothers. Are we sure they really are "flighty" and "slower"? What is it that keeps one from smiling at one's father with less than a full face? In short, what about the loved ones left behind? What about those who are *not* upwardly mobile? It is this many-sided question that upward mobility stories must either ask or avoid. The value of these narratives depends on the courage and imagination with which they ask and answer it.

This premise might seem to be troubled by the genre's well-known favoring of orphans, as in *Jane Eyre* (1847) and *Great Expectations* (1861).[9] Orphanhood seemingly extracts the upwardly mobile protagonist from any necessary or built-in ambivalence, removing the tenderness of early attachment that would guarantee a later conflict of loyalties. The dizzying liberation from prior entanglements is of course a source of the trope's charm, and the reason why writers from Brontë and Dickens to Jamaica Kincaid and Terry Eagleton so readily forget their actual siblings when they sit down to write and instead produce characters more solitary and freestanding than they themselves ever were. From the point of view of the homeless orphan, the trajectory of the plot doesn't look like the working out of a contradiction; it looks like a move from outside to inside. The outside-to-inside trajectory is also assumed when these texts are described as stories of "youth."[10] Like orphanhood, youth too is an irresistible incentive to seek shelter, a sort of natural outside that innocently calls into being a narrative pointed toward some sort of entry, assimilation, accommodation—an exercise in social integration, as the *bildungsroman* is sometimes labeled.[11] But as I've suggested, the destination is not the only image of society the novel contains. The origin too is a place *inside* society, hence a source of contradictory and specifiable commitments. We can think of orphanhood as the disguised vestige of an earlier murder. For it shoves out of sight in the past a murderous rejection that was a logical necessity in order for upward mobility to happen. And this rejection will return as guilt, ambivalence, conflicted loyalties, even if such feelings are attached to loved ones rather than blood kin (Joe and Biddy rather than Mrs. Joe in *Great Expectations*) or even to characters who are not quite loved at all—think for example of Jane's reluctant, often unconscious identification with Bessie and the other servants in *Jane Eyre*.

The question of those who do not rise is a question about what literature can do besides report on known facts. According to sociologist Stephen Edgell, the facts are roughly as follows: over the past century or so upward mobility has been by far the exception rather than the rule. Recent research has failed to show that "vertical mobility at the present time is much greater than in the past."[12] It shows instead, in Edgell's summary, "trendlessness in the pattern of absolute mobility, stability in the pattern of relative mobility, and minimal mobility evidence in support of the thesis of American exceptionalism" (101). It also shows a well-documented tendency of sociologists to hide this lack of overall upward mobility by not looking at the life trajectories of women (99). What can there be to praise, then, in the proliferation of upward mobility stories? Much has been written about why the dominant ideologies of our time might arrange to have people diverted and deluded by such stories. One cannot help asking: do these unrepresentative narratives have any use other than delusion and diversion? "Although we can boast today a considerably larger black middle class and upper-middle class, with its avenues into the professions, including elective office, some corporate affiliation, virtually *all* of the NBA, and the NFL, and a fast break into the nation's multimillion dollar 'image' industries," Hortense Spillers writes, "the news concerning the African American life-world generally is quite grim" (69). Against the background of 600,000 black people in prison, the population of a large city, what's the use of any success story, however much that story is qualified? What's the value of a story in which some representative of that population escapes to prosperity, or even fails to escape but in such a noble way as to encourage rather than discourage others?

As I have tried to suggest, these questions do not merely come from outside, from what we know independently about social reality. They are intrinsic to the upward mobility story. In his book *Mechanic Accents*, Michael Denning contrasts the "self-improvement" philosophy characteristic of the middle class with the working-class philosophy of "mutualism" (173).[13] Proof that Horatio Alger is "writing down" to his working-class readers lies in the fact that he refuses mutualism in favor of self-improvement. This is a bit unfair: the working class has always been interested in self-improvement, and Alger is more interested than he might appear in something resembling mutualism. One look at all the dead brothers shows that the opposition between the selfishness of mobility and the responsibilities of mutualism doesn't hold up. The charged possibilities of guilt, contempt, protection, and solidarity that crowd into the word *responsibility*, the relationships that Wideman neatly packs into the title "brothers and keepers," are at issue and at work all over this genre, determining the arc of the story, its choices of image, who its main characters are, and what language they speak.

"He cannot go back," Hoggart writes; "with one part of himself he does not want to go back to a homeliness which was often narrow: with another part he longs for the membership he has lost, 'he pines for some nameless Eden where he never was.' "[14] Whether or not it demystifies the lost Eden of working-class community—Hoggart himself is not always more consistent about this than his composite protagonist—the upward mobility story shows no inclination to condemn the path of upward mobility so absolutely that return would be the only ethical option. The corpses and the guilt are there, and they are important, but they are not definitive. Rodriguez ends his book with a chilly family dinner. In its last lines, Rodriguez suddenly senses his father's irrelevance to his life. The book's farewell promises a more ultimate parting: "In that instant I feel the thinness of his arms. He turns. He asks if I am going home now too. It is, I realize, the only thing he has said to me all evening" (195). Another death, this time foretold, yet a death that takes away very little from the positive value of the son's trajectory. It's as if Rodriguez were saying that reciprocal alienation is inevitable, but only because the generations must succeed one another. The implication is that his success is only that succession.

Though these narratives seem intent on exhibiting upward mobility's victims, in other words, the same passages that estimate the cost also make it evident that chastising or renouncing upward mobility will by no means be the prime or wholehearted aim. The trail of bodies may suggest that the cost of upward mobility is too high, but this remains a suggestion, one interpretive option among others; it leaves open the possibility, perhaps the necessity, of enjoying the thrill without paying full fare. After all, there is no more traditional way of protecting and thus indulging dangerous desires like social ambition than by framing them with pious afterthoughts. Moralizing helps ensure that such stories continue to be told.

I will be proposing that these narratives make a superior claim to moral seriousness, one that is both less rigorous (in that it does not demand a simple and unrealistic rejection of the desire for upward mobility) and more strenuous (in that it does demand a more creative and interesting response to that desire). This claim to seriousness is associated first and foremost with the mentor/mediator. Consider the famous moment in Balzac's *Père Goriot* when Rastignac, contemplating a rich marriage that would lift him to the heights of Parisian society but would require his acquiescence in a faraway murder, asks his friend Bianchon whether he recalls a passage in Rousseau that wonders "what the reader would do if he could become rich by killing some old mandarin in China without stirring from Paris, simply by willing it so.'

"I do."

"Well?"

"Bah! I'm well on to my thirty-third mandarin."

"It's no joking matter. Now if someone proved to you that such a thing is possible, and all you need to do is nod your head, what would you do?"

"Is he very old, your mandarin? But, my word, young or old, paralytic or healthy . . . Devil take it! All right, no!"[15]

Rastignac too will refuse the offer, if weakly and after some delay. But this refusal to acquire the object of his ambition in exchange for a death is not the novel's last word on the ethics of social climbing. On the contrary, it leaves us in some doubt as to whether it is even possible to say no. "In bourgeois society," Carlo Ginsburg comments, spelling out the consequences of the "killing of the mandarin" trope, ". . . the chain of relations in which we are all involved can make us at least indirectly responsible for a crime" (55).[16] *Can* make us, or perhaps simply *does* make us, whether we say yes or no? If we are responsible for the equivalent of murder merely by living in such a society, no matter how fully we may renounce all ambition, then there is no longer a genuine ethical dividing line between yes and no, the choice of mobility and the choice of immobility.

And in that case, why *not* say yes? This is precisely the argument of Vautrin, the would-be benefactor who has made Rastignac the offer disguised in the mandarin parable. A moral philosophy, Alasdair MacIntyre has noted, "characteristically presupposes a sociology."[17] Vautrin's sociology defines a virtuous judge (Rastignac is studying the law) as one who agrees to "bark at thieves, defend the rich, send men of spirit to the scaffold" (95). Law-abiding society, Vautrin proposes, is based on "murders without bloodshed, but somebody has been bled all the same. . . . Between what I am offering now and what you will do one day the only difference is the blood shed" (103). This reasoning does something more than merely soften the reader's eventual judgment of Rastignac. For as I have said above, what Vautrin offers his protégé, along with a means of rising in society, is an alternative model of society. The bargain he promises embodies a disinterestedness for which there is no room in Vautrin's own social theory. Yet the mysterious social bond that promises to bring about Rastignac's rise clearly has something to do with the possible meaning of that rise.[18]

Another mysterious social bond that both causes a character's rise and changes the meaning of that rise is visible in Dreiser's *Sister Carrie* (1900). *Sister Carrie* is notorious for the uncertainty of its moral judgment on its upwardly mobile protagonist. It comes closest to conclusive moral judgment a few pages before the end, and it does so by invoking *Père Goriot*.[19] Carrie by this point is a huge theatrical success. Her former lover and mentor Hurstwood, meanwhile, is begging in the streets and sinking toward suicide. Pushed away from the stage door he has stumbled through, looking for Carrie, Hurstwood slips and falls in the snow. As he gets up, the narrative switches to Carrie. "In her comfortable chambers at the Waldorf, Carrie was reading at this time 'Père Goriot,' which Ames had recommended to her" (393). Wearying, she comes to the window, where her friend Lola is gazing out.

> "Look at that man over there," laughed Lola, who had caught sight of someone falling down. "How sheepish men look when they fall, don't they?"
> "We'll have to take a coach to-night," answered Carrie absently (394).

Though the man they see fall can hardly be Hurstwood (they are on Park and Fiftieth, and he is on Broadway and Thirty-ninth), the juxtaposition is eloquent enough. In case we've missed the dig at Carrie's absentmindedness, we are recalled to it by the echo of Hurstwood's words a page earlier: " 'She owes me something to eat,' he said. 'She owes it to me' " (393).

This is not simply a rebuke of her rise by his literal and metaphorical fall. Dreiser is insisting, as he does elsewhere, that the "fallen woman" stigma has to be denied and reversed. The sequence also demonstrates the complicity—manifest as well in Dickens and Staples—between upward mobility and the literariness of the text, its reluctance to be caught in a simple act of affirmation. Literacy puts itself slyly on the side of upward mobility, which is its precondition, by continually suggesting and continually evading the proposition that the gain of one is the loss of the other. Protagonist and presumed victim are metaphorically aligned so as to produce this hypothesis, just as Pip is guiltily associated with his sister's murder. But there is no risk of formal indictment, for the alignment never quite congeals into a literal failure of responsibility, an action or inaction that might lead to charges in a court of law. As Vautrin says, the law protects those who have property. And literature protects those who have the cultural capital needed to produce more literature. Thus the tableau is slightly syncopated: Hurstwood just escapes being the man Carrie sees fall in the snow. The last time she did see Hurstwood himself, Carrie gave him all the money she had. The rest is metaphor.

But the most compelling reason for not interpreting this scene as a condemnation of Carrie is its reference to Balzac. In my account above I omitted Carrie's self-critique, which she derives, as Dreiser insists, from taking in the "sympathetic significance" (393) of *Père Goriot*. Coming to the window, she reprimands Lola's lightness. Lola has been hoping for a sleigh ride, not thinking of the effect the snow will have on the homeless. Carrie, "with whom the sufferings of Father Goriot were still keen," responds: " 'That's all you think of. Aren't you sorry for the people who haven't anything tonight?' " (393).

Whether or not this noble sentiment satisfies the reader—it's not hard to think of it as "merely literary," a passing mood, more or less inconsequential—it is seemingly intended not merely to cushion the reader's judgment of Carrie, but to try to resolve the stark ethical confrontation that the novel here comes so close to staging.[20] The reader may be surprised to recall that Carrie's sympathy for "the people who haven't anything tonight," far from being sudden and narratively inconsequential, has already been presented. In fact it has been presented as a key source of her talent, and thus a cause of her success both in the theater and in love. In this sense, her success is not merely a turning away from the fate of those like Hurstwood. It is also, paradoxically, the effect of something that first drew Hurstwood to her, and to a large extent (since Hurstwood was the invisible benefactor behind her first theatrical success) set her on her path upward. It's the secret behind her acquisition of a donor.

After all, how *does* Carrie rise? The cynical view would be that, like Richardson's Pamela as seen by Fielding, she manages to cash in on her sexual attractiveness to men—adapting Pierre Bourdieu's terms, that she manages to exchange sexual capital for economic capital, an exchange that can never be taken for granted, the currencies not always being convertible. Sexual attractiveness is also at work in Vautrin's willingness to play benefactor to Rastignac as well as in Rastignac's other successes in Parisian society. But the question of what benefits sex can and cannot be exchanged for comes under a heading that is more general and more interesting. Vulnerability to sexual attractiveness on the part of those with money and power is merely one example of the relative but real openness of power.

Let me try to clarify, taking a slight detour from *Sister Carrie*, by laying out two contrasting theories of upward mobility in relation to power. According to Bourdieu, there is no redeeming value in upward mobility stories. This is not because upward mobility doesn't happen. Though his chosen theme is "reproduction," in other words, "the stability of the basic field of relations" (Calhoun, 143), Bourdieu does not assert that upward mobility is impossible.[21] Indeed, he notes the possibility that, as in Hoggart, Rodriguez, and many others, someone's rise out of the lower classes might be enabled by institutions of higher education. Yet for Bourdieu the role of these institutions is merely to embody power. Hence upward mobility can only mean a betrayal of given values and solidarities and an identification with power, which is assumed to be antagonistic to them. This is what we see in Bourdieu's model of the upwardly mobile "oblate" in *Homo Academicus*. Originally an oblate (from the Latin for "offering" or "sacrifice") was "a child from a poor family entrusted to a religious foundation to be trained for the priesthood."[22] For Bourdieu the term refers to children without social capital whose upward mobility depends entirely on the educational institution to which they were entrusted, and who thus respond to that institution with unconditional loyalty.[23] "They offer to the academic institution which they have chosen because it chose them, and vice versa, a support which, being so totally conditioned, has something total, absolute, and unconditional about it" (100–101). According to this model, upward mobility means selling yourself, that is, selling out, within the total, absolute, and unconditional terms of all-powerful institutions.[24]

Contrast, now, the account of Jane Eyre's upward mobility in Gayatri Chakravorty Spivak's "Three Women's Texts and a Critique of Imperialism."[25] Jane's upward mobility, marked by her final replacement of Bertha Mason Rochester as the rightful "Mrs. Rochester," is made symbolically possible, Spivak argues, despite the enormous weight of patriarchy's support for legal matrimony, by Jane's commitment to the forces of imperialism, which are neither identical to nor perfectly aligned with the forces of patriarchy. The central exhibit and exemplary victim of Jane's commitment is the "Creole" Bertha, the madwoman from the Caribbean. The key to Spivak's interpretation is the willingness of nineteenth-century feminism and the nineteenth-century public sphere to subordinate patriarchal taboos on transgressive sexuality to a higher social good. Sexuality, for Spivak, means "childbearing," that is, "domestic-society-through-sexual-reproduction cathected as 'companionate love.'" Powerful as the rules governing sexuality are, Spivak argues, they can be trumped by what she calls "soul making," or "the imperialist project cathected as civil-society-through-social-mission" (244). The transgression against the sexual law of the family represented by Jane's replacement of Rochester's legal wife can be tolerated and justified because, in Spivak's words, "nineteenth-century feminist individualism could conceive of a 'greater' project than access to the closed circle of the nuclear family. This is the project of soul making beyond 'mere' sexual reproduction," the work of making "the heathen into a human so that he can be treated as an end in himself" (248). It is the project of soul making that Jane identifies herself with when she prepares to go to India as a missionary.

In making this argument, Spivak presses hard on the erotic option that the novel does not choose. "This project is presented as a sort of tangent in *Jane Eyre*," she writes, "a tangent that escapes the closed circle of the *narrative* conclusion. The tangent narrative is the story of St. John Rivers, who is granted the important task of concluding the *text*" (248–49). Rivers, you recall, is the man Jane doesn't marry, but whose proposal of marriage has a serious hold over her anyway. She and the novel pay him so much attention, it appears, not because he is personally attractive, though he is, but rather because he offers Jane a share in the knowledge and the vocation of the missionary. He offers her, that is, what she is ready to consider meaningful and desirable work—work whose desirability for Jane comes in large part from the fact that it might not *require* marriage, the fact that it replaces marriage with otherwise unavailable possibilities for personal autonomy and socially significant action. It is through this figure that a woman can begin to imagine upward mobility that would not (merely) be marriage to a man of higher station. Spivak has no more enthusiasm than Bourdieu for class hierarchy or the society that enforces it. (Spivak's Jane Eyre is another oblate, disinclined to question the value or pedagogical contents of the educational mission she has imbibed from her own teachers.) For Spivak too, upward mobility is a betrayal. But it is a more interesting betrayal, for the internally divided model of power Spivak is working with also makes upward mobility possible as something *other* than a simple and unambiguous betrayal.

I have already said something about the state of society in which upward mobility would not simply mean betrayal, the mode of social citizenship for which the protagonists and readers of modern Cinderella stories are deviously and variously prepared. Here let me simply recall how this socially visionary impulse, real if frustrated and imperfect, is associated with the patron or mentor. Liberated by their marginal or merely functional relation to the plot, shielded from the stricter scrutiny they would surely draw if they showed up in the spotlight of final marriage, it's as if these mentor figures were free to represent the text's repressed or (sometimes) its best self, social vectors that, like Jane's desire for autonomous and satisfying work, the story has been deeply invested in even though it is temporarily unable to realize them. Rivers and his ilk are of course not simply nuggets of idealism strewn across an otherwise realistic landscape. Representatives of power, they both open up and close off possibilities; they are necessarily tainted and somewhat sinister. It's not that Rivers *wants* an unpatriarchal arrangement with Jane. He enjoys and affirms the male power he possesses, even if he prefers to forgo an adoring wife. Yet his professional coldness and his desirable proposition combine to force Jane to imagine a state of unmarried collegiality, based on shared commitment to a social project and outside the normal conjugal hierarchy. And though Rivers resists it and Jane finally chooses marriage instead, the disruptive energy the novel releases in this direction must be registered in our reading. Our critical apparatus must be sensitive enough to register, that is, the effects of mediation: an intercession between power and the protagonist, working in part at least therefore on the latter's behalf, and aimed at resolving their divergent interests in some as yet perplexing and unaccustomed way.

The chilly but somehow inescapable Rivers, who disappears from the plot and yet is given the novel's last words (like Trilby murmuring the unloved name of Svengali as she dies), has an equally flimsy and equally resonant counterpart in *Sister Carrie*. Ames, who had "recommended [Balzac] to her," enjoys a similar power over what Carrie's story leaves unresolved. Like Rivers, he too never quite blazes up into a genuine love-interest, and this means that like Rivers he too remains a mentor rather than a master—which is what a potential husband risks becoming by legal definition. "It is too often true that [a woman's] one true mentor is the man who schools her in order to wed her," Susan Fraiman writes. "And finally, consequently, when the mentor is a husband and when apprenticeship reduces to the process of marital binding, it never leads the heroine to mastery but only to a lifetime as a perpetual novice" (6).[26] Carrie is willing enough to cast herself as a perpetual novice, always ready to learn from Ames's moral authority. "He liked better books than she read, better people than she associated with. His ideals burned in her heart" (317). He is extraordinarily and obnoxiously unsympathetic about Carrie's success: "He looked at her in such a peculiar way that she realized she had failed" (383). And yet, for all the distasteful little signs, what he ultimately tells her endorses a surprisingly generous vision of Carrie's accomplishment. "Mastery" is perhaps not the best word for what he thinks Carrie has or should strive to develop further. What he praises and encourages is both a self's masterly or proprietary accomplishment and, at some risk of paradox, a certain self-abandonment, a version of selflessness. Describing "the expression in your face," Ames explains: "It's a thing the world likes to see, because it's a natural expression of its longing" (385). We must understand her talent to be composed of social sympathy, for its opposite, Ames says, would be to "live to satisfy yourself alone" (386). Carrie's talent, as Ames sees it, is precisely not to satisfy herself alone, or for that matter (as the ideal of traditional femininity would have it) to satisfy others alone. Rather, it is to satisfy both herself *and* others—to do the one by doing the other. The suggestion is that, as in *The Silence of the Lambs*, she has pulled off the most esteemed, indeed the definitive feat of modern political thought: to reconcile individual self-interest with the general welfare.

Given the awkwardness of Ames's intervention in the plot, this might seem like unpersuasive moralizing. As it happens, however, it amplifies something we have already been told—notably, about why Hurstwood is drawn to Carrie in the first place.[27] The passage that explains his attraction begins, strangely, with the world of work: "Sorrow in her was aroused by many a spectacle—an uncritical upwelling of grief for the weak and the helpless. She was constantly pained by the sight of the white-faced, ragged men who slopped desperately by her in a sort of wretched mental stupor. The poorly clad girls who went blowing by her window evenings, hurrying home from some of the shops of the West Side, she pitied from the depths of her heart." The description of Carrie's attention to labor and suffering goes on for two paragraphs, taking in "her old father, in his flour-dusted miller's suit," along with a shoemaker, a blastman, and a bench worker "seen high aloft in some window, his coat off, his sleeves rolled up." "Her sympathies were ever with that under-world of toil from which she had so recently sprung and which she best understood." The punch line follows in the next paragraph. Hurstwood "never attempted to analyze his affection" for Carrie, Dreiser says: "He did not know, but it was this in her, after all, which attracted him" (116).

Carrie is notorious for not thinking of her own family, either the sister left behind in Chicago or the parents left behind in Wisconsin. Yet here she does remember "her old father," and it is this memory, strangely, that explains what her lover/mentor feels for her. The mentor who falls down in the snowy street has fallen for Carrie because of her sympathy for the people in the streets. The bond between them is not the antithesis of her bond to her family, as it seems, but rather a tribute to that bond and an expansion of it, a larger loyalty to all those who, like her family, toil and suffer. If Carrie rises by means of Hurstwood, and if what attracts Hurstwood to her is her social sympathies, then the logic seems inescapable, and just the opposite of the murderousness we began by deducing from Gissing. Carrie rises by means of her social sympathies, and her social sympathies cannot be kept apart from the meaning of her rise.

SAVING BOYS: HORATIO ALGER

> When a rich old fellow offers you money, which he
> can well afford, you had better take it.
> —*Horatio Alger*

As befits the most famous ideologue of self-reliance since Emerson, Horatio Alger offers his protagonists the gift of minimal prior attachment, a sort of zero-degree resistance to upward mobility. All the dead brothers have been surgically removed, and with them all apparent conflicts of loyalty. If the hero has a mother, like Luke Larkin in *Struggling Upward*, the decision to abandon her doesn't take long:

"Would you object to leave home?"

"No, sir; there is little or no prospect in Groveton, and though my mother would miss me, she now has company, and I should feel easier about leaving her."[28]

And yet, as many critics have pointed out, Alger's tales do not in fact embody the self-reliance with which they are popularly identified. "Alger's heroes are rarely 'alone and unaided,' " John Cawelti noted in 1965, "and do not win their success entirely through individual effort and accomplishment. From the very beginning of his career, the Alger boy demonstrates an astounding propensity for chance encounters with benevolent and useful friends, and his success is largely due to their patronage and assistance."[29]

How is it that Alger's heroes, walking or rather climbing symbols of the doctrine of "character-based success,"[30] should depend so visibly on "patronage and assistance"? Why are Alger's tales, though emptied of brothers, so full of rich old fellows offering money? We don't need Orwell to see that this Good Rich Man was "a pure dream figure." What was Alger dreaming of? According to Cawelti, he was dreaming of his small-town childhood. Though Alger was writing in the years of cutthroat capitalist competition that followed the Civil War, Cawelti argues, his imagination tended to slip the knotty uncertainties of those years and take refuge in memories of a kindlier, preindustrial America. Patrons who take a personal interest in the hero's prospects, doing the virtue-rewarding work that the market could not after all be relied on to accomplish, represent for Cawelti "a reassertion of the values of a bygone era in an age of dramatic change and expansion" (120).[31]

Alger had powerful motives to seek reassurance among images of his antebellum youth—to begin with, because he was exiled from his youthful surroundings by the pederasty scandal that ended his ministerial career, an episode that scholars had not yet uncovered when Cawelti's book was published.[32] For all Alger's remarkable achievements as a writer, he was also the son of a well-respected minister and a graduate of Harvard College, and it was thus more natural for him than for his heroes to look back fondly upon a system in which an inherited name and connections to the Old Boy network would be permitted to bolster individual merits and offset demerits. He himself benefited dramatically from the patronage of friends like Joseph Allen, a fellow Harvard graduate and publisher of Unitarian journals twelve years his senior whom he met through his family when he was still a child. It was Allen who cleverly pushed the struggling author into the expanding market for juvenile literature and (in part perhaps to protect his investment in Alger's byline) helped cover up the charges of child molestation that got Alger dismissed from his Cape Cod pulpit. Shortly after Alger's flight from Massachusetts to New York, Allen also more or less created *Ragged Dick*, Alger's most popular book, by encouraging Alger to steal its plot (that of *Ned Nevins*) from a competitor.[33]

But these acts of patronage do not seem especially characteristic of the preindustrial past. And there is another problem with the nostalgia-for-small-town-America explanation. It implies that the generosity of the patron to the patronized depends on their shared membership in the class or category of the genteel. Unlike Allen, however, the benefactors of Alger's fiction are not linked to the young men they befriend by prior bonds of familial, class, institutional, or even neighborhood solidarity. On the contrary, they tend to be total strangers encountered and acquired in the anonymity of the street. (In *Struggling Upward*, it's in the woods at night, but the woods have a very urban-anonymous feel.) The bond that suddenly springs up between young boys and their "benevolent and useful friends" is thus something of a mystery. And the precise nature of this friendly bond is worth pausing over. After all, it is the cause of nearly everything that follows in the plot. And it would make sense, therefore, to consider the bond between boy and patron, rather than the boy's "self-reliance," as the true ideological message of that plot. If so, then what we are talking about is not merely a different motor of self-improvement, but a different model of how society in general is supposed to deal with the poor and the homeless.

Early in *Ragged Dick*, the homeless shoeshine boy Dick Hunter is asked whether he has change for a quarter. He jokes to the as yet anonymous customer who will soon become the first of his patrons: "Not a cent. . . . All my money's invested in the Erie Railroad."[34] The plot makes its predictable point when, trusted with the quarter, he faithfully delivers the correct change the next morning and by his honesty (accentuated by the dramatic delay) wins further patronage. No doubt Dick also does himself some good with this businessman by portraying himself, despite all indications that he will never have anything to invest, as an investor in the railroad. In so doing, further, he displays a certain self-mastery, separable from the entrepreneurial values he facetiously announces, and this self-mastery makes a more convincing exhibit of his merit, literarily speaking, than can be revealed by any amount of assiduous bootblacking. Here as elsewhere, the scene of self-presentation to the potential benefactor seems to be the actual site where something like genuine "merit" is displayed, merit that fiction does not often display in ordinary wage-earning labor.

However we characterize this bond with the benefactor and the manner in which it is cemented, two points are clear. First, this bond does not use the same social glue that held together preindustrial small towns. And second, whatever it says about the character of the young boy, it leaves open the no less interesting question of what motivates the benefactor.

In a brilliant attempt to factor Alger's pedophilia into the substance of his upward mobility stories, Michael Moon offers an alternative explanation for why Alger's commitment to competitive individualism is upstaged by "genteel patronage" (89).[35] The reason is Alger's own attraction to "the handsome faces and comely bodies" (94) of street boys, an attraction that led him to adopt the patron's role. Alger played this role with enthusiasm. Only months after his forced departure from his ministry, his biographer writes, Alger had made himself a sort of institution among the homeless boys of New York City.[36] "Alger's room, first in St Mark's Place and after 1875 in various boarding houses around the city, became a veritable salon for street boys. . . . A generation after he settled in NY, Alger remained a kind and popular benefactor of the street Arabs" (77). Thus the "stock adult character, the Patron . . . paralleled the part Alger had begun to assume among the street children of the city. He literally projected himself into his stories" (83). To these facts Moon adds a sexual dimension.[37] Describing the crucial scene between boy and benefactor as "a mutual seduction of sorts" (94), he offers this analysis: "the ritualistic 'lucky break' that initiates the boy's rising usually takes the form of his attracting the attention of a well-to-do male patron, usually through some spontaneous exhibition of his physical strength or daring. The 'magic trick' that the Alger text ultimately performs is to recuperate the possibility of a man's taking an intense interest in an attractive boy without risking being vilified or persecuted for doing so—indeed, this 'interest' is taken in a manner that is made thoroughly congruent with the social requirements of corporate capitalism on the sides of both parties: boy and potential employer alike 'profit' from it" (101).

From this perspective Alger's patrons would not after all make sense as throwbacks to small-town New England, which was not notably more tolerant of homosexuality than New York City and offered fewer possibilities for unconventional and unscrutinized behavior. In Moon's contrasting hypothesis, the bond of patronage between man and boy is "thoroughly congruent with the requirements of corporate capitalism." But this does not follow from everything Moon has said. Consider the quick pivot he makes at the word "indeed"—a shift from his sympathy with the homosexual's desire for freedom from vilification and persecution, on the one hand, to his lack of sympathy for "the social requirements of corporate capitalism," on the other. His argument works in two contradictory directions. On the one hand, it proposes that an illicit and (to many) even monstrous sexual "interest" is in effect whitewashed by the ideology of corporate capital, which imagines interest (now in the economic sense) as nonexploitative and mutually beneficial. "Older men who might (but actually do not) stand in relation to Alger's boy heroes as fathers may 'take an interest' in them that may eventuate in actions as various as respectful advancement or rape, but none of these interactions with older men on the boys' part leaves any permanent trace in the lives of the boys except in the form of yet another accession of capital. . . . the 'rise' of Alger's hero is fostered by 'interested' older patrons, but (the informing, contradictory fantasy runs) the boy remains entirely self-fathering" (103–4). For Moon, this corresponds to "corporate culture's favorite modes of self-presentation . . . as fraternal, financially rewarding, benevolently hierarchical, open to individual talent or 'merit' " (107).

On the other hand, while pinning the rise of the Alger hero to the rise of corporate capital, Moon also unveils a hidden chapter in the history of an oppressed group. And the meaning of Alger's story for homosexuals, or for a society that has decided to recognize and correct the injustices done to groups like homosexuals, is not satisfactorily summed up by the sentences above. Where the sexual abuse of children is in question, no one will quarrel with Moon's cautious avoidance of the celebratory mode, or even of overt sympathy for those like Alger who were forced by homophobia into dangerous clandestinity. But Moon does less than justice to the rich implications of his own argument when he allows the collective interests of homosexuals to disappear into the conclusion that the bonds between older patron and street boy could only have served the purposes of corporate capital.

A more equitable and appealing alternative emerges from Moon's observations about the ambiguity of "saving." As one would expect, Alger's heroes open bank accounts and save money. But they also do something more unpredictable. They go against their own obvious self-interest, indeed often sacrificing their painfully accumulated savings, in order to "save" other boys. In *Ragged Dick*, for example, Dick drastically if only provisionally depletes his small savings account in order to take in the homeless Henry Fosdick. The all-male domesticity of Dick and Fosdick extends across three volumes of the series and includes the adoption of another street child, Mark. As Moon writes, "once the hero begins to 'rise' and achieves a modicum of domestic stability, the activity or habit that is represented as being indispensable to maintaining his personal ascendancy is 'saving.' It is by saving, i.e., thriftily and systematically accumulating bits of capital, that Dick produces his nest egg; it is by virtue of these habits that he shows himself to be a fit parent (mother) for Mark; and it is his 'saving'—by rescuing from dead-end poverty—first Fosdick and then Mark that the cycle of ascent is renewed in this series. Just as Dick has been saved in order to learn to 'save' himself, so he will save younger boys and provide them with a model of 'saving' both money and still more boys" (99).

According to Moon, this is the logic of a total social system, total in the sense that it seamlessly integrates the sexual and the economic. Saving boys offers the pleasures of a homoerotic bond in recompense for the delayed delights (and, one supposes, the delayed marriage) implied by habits of saving rather than spending money. But this instance of male bonding is not entirely reducible to a logic of corporate recruitment. For it is not, as Moon implies, a process of simple self-repetition. The boys Dick saves do not resemble him. They have noticeably less energy and "enterprise." If Dick's older benefactors admire him for his pluck, in other words, then in becoming a benefactor in his own right he is not faithfully imitating them. Dick responds to a boy's need, one might even say his *lack* of pluck, rather than his resemblance to Dick's own forceful and buoyant character. This asymmetry comes perilously close to the very antithesis of rugged individualism: from each according to his ability, to each according to his needs. Moreover, Dick becomes a benefactor *before* he can say, with the "rich old fellow" of my epigraph, that he "can well afford" to. And his recklessly premature philanthropy does not hasten his own rise. In short, this is not a self-evident image of corporate self-reproduction. Though the "all-boy families" formed around these moments of generosity may represent, as Moon says, a version of capital's own fantasy of "asexual breeding" (104), they are not founded on a simple computation of self-interest of the kind that the word *corporate* might suggest.[38] It is of course possible that this deviation from visible economic self-interest merely registers the hidden force of sexual self-interest. We need not believe it is simple altruism that allows Dick to tell Fosdick, "I guess my bed will hold two" (73). Still, even the cynical hypothesis that money is being traded for sex leaves us with a suggestive confusion between self-interest and disinterestedness, predatory sexuality and economic collectivism.

The proper referent for this confusion, I would suggest, is not corporate capitalism, but the politically ambiguous mode of social organization that arose with it and against it, in order to regulate and also in order to preserve it: the welfare state.[39] The welfare state offers something to the collective interests of women and sexual minorities, which are rendered invisible by a philosophy of sturdy independent individualism. And it is a historically specific referent, not an ideal one. In the nineteenth and twentieth centuries, the slowly developing decision to rescue society's less fortunate members, which presupposes the recognition that collective prosperity cannot be attained by the pursuit of individual self-interest, did not of course take the (to me, preferable) form of socialism. Nor is Alger's (and Dick's) erotic attraction to the weak an impulse that demands full equality. As I have noted earlier, it is an impulse to rectify extreme inequalities while maintaining a hierarchy (here, a sexualized hierarchy of "masculine" and "feminine"). In the same way, the welfare state maintains a power differential between strong and weak, rescuer and rescued, even though it also depends on redistributing from the former to the latter. As in the corporate model Moon describes, there is continuing inequality. Nevertheless, rescue is a long way from self-reliance.

The social experiments in which Alger participated, notably the Children's Aid Society, where his work is still commemorated, were part of a historical process by which the private efforts of parents and philanthropists, who could no longer cope with the proliferation of homeless children generated on a massive scale by industrial capitalism, found an eventual if still insufficient and sometimes sinister substitute in public institutions. This shift from private to public responsibility meant moving away from dependence on wealthy individuals who could afford to be charitable (and received various benefits for so doing). It meant tapping the taxpayers, who could afford less, were less likely to see the benefits, and needed more convincing. In order for this idea to enter the domain of political possibility, there had to be a momentous ethical transformation. The resistance this transformation elicited in its earliest stages can he surmised from the fear and loathing of state interference that such taxpayer-financed institutions so often continue to elicit.

The self-reliance story has of course been read as part of that resistance, and not without reason. But as Moon argues, Alger's version of that story would seem less nostalgic for past individualism than prescient about a postindividualist future. And corporate capitalism, which Moon sees him foreshadowing, overlaps significantly with the equally emergent institutions of the welfare state. The "limited liability" that gave the corporation its first English name involved a dispersal of individual responsibility that, however convenient as a device for making and protecting profits, was also about to be put to very different uses. It defended investors against demands for accountability, but it also encouraged the threateningly relativistic "no fault" view of poverty, based on a vision of ineluctable social interdependence, that support for the social welfare state would require. After all, there could be neither "systematic knowledge about poverty in America," nor the institutions to act on that knowledge, until people had begun to give up "the widely shared assumption that being poor was a self-inflicted mortification."[40] The welfare state needed "limited liability" no less than the corporation did.[41]

Alger's writings of the 1860s and after come in the period when limited liability, "traditionally considered as belonging to quasi-public undertakings" alone, had just begun to spread into all sorts of corporations—according to David Montgomery, "one of the most important innovations of the era," but one whose inconsistency with the usual view of Alger has not been pointed out.[42] Alger's astonishing posthumous celebrity came only later, in the Progressive Era. The lag time between the writing and the largest success could thus be explained by a different aspect of that era: not so much the transition from entrepreneurial to corporate organization as the rising recognition that capitalist enterprise had to be socialized and regulated. Alongside the obvious usefulness of the "virtue rewarded" narrative in combating the newly interventionist state, one has to stress the less obvious role of his benefactor figures in undermining popular, patriarchal individualism and preparing the ethical metamorphosis presupposed by the welfare state's increasing replacement of private with public responsibility—its establishment of what would look to many individuals like new zones of dangerous irresponsibility. Rather than simply celebrating the grasping individualists of Alger's own time, then, Alger's "instructive narrative" would thus be (in Alan Trachtenberg's words) "a fictive analogue to campaigns for reform."[43]

"I wouldn't keep a pig in it myself": *Great Expectations*

Robby Wideman reenters the life of his brother John Edgar as a homeless man, on the run from the law, though soon to be recaptured—in fact he is captured the next day—and sent to prison for life. The rendezvous of the two brothers in *Brothers and Keepers* bears a structural resemblance to the first encounter of Pip and Magwitch at the opening of *Great Expectations*. When Magwitch looms up in the churchyard, he too is a fugitive from justice, a homeless man begging (or threatening) for food. Next day he too is captured. When the king's officers arrest him, Pip is standing in their midst. Though he has aided and abetted the convict and agonized guiltily, he could also be suspected naturally enough of having turned Magwitch in. This is the suspicion about himself that Wideman plants in his title. "Keeper," he tells us, is prison slang for "guard." In asking whether he is his brother's keeper in the biblical sense, morally obliged to attend to Robby's welfare as if it were his own, the title also asks whether he is his brother's keeper in the penitentiary sense. Is he another guard, keeping watch, keeping order? Staying on the right side of the bars means not helping his brother stay on the loose. Is the writer's upward mobility predicated on his brother's immobility? Does he, like the respectable society he has joined, depend on prison as a solution to the problem posed by people like his brother?

The ambiguity of the keeper adds a further twist to the relation between homelessness and upward mobility. We have seen homelessness (the protagonist's) as a device that justifies the striving for upward mobility, and we have seen the homelessness of those who do not rise, or who have fallen—Dreiser's Hurstwood and Gissing's Reardon, wandering the streets of their respective cities—as an image of the dilemma of upward mobility. The suggestion here is not merely that to be homeless is to be a criminal, but that one may have to break the law in order to *rescue* the homeless. And yet both texts also hint that the rescue of the homeless man is a cause—the word is not too strong—of upward mobility, an explanation of how the rise happens.

One night's worth of hospitality to his fugitive brother earns Wideman a police interrogation: "Only after two Laramie Police Department detectives arrived at dawn on February 12, a day too late to catch my brother, and treated me like a criminal, did I know I'd been one. Aiding and abetting a fugitive. Accessory after the fact to the crime of first-degree murder. The detectives hauled me down to the station. Demanded that I produce an alibi for the night a convenience store had been robbed in Utah. . . . No matter that I wrote books and taught literature and creative writing at the university. I was black. Robby was my brother. Those unalterable facts would always incriminate me" (14). But as he knows, his situation is very different from Robby's. Accessory or not, he is released; the book does not explain why. Robby is sentenced to "life imprisonment without possibility of probation or parole" (14). The writer is free to "manufacture fiction from the events of my brother's life" (14). And when he does, the fact of being black, always incriminated, and justifiably angry about it becomes a professional resource for him. Wideman does not have to be told about the moral complications that go with benefiting from the sale of his brother's story. "Though I never intended to steal his story, to appropriate it or exploit it," he writes, "in a sense that's what would happen once the book was published" (200).

The intention to appropriate or exploit is also missing from Pip's brief dealings with Magwitch, but the same logic of delayed benefit is of course at work. In a brilliant realistic variation on a mythic motif, the hero's unmotivated act of assistance to a needy stranger who turns out to have magical powers, the fugitive convict turns out to be Pip's patron. The secret of Pip's upward mobility is his aid to a homeless man. He has unwittingly laid the foundation of his social ascent by an act both moral and criminal, and the near paradox of being both criminal and moral continues to hover over that ascent. If the opening scene of *Great Expectations* looks forward to *Brothers and Keepers*, in other words, it also looks sideways, across an apparently unbridgeable discrepancy in moral seriousness, at Alger's *Ragged Dick*. Here it is the man rather than the boy who is homeless, for the moment at least neither is wealthy, and the taint of self-interest and criminality about the rescue has nothing obviously to do with sex. But the structural parallel is still striking: Pip's meeting with Magwitch prefigures the scene of "mutual seduction" that occurs between patron and boy in Alger.

The point of saying this is, first of all, to save Dickens from a righteous but unappealing fate. Where upward mobility is concerned, he and Alger look like a cartoon contrast of thumbs down and thumbs up: Alger is the uncritical booster, Dickens the critical realist who overturns Pip's "great expectations" and turns them into "lost illusions." The overturning of the expectations gracefully acknowledges the extraliterary fact that most apprentice blacksmiths do not become London gentlemen while insinuating that it might not be a good thing for society as a whole if they did. The trajectory from expectations to illusions offers an irresistible symbol of nineteenth-century literature's self-critical achievement and of moral seriousness in general.[44] Of course, Dickens was himself "as successful an example of self-help as any in Smiles's book" (578), and no one will be surprised that he had some investment, saw some "positive element" (581), in stories resembling his own. But it has been difficult to specify what that element might be and whether it meant momentarily forgetting his moral seriousness. (Robin Gilmour, whom I'm quoting here, relates it in passing to the Victorian "impulse to improvement," which holds on to the seriousness.) It has been easier to see the upward mobility story as a betrayal. In Gilmour's words, "the burden of most modern criticism has been to stress that [Pip's great expectations] are *only* illusory, that the 'real thing' (as Trilling says) is not Pip's gentility but what goes on in the cellarage of the novel, that his expectations are indeed even dangerous and anti-social" (581).[45] When Orwell describes *Great Expectations* as a "critique of patronage" (53), he sums up an enormous body of criticism that castigates the selfishness with which both Magwitch and Miss Havisham, the true patron and the false, make Pip's expectations serve their own ends. In succumbing to these patrons, it is suggested, Pip is lured into an upward mobility that is as vain and selfish as they are, which is to say lured away from the moral center represented by Joe, Biddy, and the forge. The critique of the patron sends one back to the forge.

But this is not in fact where the novel leaves Pip, either in physical or in social space. After the great expectations have been lost, Pip ends up as something that he wasn't already. As in Alger, there *is* upward mobility. And as in Alger, a faint stigma of criminality hangs over the patron and over the spaces where patron and protagonist meet.

To begin with, the burial ground. The churchyard in which Pip, about to be surprised by Magwitch, contemplates the graves of his parents and siblings in the first scene of *Great Expectations*, like the cemetery in which Rastignac takes leave of Goriot in the last scene of *Père Goriot*, is a terminal displacement of the family, a sign that henceforth life will be lived, however guiltily, outside it. Life outside it comes under the influence of the patron. And so do other nonfamilial spaces. If the death of fatherhood in Goriot's sense is the birth of Vautrin's style of mentorship, this shift also marks the birth of a distinctive residential space. Rastignac first encounters Vautrin in a lodging house, or *pension*. Lodging houses are the special abode of people outside or temporarily irrelevant to the cycle of biological reproduction, and Vautrin, who shows a homosexual appreciation for Rastignac's "male beauty," is repeatedly associated with the quintessentially nondomestic space of Madame Vauquer's pension, that lodging house whose nightmarish description takes up the memorable and much-discussed first pages of the novel. An in-between space, it is neither the "proper" domesticity of the provincial home nor the questionable domesticity of the aristocratic *hôtel*. The *hôtel* is inhabited by the older, married women who, along with their other roles, mediate to Rastignac the power of their husbands. Like the *hôtel*, the lodging house represents how protagonists are seduced away from domesticity, or what they are seduced by. It is a midpoint that is also a new endpoint, pointing upward mobility away from domesticity.

It is in the lodging house that Vautrin makes his proposition to Rastignac. All Rastignac needs to do, in order to secure the ascent he so desires, is to acquiesce in the death of someone he need never see. Rastignac, rephrasing this proposition (misattributed to Rousseau) as the temptation to will the death of an aged Chinese mandarin halfway around the world, thereby invokes the imperial world-system, the surge of power that comes of being systematically spared the sight of your distant victims. But this is also the social logic of the *pension* itself. By the face-to-face standard of domestic intimacy, distance *is* criminality.

Magwitch, a more demure parallel to the sexualized criminal patronage of Lecter and Vautrin, brings the money from away, out of sight, in a territory provided by the empire. The empire (which Disraeli sold to skeptics as a source of upward mobility for their sons) is again where the power of upward mobility in fact comes from. Again, but even more emphatically, this territory is defined by having to *stay* out of sight. Magwitch's benefaction has taken the form of an interdiction: thou shalt not ask where the money comes from. And yet the novel's plot is defined by Magwitch transgressing the interdiction to stay out of sight, and the moral center of the plot, as critics have largely agreed, has to do with Pip recognizing and valuing the criminal who is the source of his funds, face-to-face, even as he renounces or loses the funds. This is how he is held to redeem himself for his social climbing and neglect of his loved ones.

To describe the spatiality of the plot in this way is to suggest that the novel is critical of social mobility in the name of immobile domesticity. Attention to the novel's nondomestic spaces (other than prison and Australia, where Magwitch is never actually seen) might seem to reinforce this reading. After he appears shivering in the cold churchyard, where he takes over the parental role from Pip's deceased family, Magwitch shows up in two other nondomestic spaces. He is next seen on the marshes, which come to stand for the emptiness, bleak but also somehow inviting, in which Pip must now invent himself, and *can* now invent himself. And, most interestingly, he reappears in Pip's "chambers" in London, where he seems radically out of place and yet where, unlike Joe, he quickly makes himself at home. As Sharon Marcus notes in *Apartment Stories*, the all-male legal chambers at Temple and Lincoln's Inns, where unmarried men shared the servants of the building, were among the rare exceptions to the English rule: a refusal of large multihousehold dwellings that dramatically distinguished mid-nineteenth-century London from mid-nineteenth-century Paris. London grew horizontally rather than vertically; it had no apartment houses, and to foreigners could thus represent the apotheosis of domesticity.[46]

The prejudice against public space and in favor of private, domestic space is one for which there is considerable evidence in *Great Expectations*. The novel's nondomestic spaces are set off against Wemmick's happy domesticity as well as against the forge. When Pip returns home, his moral failure is signaled by his going not to the forge but to the inn. From the viewpoint of the forge, an ideal fusion of residence and workplace that comes to look more and more ideal after the providential assault on Mrs. Joe, Pip's nondomestic dwelling is simply uninhabitable. Joe's somewhat inconsiderate comment is, "I wouldn't keep a pig in it myself, not in the case that I wished him to fatten wholesome and to eat with a meller flavor on him" (chap. 27, p. 212, Carlisle ed.).

This view of domesticity would seem to accord with a view of the novel that would make of Magwitch an ethical lesson about the dirtiness of money, and thus also about social aspiration. In this view, Miss Havisham's money is always really Magwitch's money, that is, money wrung from misery, hard labor, and injustice. One cannot take people's money because, however respectable it may look, it always comes from crime, indeed from theft. But if this moral seems radical on one level, is not very helpful on another. It suggests that it is *possible* not to take people's money. It suggests, in other words, that there exists a (meritocratic) status quo in which social climbing, snobbery, and dependence could and should be avoided, in which people therefore could and should be allowed (or forced) to stay what they already are.[47]

This is the vision of domestic self-reliance to which Dickens gives the unforgettable spatial form of Wemmick's Castle. The paradoxical villa of Jaggers's clerk at Walworth is an archaic fantasy of suburban self-containment, complete with fake battlements and a drawbridge. It has fowls, rabbits—and, conveniently, that very pig that Joe despaired of raising properly in Pip's chambers. Late in the novel, escaping to Walworth after learning that his own rooms, with Magwitch in them, are being watched, Pip is advised by Wemmick (who is off to work) to " 'have a perfectly quiet day with the Aged—he'll be up presently—and a little bit of—you remember the pig?' "

> "Of course," I said.
> "Well, and a little bit of *him*. That sausage you roasted was his, and he was in all respects a first-rater. Do try him, if it is only for old acquaintance sake" (chap. 46, 342–43).

Pause a moment over the pig. Even if it did not recall a conversation some chapters earlier in which Wemmick coolly requests a pair of pigeons from a prisoner about to be executed (chap. 32), the charming callousness of this little speech might well make one wonder at the Castle's humorous but nonetheless putatively idyllic domesticity. Politeness to a pig who has been more of a pet, politeness to a pig who, like the Aged P, both is and isn't a full member of the family, a pig who is still an "acquaintance" even now that he has taken the form of sausage—this politeness suggests that a domesticity that would truly be self-reliant would mean devouring your relations. It belongs, I would suggest, to an argument in favor of distance—an argument in favor of not eating your pets, that is, or not keeping quite so close at hand anything you are *going* to eat. It obliquely subverts the pig-keeping, anti-mobility model of domesticity by which Joe has judged Pip's "chambers."[48]

This is what a great deal of Dickens's most flamboyant language accomplishes. Critics have often wondered about the question of Pip's "progress": whether there is any, and how to feel about it, or its lack.[49] According to Franco Moretti, the narrative standpoint adopted in *Great Expectations* and *Jane Eyre*—that of the protagonists themselves, now older and wiser—in fact commits each novel to the immobility of the established order: "since point of view has its own logic—which compels the reader to appropriate the point of view that makes the text readable to him—when it coincides with a violated order, he inevitably desires the anomalies to cease, and order to be reestablished" (202). In Moretti's view, the characteristic hero of an English bildungsroman speaks rather than acts, and the manner of the speech serves as "a status symbol, a caste indicator" (195). But if so, then Dickens has given upward mobility a ringing endorsement as soon as Pip opens his mouth.

As I suggested above, what we see in the graveyard humor of the opening scene is Pip separating himself off from the (dead) family members he will leave behind. In other words, a guilt-ridden *social* distance masquerades as the innocently *temporal* distance between adult narrator and child character. Moretti is right that voice is a specifically novelistic mark of social mobility. And here the content of this form is distance, a useful or necessary brutality toward the domestic. Like Wemmick's attitude toward the household pig, Pip's imagination of his dead brothers shows a certain comic indifference to the sufferings of those beings closest to him in domestic space, an indifference that is also a source of power. The pleasure one gets from Dickens's language might be seen as earned by an individual performance. But if it reminds us of Dickens's accomplishments as performer and "self-made man," it also ought to remind us of the wider context in which that self-making took place. If his voice is a mark of merit, it is also the expression of a distance that is not personal—of impersonality, one might say, as social fact, as a form of social merit. This charming callousness, a nondomestic marker of upward mobility, can be located on the social landscape.

The character who best locates it is, not coincidentally, another benefactor figure. Jaggers is defined by the crime he works on and with; like Pip, he gets his money from it. If Pip is so often thrown together with this forbidding guardian and mentor, it is clearly because Jaggers and his nondomestic spaces invoke some of the sinister but sidestepped truth of what Pip is aiming for. He has the power to help, and he is not overparticular about which side he helps. The one case of dramatized self-making in the novel, Jaggers is someone whom we see earning a position by his efforts—not coincidentally, efforts in the use of language. What is distinctive about his use of language is the way it abstracts from the legal responsibility of particular persons. " '[I]t's not personal,' " Wemmick explains, " 'it's professional: only professional' " (192). The distance of the legal bureaucracy, which echoes that of the *pension* and of Pip's pigless chambers, takes the characteristic verbal form of "putting a case." When Jaggers puts a case, he treats situations as if the individuals concerned weren't known, or weren't present, as if they were types, suitable objects for statistical analysis. This self-making by means of impersonality, standing in as agent for invisible principals, embodies a certain denial of self-interest. He may be amoral, but we are never led to understand that Jaggers has put his own interest ahead of that of a client. His amorality is not corruption. But of course this denial of self-interest also has its own special, indirect form of self-interest. Professional neutrality is also professional profit. Little by little, Jaggers has done very well for himself.

In this way Jaggers offers instruction about the world Pip aspires to enter; and since he does Pip no other favors, that would be a minimum requirement for mentorship. Yet sordid as the world of courts and prisons is shown to be, it would not be quite accurate to say that by Jaggers's example Dickens warns Pip off. Like the disquieting coolness of the doctors in *Bleak House* and *Père Goriot*, Jaggers's professional impersonality has its attractions, for our time but also for its contemporaries. This is true even for someone as morally stringent as George Eliot. The only exception that Moretti makes, in discussing an "English Bildungsroman" that "leaves us, so to speak, with an empty stomach," is Eliot's novel of vocation, and this is because, he says, the novel of vocation aims at "the synthesis of individual expression and collective benefit" (214). Strangely enough, this "collective benefit" seems to coincide with a certain impersonality. As the word suggests, vocation belongs to an emergent nineteenth-century professionalism. Moretti observes for example that *Daniel Deronda* "turns the sociological vector of the 'family romance' toward the lower classes" (215). Instead of discovering higher origins, Deronda follows his heart toward roots that tie him to those who are poor and suffering.

This might be described, once again, as reverse snobbery. As we have seen in Alger, reverse snobbery seems to be a hidden but perversely constitutive principle of modern society. Why does Alger seek out homeless children? Why is it that Pip's relationship with Magwitch, rather than his relationship with Estella, becomes the emotional center of *Great Expectations*?[50] In each case there is something troubling or distasteful, whether a hint of the exploitative or of the goody-goody. In each case there is also a downward rather than an upward vector of desire.

In *Daniel Deronda*, the discovery of lower rather than higher origins has been anticipated by a whole professional erotics.[51] "Persons attracted him in proportion to the possibility of his defending them, rescuing them, telling upon their lives with some sort of redeeming influence" (369). Eliot does not hide the self-interest lurking in Deronda's "passion for people who are pelted" (785). But she can smile upon it anyway. For Deronda's outpouring of libido in the direction of those requiring assistance has a collective rationale that carries far beyond any personal self-seeking or eccentricity. The logic is clear: only those who are unfortunate enough to need your help can define your work, or your life, as intended for "collective benefit." And that is a highly desirable quantity. In other words, the logic of Deronda's emotions is the logic of the benefactor, a benefactor who can be confused with a private philanthropist only because he anticipates the institutional and state forms of a professionalism that, though already a reality, had not yet been put firmly in place.

Although Deronda seems intended as a hero of unblemished character, this logic of the benefactor is by no means identical with moral virtue, or at least with moral virtue of a domestic or preprofessional sort. Deronda's professionally seductive eyes, impersonally personal, "*seemed* to express a special interest in every one on whom he fixed them" (377). Only *seemed*—we don't know whether the interest is real, any more than we know this about Bianchon's devotion to Goriot or Alger's to the street kids he accosts and takes home.[52] And yet it is "special interest" of this peculiarly indeterminate kind to which dedication to the "collective benefit" has seemingly been entrusted.

The heroic Deronda and the less-than-villainous Jaggers share a mode of reconciling self-interest and the general welfare that is neither a humane ideal nor an appalling imitation of upper-class gentility. They operate in the same zone: the zone between the moral and the criminal where Pip's initial act of assistance has placed him. In this sense, they define an alternative telos for Pip's upward mobility. If so, then in spite of appearances, Dickens is not after all opting for the walling off of domestic space, site of true, private feeling and moral sensibility, as opposed to rising into the inhumanity of the social system outside. The problem of space would not be described as maintaining proper enclosure, segregation, separation of spheres, as the ideology of domesticity suggests. (Nor could Dickens's accomplishment be seen, as it sometimes has been, as a simple deconstructing of this binary.) Space in *Great Expectations* would be animated, rather, by a problematic of circulation.

The novel's inns and pubs are nightmarish enough to have come out of an antiurban, prodomestic tract.[53] When Pip obeys the resonant directive "DON'T GO HOME," he goes instead to a hotel in Covent Garden (chap. 45), where he spends a sleepless night in a room with "an inhospitable smell." He is tortured by the sentence "Don't Go Home" in all its variations, by the fact that he isn't at home and will not have one. The difference between hotel and home is at the forefront. His thoughts are of the room's many other tenants, real or hypothetical, including a suicide: "It was a sort of vault on the ground floor at the back, with a despotic monster of a four-post bedstead in it, straddling over the whole place, putting one of his arbitrary legs into the fireplace and another into the doorway, and squeezing the wretched little washing-stand in quite a Divinely Righteous manner." The monarchical is not for him. If it's like a castle, then it can't be anything like a home.[54]

But what is it exactly that is so nightmarish about these nondomestic spaces? Describing the public house on the river where they spend their last night, before the ill-fated escape attempt, Dickens writes: "We found the air as carefully excluded from [the bedrooms], as if air were fatal to life" (401). Of the room with the bridal cake in Miss Havisham's house, Dickens writes: "From that room, too, the daylight was completely excluded, and it had an airless smell that was oppressive" (94). The problem with the public space is not too free and promiscuous a circulation, as one might have imagined. It is the same as Miss Havisham's problem of complete enclosure, exacerbated domesticity: *lack* of circulation.

Jaggers of course has no domestic life. His domestic arrangements in Soho are described as follows: "he seemed to bring the office home with him . . . and to wheel it out of an evening and fall to work" (204). His home is "bare, gloomy, and little used" (203); it is professional rather than domestic space. On the other hand, we are also told, strangely, that Jaggers "never lets a door or window be fastened at night" (198). For Jaggers, despite or because of his entanglement in the prison system, one might say that walling off is no solution to the problems of social relationship. For he is always part of a larger system of circulation that makes a mockery of any effort to enclose. And there is a sense in which the rest of the novel agrees with him.

"Because she wrecks the brewery and refuses to sponsor her male relatives," Susan Walsh writes of Miss Havisham, "she blocks her financial capital from circulating within the proper channels of investment and trade, thus rendering it economically barren."[55] This insight hints at an extended connection between the circulation of air and the circulation of money, the blockage of the one and the blockage of the other. The "collective benefit" supplied by the benefactor's role in *Great Expectations* involves not so much the archaism of patronage as the anticipation of an as yet unrealized, impersonal agency. Moretti notes how dry and legalistic Pip's time in London is, ending as it does "with the legal confiscation of Pip's assets" (208). Counterintuitive as it may seem, I think this has to be turned around. As they say, follow the money. The money doesn't just disappear into the coffers of the Crown, though that is not a totally inappropriate destination for it. Pip's only significant actions in the novel involve talking Miss Havisham into a redistribution of funds on behalf of the more deserving Mr. Pocket and giving a portion of Magwitch's money indirectly to Herbert Pocket. Herbert is not one of the brothers born with their hands in their pockets, but his name and befuddled lack of enterprise bring him as close to them as the novel permits. It is through him, one might say, that some portion of the debt to the brothers is repaid.[56] The money circulates through Pip, and though his role in the circulation is not traced, a portion of this money eventually and indirectly comes back to him. In diverting the funds to Herbert, Pip unintentionally makes possible his own future as a clerk and eventually a partner in the same enterprise.[57]

Pip has learned from Magwitch, it would seem, the role of benefactor. The difference is that he is a benefactor-without-money. He is a benefactor without money of his own, that is—a benefactor who merely circulates other people's money. From one perspective, this might be seen as his apprenticeship for the role of clerk (a rich theme in upward mobility stories from Gissing through the slacker film *Clerks* and its sequel, *Clerks 2*). But the clerk's subordinated skill, or skill without ownership, describes a social position that extends from Wemmick up through Jaggers himself. Jaggers's function in the plot has been, like Pip's own when he uses Magwitch's money to arrange for Herbert's partnership, to stop anyone from following the money trail back to its source. Rightly or wrongly, this is what the law does. It is also what Pip does. Pip's good deeds are deeds of *non*transparency; they obscure the source of funds. And in doing so, they turn bad money to good causes. In short, Pip acts not like someone who has finally seen the light of domestic morality, but like a money launderer. Or, let us say, like a fund-raiser for a Non-Governmental Organization, a person of good conscience and good causes whose raw materials include the funds accumulated by the Ford or the Rockefeller foundation. At this level of ethical abstraction, the two activities are not incomparable.

This is how the property-is-theft idea works its way most successfully into the upward mobility narrative. If property comes from Magwitch, then the acquisition of property cannot be what upward mobility is about. Hence there is a certain selflessness about the hero. But this selflessness expresses itself in a peculiar form: by valuing a more equitable *circulation* of property over the personal *possession* of property. And this selflessness is not total; it allows for a certain indirect self-interest. Like Jaggers's actions on Magwitch's behalf, Pip's providing for Herbert unintentionally allows Herbert later to provide for Pip. Some selflessness is bartered for some (unacknowledged) self-interest, which shapes the actual, sober, undramatized upward mobility that follows the collapse of the great expectations.

This administrative or professional impersonality is arguably the closest we have come to solving the problem dramatized by Wemmick's domesticity: the "good" person who does "bad" things—bad at work, good at home. The solution is not negligible. Even the most democratic state would require the impersonality of statistics. Even at their best, the professions and the state engage in a mode of rescue that depends on being able to treat people as if they were not there. I am suggesting, very schematically, that Pip finds his oblique, impersonal self-interest in the sort of function that will come to be supplied by the institutional machinery of the welfare state—that he will receive his long-delayed inheritance, if you like, as his share in the impersonality of the Crown, which does inherit the money from Magwitch that Pip cannot inherit.

This sort of point has been made before, but is usually made with a strong dose of Foucaultian cynicism. D. A. Miller speaks without enthusiasm of Dickens's support, in *Bleak House*, for "the expanded development of the Victorian state bureaucracy" (64).[58] In the same antiinstitutional spirit Tony Bennett speaks, in an essay on the spread of nineteenth-century museums, of how "the development of new capillary systems for the distribution of culture would help cultivate a capacity for voluntary self-regulation in the general population."[59] It is with pronounced disapproval that Mary Poovey, writing about domesticity in Chadwick's 1842 *Sanitary Report*, notes that Chadwick's version of domestic reform did nothing to harm his own professional ambitions. "The twin effects of every component of Chadwick's sanitary plan were, on the one hand, to limit the ability of working-class men to organize themselves into collective political or economic associations and, on the other, to empower the kind of professionalized bureaucrat that Chadwick himself represented" (130).[60]

But the empowering of professionalized bureaucrats is not, after all, a self-evident evil. The insinuation of the state into domestic privacy is not a zero-sum game in which every gain for a bureaucrat's career was a loss for a woman and for the working class. As Carolyn Steedman argues, to see the working class as a cozily united collectivity beset by the external threats of professional experts and state officials has always been a gendered choice that ignored the actually and potentially positive meaning of state and professional intervention for working-class women.[61] Indeed, this is not so different from a point that Mary Poovey herself makes, in an earlier book, about Florence Nightingale.[62] "In mobilizing the Victorian domestic narrative to reform the poor, Florence Nightingale activated the altruistic language that women's maternal nature underwrote" so as to turn paid nursing into "a quasi-religious calling" (196–97). This was a means of aggressively seizing power and authority from medical doctors, but it was also a strategy that made public space for women's nondomestic expertise and careers. It is in this sense that a narrative of upward mobility could be conceived as involving, at least to some degree, reaffirming loyalty to one's origins rather than forsaking them.

This is the mode of middle-class membership, I have been arguing, that one sees in *Great Expectations*. The novel's version of the upward mobility story is thus not Pip's linear ascent. Nor is it, as readers have more often assumed, the ethical blockage of that ascent. Located in the unpretentious but respectable clerkship, it takes its moral bearings from another act of rescue, again one that is criminal, again one that fails: the attempt to get Magwitch out of England. Circling back to rescue Magwitch *a second time*, Pip self-consciously recognizes himself in and tends to another orphan, generalizing the individualized uplift of the upward mobility story into a rescue of all by all. The endpoint of this story, becoming a benefactor-without-money, is thus not an enclosed domesticity, nor an ideal democracy; it is merely the space of a modest improvement in the circulation of resources. The position Pip is moving toward, though of course not actually filling within the novel, is that of an administrative reformer, public or semipublic servant of a welfare state—not the actual state that was ready to execute Magwitch if he didn't die first, but the reformed, as yet unrealized state that would take over Pip's own role of rescuing Magwitch and all those like him. The criminality of both rescues is a mark of how far from the legal order such a role remains.

CHAPTER THREE

"It's not your fault": Therapy and Irresponsibility from Dreiser to Doctorow

Styles of Radical Antistatism: D. A. Miller and Christopher Lasch

A more democratic circulation of power, which the last chapter proposed as an effect of the reforms leading toward the welfare state, is the prime target of critique in D. A. Miller's brilliant and influential essay on *Bleak House*.[1] In Dickens's early novels, Miller suggests, the walls of the prison, the workhouse, the factory, and the orphanage draw a line between an inside and an outside, positing a space of "freedom and domestic tranquillity" where these oppressive institutions could be escaped and from which they could be criticized—making possible, that is, an emancipatory politics. In *Bleak House*, however, the intrusive, ubiquitous, all-permeating fog that emanates from the Court of Chancery blurs that line and subverts that politics. Miller writes: "what is most radically the matter with being 'in Chancery' is not that there may be no way out of it (a dilemma belonging to the problematic of the carceral), but, more seriously, that the binarisms of inside/outside, here/elsewhere become meaningless and the ideological effects they ground impossible" (62). The dominant form of social power had spilled over the walls of such institutions, sometimes in the guise of reforming them. Following Foucault, Miller argues that power no longer works by repressive confinement; it now circulates freely, as do its objects.[2] In this sense, circulation has succeeded, and has succeeded in democracy's name. But the result is democratic in name only.

It has thus become difficult or counterproductive, Miller concludes, to mobilize notions of accountability, opposition, and critique. He does not pause to ask which it is, difficult or counterproductive: whether one must try to mobilize these notions, or notions like them, in spite of the difficulty, or whether such an effort would be a political mistake. But the answer seems to be that any subsystemic quest for accountability would be mistaken. For Miller goes on to criticize *Bleak House* on the grounds that its shift in focus from Chancery to the Police is also a retreat from its own insight. In its second half, the novel turns into a detective story. Thus it does mobilize a language of accountability, guilt, and innocence. And that is its problem. Finding a culprit and putting a face on a crime, Inspector

Bucket and the Detective Police refuse the "facelessness" of "a system where it is generally impossible to assign responsibility for its workings to any single person or group of persons, where even the process of victimization seems capricious" (69). In short, the novel employs a form of scapegoating, the arbitrary assigning to an individual of responsibility that should properly be seen as systemic.[3]

In the final chapter of *The Novel and the Police* (1988), where the *Bleak House* essay is reprinted, Miller applies his argument to the upward mobility genre. The conclusion of *David Copperfield*, he notes, presents two upwardly mobile characters, David and Uriah Heep, one innocently enjoying domestic bliss and the other in prison. Heep, the exemplary parvenu, says from his cell how good prison has been to him and for him: "It would be better for everybody, if they got took up, and was brought here" (218). In effect, Miller suggests, everybody *has* been "took up." David certainly has. Hardworking and self-policing, he too has submitted to society's discipline, a form of imprisonment without walls. "Faced with the abundance of resemblances between the liberal subject and his carceral double, the home and the prison-house, how can we significantly differentiate them?" (219). We cannot in fact distinguish the so-called responsible citizen from the prisoner punished for his criminal responsibility. Upward mobility can aim at nothing more satisfying than life within an overly illuminated bureaucratic rationality that now fills all available social space.[4]

Though these essays were published in the 1980s, their demoralizing conclusion still has a provocative Nietzschean ring. But at least as I've paraphrased it, Miller's desolate social landscape should also look like somewhere we have already visited, and more than once. In 1983, when the *Bleak House* essay appeared, American readers did not need to be informed that state bureaucracies and state surveillance had expanded dramatically and were now intruding into what was once considered the private domain. Nor did they need to be told that the ethical result was a systemic, organized irresponsibility, a situation in which individuals could no longer be held directly responsible for their actions. These were clichés widely disseminated by a number of popular mid-twentieth-century books, among them David Riesman's *The Lonely Crowd* (1950), William H. Whyte's *The Organization Man* (1956), Philip Rieff's *The Triumph of the Therapeutic* (1966), and Christopher Lasch's *The Culture of Narcissism* (1978). In one way or another all of these books announce the rise of a new, socialized, other-directed model of American character that has replaced or is fast replacing sturdy American individualism. To varying degrees, they see people asking for help from government and experts instead of doing it themselves. They see the rise of the welfare bureaucracy taking the place of the ethic of self-reliance and undermining the characteristic expression of that self-reliance, the Horatio Alger or "American Dream" story of upward mobility.

It may seem farfetched to juxtapose these homegrown individualists, who sometimes complain about the very idea of "society," with so fundamentally European and collectivist a thinker as Michel Foucault. And thus it is with a mild sense of shock that one reads, in the introduction to the seminar entitled "Technologies of the Self," that Foucault gave credit for inspiring this project to Christopher Lasch's *The Culture of Narcissism*, a book that quotes and to a degree sums up the others.[5] Foucault was no doubt being diplomatic; Lasch visited the University of Vermont during the three weeks Foucault spent there in 1982. But there is still something intriguing about his momentary intersection with the tradition of American individualist outcry against state and professional intrusion, against what Lasch calls the "social invasion of the self" and the rise of a "therapeutic sensibility." Lasch writes: "The atrophy of older traditions of self-help has eroded everyday competence, in one area after another, and has made the individual dependent on the state, the corporation, and other bureaucracies" (37). Other figures of authority have been supplanted by the figure of the therapist: "Therapy has established itself as the successor both to rugged individualism and to religion" (42). What Lasch calls the therapeutic sensibility finds its apotheosis in the institutions of the welfare state, key example of "the new paternalism": "Capitalism has severed the ties of personal dependence only in order to revive dependence under cover of bureaucratic rationality." The ideology of "welfare liberalism," Lasch concludes, "absolves individuals of moral responsibility and treats them as victims of social circumstance" (369). The result is "new modes of social control" dealing with "the deviant as a patient" and substituting "medical rehabilitation for punishment" (369–70). "Therapeutic modes of thought and practice exempt their object, the patient, from critical judgment and relieve him of moral responsibility" (388).[6]

Lasch's chapter on the fate of the Horatio Alger story in contemporary America speaks of the eclipse of the work ethic and personal achievement and the corresponding dissolution of the responsible individual into an object of official therapeutic attention. It's hard not to hear some faint anticipation of Miller on *David Copperfield*. One may also find oneself recalling Gus Van Sant's film *Good Will Hunting*, a memorable recent instance of the upward mobility genre. Aimed at the slacker anxieties of the 1990s, *Good Will Hunting* locates the obstacle to success not in Will Hunting's merit—the premise is that he is "boy genius"—but, as his name implies, in his will.[7] He lacks the desire to leave behind his working-class life in South Boston and take up the sort of white-collar position that his talent puts within his grasp.[8] The work of resolving this ideological dilemma is located in a series of therapy sessions between Will (played by

Matt Damon, who also coauthored the script) and a psychologist named Sean McBride (played by Robin Williams). In the climactic session where the therapist finally gets through, breaking down the defenses of his clever and seemingly impregnable patient and making upward mobility possible, the magic words he pronounces, repeated over and over until his patient is in tears, are "It's not your fault."

This may come uncomfortably close to psychobabble, but it is nonetheless a decent popularization of the message of generalized irresponsibility that Miller deduces from Chancery. And it does not seem haphazard that, giving such prominence to limited liability, the upward mobility story should place this rejection of individual responsibility at its decisive turning point. Nothing underlines more precisely the cultural work that the upward mobility genre seems appointed to accomplish. "It's not your fault" is a proposition that a society of proudly rugged individualists will resist. The genre seems intent on breaking down that resistance. To do so is not merely to release the individual from misguided guilt, but to win agreement to a counterproposition: that, because society is interdependent, what the individual is and does is neither entirely his fault nor—as the doctrine of self-reliance had insisted—his achievement. As I've suggested, this dispersal of responsibility is just what citizens had to be convinced of in order to divert their resources into rescuing society's less fortunate members from what had previously been seen as the results of their own actions and inactions. It is by trading in his heroic self-reliance for this less heroic view of society, which no longer claims that anyone fully deserves their rewards or punishments, that Will Hunting becomes able to rise within his society. He is allowed to rise when he acknowledges that the rise is not really his. His story recapitulates the passage from "self-reliance" to the mentality of the welfare state, for which "it's not your fault" might seem to serve as a motto.

A self-evidently disastrous motto, according to Lasch.[9] "Is it really necessary to point out, at this late date, that public policies based on a therapeutic model of the state have failed miserably over and over again? Far from promoting self-respect, they have created a nation of dependents. They have given rise to a cult of the victim in which entitlements are based on the display of accumulated injuries inflicted by an uncaring society" (210). And according to Miller? Miller's vision of a society full of Uriah Heeps, all insisting it would be good for everybody to be "took up," would seem to throw him into agreement about "the therapeutic model of the state." Aside from Lasch's nostalgia for the self-reliant individual and his rage against self-proclaimed "victims" claiming "entitlements," what distinguishes Miller's antistatism from Lasch's?

A good deal, of course. Having arranged this unexpected and I hope mutually disagreeable meeting of the minds between Miller and Lasch, I must now accent—it was the point of the exercise—a feature of Miller's critique that evades Lasch's antistatism but that is generally drowned out by Miller's and his readers' easier outrage against "the system." In the *Bleak House* essay, the word *system* is asked to stand for two distinct levels of social reality. It stands of course for Chancery, or the "emergence of a new kind of bureaucratic organization" (75) that frustrates all efforts to assign responsibility. But it also stands for the larger metasystem that contains both Chancery and the Police. It is by the putative logic of this metasystem that Chancery seems to call the Police into being both to serve it and to compensate for it. This second, larger sense of system, according to which the Police polices "for" Chancery, satisfying the desire for responsibility that Chancery frustrates, is described by Miller as merely a "possibility" (75). It thus remains possible, by Miller's own admission, that the two organizations are significantly independent of each other. But if so—and there is evidence for this proposition—then there *is* no "system" at the higher level. Thinking this unfamiliar thought, which will require suspending the well-known paranoid protocols that ask only a wink and a nod in order to be certain of systemic culpability at the highest possible level, means entertaining the hypothesis of a Chancery *without* the Police. And in that case, the grounds for Miller's critique of Chancery as such would become difficult to specify. Take away the Police, separate off these two governmental functions, and in Miller's view, if I may put my own words in his mouth, *Chancery is right*.

Making some allowance for hyperbole, let us say that attempts to make individuals responsible must often if not always be frustrated, much as Chancery frustrates them. Endless interpretation, which is the Chancery way, corresponds to the infinite richness of reality. The truth about responsibility is that it is dependent on too many other people, too many interlocking histories, many of them invisible to any single observer. Only some callously impersonal, many-headed collectivity could even be imagined marshaling the breadth and diversity of vision necessary to see how complex any given case of responsibility is and allow a final finger to be pointed. That collectivity would perhaps resemble the maddening Chancery lawyers, notorious butt of Dickens's satire. Thus the satire of Chancery as a paradigm of bureaucratic hyperrationality begging to be reformed or abolished is at most half the story; it misses Chancery's equal and opposite role as the very model of what it must always and everywhere mean to live in a complex modern social system—neither the word *bureaucracy* nor the word *capitalism* is quite adequate—where responsibility is never fully present, always more or less deferred. A role whose tag line could very nearly be expressed in the words "it's not your fault."

In a wonderful footnote to the introduction of *The Novel and the Police*, Miller quotes at length from the scene toward the end of *Bleak House* in which the case of Jarndyce and Jarndyce is finally closed, the estate dissipated in legal costs, and all of Chancery's counselors, clerks, and other officers stream out of the courtroom, doubled up with laughter. Miller's point is that farce, which seems to protest against Chancery, is in fact on Chancery's side, one of its own effects. "This fact must cast a long shadow on the novel's efforts to satirize the court in ways not already foreseen and put to good use by the requirements of bureaucratic operation" (xii–xiii). Since more than one character has died trying to force Chancery to live up to its official responsibilities, indignation is certainly in order. Yet Miller's own ingenious and persuasive efforts to read Dickens against the moral grain encourage a similarly risky or "irresponsible" reading here. What do we make of the image of the laughing bureaucrats? They are neither David Copperfields nor Uriah Heeps. Though they have no doubt aspired to rise into the posts they are seen in the act of leaving for the day, they do not seem excessively policed. For a moment at least, here we do seem to get, as predicted, Chancery without the Police.[10] Moreover, a social theory that might account for all this unpoliced irresponsibility has a well-marked place in *Bleak House*. It is articulated and embodied by Harold Skimpole, unembarrassed debtor, parasite of the system, and antithesis of both David and Uriah Heep. I have written about Skimpole as social theorist elsewhere.[11] Here let me simply note the rough fit between Skimpole's amoral theory of society as total system and Miller's Foucaultian premises, which (to continue speaking roughly) refuse any extrasystemic norm or standard as well as any possibility of dividing the system up so as to attribute more or less responsibility, more or less capacity of significant action, to individuals or institutions within it. Looking at these premises and at *The Novel and the Police*, one would have to conclude that, despite Miller's obvious lack of enthusiasm for the institutions of the welfare state, in Lasch's view he would probably have to be placed inside, not outside, the welfare state's ethic of irresponsibility.

And inside that ethic is where I would like to place him. Reserving the right to elaborate the meaning of this phrase as I go, I would suggest that the ethic of the welfare state seems one very useful context both for Miller and for Foucault. This means rescuing both from their admirers. In his familiar antistatist posture, Foucault encourages serious mistakes about how power works today. Scandals like Enron, for example, resulted from a *failure* of government regulation: not too much surveillance, as Foucault has always seemed to suggest, but too little. Yet Foucault appeared to some of his French contemporaries as a technocrat, and he could on occasion be more daringly neutral toward objects of analysis like the rise of "biopower" than hasty readers have wanted to acknowledge. Interviewed for a volume on the French social security system (also published in 1983), Foucault agreed that one perverse effect of this benevolent social protection was "a growth in dependence" at the expense of "autonomy."[12] Here his accents are very close to Lasch's. But Foucault explicitly rebukes his questioner for the "very optimistic notion of society" (168) that encourages a crudely negative view of the state. Rejecting the state does not mean avoiding the relevant problems of power. Which means that the state itself is not in principle to be avoided. In short, Foucault refuses the option of an easy or populist antistatism. His goal, he says, is "optimal social security combined with maximum independence," a goal that can be approached by experimenting with decentered decision making and otherwise fiddling in an empirical and reformist spirit with existing state machinery: "which taps need turning, which bolts need to be loosened here and there" (165). This is the sort of goal, he suggests, that in part at least has *already* been achieved within existing bureaucracies. If one considers today's public provision for old people, for example, comparing it with the way families before World War II "pushed their old people into a corner of the house," one must conclude that "the condition of old people has improved a great deal in the last few decades" (176). On this evidence, Foucault can be claimed as a sometimes reluctant but always valuable ally in the "reformist" project of defending and extending the welfare state—as certain interpreters of Foucault on governmentality have tried to do.[13]

A strong if only implicit condemnation of all institutions, especially governmental ones purporting to do the work of benevolent reform, has too often provided the working definition of the Foucaultian school in the United States. Whether or not I succeed in embarrassing the holders of this position by underlining their unwilling proximity to Christopher Lasch and other state-hating individualists, my intention is to see the Nietzschean critique of responsibility developed by Foucault and Miller in a different light: to value it as a positive contribution to the ethical repertoire of the welfare state, and in particular as a means of interpreting the swerve away from self-reliance both in twentieth-century stories of upward mobility and in twentieth-century politics. I'm not suggesting that the critique of responsibility is adequate to this project or its key. As always, it's easier to see what is being turned away from than what is being turned toward, either in upward mobility stories or in the larger political hopes that help structure them. My premise is only that something like a Nietzschean/Foucaultian irresponsibility is a useful and perhaps necessary step in the prolonged process of reversing our society's present priorities: too much individual responsibility, not enough collective responsibility. Necessary, though this may seem paradoxical, in order to overturn what Ann Oakley correctly calls "the irresponsible society."[14] I take over Oakley's adjective as a token of how perilous the project is of melting down existing loyalties in order to reshape them and give them some other social content—a project fiction shares with politics.

If the words "it's not your fault" and the ethic for which they stand have seeped into the upward mobility story, as suggested by a Hollywood blockbuster like *Good Will Hunting*, they would seem to mark a significant change in the prevailing common sense. One would like to know how and when this change occurred. This chapter will examine three American texts that mark three stages in this process: Theodore Dreiser's *The Financier* (1912), Budd Schulberg's *What Makes Sammy Run?* (1941), and E. L. Doctorow's *Billy Bathgate* (1989). But let us note at the outset that this is neither an exclusively American story nor a story of simple linear transformation. In the person of Hannibal Lecter, we have already noted the therapist as a characteristic figure of the twentieth-century upward mobility story. But as the formal abstraction of the "donor" helped reveal, there is a relative consistency of function across a considerable historical span—from *Good Will Hunting* and *Silence of the Lambs* back to Rousseau's *Confessions*. The therapist is one in a long but recognizable line of benefactors, all of whom do to some degree what Lasch says the therapist does. They spread responsibility around, socialize it, transfer it from the individual to society. So this common sense would appear to have been developing quietly for some time.

The sudden salience of the therapist as benefactor is also an index of at least one thing that has changed. The prospect I anticipated in *Great Expectations* seems to have come to pass: it is currently possible, imaginatively speaking, to be a benefactor without any money. This is the largest historical gulf between the rich old men of Alger and Dickens and *Good Will Hunting*'s therapist, who performs the work of upward mobility without himself possessing anything like Minnie Driver's millions. Indeed, as we see in *Good Will Hunting*, it is now of positive importance that the benefactor *not* be rich. The catchphrase "it's not your fault" does not simply let Will off the hook as an individual. Worried as he rightly is that his upward mobility may lead both directly and indirectly to harm for his buddies, it also offers him a vision of society in which his will to make use of his talents might nonetheless be a "good" will, a will directed toward the good of people like himself back in South Boston. It does so by means of the therapist. We do not see the work Will eventually takes up; what we have continually before our eyes is the work of the Robin Williams figure, a man who is making use of his talents and yet doing something "honorable," to use Will's term. He is also a representative of the state, and even of the state in its punitive function, if only an indirect representative; the therapy sessions are part of a deal cut with prosecutors to get Will out of serving his jail time. Yet this work as teacher and therapist is public service, consistent with what the state at its honorable best can do. As a fellow son of Southie, he is working with, and on behalf of, people like himself. Like many a writer who writes about the family left behind, the therapist fashions a white-collar life in the present out of his blue-collar past, and a life that can always be suspected of betraying that past. The fact that he has won little money or fame, which is underlined by the running contrast with the prize-winning mathematician Lambreau, who tries and fails to be Will's mentor, is an answer to the hovering suspicion of betrayal. In making his work more honorable, the relative "failure" also gives his example more power over Will.[15]

The contrast with the nineteenth-century novel is anything but absolute. Exiting their novels under arrest, Magwitch and Vautrin could both be considered versions of the benefactor-as-failure. And at other moments both of these, like the therapist, also move through upward mobility stories of their own, however sketchy the account of them. What seems decisively different (though even here Vautrin could be argued as a counterexample) is that the therapist is a figure who has risen *because* of the function of benefactor. He is not dispensing at whim profits that were made elsewhere. Being a benefactor is how he makes his profits, how he gets ahead. Consider two examples, neither of them from the United States.

The Mystic Masseur (1957), V. S. Naipaul's first novel, is a darkly sarcastic specimen of the upward mobility genre. With an aesthetically dazzling disorientation, it balances its clear and overwhelming disrespect for its protagonist against a perhaps even more scathing contempt for the society he is attempting to rise out of. There seems no firm ground anywhere. Yet Naipaul permits his hero one chance to display what demands to be called by the old-fashioned name of *merit*—a display that, surrounded as it is by so much ignorance, corruption, and ineptitude, is almost shocking. The turning point of the novel, the moment when the protagonist, who up to this point has seemed merely a hapless and dangerous would-be charlatan, does actually begin to rise in the world, is the moment when he performs a bizarrely effective cure on a small boy. The boy thinks he is being pursued by a deadly cloud. It comes out that the boy's brother has recently been killed by a truck while on an errand that the boy himself was supposed to run. The mystic's key words are as follows: "Remember, you wasn't responsible. Wasn't your fault."[16]

Hanif Kureishi's *The Buddha of Suburbia* (1990) is again an upward mobility story, again involving an amateur guru who is more or less of a charlatan, and again it gives to the guru/charlatan a power to rise in the world that is not quite reducible to a gift for deceiving the gullible. In a scene that's representative of his message, the suburban buddha tells his brother-in-law, "There's too much work in the world. . . . Under no circumstances make an effort" (49).[17] The refusal of work works. The brother-in-law breaks into sobs and is "released." And the minor government functionary who has played guru to him thereby enters into a new life. It's Christopher Lasch's worst nightmare: a self-reliant figure who rises in the world and yet does so only by preaching the evils of work, effort, and self-reliance.

The sense of paradox here goes further. On the one hand, the cures are real, and though both novels treat the guru's prescribing of a curative dose of irresponsibility with at least some irony, the effect is far from ironic. There is real if reluctant approval for a euphoric escape from over-individualized responsibility, an approval that is necessary to the welfare state. On the other hand, however, neither self-reliance nor self-interest has been abandoned. A few pages later, Kureishi's hero is told, "you're beautiful, and the beautiful should be given everything they want." He objects, "what about the ugly ones?" And he is told, "It's their fault if they're ugly. They're to be blamed, not pitied" (93). It's a joke, of course, but it's also a commentary on the "no fault" philosophy. Directed to the beautiful and talented, "it's not your fault" can be interpreted as removing any social loyalty or standard of justice that might stand in the way of competing for and winning whatever prizes are on offer, for example by calling attention to the equally undeserved fate of those who are not so lucky.

Karim insists on asking about the ugly ones, or the other ones. So does Will Hunting. One of the film's finest moments is the "this is why I won't take your job" speech Will delivers—or fantasizes delivering—to the interviewers of the National Security Administration. The use the NSA wants to make of his mathematical ability, Will foresees in a swift comic improvisation, could logically lead to injury (shrapnel in the ass), then unemployment, then higher gas prices, and finally ecological disaster: all this for someone just like himself back in South Boston. This sequence of events *would* be his fault. And this oblique but no less compelling sense of fault lurks behind the clichés of childhood trauma that the therapist explicitly addresses. When Will's resistance is overcome and he is released into upward mobility by the phrase "it's not your fault," therapist and patient are talking about the violent abuse Will suffered as a child from his stepfather, which has ostensibly left him subject to violent impulses (we see him start a meaningless playground punch-up) and thus with a lengthy record of arrests. The therapist confesses that he too has suffered such abuse. Abuse would seem to stand in for working-class membership, which becomes a pathology requiring medical treatment. Treatment for child abuse is really treatment for the disease of belonging to the working class. The self-evident proposition that Will did not cause or deserve the beatings can thus be mistaken for the plausible but more debatable proposition that "It's not your fault you want to walk away from manual labor and from your working-class friends; it's not your fault that in the universal competition, they are predestined to lose and you are predestined to win." What Will has to be cured of is not violence, but loyalty to those who will not rise with him.

The point cannot be overemphasized. "It's not your fault" expresses more than a refusal of entrepreneurial self-reliance. It's also a motto of capitalism itself, at least in its corporate, finance, post-Alger phase. The Reagan-era moral is the underlying subject of the film *Interview with the Vampire*: sucking blood is our nature as vampires, and that which is our nature cannot be our fault. How can it be that the same release from responsibility acknowledges social interdependence on the one hand even while it encourages no-holds-barred competition on the other? The contradiction serves as a reminder that what I have been calling the welfare state can and must also be thought of as welfare capitalism: at best a means of managing capitalism from within, not a magical antidote to it or escape from it.[18] This is one reason why the moral history to which the upward mobility story belongs is so obscure, indeed sometimes almost invisible. It is why responsibility needs to be redistributed, not simply evaded. And why blame remains necessary, however difficult. One might say that there is no greater challenge, under welfare capitalism, than learning how to blame well.[19]

LOYALTY AND BLAME IN DREISER'S *THE FINANCIER*

In his brief but resonant introduction to *Sister Carrie*, novelist E. L. Doctorow pauses to note that the young Dreiser arrived in Pittsburgh in "the aftermath of the Homestead strike in which armies of Pinkerton detectives and striking steelworkers had fought pitched battles."[20] The remark raises an interesting question about a scene in *The Financier* (1912) when there is another mention of the Pinkertons. Edward Malia Butler, who has been informed that his daughter Aileen is carrying on an illicit relationship with Frank Cowperwood, reluctantly decides to go to a detective. Seeking one not in Philadelphia but in New York, where he can pass unknown, he nevertheless hesitates to give his name at the Pinkerton office or "to take anyone into his confidence in regard to Aileen" (35).[21] It's not hard to see why. In practical terms, all the major players in this novel, Butler included, subscribe to Frank Cowperwood's motto, "I satisfy myself." And in a world of self-interested self-satisfiers, why should anyone have confidence in anyone else, confidence in other words that others will do anything other than satisfy the urge to make as large a profit as possible, if necessary at one's expense?

In seducing Aileen, Cowperwood could certainly be said to have betrayed the confidence of Butler, whose hospitable patronage helped make Cowperwood's fortune, and his other patrons in Philadelphia's Republican Party betray him in their turn. They might have been expected to make some effort to save him from his financial and legal difficulties, if only in order to spare the party an election-time embarrassment. Instead, they decide to use their insider knowledge of those difficulties in order to make a financial killing, buying up Cowperwood's streetcar holdings cheap while he loses everything and goes off to prison. Butler has every reason to suspect that someone coming into knowledge of his family's dishonor would similarly decide, without any personal animosity but simply playing the universal self-satisfaction game, to use that potentially explosive knowledge to blackmail him or by some other means turn it to his or her personal advantage.

It's something of a surprise, therefore, that as Butler listens to the head of the Pinkertons' New York office, he allows himself to be reassured: "so far as your private affairs are concerned, they are as safe with us, as if you had never told them to anyone. Our business is built upon confidence, and we never betray it" (35). And so it comes to pass. Aileen and Cowperwood are caught in their love nest, and though this exposure makes little difference in the end, Butler's confidence is not betrayed. Like the dog that didn't bark, this absence of betrayal begs to be treated as a clue within a larger mystery. The mystery is this: how can the novel account for Butler's justified confidence in a stranger? The mere fact of paying for services rendered is clearly inadequate to guarantee such a social bond; Frank has no loyalty whatsoever to his first employers though they pay him very well. How then can the novel account for the existence, within the world of "business," of loyalty among nonkin? Unless it is seen as simple masochistic foolishness, which is of course a possible interpretation, any loyalty that stands firm against the "I satisfy myself" philosophy, even a loyalty that may not appear to rank very high on the scale of moral development, would seem obliged to throw an interesting new light both on Dreiser, whose conspicuous failure to blame Cowperwood for anything has so long puzzled his critics, and on the literature of upward mobility in general.

Loyalty is of course visible enough in *The Financier*, even in the world of business. On the novel's first page we are told that the hero's father, a teller at a bank, is "exceedingly grateful" (1) for the promotion that enables him to move his family into a larger house. Gratitude to his employers is a sure sign that, unlike his son, he is going nowhere. Gratitude toward those above you will keep you loyal to them. Loyalty will keep you in or near your place. There is no evidence in Dreiser of enthusiasm either for conventional morality or for the immobility that seems to follow from it. For Dreiser both conventional morality and immobility belong to the domain of the family, which is a domain of self-sacrificing and self-reproducing stasis. The loyalty of Cowperwood Senior to his employers, built up over long acquaintance, seems modeled on his loyalty to his wife and children. As one recent critic has noted, this circumscribing of individual ambition makes Frank's father resemble the heroes of Horatio Alger, while Frank himself, who moves from opportunity to better opportunity without a qualm or a backward glance, does not.[22] In Frank the vestigial principle of family loyalty, though not totally lacking, is certainly not well developed. Without his care and attention, he muses, his children "would probably do as well as most children." In any case, he will not allow them to stand in the way of "his own personal freedom . . . to go off and set up a new world and a new home with Aileen" (51). Dreiser does not seem very tempted to speak up on behalf of bonds to one's offspring.

Like Dreiser himself, his critics have been more interested in Frank's erotic bonds, or erotic loyalties: his relationships with Lillian and Aileen, his wife and his mistress. If the proper model of life, as suggested by the famous allegory in chapter 1, is a lobster and a squid locked in the same tank, with the lobster biting off piece after piece of the helpless squid, then what is Dreiser suggesting about love? Does the same model apply? And if so, what's in it for the squid—let's say, the woman—who chooses to enter the tank of her own free will? Is the world divided into those who are smart enough to satisfy themselves and those who are dumb enough to sacrifice themselves? Or is love on the contrary an exception to the self-satisfaction rule and thus perhaps also a compensation for it, offsetting the relentless struggle for survival that would otherwise seem to make life almost unlivable? Here if anywhere we should be able to test whether Dreiser bestows genuine libidinal power upon any principle of loyalty (freely chosen rather than predefined by kinship) that might undermine, interfere with, or at least distinguish itself from the inconstant, faithless world of finance capital.

This is another way of phrasing the "it's not your fault" question, the absence of moral commentary that has never ceased to haunt Dreiser criticism. Does Dreiser suggest that pure self-interest is a viable life philosophy, that one can live and should live without any overriding commitment to others, with nothing but such limited, provisional alliance as is defined by moments of *shared* self-interest? Or does he judge self-interest from the outside, setting the "I satisfy myself" philosophy in the context of some higher and countervailing principle?

In his influential reading of *The Financier*, Walter Benn Michaels answers this last question with a resounding no. Cowperwood's love life is just the place to look for such a principle, Michaels suggests, and one seems to find there precisely what one is looking for. It's Frank's sudden valuing of productivity that makes Lillian (another Older Woman, it should be noted) seem a stable anchorage amidst capitalist turbulence.[23] As a principle of value, productivity posits an open, stable relation between labor (or virtue or payment) and its due reward. It is assumed that the first can always be exchanged for the second. But if this is the rule for the wife, it does not hold for the mistress. "The difference between a wife and a mistress, according to Dreiser, is the difference between a woman who gives her love in a 'sweet bond of agreement and exchange—fair trade in a lovely contest'—and a woman who loves without thought of return; 'sacrificial, yielding, solicitous,' she is motivated only by 'the desire to give.' "[24] In courting his wife, Lillian, during a period of financial panic, according to Michaels, Cowperwood is seeking an "absolute security" (63) outside the aimless fluctuation of his daily business of securities trading—just such a fixed, normative point as is represented in Thorstein Veblen by efficient industrial production.[25] Cowperwood's later attraction to the "vitality and vivacity" of Aileen, however, presents him in an unconscious form with his attraction to speculation, to instability, which is the actual source of his profit. Frank's choice of Aileen and his loyalty to her—a loyalty that is sustained at least through the first third of the *Trilogy of Desire*, if not much longer—thus becomes evidence that Dreiser is committed not to production but to speculation.

In a bold if questionable move, Michaels associates speculation (seemingly the epitome of ever-shifting, uncommitted, short-term investment) with what is usually taken to be the absolute, unwavering relation between parent and child, which might seem the antithesis of unprincipled moneymaking. Speculation, Michaels asserts, means getting something for nothing. That's not how husbands love wives, he goes on, but it is how parents love children—and how mistresses love their lovers; they give without thought of return (75). In other words, the truth about capitalism is speculation, and speculation is rooted in the nuclear family, which is to say in nature itself. Speculative capitalism is nature's way: not an economy of exchange, but an economy of the gift, outside of all calculation. Michaels concludes that "there is no refuge from the instability of the market" (83), but there is also no *need* for such a refuge. Frank's most "natural" erotic urges are aimed at just what "finance capitalism" (83) is already prepared to give him. The loyalty Frank wants and needs is the loyalty of the mistress, which is both sexier than that of the wife (because associated with ever-increasing profit) and also stronger (because irreducible to mere exchange, it cannot be outbid or exceeded). We are not told whether this is also true of the lover's loyalty *to* the mistress.

So yes, there is loyalty within finance capital. But it is a loyalty that expresses nothing *but* finance capital. It is not a loyalty that might stand *against* finance capital.

As I've been suggesting, the result of this line of argument is a "no fault" view of upward mobility. Fault would seem intrinsic to the upward mobility story, for every passage out of the society of origin, even that of an orphan like Alger's Ragged Dick, would seem to involve the betrayal of some prior loyalty. But if loyalties are free gifts, which create no obligation, then there is no betrayal and there is no fault.[26] In the world of Horatio Alger, reward for one's labors was the central moral principle—though one not often observed by Alger in practice, as many readers have noted. Dreiser pushed Alger's practical neglect of this principle to the point where it became theory; readers could no longer miss the glaring fact that the principle of "no labor, no reward" was no longer functioning. As Doctorow observes, *Sister Carrie*'s representation of sexuality was less threatening to early readers than its manifest unhooking of reward from virtue (viii). Like *An American Tragedy*, *The Financier* is centered on a courtroom drama in which the question is whether the protagonist is guilty or innocent, which is to say, generically speaking, whether his upward mobility is guilty or innocent. In one case the means to that upward mobility is a perhaps-murder, in the other a perhaps-swindle, but in both cases what is questioned is "fault" as the key to upward mobility. Didn't someone have to be victimized or betrayed? D. A. Miller might have seen Heep, in prison, as the necessary victim of David Copperfield's success. Instead, he sees both as equally and unhappily imprisoned. For Michaels, the unhappiness disappears and the equality remains: upward mobility is victimless, hence blameless. Responsibility cannot be assigned.

In convicting Cowperwood, Michaels says, the court "is punishing him for something he never meant to do, making him responsible for events that he did not, in his own words, 'create': 'I did not create this panic. I did not set Chicago on fire.' But to put the argument in this way is, in Dreiser's terms, to expose its weakness. For what does the financier create? His 'harvest' depends not on hard work, not even finally on his 'subtlety,' but on his happening to be in the right place when a crisis comes. If the financier has neither earned nor deserved his success, then the fact that he has not created the conditions of his failure ceases to count as a mitigating circumstance. . . . The court's decision reduces the difference between the businessman and the thief to a matter of 'accident'" (78). In other words, upward mobility is not an achievement, but by the same token neither is it an instance of moral lapse or culpability. Michaels concludes: "In an economy where nature has taken the place of work, financial success can no longer be understood as payment for goods or services. It becomes, instead, a gift, and for Dreiser the economy of the gift functions at every level" (78). The "love of a parent or mistress" should be taken as a gift, and so should the source of "speculative fortunes" (78).

Now it is important to note that this conclusion, while quite compelling in a sense I will come to in a moment, is arrived at by a certain sleight of hand. First of all, it involves a serious misunderstanding of the actual nature of gifts. Gifts are never free. Even someone as notoriously individualistic as Ralph Waldo Emerson understood this perfectly well. It's because gifts do create obligations, allow one to be put at a disadvantage, compromise one's self-sufficiency, that Emerson describes himself in "On Gifts" as resenting both gifts and the giver. "How dare you give them? We wish to be self-sustained. We do not quite forgive a giver."[27] The anthropologist Marcel Mauss is credited with establishing Emerson's insight on a more or less scientific basis; as Mauss showed, gifts are indeed part of an indirect system of exchange that is always understood to confer obligations.[28] The phrase "economy of the gift" is thus deeply misleading, for what is asserted here is that there exists no economy, no need to give something in return for something you take, no law or rule that governs gift giving. In this sense of the word, the phrase "economy of the gift" is merely an excuse for escaping from any and all economy.[29]

One such economy is that of gender. Seeing loyalty as a free gift is convenient for men, who can unconsciously expect that they will receive loyalties and other services from their womenfolk for which no recompense or remuneration of any kind will be required. It encourages men to think of themselves as children to whom everything is owed. The assumed or ideal perspective here would seem to be that of the male (as) child. For the male child, love is not only speculation, entailing no reciprocal obligations, but—to the extent that he functions within a gender system or economy—it is an *inevitably successful* speculation, an investment with a high and guaranteed return. This point helps explain the direction in which loyalty or emotional capital will flow between Frank and his wife and mistress.[30]

But from the perspective of Frank's public guilt or lack of it, the most important economic reality that is evaded by speaking of an "economy of the gift" is that which links finance via gifts—or bribes—to the power of the state. It is in the name of the state, or the public, that blame becomes possible. No, you cannot steal that which is freely given. But who gives Frank Cowperwood the funds he is accused of stealing? The only plausible way to use the word *gift* in this context is if one identifies the giver as city treasurer Stener, a corrupt pawn of the Republican political machine then ruling Philadelphia. Stener did not have the right to profit from, or to allow Cowperwood to profit from, money that belonged to the people of the city of Philadelphia. Like so many other financiers, Cowperwood makes his fortune not on the open market but by using political connections to obtain illegal access to public funds and thus manipulating the market. Butler's upward mobility story, which makes possible Frank's own, differs from it only in minor details. Butler is "a poor young Irishman" who collects garbage for free and feeds it to his pigs and cattle until "a local political character, a councilman friend of his," has an idea. "Butler could be made official garbage-collector. The council could vote an annual appropriation for this service. Butler could employ more wagons than he did now—dozens of them, scores. Not only that, but no other garbage-collector would be allowed. There were others, but the official contract awarded to him would also, officially, be the end of the life of any and every disturbing rival" (11). Like Butler, Cowperwood derives his profits from the fact that the market is *not* open but on the contrary closed down with help from official friends, made into a monopoly by the direct exercise of state power. Understandably enough, Michaels underplays this state-oriented side of "finance capitalism," for it gives the supposedly victimless crime both a source and a victim: the inhabitants of the city of Philadelphia.

But can the city of Philadelphia be properly described as a victim? In response to the argument above, one might well object that the city does not manifest collective consciousness of its interests or otherwise assert its existence and rights, thus proving it is an entity capable of sustaining injury. The ethical standards by which such an act might be judged are appropriate to it only if it is a real entity. But a city is not real in the way a person is real. Even now, who would suggest that one should be loyal or even *can* be loyal to a city in the way one is expected to be loyal to a person? And in historical perspective, the incongruity is even more stark. It might be proposed, that is, that people had not yet come to see the abuse of the municipality for private advantage as illegitimate. "There was a political ring in Philadelphia in which the mayor, certain members of the council, the treasurer, the chief of police, the commissioner of public works, and others shared. It was a case generally of 'you scratch my back, I'll scratch yours.' Cowperwood thought it rather shabby work at first, but many men were rapidly getting rich and no one seemed to care. The newspapers were always talking about civic patriotism and pride but never a word about these things" (10). "No one seemed to care": in the period Dreiser was describing, in other words, there existed little if any organized public opinion that defined such behavior as a crime, few if any representatives of the city of Philadelphia who were ready to contest the legitimacy of what Butler, Cowperwood, Mollenhauer and their cronies were doing. The newspapers are silent. The Municipal Reform Association is described as ineffectual. For all intents and purposes, the relevant ethics was not yet in place. And not all that much has changed. Outcry against the immense corporate scandals of our own time, such as Enron and WorldCom, again involving direct collaboration between financiers and their friends in the government, again involving a failure to rescue the victims from statistical anonymity and put faces on them, has again been pitifully weak, thus suggesting that such an ethics is still very flimsily implanted in the public sphere, that the public is still very much at risk of underrepresentation and underprotection. All the more reason, then, to

understand Dreiser's lack of outrage against Cowperwood and the unin-
hibited excitement Dreiser seems to permit himself at the possibility of
making fortunes in an ethical area still thought of as gray.

All of this is true enough, and yet the history is in fact a bit more complicated. In the period in which Dreiser was writing, elements of this new
ethical sensibility were already starting to emerge, even if they had not
yet quite cohered. Large institutional entities suddenly demanded to be
treated as real persons. They demanded loyalty, and in doing so they also
redefined loyalty. The claims made for these newly emergent entities—I'm
speaking most obviously of corporations—were necessarily accompanied
by strenuous ethical rearrangements. The very concept of a corporation
required a redefinition of what was and was not criminal or blameworthy.
Even the patrons of Horatio Alger, who represent the power of the market, tend to place their charges in a secure and respectable niche rather
than bestowing pots of bullion upon them. This restraint would seem to
correspond with historical developments during and after Alger's lifetime
that were busily transforming the nature of merit. As Martin Sklar points
out in *The Corporate Reconstruction of American Capitalism, 1890–
1916*, reformers at the end of Alger's life were already arguing that society
could not acknowledge merit as long as it was organized around the holding of individual property. For bad reasons (defense against direct democratic demands) as well as better ones (rationality and efficiency as opposed to client-patron favoritism), they decided it was in the interests
of society as a whole to separate merit off from outside influences like
demagoguery and the possession of inherited wealth. Instead, merit
should be associated with patterned behavior inside large semi-autono-
mous organizations.

> On the one hand, capitalists in large corporations operating in major
> sectors of production and trade had changed from the entrepreneurial-
> debtor outlook to the administrative-investor outlook, strengthening a
> growing consensus . . . in favor of government regulation of the market.
> . . . On the other hand, captains of industry and finance joined reformers,
> moralists, and professionals in wanting "efficient" government, standing
> above the "corruptions" of party politics; they wanted government bu-
> reaucracies, like those of the better-managed corporations, based solely
> on merit instead of on clientage, patronage, or immediate popular de-
> mands, especially as government was assuming a greater role in adminis-
> tering the conduct of social life and business practices. (30–31)[31]

Benefactors who are not rich, like the therapist, mediate between the
old system of patronage, where money and power expressed themselves
directly and shamelessly, and the new system of bureaucratic rationality,
which at worst forced these underground and at best made them illegal.

As Sklar notes, this new system was a cross-class project, one that could only work because it made some concessions to the working class (including the regulation of big capital) while also favoring some (not all) interests within the capitalist class. So-called corporate liberalism could offer, as "small-scale competitive capitalism" could not, "opportunity for employment and advancement based on 'merit' without the obstruction of nepotism found in proprietary enterprise. To labor, corporate capitalism could offer greater stability of employment and better wages with higher productivity, as well as pensions, profit-sharing, recreational facilities, and even advancement from blue collar to white and prospective advancement up the corporate ladder" (23).

As noted above, limited liability had been opposed initially on the grounds that it subverted proper personal responsibility for one's debts, that is, for one's actions. With the rise of the corporation, the conventional system of exchange between an action (for example, a piece of work accomplished or a theft) and its reward or punishment was disturbed, and the meaning of loyalty along with it. It is this disturbance that Michaels's argument both reflects and misinterprets. For the subverting of a previously transparent relation between an action and its reward or punishment does not happen solely at the behest of corporate capitalism. Rising along with the corporation are similarly large, abstract, impersonal entities like the city government of Philadelphia.[32] And, somewhat more slowly, at the federal, state, and municipal levels, what will come to be called the welfare state.

Often these official entities seem to come after and in response to capitalism. But as we have seen, they may also serve as hidden source of the funds that will then be displayed as the supposed fruit of a capitalist's hard work and financial wizardry. In terms of timing, the period of what Michaels calls "finance capitalism" more or less coincides with the period of the expansion of government and the rise of the welfare state. And in order to rise, the welfare state too needed to shift decisively the meaning of individual responsibility. To put this as pithily as possible: once upon a time, if you were homeless, it was because you refused to work. Poverty was equated with moral failure. There could be no move in the direction of what we now call welfare—state responsibility to care for those most in need—until the equation of poverty with immorality had been broken, until responsibility for poverty had come to be seen as (at least in part) systemic and shared rather than exclusively individual, until the general ethical sensibility had swerved in the direction of "no fault."

The modifications thus entailed in the notion of the accountable self are a central theme of Howard Horwitz's *By the Law of Nature: Form and Value in Nineteenth-Century America*, which finds illustrations in Dreiser's financier. Though Cowperwood is "frequently called self-reliant and self-sufficient," Horwitz shows, his upward mobility story is not in fact an example of "Emersonian self-reliance."[33] On the contrary, it is achieved by "an effacement of agency" (197). Cowperwood exercises power "by taking himself off the market" (198). Though the example Horwitz is mainly interested in is the trust, he shows that this new, effaced, off-market agency is also mirrored in those government agencies that arose and expanded in order to restrict the new monopolistic corporations and to deal with the new scale of human disasters they left in their wake. "To catch insiders like Boesky, Boesky's lawyer remarked, the Securities and Exchange Commission must be 'everywhere at the same time,' must, that is, be more trust-like than the monopolist."[34] It is precisely the trustlike power of the city, in Horwitz's argument, that attracts Cowperwood's imagination and money as an alternative to other, more strictly corporate forms of speculation. In his first rise, he makes his fortune by means of a "privileged relationship with the city treasurer" which "involves, like the city treasurer's own activities, control without 'actual ownership' " (199). However unethically, Cowperwood acts here both as and like an agent of the government. And the secret of his second rise, after he gets out of prison, is his investment in "streetcar and gas lines," which "are less individualistically based than stockjobbing."

> Whatever the problems tracing ownership in the period, and however much ownership and control were diverging, ordinary speculation and investment always retain the risk of liability, since they point to assets (or the lack thereof) and persons. Albeit "fictitious persons," corporations still point to persons, fictitious or otherwise. This fact, after all, is what returned Cowperwood to fortune after his prison term. During the panic of 1878, Jay Cooke's investment house closes. The problem with Cooke's house, in Cowperwood's view, is that it is "dependent upon . . . one man." It is such dependence and traceability—that is, conventional individuality—that Frank seeks to eschew in his obsession with surpassing speculation. In urban utilities he sees an opportunity to disappear entirely, to become an element in the city's inexorable expansion and thus endlessly satisfy his insatiable, because unlocalized, self. (202)

To say that "gas and street railways are public services tied to cities" (202) is to say that they are tied to "an entity less volatile than the market" (202). But if so, then the self involved is not really "unlocalized" or "insatiable." However characteristic it may be of the market, the word *insatiable* is less perfectly matched to the new sort of self that arises together with the "less volatile" institutions of public service and municipal governance.

Here it may be helpful to remember Cowperwood's somewhat prolonged interaction with another branch of government. He spends a substantial number of the novel's pages in prison. And while in prison, he conducts himself in a modest and orderly fashion. His conduct is satisfactory to his guards, and the experience is not all that far from satisfactory to himself. A truly insatiable protagonist might well have been crushed by his imprisonment or rebelled angrily against it. Aside from one tearful collapse in Aileen's arms—a moment that reveals Aileen as a nonspeculative parental harbor, as much a mother as a lover, and in this sense indistinguishable from Lillian—Frank adapts to prison pretty easily, blaming neither himself nor those who put him there. (One notes the uncanny repetition of the "happiness in prison" motif from Stendhal.) With a certain civility, he seems to accept being a prisoner as more or less continuous with his earlier life.[35]

This surprising pliability in prison is a reminder of certain quietly remarkable moments elsewhere in the novel. Despite fierce conflicts of interest and desire, Frank refuses to talk to either Butler or Lillian as if they were his enemies. Despite Stener's betrayal, we are told that Frank alone would have set him up in business again, on Stener's release from prison, when the latter's allies fail him: "The man who would have actually helped him if he had only known was Frank A. Cowperwood. Stener could have confessed his mistake, as Cowperwood saw it, and Cowperwood would have given him the money gladly, without any thought of return" (57). Slow to feel outraged by the aggressions of others, Cowperwood seems less representative of a robber baron than of a parole officer or a court-appointed therapist. The "one thing that Cowperwood objected to at all times" was the fact that Lillian is "moral," which is to say "reproachful" (56). Cowperwood is himself not reproachful. He is described as "shameless" (56), but it is just as noteworthy that he is unwilling to shame others.

If this refusal to subject others to shame or reproach seems amoral, its amorality is not simply that of naturalism's insatiable, power-hungry competitor; one would be more inclined to think, once again, of the "therapeutic" sensibility that Lasch sees as marking the decline of self-reliance and the work ethic. Reluctant to blame or punish, Cowperwood cannot be called civic-minded, but he is strangely *sociable*. And thus representative, one might say, of a new sort of "no fault" sociability that has become increasingly characteristic—for better as well as for worse—both of public policy and of private life.

Cowperwood's prison display of humble adaptability, rather than the undaunted fire that might have been expected of a ruthless and titanic financier, is entirely consistent with one of the novel's most explicit natural images for him. In the novel's afterword, "Concerning Mycteroperca Bonaci," we are told that the Black Grouper lives long and grows very large "because of its very remarkable ability to adapt to conditions. . . .

Lying at the bottom of a bay, it can simulate the mud by which it is sur-rounded." In his business success, Frank too is a bottom feeder. Proud gestures and noble risks are taken by others around him, but he "did not want to be a stock gambler" (7). To pursue the gambling analogy, we might say that he is not a gambler but the house: whatever happens, he always gets his cut. And if so, then he would also have to be assigned a different role in the better-known allegory of the lobster and the squid. This allegory answers the question "'How is life organized?' Things lived on each other—that was it. Lobsters lived on squids and other things" (1). Frank is not the lobster, after all; he is the hand that put the two together in the tank. In nature, the squid had a chance of escaping. It has no chance here precisely because this competition is not natural but man-made. It's not that life *is* organized, but that it has *been* organized, and organized in a particular way. People, who live on lobsters, have placed lobster and squid in the tank together, and it is presumably those people who benefit in some sense from the competition in which they do not themselves participate. The same might be said of Cowperwood, who uses city funds to profit safely from the rising and falling investments of others who must risk their own money. And who in doing so acts both illegally and in imitation of the state itself. After all, what is the state but a transparent tank which shapes the struggle for existence for all those within it?

Here we can return to Butler's relations with the Pinkertons. What is intriguing about the Pinkerton interview is that, unlike bonds within fami-lies or between lovers, it seems to represent a new, socially emergent prin-ciple of loyalty. Once the initial arrangements have been made, Butler says, " 'I'm much obliged to you. I'll take it as a great favor, and pay you well.' " The reply is " 'Never mind about that. . . . You're welcome to anything this concern can do for you at the ordinary rates' " (35). The Pinkerton representative takes Butler out of the realm of the personal, where the firm's action would be a "favor" and, as the other side of the same coin, would also suggest the danger of someone taking personal advantage. This is not a favor; it's what's done at the "ordinary rates." In other words, the loyalty the detective agency offers to Butler is clearly not a gift. "Confidence," a refusal to take advantage of insider informa-tion that contrasts starkly with how things are done by the leaders of Philadelphia, is simply normal business practice for the Pinkertons.

There is a strong hint of amorality in this everyday professionalism. Though Butler happens to be an outraged father who wants evidence that the standards of traditional morality are being violated, he could just as easily have come as a criminal—as indeed he is, one might say, though no law he might be breaking is ever made explicit. Professionalism in its most amoral, mercenary sense is what Dreiser might have associated with the role the Pinkertons had played, seven years after Pinkerton's death and two years before Dreiser's arrival in Pittsburgh, as violent strikebreakers at Homestead.[36] Even Pinkerton's biographer describes this as "the blackest episode in the history of American labor" (120). As a former friend said, "it became his unlucky destiny to give his name to an army of illegal soldiers not under the command of the nation or the state, an impudent menace to liberty: an irresponsible brigade of hired banditi" (213). The factory owners could afford to hire a private army, and money guaranteed its loyalty. Civic loyalties seemed weak by contrast, much as in *The Financier*; the public authorities were irrelevant. The Pinkertons could thus been seen as professionally neutral in the sense that they were awaiting a paymaster. But the paymaster, upon arrival, would inevitably turn out to be a wielder of naked, brutal power.[37]

Still, there are other, very different things Dreiser would also have known about the Pinkertons. In 1867, which is to say early on in Frank Cowperwood's career as a manipulator of financial markets, Allan Pinkerton solved a high-profile case that involved, of all things, fraud on the financial markets. Pinkerton was hired by Western Union "to investigate a group of criminals who were tapping the company's wires somewhere on the western frontier, and either using the information thus gained for insider trading, or transmitting false messages to the eastern newspapers which had an adverse effect on the New York stock market. Many companies, notably the Pacific Steam Navigation Company, were driven to the edge of bankruptcy, and fraud on a massive scale was estimated to run to many millions of dollars" (183). Pinkerton solved the case by locating "a broker who had made a fortune by buying up the vastly depreciated stocks of companies named in the more sensational disaster stories" (183–84). If one remembers who Butler and his friends are and how their fortunes were made and continue to be augmented, one starts to balance the reassurance the Pinkerton agent offers Butler against a certain ethical threat. It's as if only the Pinkertons were acting effectively against just the sort of financial fraud that the novel takes as its central subject. And as if, though acting at the behest of a huge monopoly, Pinkerton were also acting on behalf of the public. His public-spiritedness was in fact surprisingly and disquietingly genuine. After the trial of the ringleaders, Pinkerton "drafted a twelve-page document outlining the case for Federal legislation to protect and control the telegraph lines." This document "was never implemented" (184), but the responsibility for its nonimplementation lay with the public's elected representatives, not with Pinkerton.

In short, there is an area of considerable overlap between the seeming professional amorality of the Pinkertons—their willingness to work for anyone, no questions asked, taking their small but secure cut from the riskier competitive activities around them—and the still embryonic public

ethics of the state, which the Pinkerton agents exemplify by their principled refusal to use their knowledge for personal profit.[38] One could thus
describe their professionalism both as existing within finance capitalism
and as operating against finance capitalism. What we see here is neither
amorality nor conventional morality. What we see, as it emerges, is precisely an *un*conventional morality—not the absence or negation of morality but rather a protoprinciple, not yet agreed upon, not yet conventional,
not yet quite a principle at all.

Professional loyalty is of course monopolistic. In this it resembles love.
And one might speculate that the professionalism of the Pinkertons shares
in the amoral excitement, or in what is exciting about the escape from
morality, of Cowperwood's attraction to Aileen. But there is a moral element to this loyalty. Let me try to emphasize this point by a sort of short-
cut. It might be argued that Frank's relation with Aileen is in some sense
really a relationship with her father, who has given him the necessary leg
up in the world of municipal politics and has thus done more than anyone
else to make Frank's fortune.[39] And behind this loyalty to both Butlers,
father and daughter, is an equally libidinized relation to the city of Philadelphia itself. For what his investor's heart first falls in love with is the
city's expanding network of streetcars. And it is the city's (corrupt) government that temporarily allows him to realize his amorous dream of
merging with the young and growing metropolis, fostering it, possessing
it, controlling it. Frank's love for the city of Philadelphia—the city of
brotherly love—is not quite fraternal or morally chaste. But it can make
the reader feel, even in the midst of so unpromising a story, the subtle
emergence of a loyalty and an ethical sensibility that cannot be reduced
to unscrupulous Enron-style profiteering.

". . . TAKE HOSPITALS, THE COPS AND GARBAGE COLLECTION": BUDD SCHULBERG'S *WHAT MAKES SAMMY RUN?*

In *The Cultural Front: The Laboring of American Culture in the Twentieth Century* (1996), Michael Denning uses the phrase "ghetto pastoral"
to describe "the most important genre created by the writers of the proletarian literary movement," a movement centered in the 1930s.[40] "Ghetto
pastorals were tales of growing up in Little Italy, the Lower East Side,
Bronzeville, and Chinatown, written by plebeian men and women of these
ethnic working-class neighborhoods. . . . they were not explorations of
how the other half lives. Rather, they were tales of how *our* half lives"
(230). At the end of the chapter, Denning takes the classic film *On the
Waterfront* (1954), directed by Elia Kazan and written by Budd Schulberg, as the genre's culmination and as proof of its lasting impact.

A number of the authors Denning discusses under the rubric of ghetto pastoral produced what have also been described as upward mobility stories: Anzia Yezierska, Abraham Cahan, and Carlos Bulosan, for example, as well as Tillie Olsen, whom I take up in a later chapter, and later novelists like Budd Schulberg and E. L. Doctorow, whom I'll discuss here. Denning is aware that often "the ghetto pastorals were not seen as proletarian novels" (239). The reason is that though the writers may have been raised in working-class families and communities, they ended up writers rather than factory workers, which is to say (in the eyes of many critics) no longer working class, but middle class. Perhaps in order to compensate, Denning eliminates from his account all reference to their upward mobility. What counts is where the authors came from, not where they landed. "It was the memory of a proletarian childhood that lay at the heart of these books" (240). A character from Daniel Fuchs's *Summer in Williamsburg* (1934) is quoted as saying "[L]ook how I worked my way up in four short years. . . . where in the world could a Jew make such a man of himself as right here in America." He turns out to be not a writer, but a gangster (255).

Denning's avoidance of the tainted concept is understandable enough. Upward mobility seems too close to the self-evident irresponsibility of the gangster, a figure not notoriously anxious about the consequences his own rise might have for the community he rises out of. Yet gangsters and writers have their loyalties, and these loyalties are entwined in their social ascent, sometimes in similar and surprising ways. Doctorow's fifteen-year-old Billy Bathgate, a moment after being singled out by Dutch Schultz's gang and thus set on his way upward, looks at his friends and thinks, "Oh you miserable fucking louts, that I ever needed to attach my orphan self to your wretched company, you thieves of the five-and-ten, you poking predators of your own little brothers and sisters. . . . fuck you forever" (41). Upward mobility's good riddance to the society of origin was never expressed with less indirection. Yet notice how this passage blends different flavors of contempt: for example, an amoral contempt for the pettiness of their criminal ambitions as compared (already) with those of Schultz, which collides with the ethical contempt for the disloyalty that allows them to prey on their own brothers and sisters. There is a perceptible hint, if only a small one, that disloyalty like this should and could be avoided, perhaps by taking crime to a higher level. Unlikely as it may seem, Billy's act of rising above his companions merges with the act of enunciating a moral standard, a standard of loyalty to the family and/or the community that neither the family nor the community has perhaps enunciated for itself. And though here this emergent standard judges his friends, it also has the potential eventually to judge Schultz, and perhaps Billy himself.

Upward mobility seems to stand in direct contradiction with the double aim of representing working-class experience and mobilizing that experience politically, for example by commitment to a party or labor union. Yet no materialist can neglect the awkward material fact that a working-class childhood was also a form of capital for these writers, providing them with something they could work up and sell, and thus was also a means by which they rose. Indeed, the possibility of exchanging proletarian experience for a financial reward often takes up a prominent place in the fiction itself. And as the Doctorow passage suggests, there is also a strong supplementary motive for writing upward mobility back into the representation of working-class ethnic community: rising can also involve the discovering, affirming, and refashioning of loyalty.

The loyalty to the public welfare that remains largely embryonic in Dreiser's *Financier* (1912) and in the Progressive Era has clearly evolved by the period of the New Deal, which finds forceful articulation in Budd Schulberg's *What Makes Sammy Run?* (1941). Sammy Glick, newspaper copy boy turned Hollywood mogul, offers a better approximation of Dreiser's lobster than Frank Cowperwood. We watch as he takes large and bloody bites out of everyone around him, beginning with his girlfriend and the writer whose first script he steals and ending with the mentor he stabs in the back and replaces as Hollywood studio head—perhaps a reference to the fall of Schulberg's producer father, B. P. Schulberg. In between come the members of the Writers' Guild, to whom I will return. One of these is the novel's narrator, a gentle alcoholic named Al Manheim who begins as a newspaper theater critic and corrects Sammy's grammar. Like *The Great Gatsby* (1925), *What Makes Sammy Run?* is someone else's upward mobility story, told from the inherited position of someone who doesn't need an upward mobility story himself, or at least not so dramatic a story. University-educated, without much money but with considerable cultural capital, Al can afford to believe in the New Deal. And he knows it. Self-consciousness about this prerogative tinges his upward mobility sermon early in the novel, a sermon that sets Sammy's bad habits against an ethical vision of the welfare state: " 'Sammy,' I began wisely, 'society isn't just a bunch of individuals living alongside of each other. As a member of society, man is interdependent. Not *in*dependent, Sammy, *inter*dependent. Life is too complex for there to be any truth in the old slogan of every man for himself. We share the benefits of social institutions, like take hospitals, the cops and garbage collection. . . . We can't live in the world like a lot of cannibals trying to swallow each other. Learn to give the other fellow a break and we'll *all* live longer' " (9).[41]

The plot of *What Makes Sammy Run?* makes this official-sounding New Deal moral sound like the novel's last word. Underlining just the conclusion that Dreiser is led up to but refuses to allow his novel to endorse—that real love is irreconcilable with absolute self-interest—Schulberg arranges for Sammy to be betrayed at the very moment of achieving his prize, and betrayed by the prize herself. His rich, beautiful, and sophisticated new wife, who is also the daughter of a big Wall Street funder, turns out to be coldly playing by Sammy's own rules, which is to say promiscuously seeking ever higher returns on her personal capital wherever she can find them. In effect, she is Wall Street's female face. And yet the relationship that occupies the heart of the novel is not between Sammy and his bride, but between Sammy and Al. And the fate of that relationship does not lend itself to such easy morals.[42] For one thing, the relationship seems indestructible. For another, it is full of a surprising amount of give-and-take. We are eventually shown for example that Sammy has long ago learned Al's lesson about interdependence. And we are shown that Al himself has yet to learn it.

Late in the novel, in an italicized flashback that results from Al's private investigation into Sammy's childhood, we get a scene that is reminiscent of Dreiser's Pinkertons. Sammy has been beaten up repeatedly by a bigger boy named Sheik, who calls him a "dirty kike" (214).

> *Two years before when they had been the heads of rival gangs, Sammy's men had cornered Sheik on a roof. Everybody knew what Sammy had taken from him and they were all ready for Sammy to tell them to send Sheik back to his block with a hole in his head. But Sammy just looked at Sheik kind of funny and said, "Go on, get runnin', you bastard, get the hell outa my block."*
>
> *It meant that Sammy was beginning to understand the secret of power. Having Sheik beaten to a pulp would only have evened the score. Without ever having thought it out, Sammy seemed to know intuitively how this gesture would leave him one up on Sheik.* (220–21)

Sammy's rise, as the novel presents it, does not in fact depend on moments like this. The success we see results from ceaseless and shameless self-promotion as well as lying, stealing, and other forms of betrayal. So no, sending Sheik off with a mere warning is not "the secret of power," or at least not the secret of the power Sammy comes to exercise. On the other hand, it *is* the secret of a sort of loyalty. Sheik ends up years later as Sammy's "Man Friday . . . a sort of combination secretary, valet, business manager, companion and procurer" (228).[43] And Al himself, to whom Sammy shows a notable lack of vindictiveness, is the only person whose loyalty Sammy openly claims. This loyalty is interesting because, once again, it represents a principle of social bonding that the upwardly mobile protagonist will need but for which his philosophy of self-interest leaves no room.

Structurally speaking, if not in its tonality, Sammy's decision to let Sheik go parallels the decision of the judge who lets Will Hunting off with therapy. The letter of the law is softened in the name of some future hypothetical good or improvement to be shared between the punisher and the punished. This is a scene out of Nietzsche's *Genealogy of Morals*—as many upward mobility scenes are. Into a world where birds of prey eat tender lambs and the word *good* refers extramorally to how they taste, something like a morality is born. Not quite morality itself, for unlike Nietzsche's Judaeo-Christians Sammy will not now begin to use "good" and "bad" in the moral sense. What he seems to recognize, rather, is a motive—perhaps we could call it protomoral—urging the one who is powerful to withhold the full exercise of his power. Today he is stronger than Sheik. Yesterday, when Sheik beat him up, Sheik was stronger. To-morrow Sheik may be stronger again. The identities of lamb and bird of prey have become interchangeable and uncertain. This is not so much morality as sociology. The motive for restraining his self-interest that Sammy seems to have discovered is the one Al lectured him about, and the one Dreiser's New York Pinkertons seem to abide by: continuing social interdependence.

With a certain symmetry, Al refuses the interdependence he says he believes in. This refusal takes the form of his resistance to the union. Like Sammy, he is too much of an individualist. He describes himself at the outset as "a guy who didn't care six months ago whether the screen writ-ers were organized into a Guild or a sewing circle. . . . I had come out here to be a writer, not a second John L. Lewis" (183–84). He "didn't see much need or much chance for a screen writers' association" (133).[44] It is his own individualism—an error for which Schulberg himself was repri-manded by his then-comrades in the Communist Party—that he's work-ing through, so to speak, in his relation to Sammy.[45] He tells Kit, who is on the front lines of the organizing effort, "that I liked a lot of people, but I liked them one at a time, not all bunched together" (130). The image of people "all bunched together" comes back at him three pages later when Sammy describes the union members as "nothing but a bunch of sheep" (133). That's when Al joins. Sammy is also the reason why he later tears up the resignation from the Guild that he has privately signed. It's as if Sammy were a fiction he required in order to talk himself into doing the right thing.

The union *is* the right thing, for Al and for Schulberg, only because it preserves some of Sammy's individualist commitment to the upward mobility story. Here, as in Cahan's *The Rise of David Levinsky*, Naipaul's *Mystic Masseur* (where the protagonist's political rise is blocked by a strike), and Doctorow's *Loon Lake*, upward mobility and labor union solidarity seem destined for a head-on collision. A studio manager speaking at the crucial Writers' Guild meeting "seemed to feel that the story of how he had risen from truck driver right here at this studio to his present importance was a devastating argument for writers giving up the Guild foolishness and making the studio one big happy family" (175).[46] This is sarcastic, but Al too wants a career and a sense of individual "importance." Liberty for all, as Stendhal put it, but also distinction for himself. So the issue is genuine. The novel confronts it most squarely by means of the character of Julian Blumberg. Sammy gets his start in Hollywood by taking a script written by Blumberg and peddling it as his own. The state will not stop this from happening. Though Sammy is utterly unscrupulous, in this sense he walks a fine line within the law.[47] But there is a force that can constrain Sammy, and that force is the union. Kit, leader of the Writers' Guild, successfully uses its clout to force Sammy to offer Blumberg at least some of the credit and money he deserves. "Julian might still be ghost writing if it weren't for the Guild" (171).

Julian's upward mobility story is cut short—by Sammy's conspiracy to subvert the Guild—and at the end it is left hanging. But it nonetheless provides the crucial baseline against which Sammy's upward mobility can be morally measured. It can perform this function because it is not merely a moral standard, but a standard that is empowered by its own success in the world—not quite Sammy's success, but *some* success. In other words, merit cannot serve as a measuring stick unless it can contrive to get itself rewarded. Sammy uses the phrase "survival of the fittest" to justify his behavior (122). Al replies: " 'What do you mean, survival of the fittest? . . . Who's more fit to write screenplays, you or Julian?" (123). It's clear that fitness in this sense will not lead to survival, let alone triumph, when set against "ways of reaching the top without creating anything" (152). Julian's is a story of merit rewarded., but it is not a story of self-reliance. For the merit standard is not natural to this system: it has to be constructed, regulated, enforced—in short, imposed by outside intervention. That is the mediating or "donor" role of the union. The real moral center of the book is this not quite magical intervention, without which Julian would have no upward mobility story. It seems like magic, but it is only human effort that enables the writers to play the role of their own collective mentor/benefactor, the role they *had* to play in order for anyone's individual talent to reap its due reward.

To put this another way, the norm against which Sammy's career is judged is not a presumed stasis in which everyone would stay who and what they already are. The norm is another upward mobility story. This norm is a story of empowerment, but one that works according to a different "secret of power": the interdependence that Sammy discovers on the rooftop with Sheik. Like Pip's long if briefly noted occupation as a clerk after the failure of his great expectations, Julian's is a chastened upward mobility story, an undramatic compromise arrived at by trading some embrace of social responsibility against some improvement in status and opportunity. The same holds for Al's own career—which is to say that he too has one, though it is less than stellar and indeed almost imperceptible in the dazzling radiance of Sammy's. Al's trajectory does not depend, like Julian's, on the visible intervention of the union. All we hear of Al's writing is reference to an anti-Fascist script that does not get produced. Instead of achievements, we watch his relationship with Kit and his research into Sammy's past. And that pairing of love and sociological research is where we have to look for the meaning of his career.

When Al and Kit finally decide to marry, the gesture is more than cursory or conventional. Though Al has long ago declared his honorable intentions, the unexplained delay in acting on them underscores three areas in which one might say it is his resistance, rather than hers, that had to be overcome. First, Kit is or at least first appears "mannish." Second, she has been sleeping with Sammy and liking it. And third, she is the leader of the union. Each of these items translates into individual erotic terms a move in the direction of democracy. It's not exactly "bad sex" in the Rousseau sense, but it does involve "sharing," and the structural resemblance goes further. Each item requires that Al surrender some of his prior and gendered sense of being singular, superior, an individual set off against all others. When Al marries Kit, what he is really marrying is the Guild. And in doing so he is reminded that even the Guild's guiding spirit has never lost her soft spot for Sammy, that is, for self-interested upward mobility.

A certain political incorrectness is also an ingredient in Al's research. As Denning says, the depiction of the New Jersey longshoremen's community in *On the Waterfront* offers a powerful finale to the ghetto pastoral mode. Denning does not say, but others have, that the film's triumphant success was made possible in large part by Schulberg's long and painstaking research among the dock workers. Research was necessary; unlike Denning's idealized writer of ghetto pastoral, Schulberg did not belong to the community he was describing. Indeed, his role as an intrusive questioning outsider is something like that of the Federal Crime Commission investigators in the film who try to get Terry Molloy (Brando) to testify.[48] The film makes no effort to get the audience to like or admire these uncharismatic representatives of the state. Yet it's worth reflecting on the means of their success. Their breakthrough, the moment when Brando's resolve to keep silent unmistakably starts to weaken, is the scene on the roof, among the pigeons, when one inspector turns the conversation to Brando/Molloy's career as a boxer. The Feds get to him, in other words, not by appealing to him as a longshoremen, but by reminding him of the period when, to quote his big upcoming line, he could have been a contender. What is the logic here? Yes, the same corruption that fixed his fights and kept Molloy back (symbolized by Friendly, the Lee J. Cobb figure) also tyrannizes over the longshoremen. But for Molloy to have had a shot at the title would have done nothing for his fellow longshoremen. "I could have been a contender" is so heartbreaking in part because it is so modest. Even at the height of his aspiration, Brando/Molloy is not asking for the championship itself. But even so, his success as a fighter would have defined an individual trajectory, not a collective one. The stirring final spectacle of individual courage and group solidarity, when the severely injured Brando limps through the gate and is followed by the rest of the workers, thereby breaking Friendly's grip on the union, is not easy to reconcile with the film's single most memorable line. The state, with which Schulberg himself is so obliquely identified, intervenes to save the workers from their (corrupt) union only by appealing to the desire for individual upward mobility.

In *What Makes Sammy Run?* Al Manheim's merit echoes that of his state-identified investigator-creator. It is most manifest, that is, in the sequence when Al also comes closest to acting out the ethics of the welfare state. He does so by playing retrospective social worker. In search of an answer to the enigma of what makes Sammy run, he penetrates into the slums of the Lower East Side, questions Sammy's mother, his brother, and his old teacher, tries to make sense of Sammy's childhood. The general conclusion Al boozily draws for the bartender afterward is that this experience should be generalized: "Now the world is full of people hating other people's guts. Now, Henry, answer me this, what if each of them took the time to go down to Rivington Street—I mean each person's particular Rivington Street, Henry? We would begin to have compassion in the world, that's what. Not so much soda this time, Henry" (224). It is not quite an epic descent into the underworld, but it can claim to explain both Sammy's upward mobility and—in a different sense—Al's own.

What Al discovers on Rivington Street is a family that, despite difficult circumstances, had survived more or less intact, but was finally broken because of the failure of a glass cutters' strike. The brother tells the story: "Papa was a foreman, making sixteen, but he remembered how it was to live on ten dollars a week. And now it was even worse with the war boom started and prices rising. He walked out with his men" (211). The owner tells him not to be a dope, soon he'll be partner. He answers: " 'To be a partner in a sweatshop, such honors I can do without" (212). The failure of the strike explains his failure to support his family, and his failure to support his family explains what makes Sammy run. One might conclude that Schulberg puts the blame on the union, which made unrealistic demands. This would be consistent with Al's own ambivalence toward the Writers' Guild as well as his own implicit demand for realism—that is, the probability that a given action will result in obtaining some degree of power. Or one might conclude, emphasizing the father's initial position of relative privilege, that Schulberg puts the blame on the father's left-wing principles, his solidarity, his foolish nobility. In other words, he blames anyone surrendering the power he was lucky enough to start out with. But blame is perhaps not the right word for a compassion in the father that embodies Al's own relative privilege, his own top-down solidarity. The moral that comes closest to articulating the many givens Schulberg has provided takes us back to the New Deal, and does so by giving a special role to those privileged to look down from the top. That moral is—as in *On the Waterfront*—that on its own the labor movement will fail, and that its failures must be supplemented by intervention from above, intervention by the privileged and compassionate, intervention by the state.[49]

Walter Benn Michaels suggests that the interdependent society he identifies with finance capitalism is a society in which all debts and responsibilities are canceled. Within the limits this premise sets on any praise and blame, Michaels seems to praise this universal cancellation or floating of responsibility. We can think of this as the Sammy Glick position. Christopher Lasch sees much the same generalizing of irresponsibility as characteristic of the welfare state, but he of course condemns it. He would presumably also condemn Al Manheim, who seems a faithful voice of the somewhat paternalist welfare state at a point when it was still a recent and very uncertain project. It seems clear that this interdependence and the "no fault" impulse that is its ethical shadow are characteristic at the same time both of finance capitalism and of the welfare state. The challenge around which the upward mobility story molds itself is therefore that of first loosening responsibilities, and then reallocating them. From this perspective, I would suggest that Al Manheim rises not merely by riding Sammy's coattails or by satirizing him, though his story has elements of both. He also rises by coming to an understanding of Sammy, seen against the community from which he emerged, that despite the Thirties wisecracking style would have to be called compassionate. This is to say that he rises, in his moderate way, by fulfilling a responsibility that is characteristic of the New Deal.[50]

"I LIKE . . . TO BE RELIABLE": E. L. DOCTOROW'S *BILLY BATHGATE*

Perhaps because E. L. Doctorow's protagonists are so often upwardly mobile, they tend to be evasive about what they are committed to.[51] Uneasily balanced between the consciousness of the proletarian, the gangster, and the writer-to-be, they sometimes call the object of their desire "life."

Only something as vague as "life" can cover, for example, the amoral jumble of desires that opens Joe of Paterson's narration in *Loon Lake* (1980): "I stole what I needed and went after girls like prey. I went looking for trouble and was keen for it, I was keen for life, I ran down the street to follow the airships sailing by, I climbed firescapes and watched old women struggle into their corsets, I joined a gang and carried a penknife I had sharpened like an Arab, like a Dago, I stuck it in the vegetable peddler's horse, I stuck it in a feeb with a watermelon head, I slit awnings with it. . . . I only wanted to be famous!" (2). Here, as in Billy Bathgate's apostrophe to the "miserable fucking louts," the cascading rush of clauses won't let you pause to distinguish between commonplace sadism and aesthetic spectatorship (the dirigibles and the firescapes), between the disinterested or perhaps even sympathetic contemplation of the old women struggling into corsets and the appetitive scrutiny of girls as prey, between the budding criminal's need to dominate and the budding writer's need to see for himself. This daredevil indiscriminateness, which flows from but also overflows the standard moral confusions of the picaresque first-person, is a kind of "no fault" style. It can lead you to see the writer as criminal, or the criminal as writer, or the aspirant to upward mobility as some combination of the two. In any event, it leaves the object of their commitment anything but clear.

Perhaps that is just Doctorow's point. One of the strongest arguments for his political seriousness rests on the premise that the endpoint of his plots is still more unreliable than the narrative voices that seductively lead us there. Joe's upward mobility story ends, for example, in a dark inversion of Horatio Alger. Like Billy Bathgate, who identifies with and attaches himself to the gangster Dutch Schultz, Joe chooses in the end to become son, heir, and successor to the man we have come to recognize as the ruthless and virtually omnipotent center of an evil social system. Despite the richness of "life" that Joe's voice and adventures ensure, the reader seems intended to recognize the costliness of his error, to see a fault even if Joe is never punished for it. Deciding that the protagonist is the very opposite of an eligible role model, we can reflect on the politically demobilizing consequences of upward mobility aspirations for the working class: not just the ease with which a keenness for "life" can come to mean aiding and abetting CIA campaigns of liquidation—an item on Joe's curriculum vitae—but also a loss of respect for the parents, who are inescapably seen as failures, and a loss of the sense of cross-generational continuity that radical politics requires.

There is clearly something important here. Yet it can hardly be the whole story of Doctorow's strenuous wrestling match with American society in the unscrupulous free-market era. Moreover, the adventurous energy that flows between Doctorow's narrators and the American Dream forms a high-voltage circuit; even at the end of the novel, many and perhaps most readers will have trouble pulling away into respectably buffered alienation. Thus it is perhaps necessary to seek for Doctorow's political commitments in as well as against the narrative force of the American Dream. On the first page of *Loon Lake*, Joe describes Paterson, the nightmarish neighborhood of his parents: "What, after all, was the tragedy in their lives implicit in the profoundly reproachful looks they sent my way? That things hadn't worked out for them? How did that make them different from anyone else on Mechanic Street, even the houses were the same, two by two, the same asphalt palace over and over, streetcars rang the bell on the whole fucking neighborhood. Only the maniacs were alive, the men and women who lived on the street."[52] Reinventing his world metaphor by metaphor, Joe seems to share with the street people all the available "life." His parents at any rate seem entirely deprived of it. His case for leaving natural parents behind and fleeing toward a parental surrogate like auto magnate F. W. Bennett seems open-and-shut. Yet the novel does not in fact allow Joe to put his neighborhood behind him. It obliges him to act out his commitments to the neighborhood even while submitting to the impulsive violence of unconsidered desire.

He is a homeless person, and thus a kind of neighborhood representative in spite of himself, when he arrives at Bennett's mansion on Loon Lake, and it's as if only that arrival can make sense of the violence he has already revealed in himself. Penfield, the poet who self-consciously parallels Joe, dots the i's and crosses the t's: he too arrived at Loon Lake, treed by Bennett's dogs, in order to murder Bennett, and he did so because homelessness like his is the result of Bennett and his corporations.[53] "People I loved died because of the policies of one of his companies" (53). Does that mean the death-in-life of Joe's parents can be blamed on Bennett as well? This is precisely the suggestion when the flight from Loon Lake takes Joe and Clara Lukacs to Jacksontown. Here the plot borrows from the paranoid thrillers of the sixties and seventies, which offer their own interesting accompaniment to the advent of "theory." Running away from Bennett, Joe and Clara find themselves stuck in a Bennett company town, where Joe works on an assembly line in a Bennett autobody factory and his friend and next-door neighbor turns out to be a Bennett company spy. But if the hint of inescapable total system, with police and company working hand-in-glove, prepares for Joe's final offscreen conversion, or anticonversion, into a CIA director and Bennett's successor, the episode also plunges Joe back into the lifeless life of his factory-worker father that he had tried so hard to avoid. And he now learns to look at it with more respect: "It was enough to make me think of my father. The man was a fucking hero" (188). The novel will give this recognition nowhere to go, politically speaking, but that does not cancel the power of this inadvertent return to the parents' neighborhood.

The world left behind by his mobility also reasserts itself, at the very heart of the mobility story, as the disguised social substance of Joe's passion for Clara. Clara echoes Joe's own desire for mobility and also justifies it. But she does so by means of Joe's epiphanic quasi-memory (we are not told that Clara herself remembers it) of the "outrage" her face registered when she was forced, as a small child, to urinate before strangers in the street. Returning obsessively to this image, Joe turns mobility itself into an expression of outrage at casual, taken-for-granted indignity. The struggle for possession of Clara is thus something more than what it sometimes seems, a struggle between men over an abstract feminine trophy. In a sense, Joe's love for Clara can be taken as an indirect mode of political commitment.

In *E. L. Doctorow's Skeptical Commitment* Michelle Tokarczyk points out how Joe, like other Doctorow heroes, concentrates his desire on the act of stealing or rescuing a beautiful woman (the two acts are difficult to distinguish), a woman who belongs to an older and more powerful man. Clara belongs to the union-busting gangster Tony Crapo, and perhaps also to Bennett himself; Drew Preston in *Billy Bathgate* (1989) belongs first to gangster Bo Weinberg, then after Weinberg's murder to Dutch Schultz. Within *Loon Lake*, the same scenario comes back with a minor twist when Joe takes to the road with Red James's recent widow. Joe himself is "not unaware of his attraction to other men's wives, he was not unmindful that his life since leaving Paterson had been a picaresque of other men's money and other men's women, who in hell was he to get righteously independent with anyone?" (272). If righteousness requires independence, then this flagrantly Oedipal fantasy structure entails a "no fault" policy on upward mobility. Yet there is much here of which both Joe and Doctorow do indeed seem unaware, including the way it teases the rags-to-riches story back in a more righteous or praise-and-blame direction. On the psychological level this motif registers a simple displacement of Oedipal conflict (it is more palatable to imagine stealing a woman from a surrogate father than from a natural father). But on the political level it also registers an undeclared assault on the powerful surrogate father. And this assault can then be interpreted as an indirect defense of the natural or lower-born father—the scenario that Doctorow stages with more direct political implications in *The Book of Daniel*. Instead of simply displaying contempt for the family of origin, then, the upward mobility plot turns out to channel the energies of personal ambition into a devious but erotically charged vector of neighborhood loyalty.

The fact that Joe's story does not end well means that Joe is no positive hero, but it does not erase the intermittent elements of attractive, even compelling moral sensibility with which Doctorow has infused his character. A central scene of the novel, announced early, delayed, and finally repeated in detail, presents Joe stealing a large wad of bills from a woman with whom he has just made love, then tossing the money away into the wind. The money, we learn, comes from the sexual exploitation of a third party. The sex that precedes the theft is itself unmistakably and a bit shockingly sadistic. On this evidence, Joe is a sadist, a thief, and at the same time a disinterested agent of justice, refusing to share in these ill-gotten gains. He does not simply play to win.

A similar scene and a similar moral organize the narrative of *Billy Bathgate*.[54] The novel opens with Dutch Schultz's murder of his trusted lieutenant, the handsome Bo Weinberg, then his confiscation of Weinberg's girlfriend, Drew, all of it witnessed by the young Billy. Cut up and surrendered only in reluctant bits, this primal scene becomes an organizing center of the novel, like the bills in the wind in *Loon Lake*. Indeed, Billy's power over Drew—another somewhat older woman of absolute beauty whose possession stands in for all the promises of upward mobility—seems to reside largely in the power of having witnessed and being able to narrate Weinberg's death. Weinberg, another father figure whose woman our hero will inherit, is aligned by the imminence of that death with the poor natural fathers, not the rich parental surrogates. Billy's narration, neither entirely false nor entirely true, bestows upon him a dignified death—a death singing "Bye, Bye Blackbird." And this is how Billy achieves his most novelistically gripping success. As in the short story "The Writer in the Family," which comes closer than the novels to the facts of Doctorow's own downwardly mobile childhood in the Bronx (see his autobiographical book, *World's Fair* [1985]), the young man gives himself a place in the world by lying, imaginatively and responsibly, about the death of a father whose life has been a failure. Here too, the son's upward mobility is secured, in part at least, not by setting his "life" against the father's lifelessness, but by using his lively creative powers to invest the father's death, or failure, with the dignity it deserves.

Doctorow never lets the reader forget the odds against finding anything like justice at the center of the upward mobility story. For Bennett, crime, including his own, is the only alternative to the breadline: "If you can't steal and you can't sap someone on the head when you have to, you join the line at the flophouse. You get on the bread line, you sit at the curb and hold out your hand" (*Loon Lake*, 125). Doctorow leaves it unclear whether Bennett is here describing the institutions of the welfare state or, as seems more likely, a society that does not yet have them. In the latter case, the welfare state would offer a more dignified alternative just where Bennett says that none exists. On the other hand, Doctorow also underlines the fact that Bennett's wealth endows "hospitals universities libraries

museums planetaria parks think-tanks and other institutions for the public weal all of which are the benefactions of the utmost class" (184). These
are the dignity-preserving places, so to speak, between crime and the
breadline. But how independent can public institutions pretend to be of
the capitalist surplus that pays for them, whether directly through philanthropy or indirectly through taxation? For that matter, how independent
can literature pretend to be? Penfield, who admits to wanting to kill Bennett, says, "I'm a poet and the Bennetts are my patrons" (53).

The moral price to be paid for upward mobility is illustrated early in
Billy Bathgate when Billy watches a window washer falling to his death
from a scaffold "maybe fifteen stories up" (106–7). Doctorow then makes
a characteristic diversionary move. Billy's account of the death is immediately followed by an appreciation of the way Mickey, the gang's driver,
moves through traffic "with the authority of a professional": "I knew
that Mickey would drive a car as calmly at a hundred miles an hour as at
thirty, that whatever he called upon a car to do it would do, and now
with the vision in my mind of the helpless window washer falling to his
death, Mickey's competence stood in my mind as a silent rebuke in confirmation of Mr Berman's remark" (108–9). He has been caught paying
too much attention to the "accident," engineered by Dutch Schultz's gang
in its bid to muscle in on the union. Mr. Berman, the financial brains of
the gang and Billy's mentor, has rebuked him for gawking.

As we have seen, there is nothing strange about setting upward mobility
against union solidarity. But the place of professionalism in *Billy Bathgate*
is odd. For it might seem that professionalism would be on the side of
upward mobility. Here professionalism seems to have more in common
with union solidarity.

Professionalism is odd in *Billy Bathgate* first of all because it seems to
have displaced the usual rewards of gangsterdom and become itself a reward, and a very desirable one. The epigraph to this section comes from
Bo Weinberg's last words, which are reported at almost the exact center
of the novel and seem intended to exercise their full traditional authority:
"I like best of all to be reliable, that is the purest pleasure" (234). There
is an overlap here with self-reliance, but the emphasis is different. One is
reliable for or on behalf of others. Reliability is what they want out of
you. Thus it is a happy coincidence if it is also what you want, what
you take "the purest pleasure" in. When it becomes a pleasure, reliability
resolves the contradiction between individual self-interest and the general
welfare. Billy refers to this social pleasure as a form of love. In him too
the desire to fit in with the others is stronger than the pleasure of the new
clothes, the glamour, the ability to inspire fear. What Billy tells us he wants
is to be treated "as another of Mr. Schultz's men, a professional" (94). "I
had the avid desire to reconnect with the gang, I felt love for every one of

them, there was a kind of consistency to their behavior that made me feel grateful for their existence" (389).

In *The Great Gatsby*, Nick explains his stubborn loyalty to Gatsby by referring to Gatsby's underlying indifference to the piles of shirts and other possessions he has amassed in order to mark his social ascent. What Gatsby really cares about, Nick says, is "some idea of himself that has gone into loving Daisy" (117).[55] And it is this idea that redeems the enterprise of upward mobility. Doctorow's version of loving Daisy is not, as might be expected, loving Drew. The redemptive idea is loving to be reliable, loving to belong with one's fellow professionals.

The contrast with Schultz's philosophy of self-reliance is highlighted again and again. "'Christ, I had to earn everything I got, nobody gave me a thing, I came out of nowhere and everything I done I done by myself,' Mr Schultz said" (100). Shortly before his death, he announces again: "I was never a joiner. . . . I never asked anybody for anything. Everything I got I got for myself. I have worked hard. And how I got where I got is I do what I want, not what other people want" (437). In other words, Schultz's downfall is also the downfall of the heroic individualist. As Weinberg says, others have "better ideas for the future than this wildass. He is obsolete kid" (231). Foremost among these others is Berman, who dies with Schultz but whose ideas are picked up again in the conclusion by Billy himself.

> "The modern businessman looks to combination for strength and for streamlining," Mr. Berman said. "He joins a trade association. Because he is part of something bigger he achieves strength. Practices are agreed upon, prices, territories, the markets are controlled. He achieves streamlining. And lo and behold the numbers rise. Nobody is fighting anybody. And what he has a share of now is more profitable than the whole kit and caboodle of yore." (433)

Can this count as a redemptive idea, something worthy of love? If the Mafia is a figure for ordinary everyday capitalism, as Fredric Jameson has suggested, it hardly needs saying that Berman's vision of an end to violence and a restraint of competition is not a vision of an end to capitalism itself.[56] But it does fortify hints about the value of professional belonging, building them into a structure of feeling that transcends professionalism.[57] "People will work things out quietly, with not so much fire in the streets" (212). "'Cooperation,' I said. 'Exactly. What happened in the railroad business is a perfect example, you look at the railroads, they used to be a hundred railroad companies cutting each others' throats. Now how many are there? One to each section of the country'" (213). This is not quite "monopoly capitalism." The abstraction that Berman calls "the numbers" is a force against unnecessary competition, but also against ethnic prejudice and rivalry, like that between the Jewish and Italian mobs. And it is a force on behalf of what I will call, for want of a more inspiring term, civic loyalty.

The beginning of the end of Dutch Schultz's career as a gangster is the moment when on sudden impulse he murders a "city fire inspector" (122) who has picked the wrong time for an inspection. The absolute end of that career is determined when Schultz vows to murder the public prosecutor, Thomas E. Dewey, who is trying to put him in jail. Schultz complains that the city is against him. "I mean the fucking fire inspectors? What next, I mean the mailmen?" (125). In a sense, this is not paranoia. What is against him is indeed the city. The city has become a moral and political entity, as it arguably was not in the late-nineteenth century Dreiser described in *The Financier* or even the early-twentieth century in which that novel was written. Looking back at the period of the New Deal (the mid-thirties) from the period when Reagan was busy trying to eviscerate its institutional legacy (the eighties), Doctorow sees, as the Italian mobsters who kill Schultz also see, that the public had evolved. Schultz thinks the law is just another racket—and many Foucaultians have agreed with him. But the law now has its crusaders, like Dewey, and the city will not stand to see Dewey assassinated. It is ready to defend itself against the most violent results of heroic individualism and competitive self-reliance. The possibility has arisen for a better level of "cooperation" within what has been an urban jungle. This is the narrative that underlies Dutch Schultz's fall—and that begins, as Billy notes, with his own arrival on the scene.[58]

Billy's relation to all this is ambiguous. He presents himself as a cause of the failure of Berman's prophetic plan. "Oddly enough the person I felt bad about was Mr. Berman, the moment I had chosen at the Palace Chophouse to reveal what Drew Preston had told me he must have perceived as an act of treachery, the moment of his ruination, it was the end of all his plans, when his man would not finally be brought along into the new realm he foresaw, where the numbers ruled where they became the language and rewrote the book" (443). Billy also presents himself as an antistatist. He says he admires Schultz for "living in defiance of a government that did not like you and did not want you and wanted to destroy you" (99). Considering the possibility that Schultz could be found guilty and that he would thus be "freed of him," (382), he goes on: "If something as ordinary and mundane as government justice could tilt my life awry, then my secret oiled connections to the real justice of a sanctified universe were nonexistent" (383). Like other romantic antistatists, Billy needs government justice to show itself to be a faulty and disappointing thing so that he can continue to believe in a higher and more personal brand of justice, one that will offer him more distinction. This is why he says he "felt real love" (440) for the personal Schultz and not the impersonal Berman, even though he agrees with Berman.[59] "Mr. Berman had been my mentor ever since, generously bringing me along, nurturing me, and yet I still did not forgive him that loss of a boy's few pennies" (441). One might nevertheless say that Billy acts against or outside of his love, and perhaps even as Berman's agent. Getting Schultz killed means saving Dewey's life, and in this backhanded way acting as agent for the public. As elsewhere in the Rousseau "bad sex" line, working for a less violent or more democratic future seems to entail a detour from satisfaction in what one thinks is one's love.[60]

How much of a moral life is possible within the gang? This is the same question as: How much of a moral life is possible within capitalism? Doctorow does not foreclose this question. Billy has a surprisingly active moral life. Like the welfare state in relation to capitalism, his moral life both pulls away from the life of the gang and remains inescapably limited by it. He saves someone from being killed by the gang (Drew), and he saves the memory of someone who was killed by the gang (Bo Weinberg). On the other hand, the "cartwheeling body of the window washer in the sun coming down alongside the office building on Seventh Avenue" (117) stands beyond the limit of the memories this narrative allows Billy to honor, and even further beyond some more significant action on the workers' behalf. From the point of view of the window washers' union, this novel is *On the Waterfront* without the happy ending. The limits are narrow. Even enlarging the domain of "cooperation" would not seem capable of pushing those limits back enough to produce a happy ending.

When he is trying to rid his mind of the image of the falling window washer, Billy remembers a comment from Berman that seems relevant to what he has just seen. " 'Nobody dies who doesn't sin,' Mr Berman had said to me in the diner. 'And since that covers everybody, it's something we can all look forward to' " (110). Putting the window washers and their murderers on the same moral plane, Berman offers a manifesto of irresponsibility. Yet he himself is trying, within the limits of competition, to create more responsibility and to diminish the violence and pervasiveness of competition. The historical vector he imagines so hopefully seems to fit the welfare state at least as well as corporate capitalism. It would be satisfying to say the same about Billy. But Billy's irresponsibility is also that of the child, assumed to be incapable of taking on full adult responsibilities. And it is that of the performer. The act of juggling, which first gets Billy noticed by the gang and in this sense begins his story, is also an act in the theatrical sense, an artistic spectacle. "It was juggling that had got me where I was" (32). More important, juggling was "something that marked me but after all wasn't my fault" (33).[61] The rest of us "miserable fucking louts" want to know: can juggling offer Billy distinction without that distinction being his fault? Can we accept the "no fault" version of upward mobility it appears to offer?

The question must be directed to Doctorow himself, for juggling is one of the many parallels to his own literary vocation that he democratically invites the reader to detect among his characters. A spectacle of strenuous stasis rather than historical dynamism, juggling is both a personal way up in the world and a defiance of gravity that exerts a universal appeal. At the very least, it encourages us to think that in the social world, too, things are not fixed at their natural and unalterable level. But what is its relation to more directly political solutions? Tokarczyk sums up the family romance theme of natural versus surrogate fathers by suggesting that Doctorow's "search for a father-figure to complement or replace an inadequate one" is "resolved through the representation of writing as the ideal parent" (243–44). This formulation makes sense of Tateh's trajectory in *Ragtime*, where upward mobility can be legitimately embraced, it seems, if and perhaps only if it can be seen as the story of an artist successfully marketing his vision. But to see writing as an ideal parent does not of course settle the political question. In the next chapter, we will have to ask whether literariness signifies a public or a merely personal solution to social conflict, whether it is more than a synonym for playful disengagement.

CHAPTER FOUR

A Portrait of the Artist as a Rentier

"WHERE ARE YOUR NOBLES NOW?": BOHEMIA IN *KIPPS*,
   MY BRILLIANT CAREER, AND *TRILBY*

H. G. Wells's novel *Kipps: The Story of a Simple Soul* (1905) describes a
lowly young draper's assistant (Wells's own occupation at the same age)
who receives an unexpected inheritance and suddenly finds himself rich.[1]
As a result, he becomes engaged to the upper-class woman he has long
adored from afar. However, his efforts to adapt to the conventions of the
genteel world soon begin to weary and oppress him, and he goes back to
his childhood sweetheart, who has meanwhile found work as a servant.
He then loses most of the inheritance, swindled by the former fiancée's
brother. The loss of the inheritance does not prevent him and his sweetheart from living happily ever after.

The apparent moral of this story—a cheerier rewrite of Dickens's *Great
Expectations*—is that happiness depends neither on acquiring a lot of
money nor on climbing the social ladder. Late in the novel, after Kipps
has renounced his fiancée but before he loses his riches, this moral is articulated for him by a character with the Nietzschean name of Masterman,
a figure of the working-class intellectual apparently modeled on George
Gissing. "'You were starting to climb,' [Masterman] said at dinner. 'That
doesn't lead anywhere. You would have clambered from one refinement
of vulgarity to another, and never got to any satisfactory top. There isn't
a top. It's a squirrel's cage. Things are out of joint. . . . You'd have hung
on, a disconsolate, dismal little figure, somewhere on the ladder, far below
even the motor-car class, while your wife larked about, or fretted because
she wasn't a bit higher than she was. . . . I found it all out long ago. I've
seen women of that sort. And I don't climb any more'" (242–43).[2]

Aside from its somewhat dated misogyny, this little speech might have
been pronounced by a critic or novelist today, explaining (though one
wonders to whom) why the theme of social climbing no longer holds
much critical appeal. Who believes that there *is* a "top"? Who would
suggest that even the fate of a "simple soul," if there is such a thing, can
be accounted for by the crude social topography of "up" and "down"?
We know that every once in a while an unrepresentative upstart makes the
leap from something like rags to something like riches. Whether readers

conceive of such stories as an absolute economic improvement, as a relative gain in status that allows one to exult over others, or as something else entirely, most of them would not conclude that sophisticated fiction should be or has ever been centrally "about" anything so coarse and uncommon. Fairy tales and satire, yes; the realist novel, no. Suspicious of ladders and of stories that involve climbing them, educated common sense today tends to prefer categories that overlap with upward mobility but put the emphasis elsewhere. The young person's "coming-of-age" story and the immigrant's "coming-to-America" story, for example, are also concerned, if only inadvertently, with attaining greater access to economic goods and services. But focusing on the individual life cycle and personal development or on national belonging and cultural assimilation seems to leave more space for the proper exercise of literary imagination.

Even the *künstlerroman* or portrait of the youthful artist, which might look like a more specialized category, probably resonates with more actual experience of novel reading than a phrase like "upward mobility."[3] And this makes intuitive sense, given how much of what is called upward mobility in fact takes place in more or less autobiographical first novels (sometimes the author's only novel) that recount the protagonist's struggle to overcome various obstacles, get an education, achieve a certain distance from his or her society of origin, discover a sense of artistic vocation, produce the book one is holding in one's hands. In addition to *A Portrait of the Artist as a Young Man*, Joyce's prototype, one thinks of such interesting variants as D. H. Lawrence's *Sons and Lovers*, Ralph Ellison's *Invisible Man*, Tayeb Salih's *Season of Migration to the North*, Tsitsi Dangarembga's *Nervous Conditions*, and Zadie Smith's *White Teeth*. In cases like these social distance up or down the ladder seems indistinguishable from literary or intellectual achievement.

Should we conclude, then, that the real subject of Masterman's speech on social climbing is his own (and Wells's) situation as writer and intellectual? Not quite. The ambiguity of the story's endpoint cannot be escaped simply by expressing a preference for one theme (the literary) at the expense of the other (the social). The argument swings both ways. If the real kernel of the upward mobility story is often the emergence of the writer, the reverse is no less true: becoming a writer will mean some sort of change in one's social position, usually for the better. Thus even the novel's most reflexive or inward-looking treatments of the writer's formation are often oblique treatments of upward mobility. This chapter will suggest that, along with their other virtues, stories that oscillate on this axis are among the most intriguing discussions of upward mobility, and precisely because it is so difficult to locate on a social grid the endpoint called "becoming a writer."

Wells's case against social climbing is not as open-and-shut as it might appear. To begin with, its reference to "women of that sort" leaves a gaping loophole: the possibility that social climbing fails to make men happy only because women, or the particular women men want as the reward of their striving, *are* "of that sort"—because women are more intent than men on an endless, insatiable accumulation of the signs of higher and higher status. Here a not very convincing gender stereotype is imported into the scenario in order to rescue men from recognizing that they themselves are ambivalent about, and cannot simply repudiate, social climbing.[4] As might be expected, this effort to conceal the positive attractions of social climbing does indeed fail to convince. In suggesting that marriages founder when the female partner cannot rest content with what she has and keeps striving for more, Wells's mininarrative hints that though *more* is bad, *some* of this unnamed ingredient may be good, and even necessary. It hints that social climbing may after all mean acquiring something of value that men as well as women will rightly want.

This hint is confirmed by the terms in which Masterman abjures social climbing. Society is not a ladder, he says, but a squirrel's cage. When you think you are climbing, you are in fact staying in place while one "refinement of vulgarity" after another whirls around you. There is no "top," or no "satisfactory" top—not quite the same thing—that would make the climb worth undertaking. And yet we know that Masterman himself *has* done some climbing in the past, for he tells us that he doesn't climb "any more." Was the former episode of climbing alluded to here simply an embarrassing mistake? It appears not. His story goes as follows: "I found myself at thirteen being forced into a factory like a rabbit into a chloroformed box. Thirteen! . . . But even a child of that age could see what it meant, that hell of a factory! Monotony and toil and contempt and dishonor! And then death. So I fought—at thirteen! [. . .] I got out at last—somehow [. . .] Some of us get out by luck, some by cunning, and crawl on to the grass, exhausted and crippled, to die. That's a poor man's success, Kipps" (210–11).

If, as Masterman hints, he has reason to expect a rapid and premature death, then "a poor man's success" is of course not a success at all. On the other hand, his resignation is also described at one point as a "pose" he can "abandon" (207). But whether or not the expectation of imminent mortality is a pose, one must risk a certain callousness by declaring that in an important sense, Masterman's is indeed a success story. He has managed to educate himself. Despite his exhaustion, he is no longer doing exhausting work. Now he has access to such authoritative judgments as "Things are out of joint." "All the old tradition goes or has gone," he opines, "and there's no one to make a new tradition. Where are your nobles now? Where are your gentlemen?" (206). In order to know that there once existed an "old tradition" of nobles and gentlemen that is now going or gone, one must command a view of history and a view of the social whole. That is, one must have knowledge of the top as well as the bottom of the social ladder. Such a view is not available, at least on Masterman's telling, from the floor of a factory, where all is "monotony and toil." Something very much like social climbing has to have happened in order for him to have seen enough of the world so as to judge whether it is indeed a ladder or a squirrel cage or something else entirely.

Moreover, these ambitiously comprehensive opinions are imbued with a palpable nostalgia for the era when gentility had not yet disappeared. In what he reveals of his values, Masterman aligns himself with the real gentility that has been lost: "there's no place or level of honor or fine living left in the world, so what's the good of climbing?" (208). Once upon a time, he implies, there *was* a place or level of honor, there was such a thing as "fine living," and it was done by "nobles." At that time these values were authentic and deserving of respect, and thus social climbing made sense. As it still would, one has to infer, if only these gen-teel values had not been kidnapped and perverted by the newly moneyed classes. The one who knows this is the one who carries those values forward into the present. In other words, the torch of authentic gentility has passed from the people at the top of the ladder to the educated person without (much) money. If the rise of uneducated people with money seems a perversion—Kipps himself would seem to furnish a convenient model—there is no suggestion that Masterman would strenuously object to the upward mobility that has produced people like himself. His story cries out for that alternative resolution.

Masterman's self-flattering decline narrative should sound familiar to academic readers, for it reproduces a founding myth of literary criticism in the academy. It explains both to the general public and to upwardly mobile academics themselves why society benefits from offering them a discipline to inhabit, along with its new career opportunities. Like *The Waste Land* as read by F. R. Leavis and his friends, the sad conviction that "the world is out of joint" becomes a source of pleasing self-legitima-tion to those who can claim to know through literature that once upon a time the world was not yet out of joint, and who thus can sell the memo-ries they have preserved (in other words, knowledge of the canon) to a society now convinced of how much it has lost.[5] In other words, the case *against* social climbing that Masterman makes to Kipps disguises a case *for* the social ascent of critics like Masterman himself, or like those later intellectuals and academics whose monastic self-image of dead-to-the-world disinterestedness gives collective institutional form to Masterman's debilitated asceticism.[6]

In effect, literary criticism has identified with the figure of the aristo-cratic rentier, and this identification has served its ambitions relatively well. For whatever reason, there has been little attention to this identifica-tory logic within literary criticism. I think it is safe to say that novels are wiser about it than critics, whether inside or outside the fictional frame. Neither the logic by which mobility is attained nor even the fact that it *is* attained appears to register in Masterman's consciousness. Denial that one occupies any place on a social ladder, or that such a thing as a social ladder exists, is of course not restricted to the guild of intellectuals and writers. But the writerly version of this general ideological formation is pervasive. Masterman insists that he has climbed out, not up, and his prototype Gissing often has his heroes declare that they are social aliens, at home nowhere. The protagonist of *Born in Exile* (1892) believes he is an exile both from his own former class and from the class system in general: "I myself belong to no class whatever" (296).[7] As *Kipps* suggests, however, the novel tends not to accept statements like this at face value. For better or worse, the genre's commitment to densely textured social determinations leads it to flesh out the ways in which such characters are ineluctably determined by the social locations they claim to have escaped. Even a novelist who believes that one can belong to "no class whatever" is likely to be betrayed into presenting the character who affirms this as self-deluded and unintentionally comic. Self-betrayal like this is one of the virtues of the upward mobility story.

Consider for example an autobiographical first novel, roughly contem-porary with *Kipps*, by the young Australian novelist Miles Franklin.[8] The teenage heroine of *My Brilliant Career* (1901), raised "up country" in a family beset by drought and squalid privation, wants only to be permitted to read and write, for in books she finds "the unspeakable comfort and heart-rest of congenial companionship" (61) that her actual companions cannot provide. She accepts a marriage proposal from a wealthy suitor only after he loses everything, telling him, " 'Do you think I am that sort, that cares for a person only because he has a little money? Why! that is the very sort of thing I am always preaching against' " (173). The truth is that she knows she cannot attain "the dream-life with writers, artists, and musicians" (21) she longs for without moving away from a life ruled by necessity. In order to live among the educated, she must move up the social ladder: "I was always desirous of enjoying the company of society people who were well bred and lived according to etiquette, and possessed of leisure and culture sufficient to fill their minds with something more than the price of farm produce and a hard struggle for existence" (74). If other people will perhaps value these same amenities for other, less disinterested reasons, that is their affair. This is the same irony that Wells applies to his would-be superman in a neatly balanced sentence: " 'I don't

climb,' said Masterman, and accepted Kipps's silent offer of another ciga-
rette" (206). One must not appear to be arranging to have cigarettes provided, yet it is convenient that a listener who possesses both an inquiring
mind and a sizable inheritance is there to provide them.

Cultural history has a well-known name for this partial disavowal of
social situation and social ambition, a simultaneous impulse to veil the
mystery of how artists and writers manage to get themselves provided for
and to offer that mystery as a tourist attraction. Since the early nineteenth
century, the mysterious location of art on the social scale or in the social
landscape—the choice of metaphor cannot be innocent—has been assigned the floating place-name of bohemia. An urban underworld, a miraculously self-sustaining countercultural neighborhood, both glamorous
and impoverished, where avant-garde art is produced and the usual social
rules are suspended, bohemia has often been described as a myth.[9] If so,
it is a myth that since the nineteenth century has been useful both to artists
and to bourgeois society. It has been useful to artists because it permitted
them to believe they could sustain themselves without compromising
themselves. And it has been useful to bourgeois society because the bohemian artist preserved the ideal of the autonomous, self-reliant individual,
performing a particular kind of unalienated labor that makes the matching of merit with reward seem just and proper, if always in jeopardy—a
view of labor increasingly difficult to see embodied elsewhere in the capitalist economy. This double usefulness helps explain the little-noticed fact
that, from Balzac's *Lost Illusions* and Flaubert's *Sentimental Education*
to Hanif Kureishi's *The Buddha of Suburbia* and Jamaica Kincaid's *Lucy*,
the protagonists of upward mobility stories so often pass through a bohemian setting, sometimes spending a significant portion of their time in it,
and sometimes paying a price for being denied access to it. By translating
upward mobility into the unique, category-breaking language of art, it
was possible to sustain the apparent paradox of rising *without* rising, of
success that would somehow evade both dependence on the ruling order
and the ethical self-betrayal associated with such dependence.

According to Pierre Bourdieu, bohemia is the place where commercial
failure signifies artistic success and commercial success signifies artistic
failure. Like a latter-day Masterman, Bourdieu asserts confidently that
art and thought can be true to themselves—that is, to their oppositional
role. But they can do so only by failing to be recognized by a society
whose values are conventional and mercenary. And again like Masterman, Bourdieu fails to tell us what many of us novel readers most
want to know: how the residents of bohemia in fact keep body and soul
together. That's why, like Wells's era of genuine gentility, bohemia's
"golden age of authenticity . . . untainted by commercialism and tour-
ists" (9) is always seen as already gone or at the point of disappearing.

And it is why Bourdieu must offhandedly concede that bohemia's secret, the only way in which the paradox can be sustained, is the artist's offstage possession of an independent income. "The artist cannot triumph on the symbolic terrain except by losing on the economic terrain (at least in the short run)," Bourdieu writes, "and vice versa (at least in the long run). It is this paradoxical economy that gives inherited economic properties all their weight—also in a very paradoxical manner—and in particular a private income, the condition of survival in the absence of a market. . . . As in *Sentimental Education*, 'inheritors' hold a decisive advantage when it comes to pure art: inherited economic capital, which removes the constraints and demands of immediate needs (those of journalism, for example, which overcame a Théophile Gautier) and makes it possible to 'hold on' in the absence of a market, is one of the most important factors in the differential success of avant-garde enterprises, with their doomed or else very long-term investments" (83–84).[10] If even the bohemian is dependent on unearned income, then pace Bourdieu, there can be no such thing as "pure" art. But if there is no such thing as pure art, then there is also reason to doubt the other side of the opposition, the *im*purity that Bourdieu discerns in all accomplishments on "the economic terrain," which for him can only be described as "artistic failure" or selling out. In short, there is a logic behind the novel's toned-down version of bohemia: a more or less modest, more or less realistic version of the bohemian hypothesis that rising in the world and refusing the laws of the world might be somehow compatible.[11]

One of the few novels Miles Franklin mentions by name is George Du Maurier's *Trilby* (1894), which contributed enormously to the already popular image of the artistic life of Paris's bohemia, the Quartier Latin.[12] At the ostensible center of *Trilby* is the unconsummated love between Little Billee, one of three British artists sharing a Parisian loft, and Trilby, an enchanting and impoverished English girl who delivers milk, chatters away in French slang, poses for painters in the nude, and lives in gay bohemian innocence without the benefits of respectability. When she comes to the attention of the Englishman's highly respectable family, they suspect her of scheming to catch a rich husband and arrive in Paris to head off the *mésalliance*. Trilby nobly renounces all claims and disappears without a word. Five years later, however, she reappears. She who could not sing a note is now the greatest singer in Europe thanks to her musical mentor Svengali, the talented but sinister Jew who once lived in the same bohemian poverty but now rides the wave of her, or rather their, artistic accomplishment.

This artistic upward mobility story is easily missed, distracted as the reader is by the picturesque delights of bohemian love and by a tour guide voice that is solidly and complacently aligned with the three respectable

Britons. They have no need of upward mobility. They are slumming in Paris, absenting themselves for a time from gentility. Once they have returned to England and their habitual levels of comfort—"well groomed, frock-coated, shirt-collared within an inch of their lives" (175)—they will look back on bohemia as a stage of life whose loss, though painful, was no less inevitable than the passage from youth to maturity. In spite of them, however, and almost in spite of itself, the novel obliges us to imagine bohemia as something that persists and indeed follows after them. In so doing, the novel gives to social relations not just an alternative style but an alternative content. This is accomplished by the provocatively shared trajectory of Trilby and Svengali.

The revulsion the three friends come to feel for their fellow bohemian Svengali when he shows up in London expresses more than respectable anti-Semitism. It also includes the establishment's disgust for the Uriah Heep–like figure of the parvenu, here consolidated into one of literary history's most sinister and memorable benefactors. Svengali lacks the gentlemanly dignity of the British artists precisely because he is a true bohemian. Acting out bohemia's two-faced relation to the bourgeois world, Svengali fawns (for he is weaker than society) but he also mocks (for he is also stronger than society). He possesses neither inherited status nor money, but he does possess talent. His place in the history of the benefactor that leads toward criminal therapists like Hannibal Lecter is defined by the fact that, according to his narrative, talent can be transmitted, producing in turn both money and status. It is talent in the domain of art, detached from his own racially stigmatized body and relocated by means of mesmerism in his surrogate, that makes possible the conjoined social rise, or makes it possible as something more than a simple abomination. Socially speaking, his ability to detach himself from his unpresentable body via mesmerism *is* his talent, just as ventriloquism, which accomplishes much the same thing, is the talent of his more hideous analogue, the Phantom of the Opera (1910).[13] In both cases, the musical gift itself seems secondary. It can only be reported secondhand, whereas what the reader sees and feels most intensely is the invisible mentor's power over the very visible singer. The abhorrent mentor's art of self-separation and reembodiment in a beautiful surrogate turns the couple into a tableau of upward mobility's full before-and-after.

The pairing of Trilby and Svengali strikes the British artists as incomprehensible. But if Trilby is not the designing villain of a classic female upward mobility plot, as she appears to Little Billee's family, she does bring along with her a social disturbance that transcends her own personal innocence. By acting as Svengali's stand-in, Trilby forces a general acceptance and even celebration of his rudely upthrusting ambition, and does so in spite of everything else society feels about him. And though she pays a high price for her surrogacy—via mesmerism she is merged into her male counterpart with almost supernatural thoroughness, more so than she would have been in a conventional marriage—she is strangely unable to let anyone forget the blow she has struck against society. She cannot let them forget the countersociety she and Svengali together embody. Even after Svengali's cruelty has been exposed to her friends and Trilby is on the point of death, the fact that Svengali and not Little Billee has carried her off vibrates with a truth that cannot, it seems, be taken back. It is Svengali's name that Trilby murmurs as she dies. "[T]hat ruffian's name on her lips!" (264), Little Billee exclaims, expressing the intensity of the author's own apparent sense of irreparable violation.[14]

Thus the mention of *Trilby* in *My Brilliant Career* is unexpectedly pertinent. For though that novel never passes through any actual bohemia, its resolution offers a bohemian twist. The heroine suddenly refuses to wed the same highly desirable man, his wealth now restored by a timely inheritance. She announces instead that she has chosen a life of writing. However abrupt and awkward, this decision to become a writer rather than to marry can be said to work, narratively speaking, and the reason is that here, as in *Trilby*, art becomes a figure for a social relation. *My Brilliant Career* turns success as a writer into a defiant identification with the lives of Australia's ordinary working people and the task (both literary and political) of representing those lives. Writing is work because it is about those who work: "I am proud that I am an Australian, a daughter of the Southern Cross, a child of the mighty bush. I am thankful I am a peasant, a part of the bone and muscle of my nation, and earn my bread by the sweat of my brow, as man was meant to do. I rejoice I was not born a parasite, one of the blood-suckers who loll on velvet and satin, crushed from the proceeds of human sweat and blood and souls" (257).

The implicit term of contrast is the proposed marriage, though the narrator seems to forget that her suitor cannot be accurately described as a lolling blood-sucker. More important and more surprising, however, is the implicit continuity with her own childhood, which she had once seemed so eager to leave behind. In the beginning, writing seemed to acquire its value by effecting a total separation from the heroine's laborious childhood. Now on the contrary it is presented as reaching back to include that childhood, indeed as an ideal synthesis between the contradictory values of labor and leisure, of her (lower) social origin and her (higher) social destination. What she wants out of writing (something writing is not guaranteed to provide) is an answer to the implied charge that success will mean self-betrayal: a plausible means of remaining loyal to her society of origin while also leaving it.

There are no such visions at the end of Wells's *Kipps*, yet the conclusion again differs slightly and interestingly from a mere renunciation of upward mobility. Kipps ends the novel as the proprietor of a bookshop. In so doing, he fulfills a dream that has been slowly nurtured by his acquaintance with Masterman. This cultural self-employment is made financially possible because, as I said, Kipps does not lose all of the money he has inherited. We discover well after the fact that in his brief period of prosperity he had given money to one Chitterlow, an aspiring playwright who had knocked him down with his bicycle while he was still poor and then befriended him. The gift was presented under the fiction of investing in a quarter share of the latter's as yet unproduced play. Chitterlow's character is almost inconceivable without the category of bohemia. He both does and does not belong to the society into which Kipps is ascending. He is an educated man, but it is clear that when Kipps attains full and fearsome gentility, Chitterlow will be discovered to be unpresentable. When he "loom[s] up" suddenly in Kipps's "new world" (166) and is explained as "a Nacter chap" who "writes plays" (167), the genteel fiancée quickly insinuates that he does not "compel her complete confidence" (168). Once again, the bohemian is at the margins of social respectability. And once again, he is also somehow a source of funds. Kipps was completely disinterested when he invested in Chitterlow's play. Yet in a variant of the last-minute inheritance motif, the long-forgotten play turns out in the end to be an enormous success, and the philanthropic pseudoinvestment, which Chitterlow respects as real, turns out to be a gold mine. The only part of his inheritance that Kipps retains is the part that he had freely given away, and given away in the interest of art.[15]

"I Don't think I should be unhappy in the workhouse": George Gissing, Perry Anderson, and the Unproductive Classes

If the happy ending of Wells's *Kipps* arrives by way of bohemia, the reverse is true of Gissing's *Born in Exile* (1892).[16] The novel has no access to bohemia, and this deficit is presented at least semiseriously as the reason why the protagonist's hopes of upward mobility are thwarted. Godwin Peak claims that only genteel women, who look down on him and his unconventional beliefs, are sexual. Women who share his skepticism are not: "The truly emancipated woman . . . is almost always asexual" (202). The ideal synthesis of sexuality and emancipation is explicitly associated with bohemia, but he denies that any such thing exists: " 'An ideal!' exclaimed Peak. 'An ideal akin to Murger's and Musset's grisettes, who never existed' " (114). His eventual benefactor, Marcella, feels the same disappointment when she seeks out an author who sounds like a kindred spirit but is discovered to be not a free-thinking salonnière but a proper lady in her parlor (237). What matters here is less the actual crowding out of bohemian options by English stuffiness—verifiable existence has never been bohemia's key virtue, even on the Continent—but rather that even the *idea* of it doesn't excite Gissing's protagonist. Peak finds no emancipated women who are sexual not because there are none, but because the women he *does* sexualize are their opposites: ladies of great respectability who are firmly fixed high in the social hierarchy. He has invested his desire in that code of gentility in terms of which he himself does not and cannot measure up. If Peak's erotic object choices can come only from the society far above him (in interesting contrast to the choices of his author), then he is neither going to enter that society nor, like Kipps, find happiness somewhere below it.[17]

One context that might be usefully applied both to this blockage of upward mobility and to the upward mobility story in general is Perry Anderson's notion of a "symbiosis" (22) between new bourgeoisie and old aristocracy.[18] In an essay called "Origins of the Present Crisis," written in 1964, Anderson offered what he called a "crude schema" of modern British history in order to explain why the then Labour government had proven so ineffectual. Instead of a proper domestic evolution in which politics, economics, and culture were organically fused, Anderson suggested, Britain had experienced an off-center development characterized by the lingering political and cultural influence of the landed aristocracy, which an all-too-deferential bourgeoisie has preferred to merge with rather than supplant, and a passive, quiescent working class that chose defense of its cultural identity rather than revolutionary change. Britain's supposedly industrial economy in fact depended on the exploitation of its colonies, and then in the mid-twentieth century shifted its capital out of domestic industry and into the sector of international finance. This massive outflow of capital into the City of London abandoned most of the country to deindustrialization and left the Labour government at the mercy of international investors, hence unable to realize its political program. Political blockage also entailed cultural blockage. According to Anderson, the English aristocracy continues to wield a disproportionate amount of cultural influence long after a supposedly triumphant bourgeoisie was to have generalized the middle-class values of Weber's Protestant Ethic. An ideal that "was naturally secreted by a leisured landowning elite" (24) was extended, with the help of imperialism, to the national culture in general. And even, Anderson insists, to the working class. "If the mythologies of rank captivated the middle class, producing a notorious social-climbing and craving for titles, they also powerfully mystified real social relations for the working class as well" (30–31).

Social climbing there was, but divorced from the sort of principles that might make its adventures worth serious attention—such principles as might be expected in particular from working-class protagonists. Given their different historical experience, such protagonists would not be presumed to embody an identical middle-class ideal of hardworking self-reliance. But neither would anyone anticipate that, like the protagonist of *Born in Exile*, they would continue sexualizing the genteel world of the leisured, a world supported by independent income emanating from undeclared sources, so long into the period of realism. Who would have imagined that Wells, whose hero does escape from sexual enthrallment to his superiors, would rewrite Dickens from a perspective that is more patronizing toward his protagonist (that "dismal little figure") than Dickens had been to Pip forty years earlier?

Anderson was inspired by Arno Mayer's *The Persistence of the Old Regime* (1981), which deals with Europe in general. But he suggests that there is something exceptionally English about the persistence of aristocratic cultural hegemony.[19] In the larger landscape of world literature, however, the stubborn cultural power of a seemingly outmoded aristocracy makes the English case less exceptional. Even a quick survey of other national traditions reveals that much of the novel's treatment of upward mobility continues to come from the perspective of the aristocracy, if often a declining aristocracy. The Older Men of Gothic romance are not restricted to any one national literature. Gaston Leroux's *Phantom of the Opera* is a French version of the top-down artistic Cinderella story, inviting comparison with *Trilby* and *Pygmalion*. The great Italian realist Giovanni Verga, whose *Mastro don Gesualdo* (1888) was translated by D. H. Lawrence, features a protagonist who "started as a navvy, with stones on his shoulder," yet as a character correctly prophesies, "in a very little while you'll be able to say that Mastro don Gesualdo is the boss of the place!" (42). How is this ascent seen? "Nowadays there's no respect for anybody. Nowadays it's whoever has got the money is in the right. [. . .] Today there's no other God. You can be a gentleman—or a girl born of a good family! But if you've got no fortune!—Whereas one who has sprung from nothing—like Mastro don Gesualdo, for example—!" (24).[20] Though Verga is not uncritical of the people of "good family" who make statements like this, and though he might insinuate that by its bad behavior the falling nobility has forfeited its right to judge, there is no class perspective in the novel to which he is closer.

Writing in Hungary in 1942, Sándor Márai centers his novel *Embers* in an aristocrat's view of his best friend's upward mobility. The friend, Konrad, has disappeared mysteriously. The disappearance comes after a hunting incident in which the aristocrat, Henrik, thinks that Konrad has wanted and perhaps even planned to kill him. Later he visits Konrad's apartment and decides that this is because Konrad has been having an affair with his, Henrik's, wife.[21] If there is an erotic entanglement between friend and wife, as seems likely, is it the work of Eros or ambition? Nothing other than ambition is allowed onstage to explain it. The one active ingredient in the men's friendship, the only instability pointing toward a possible passage from absolute loyalty to suspicions of attempted murder, is the much-stressed fact that, though both are from well-born families, Konrad is poor and Henrik rich. But this action-oriented and even melodramatic account gives precisely the wrong idea of the novel. The friendship between Konrad and Henrik is presented largely in retrospect, and from Henrik's point of view. At the time of the retrospective narration, forty-one years after the action takes place, both men are seventy-five years old, and Konrad too has acquired—via inheritance, then years of work in Southeast Asian colonies—all the material possessions he requires. There is an upward mobility story here, indeed one that is central to the plot. But this story is almost totally concealed by the facts of Konrad's high ancestry and by the narrative viewpoint of Henrik, who is born with everything a human being could desire and thus has no need to rise. Upward mobility disappears into their shared old age and into the articulation of a matching philosophy: an old man's philosophy of disinterestedness or generosity so profound as to become almost indifference, indeed almost deathlike. It's as if the novel equated an Old World aristocrat's wisdom with an old man's wisdom: the passive wisdom of the futility of striving, coupled with active contempt for a new world in which material striving has become all-pervasive. Extraneous to the plot but central to the exposition of this philosophy is the figure of Henrik's ninety-one-year-old servant, Nini. Nini embodies a happy, self-forgetful subservience. She lives, indeed has always lived since she arrived at the age of sixteen, only in order to offer perfect service to her employer. Omniscient, she is also perpetually unmoved, thus echoing Henrik's willingness to pardon and even find value in Konrad's passion from a position of utter withdrawal from all passions, including the passion for revenge.

Writing her *Rahel Varnhagen: The Life of a Jewess* in roughly the same period, Hannah Arendt used the word *parvenu* to sum up Rahel's eager efforts to assimilate into aristocratic German society, culminating in her baptism. Arendt prefers to describe herself as a pariah. Judith Shklar comments: "The choice of the word parvenu to describe this humiliating behavior is not insignificant. It is *the* classic snob word, which is thrown at the *bourgeois gentilhomme* by the aristocrats whom he tries to join, and at the 'new rich' by those who have inherited their money. The parvenu is a universal figure of ridicule and contempt. That she should have used this word for assimilated Jews tells us a good deal about Arendt. The pariah is so sure of her superiority that she no longer wishes to make efforts to join the larger society. She has, in fact, absorbed the attitudes of its upper class so completely that there is no impulse for her to rise from her actual condition" (363).[22]

To put these three texts side by side is to feel the power that an aristocratic perspective continues to exert upon various national traditions well into the twentieth century. And to add Arendt to the other two is to feel how strongly this force works in particular upon those who, like Gissing, are specifically *literary* pariahs, falling into the ideological orbit of the so-called parasitic or unproductive classes while and because they are becoming writers and intellectuals. The viewpoint of the aristocracy rhymes handily with the viewpoint of literature itself. This is precisely the transfer we observe in Wells's Masterman: the writer or intellectual identifying himself with the declining gentry or aristocracy (intimations of mortality included) at the expense of the new money, which is to say at the expense of those with whom his own location among the aspiring have-nots would otherwise seem to ally him.[23]

Bohemian assertions of artistic independence will thus have something perversely in common with the philosophy of Miles Franklin's "parasites" and "blood-suckers." More interesting still, they will adapt that philosophy to a new set of social circumstances. Consider the description of Gertrude Stein by a young American friend: "She was a rentier, and possessed a rentier mentality in matters of taxes, jobs, and governments. . . . Without her fixed income we might never have heard of the rue de Fleurus, but with it we should not be surprised to find her disapproving of Roosevelt and the New Deal, believing in rugged individualism, favoring a gold basis for the dollar, regarding a man out of work as lazy or incompetent, thinking every American could take care of himself."[24] Recounting how the famously un-self-reliant rentier was assisted in renting her dream house in the south of France, Janet Malcolm quotes the words Stein put in the mouth of Alice B. Toklas about "the faculty of Gertrude Stein of having everybody do anything for her": "Gertrude Stein said that the others looked so efficient, of course nobody would do anything for them. Now as for herself she was not efficient, she was good humored, she was democratic, one person was as good as another, and she knew what she wanted done. If you are like that she says, anybody will do anything for you" (64).

This self-description echoes the self-conscious helplessness of *Bleak House*'s Harold Skimpole, an aesthete and amateur artist who identifies himself, and is in turn identified by his helpful friends, as a "child."

His good friend Jarndyce and some other of his good friends had helped him . . . to several openings in life; but to no purpose, for he must confess to two of the oldest infirmities in the world: one was, that he had no idea of time; the other, that he had no idea of money. In consequence of which he never kept an appointment, never could transact any business, and never knew the value of anything! . . . All he asked of society was, to let him live. *That* wasn't much. His wants were few. Give him the papers, conversation, music, mutton, coffee, landscape, fruit in the season, a few sheets of Bristol-board, and a little claret, and he asked for no more. He was a mere child in the world, but he didn't cry for the moon. (119)[25]

Like Stein, Skimpole speaks of himself "as if he were not at all his own affair, as if Skimpole were a third person" (120). And like Stein, Skimpole seems to see art as an adequate rationale for this self-dispossession, a proper alternative to the sordidness of possession in the crude everyday sense: "Possession is nothing to me. Here is my friend Jarndyce's excellent house. I am obliged to him for possessing it. I can sketch it, and alter it. I can set it to music" (120). Unlike Stein, however, Skimpole does not in fact possess an independent income. One wonders whether Dickens would judge him so harshly if he did.

Stein's demand that things be done for her, her refusal to act out the self-reliance she is so ready to force on those without trust funds, may strike the reader as equally insufferable. But if, as I suggested above, Dickens distracts us from moral judgment when he allows Skimpole to speak as an intriguingly impersonal voice of the Chancery-centered social system, then perhaps the same holds for Stein. Perhaps what is so odd about the stylistic echo between the two self-serving confessions of helplessness, in other words, is that Stein too sounds like a voice of the emergent social system—and precisely the system of "Roosevelt and the New Deal" of which she so sternly disapproves. Flaunting her inability to take care of herself and demanding that others assume that responsibility, she seems to be impersonating nothing so much as a welfare recipient, or what a welfare recipient looks like to an opponent of welfare.

Is this merely a perverse coincidence? Anderson, as I read him, suggests obliquely that it is not. His argument leaves open the possibility that the dominant culture's divergence from a middle-class ethic of productivity and independence, and the divergence of the ideal of literature along with it, does not after all happen fully or precisely by means of an identification with the old aristocracy. From the end of the nineteenth century on, the aristocratic ethos might also be described as a *financial* ethos—in other words, something that looks old but in fact corresponds to a new social alignment. In "The Figures of Descent" (1987), a reconsideration of his original theses formulated almost twenty-five years later, Anderson puts further emphasis on how, as the English industries that had sparked the Industrial Revolution stagnated, British hegemony came to be propped up by the Empire and finance capital. "Instead of organizational or technological renovation, British industry drew on the assets of empire, settling into an easy reliance on customary and (in the case of India) captive markets. This turn in the pattern of trade was accompanied by a surge of overseas investments" (149). Among the results were huge "rentier revenues" as well as huge profits for the City, which "cushioned the crisis of aristocratic incomes" (149). "Instead of a redressment of the position of British manufacturing, the end of the Belle Epoque . . . witnessed the apogee of rentier returns on overseas investment" (151). Summing up this rewrite of his thesis, Anderson says: "When agrarian property lost its weight it was not industry but finance which became the hegemonic form of capital, in a City socially and culturally in many ways closer to the wealth of the estates than of factories" (167–68). In the last decades of the nineteenth century and the first decades of the twentieth, the City looks closer to the world of landed property, at least "socially and culturally," than to the world of manufacturing. The new ethic of gentlemanly parasitism, largely based now on revenue from overseas investment rather than on revenue from land, shares the same aversion to the industrial ethic of self-reliance. In either case one can speak, with Miles Franklin, of parasites and bloodsuckers. But finance capital, which has concealed the enormity of the shift away from the old agrarian basis of aristocratic hegemony, is part of a social settlement that implies a different location for the working class. (As we saw above in examining Dreiser's *The Financier*, the world of finance capitalism can also be described as the world of welfare capitalism.) It also indicates an ambiguity in the aristocratic identification of the writer.

Recipients of welfare do not in fact tend to argue, like Skimpole and Stein, that they are irresponsible by nature, hence the system should take them in charge. (Their expressed opinions on this subject will come up in the next two chapters.) On the contrary, they tend to be eager to work and to feel frustrated that the system offers them no opportunity to earn a living by doing so. But for someone in this position, accepting the solicitude of the state would be perfectly logical. The same would have been true for Stein herself. Her writing was considered difficult and (at least until *The Autobiography of Alice B. Toklas*) didn't sell in appreciable quantities. The market did not give her the opportunity to earn a living by doing the work at which she was skilled. That is no doubt one reason among others why she took so well to the fate of being a rentier. In Gissing's *New Grub Street* (1891), this is also the case of Harold Biffen, the uncompromisingly realistic author of the unsalable novel *Mr. Bailey, Grocer*. And Biffen draws the appropriate conclusion. He might as well be supported by the state, for being supported by the state is "very much the same" as being supported by inherited income from investments: "I don't think I should be unhappy in the workhouse. I should have a certain satisfaction in the thought that I had forced society to support me. And then there's the absolute freedom from care! Why, it's very much the same as being a man of independent fortune!" (416).

Biffen and the protagonist Reardon, both of them authors who cannot expect an enthusiastic embrace from the current market, are of course trying to console themselves for their poverty. But this fanciful equivalence between possessing an independent fortune and seeking refuge in the workhouse is more than a piece of self-protective wit. It is also a serious way of renegotiating the fundamental dilemma of upward mobility. His horror of sexual vulgarity aside, Gissing often appears paralyzed by that dilemma. Rachel Bowlby writes: "There is nothing outside the rigid dichotomies of value and class entailed by the starting assumption that culture is incompatible with the new commerce and the mass society it caters to: no way out of the impasse which offers an impossible choice between 'practical' adaptation to profit-seeking vulgarity, and the noble resistance of starving, embittered authenticity" (117). Raymond Williams describes this impasse in similar terms: "The one fate is different from, but no better than, the other. The only way out is for the exceptional individual, but his fate is a scrambling and ambiguous mobility, in which more often than not he will either go under, after years of effort (Reardon or Biffen in *New Grub Street*), or prosper but deteriorate morally (Jasper Milvain in *New Grub Street*), since from the destructive general condition the only forms available, for a successful career, lead to an exploitation of labour or of the minds of others" "If one succeeds materially," as Christina Lupton and Tilman Reitz put it, "one fails morally."[26]

Biffen's imagining of workhouse happiness effects a slight shifting in the terms of the impasse. If writers have traditionally identified with rentiers, what is to stop them from now identifying with the beneficiaries of a not-quite-emergent welfare state—that is, abandoning privileged status in favor of a guaranteed minimal standard of survival? By the criterion of whether they produce anything of commercial value to society, men of independent fortune are no different from workhouse inmates; both force society to support them. Why shouldn't the "serious" or "difficult" writer who finds himself in the same situation take immediate advantage of the state (even in its most meager, deliberately ineligible offerings) rather than pining for the distant aristocracy?[27] It's not what is usually meant by "success." The amenities are less lavish. But both Reardon and Biffen are ascetic in their needs.

The crucial comfort that a private income would permit but that the workhouse would preclude is genteel female companionship. As if in anticipation of Wells's Masterman, Gissing allows this factor to be decisive. Reardon has chosen to marry, and to marry a woman from a good family. That, and not the difference in habits between inside and outside the workhouse, is why he knows he could not be happy inside one. "I have a horror of the workhouse. Remember the clock at Marylebone I used to tell you about" (416). As he lies in bed at night, the workhouse clock reminds him of the work he has not accomplished: "no sooner had the workhouse bell become silent than he began to toil in his weary imagination" (152). For all the rest he gets, or the comfort from his wife's presence at his side, it's as if he were *already* in the workhouse. But inside he would have no hope left of winning back Amy's affections. Biffen, on the other hand, is described as indifferent to women and marriage, for most of the novel at least.[28] And this brings him closer, if not quite close enough, to what might be called a state-centered solution to the dilemma of the artist and the market.

Biffen actually makes a living, if not a very good one, training ambitious young men for examinations that will enable them to take jobs in the civil service. Like Henry Higgins in Shaw's *Pygmalion* (1914), who teaches proper pronunciation to social climbers, he too serves the desire for upward mobility, though at a lower level of remuneration.[29] He makes his living off the state, and can do so precisely because the state has now, via the still recent civil service exams, become an avenue of upward mobility. He is not himself upwardly mobile, but neither does he starve. And he has the leisure to write. It is something less than success, yet an eligible option. There is a strong suggestion that Reardon too could be saved in this way, or to this limited extent, if only he could free himself from Amy and what she represents. Had it not been unacceptable to Amy for reasons of status, his job as a clerk in a hospital, which Reardon in his decline is happy to have back, could have satisfied his basic needs while providing him ample time to write. Here public or semipublic institutions perform much the same unofficial function that the welfare state would eventually make official. They provide a social sufficiency; they do not facilitate rising, but they prevent too drastic a fall. In 1897, six years after *New Grub Street* was published, Beatrice and Sidney Webb introduced their "national minimum" scheme, which "wanted the government to provide a floor of services, a national minimum standard beneath which no one would be allowed to sink in the areas of work, housing, health, and education."[30]

Gissing will not quite go in this direction, but he at least indicates its existence by means of the novel's most state-oriented figure of the writer, Marian Yule. Marian is insistently associated with her workplace, the British Museum Reading Room. She doesn't like the Reading Room; she works too long and hard in it, for too little reward, and at the expense of all sentimental satisfactions. Yet all this cannot conceal the deep logic of her presence there. Her real or potential independence as a working woman is made possible by the existence of a publicly supported institution. In this sense, as in its attention to Biffen's job and to the playful parallel with the workhouse, the novel offers, somewhere in the semi-utopian distance, the solution of state funding for the arts, which would allow survival, respectability, some degree of independence from the market. It is not quite the kind of comfort Milvain enters into by his marriage to Amy, but it is a chastened, scaled-down substitute for an "independent income."[31]

"You're a Town Hall wallah, aren't you?": *Pygmalion* and *Room At the Top*

Thanks to its musical sequel *My Fair Lady*, Shaw's *Pygmalion* is probably one of the twentieth century's most famous narratives of upward mobility. Not quite as well known, but hardly a secret either, is the role Shaw played, along with his friends and fellow Fabians Sidney and Beatrice Webb, in formulating the principles of what was to become the welfare state. It is puzzling, therefore, that readers are not more in the habit of combining these two pieces of information and thus treating the argument of the present book as a commonplace: that is, considering the upward mobility story against the backdrop of the welfare state.

Like *The Silence of the Lambs*, *Pygmalion* might be described as a Cinderella story that ends without the expected marriage. Eliza's father is married, but Eliza herself is not. Since the play first appeared, readers and audiences have demanded to know why the happy ending announced in advance by the title, the amorous joining of the mentor/benefactor and the flower girl whose upward mobility he has made possible, is withheld. The quick answer is Mrs. Higgins, Henry Higgins's mother.[32] Higgins is reminded—and reminded *by* his mother—that he never falls in love with "anyone under forty-five" (70). He replies: "My idea of a lovable woman is somebody as like you as possible" (70). In his concluding remarks to the play, Shaw explains: "If an imaginative boy has a sufficiently rich mother who has intelligence, personal grace, dignity of character without harshness, and a cultivated sense of the best art of her time to enable her to make her house beautiful, she sets a standard for him against which very few young women can struggle, besides effecting for him a disengagement of his affections, his sense of beauty, and his idealism from his specifically sexual impulses" (141–42).

In terms of her wit and other graces, Eliza Dolittle would seem to meet Mrs. Higgins's standard quite nicely. If Higgins doesn't love her as Pygmalion loved Galatea, it is perhaps because of what he calls "the coldness of my sort of life" (136)—an emotional temperature reading that has scrolled across our screens before. Mentors, like mothers, often encourage "the disengagement of . . . affections" and "idealism" from "specifically sexual impulses." Some such disengagement has accompanied and re-channeled upwardly mobile desires since the chilly idyll of Rousseau and Madame de Warens.[33] There is reason to suspect that something similar is happening here. Another important clue is the phrase "sufficiently rich." With so much else going for them, why do mothers need this added embellishment? The seemingly needless qualification suggests that, like Gissing, Shaw has given his hero something less avowable than filial devotion: not just a love of the mother, the older woman, or the genteel woman, but a love of the genteel woman *who has an independent income*.

Higgins makes his own living, he says, by exploiting the fact that "[t]his is an age of upstarts. Men begin in Kentish Town with £80 a year, and they end in Park Lane with a hundred thousand. They want to drop Kentish Town; but they give themselves away every time they open their mouths" (26). But his cavalier attitude toward money and the feelings of others does not reflect this material reliance on selling his services to upstarts. On the contrary, it makes him sound like someone who doesn't need to earn a living at all, as if phonetics were nothing more than what he suggestively and repeatedly calls it, his "hobby" (27). He makes a show of having an independent income—enough of a show so that one can doubt it. And his mother, with whom he declares himself in love, seems to represent that income. Eliza, despite all her other attributes, cannot compete. For the play gives Eliza "the manners and habits that disqualify a fine lady from earning her own living without giving her a fine lady's income!" (87). That is, it comes strangely close to making her a feminized figure for Shaw himself, a self-made man who often despised what he had to do to earn his living, for example writing the "pot-boiler" *Pygmalion*.[34]

Here, as in Gissing, upward mobility appears blocked by the text's furtive but unmistakable commitment to "inherited economic capital." Both texts thus offer evidence in favor of Anderson's revisionist narrative, a story of upward mobility forestalled by aristocratic identification. *The Making of the English Working Class*, E. P. Thompson's classic history, suggests that the English working class can be considered the protagonist of an upward mobility story. And not merely *an* upward mobility story, but *the* upward mobility story: the rising meta-narrative around which the history of English society as a whole will naturally organize itself and from which all of society's subsidiary narratives, including literary ones, will henceforth derive their proper importance and meaning. But Thompson, writing in 1963, notoriously stopped short before he had to evaluate what exactly the working class, once made, went on to *do*—which was clearly something less than the predicted overthrow and wholesale transformation of existing society. Anderson's retelling of the story, which carried the working class's autobiography into the mid- and then late-twentieth century, underlined the blurriness and disappointment of its provisional endpoint. For Anderson, making use of a Gramscian concept, the working class had gone on to become a "corporate" class, incorporated into existing capitalist society.

Strangely, Anderson also uses the vocabulary of upward mobility. And for him—this too is strange—the problem is that like the middle class before it, the working class has failed to be self-reliant. It has subsided into political inertia, and this is because it too has imitated the aristocracy, though at second hand. Imprisoning itself in tradition, it has taken on the character type proper to an economic order defined by inheritance. The point is emphasized by Anderson's metaphors. After World War I, the death of the Liberal Party as a major force meant that "Labour *inherited* the space left by Liberalism, without ever having to engage in a direct contest with it" (52—my italics). The same verb comes back in Anderson's account of what happened after World War II. "Labor in 1945 *inherited* a popular radicalization it had done little directly to stimulate" (54).[35] It may have nothing to lose but its chains, but Labor behaves with the passivity of an heir. It is this legatee-like passivity that is written into Keynesianism and the founding of the welfare state (really two versions of the same thing), which together define the unimpressive level of political development the working class has now reached. "The twin foundations of the post-war settlement—counter-cyclical demand management and a welfare state—were . . . laid independently of Labor, in a civil service-initiated consensus" (53–54). Change came to the working class "not as the fruit of conscious purpose or collective struggle, but as a historical windfall. The Party was initiated into power without having to mobilize for it; and it acquired a program without having to originate the ideas behind it" (54). Like the paradigm of the middle-class *bildungsroman*, this reduces the party of the working class to the grand anticlimax of integration into the status quo—in Anderson's words, "bettering the condition of the working-class within a social order taken as given and an imperial heritage it strove to preserve" (58). Again as in the *bildungsroman*, the efforts of the working class to better its condition involve the achievement of working-class identity—the sort of distinctive identity that the middle class, by its persistent identification with the values of the aristocracy, had forfeited. In "Origins," Anderson sums up his argument: "the bourgeoisie won two modest victories, lost its nerve and ended by losing its identity." Meanwhile the working class, after successive defeats, "evolved, separate but subordinate, within the apparently unshakeable structure of British capitalism" (29–30). The achievement of class identity coincides with and results from political failure. The "most important single fact about the English working class," Anderson writes, is "the disjunction between an intense consciousness of separate identity and a continuous failure to set and impose goals for society as a whole" (33).

The obstacle to the spread of socialism has "not been lack of class consciousness but—in one sense—excess of it" (33). By the working class's conscious pursuit of a unique "way of life" and embrace of a "separate moral universe" (33), it has made itself into a mere interest group. I will say more in the next chapter about Richard Hoggart, whom Anderson takes here as an example.

Responding to this critique, E. P. Thompson joined with other commentators in questioning Anderson's right to judge the trajectory of the British working class by comparison with supposedly more militant labor movements in other countries, the most successful of which have arguably done no better in the long run than create versions of the welfare state that are now, like Britain's, diminished and endangered.[36] Equally important, Thompson suggested that the self-transcendence Anderson associates with revolution is also visible in the welfare state, in whose institutions the working class both expressed itself and, within limits, successfully generalized its goals to the rest of society. Respect must be paid, Thompson insists, to the working class's "long struggle to attain humane welfare services" (84). Anderson's grudging appraisal of the welfare state underestimates the pressure from below that was necessary to bring it into existence as well as the real effects, including concessions in power and resources, that this entailed for large numbers of people. "The abolition of factory labor for children under the age of 11, or the institution of divorce, or the penny-post, may affect the power-model [that is, revolution] scarcely at all; but for those who were then living these may have affected them inexpressibly or quite perceptibly" (86–87). Thompson cannot see "social reforms" merely "as distractions from 'hegemonic' aspirations." For "any mature view of history (or of contemporary actuality) must in some way combine evaluations of both kinds" (87)—in other words, both ultimate goals and immediate changes in "the quality of life," in particular those provisionally enforced by the state.[37]

I will not attempt to render further judgment on this controversy, which remains much too vital and troublesome—especially in its attention to the domain of the international, taken up below—for me to want to see it closed down. Instead, let me note that the supplement Thompson here adds to his narrative of working-class history, under Anderson's provocation, has the nonpartisan virtue of recontextualizing Anderson's initial insight. Anderson had attributed the working class's political abdication, the source of its paradoxically confident sense of identity, to the cultural hegemony of the leisure class. Rather than abdication of the struggle, Thompson sees a moderate but appreciable political success, and he locates that success, along with working-class identity itself, in the welfare state. To this I add that the welfare state could come into existence only once there had been an undermining of the work ethic and the elaboration of what might be described, positively and polemically, as a new ideology of leisure. If Thompson must concede that the welfare state is a mixed entity, part failure as well as part success, then Anderson might be asked in turn to concede not just the partial success, but also the role in that success of the leisure class and its cultural influence. Anderson's own persistent if unavowed loyalty to an aristocratic or rentier view from above provides another motive, if further motives were needed, for investigating its hidden and seemingly perverse role in the formation of the British left and thus also in the left's single largest historical monument thus far, the welfare state.

One version of this hypothetical overlap between rentier and welfare state mentalities can be glimpsed in *Pygmalion*. As we have seen, the play offers striking evidence of the middle class's aristocratic identification. But *Pygmalion* offers equally striking evidence of an "excess" of working-class identity. The allegorically named Alfred Dolittle, champion of what he calls "the undeserving poor," represents the working class as happy to be exactly what it is, give or take a little extra money for liquor. Indifferent to middle-class values, he helps Shaw explode the middle-class belief that all those below it on the social ladder must inevitably yearn to climb in its direction. When Dolittle offers in effect to sell his daughter to Higgins for five pounds, Higgins asks, "Have you no morals, man?" The answer suggests, with memorable concision, that morals are relative to social location: "Cant afford them, Governor. Neither could you if you was as poor as me" (59). Yet on reflection, Dolittle himself seems an exception to this very plausible rule. For like Higgins, he speaks as if he *could* afford them. At the end of the play he will receive an inheritance, and when he does it's a reminder that from the beginning he acts as if (like the working class in Anderson's narrative) he had already received or at any rate always expected one.[38]

Where does his sense of entitlement come from? It comes, I would propose, from Shaw's explicit commitment to what would become the welfare state—and from that less conscious part of Shaw's commitment that feeds on his identification with "inherited economic capital." Welfare issues are clearly on Shaw's mind here. The reception of Dolittle's "undeserving" character has clearly been prepared by contemporary debates about how and how much to provide for the poor. In asking for his handout, Dolittle refers to oft-repeated fears: "Dont you be afraid that Ill save it and spare it and live idle on it. There wont be a penny of it left by Monday: Ill have to go to work the same as if I'd never had it. It wont pauperize me, you bet. Just one good spree for myself and the missus, giving pleasure to ourselves and employment to others, and satisfaction to you to think its not been throwd away. You couldnt spend it better" (60). Like a Cockney version of Higgins, Dolittle manages to outrage "middle-class morality"—he declares openly that he wants the money for drink—even while he also placates that morality. The result of this act of charity, he says, will not be idleness, but a return to the status quo of hard work. Much the same could be said of the welfare state itself. Its social engineering aims to relieve the hardships of daily life, sweetening rather than abolishing or transforming them. It too requires a refusal of the "middle-class morality" of individual self-reliance. Though he does not speak about himself in the third person, Dolittle is here looking at himself from the impersonal perspective of the social system. In effect, he is ventriloquizing that system. That is why his speech begs to be placed alongside the shamelessly amoral rentier voices of Skimpole and Gertrude Stein, or for that matter Gissing's less exuberant Biffen in his equating of workhouse with independent income. Dolittle too ventriloquizes an ideology that, if it is not yet official, is already moving away from "middle-class morality," and confirming the working class's sense of justified independence from it. That is arguably the key to his immense and otherwise inexplicable self-confidence.

In 1914, the working class had not yet won the sense of official entitlement that Shaw gives to his character. But what he gives his character is congruent with what he proposed society *should* give the working class. Giving is not an inappropriate verb; for Shaw it was indeed a case of noblesse oblige. As a Fabian, he did not believe that either people's morality or their opinions about their happiness, democratically canvassed, should be allowed to stand in the way of a more rational distribution of society's goods. The people could not be trusted to act in their own interest. The state, acting as "the representative and trustee of the people," would have to do that for them.[39] Somewhat surprisingly, Shaw's model for how to reform the allocation of society's resources is rent. "What the achievement of Socialism involves economically, is the transfer of rent from the class which now appropriates it to the whole people" (73). Shaw's embrace of the radical theory of rent formulated by the Fabians in the 1880s, drawing on British economists David Ricardo and J. S. Mill as well as the lesser known W. Stanley Jevons, may have had something to do with his family's background in colonial Ireland or his stint, early in life, as a rent collector. But the notion of the socialist state as landlord, the oddest and most telling of Shaw's metaphors for the state, clearly also has something to do with Anderson's diagnosis: a society in which landed property continued to wield disproportionate political and cultural power. Marx's theory of surplus value, which rent theory was intended to supplant, was of course not tied in the same ultimate and exclusive way to the land. As an alternative explanation of economic inequality and what should be done about it, rent theory not only bestowed more agency on the state, which became, in Rodney Barker's phrase, a "romantic hero." By imagining the state as possessor of land, it also presented this romantic hero, like its literary antecedents, as recognizably aristocratic: a reformed, beneficent landlord, taking in rent only in order to redistribute it more equally. According to this scheme the term "rentier," one who lives off rents received from property, applies both to the state, which receives rent from all its citizens, and to the citizens, who are thereby asked to envision their income not as the reward of an individual effort but on the contrary as their share in the whole, their portion of the common resources of society that the state watched over on their behalf. In this sense each citizen is encouraged to think of himself or herself as owning, and receiving rent on, the whole of society's wealth. It is Biffen's fantasy of enjoying an independent but not extravagant income, a fantasy that has now been generalized, democratized, and turned in the direction of public policy.

In effect, Shaw's rentier sociology combines Anderson's narrative with Thompson's. That is, it fuses the aristocratic cultural style, never quite supplanted by the middle class, with the new socialist-paternalist program by which the working class will be granted social integration—the program that later both solidified and deteriorated, under the pressure of opposition and circumstance, into the institutions of the welfare state. Thus the state becomes the ideal repository of "inherited economic capital," the latest in a long line of Good Rich Men: the ultimate mentor. From this point of view, sounding as if you had an independent income without the actual assurance of possessing one—what I call above being a benefactor-without-any-money—comes to seem less of a personal anomaly and more the representative tonality of a historical period in which the ideology of the welfare state has begun to emerge, though it remains fragile and unofficial.

The historical gap between anticipatory and official versions of that ideology offers one take on the unsettledness of *Pygmalion*'s ending. It requires no great leap of imagination to see Henry Higgins, who in act 1 is taken for a policeman, as embodying Shaw's ambivalent identification with the state. In serving the social function of upward mobility, Higgins's expertise occupies the slot that would soon be largely taken over by state-sponsored education. When he accepts Eliza as a student despite the fact that she cannot pay her way, Higgins anticipates that pillar of welfare-state policy even more precisely. Yet he is totally insensitive to feelings—Eliza's feelings most obviously, but even his own.[40] The only happy ending he can imagine is one in which he, Pickering, and Eliza will be "three old bachelors" (138) together. This has the appearance of equality, but it demands that Eliza give up much of what she is and wants (womanhood and love) in order to imitate the masculine style of life to which the two men are already habituated. In the very act of valuing her independence—

he calls her "a tower of strength" (138)—Higgins recognizes in her nothing that he himself has not put there. In his own eyes, her learning is really his teaching. And his teaching is as unidirectional as the bequeathing of an inheritance. In this respect Shaw shows how close he remains to the perspective of "inherited economic capital."

A quick concluding glance at the Angry Young Men, some forty years later, offers a chance to gauge the shift from Shaw's pre–World War I anticipation of a heroic role for the state, still dominated by the voice of "private" income, and a post–World War II situation in which interventionist state institutions are real—in the eyes of the Angries, all too real. The first literary movement that has been regularly interpreted in the context of the welfare state, the Angry Young Men are most often seen as explicitly rebelling against its drabness and ignominious security. John Osborne's target, according to critic Luc Gillemin, is "the 'Brave-New-nothing-very-much-thank-you' world, the British welfare state, gutted of its ideals and stuffed with American-style consumerism" (51).[41] In Osborne's *Look Back in Anger* (1957), the keyword of "the state of mind that the welfare state had helped to promote" is "pusillanimous" (51). Anger, allied with passion, enthusiasm, and above all defiance, strikes the very opposite note. For this school of writers, one might almost say that it is the welfare state, rather than their apparent natural enemies in the upper classes, that the working-class characters define themselves against.

But if so, then the welfare state would seem to have become a more explicit presence in the upward mobility story's ending. Consider John Braine's *Room at the Top* (1957), a minor classic of the genre that has been widely popularized by its film version (1959) much as Shaw's play has been by its musical and film remakes. *Room at the Top* readily fulfills its working-class protagonist's wish for the good life. As if scripted by Gissing's Masterman, however, the ending spoils his enjoyment of it. The narrative structure comes even closer to that of Stendhal's *The Red and the Black*. Joe Lampton wins the heart and hand of a wealthy young heiress who represents his highest dreams of social ascension. In the process he abandons the Older Woman who had been his lover. He then realizes, too late, that in choosing the wrong woman he has more or less murdered the right one (Julien Sorel's unsuccessful attempt to kill Mme de Rênal is roughly replicated in Alice Aisgill's semisuicide and Joe's self-accusation of murder). He has sacrificed his chances for true love, genuine understanding, and a life that is different from that of the "Zombies" around him. Unlike Julien Sorel, Joe ends up alive and married, but it makes little difference.[42] Again, the heart of the story is not Joe's successful move into the company of the rich, but the love story between him and the Older Woman: what draws them together, what pushes them apart, and what kind of an alternative to the empty sell-out finale their couple offers. Again, this alternative *is* an upward mobility story, not an utter rejection of the very idea but a variant on it. And again, the thing to look for is the logic of that variation, the logic of what might have been.

That logic leads, of all places, to the Town Hall. Joe is arriving to begin work there on the novel's first page. He is an accountant, hence already an incontestable member of the middle class; he has risen out of his parents' class before he gets off the train. That first stage of his upward mobility, which will soon be neglected in favor of the higher and more dramatic stage to come, is associated both with the Town Hall and with Alice Aisgill, the Older Woman. The obvious connection between Alice and the theater, where the signs of her age (which he seems unable to forget) magically if only temporarily disappear, is arguably less important than the more obscure connection of their love affair to the town. One might almost say that, as in *Pygmalion*, the stage is a figure for the government, which promises to make the theater's evanescent magic into permanent policy.

Joe, son of an industrial worker, meets Susan Brown, daughter of a rich industrialist, while both are acting in an amateur theater group. Like Eliza Dolittle, whose progress is marked by a series of acting lessons and rehearsals, he too makes embarrassing, class-defining mistakes of pronunciation on stage. And he too ends up triumphing over all obstacles. Yet it is nature, not theater, that wins the two big battles for Susan's affection. Joe seduces her by means of his looks, and he seduces her father (when offered money to leave the daughter alone) by means of an unplanned, irrational fit of working-class authenticity, complete with sudden return of his vanished Yorkshire dialect. Theater works, on the contrary, to bring him together with Alice Aisgill, overcoming his "natural" aversion to the signs of her aging body. The first or moderate version of upward mobility is again associated with bohemia. In neither text, however, does the theater stand for a green wood of unfettered imagination where you can be anything that you can mimic. Convenient as such a self-advertisement may seem, literature presents itself in both *Pygmalion* and *Room at the Top* as subject, like bohemia itself, to almost invisible logics of constraint, in particular a logic of democratic generalizability. And that logic leads back toward Town Hall. Instead of a celebration of individual ability—what Joe deserves because of what is special about him—the theater follows a logic of collective need: what Alice deserves because of what she brings (by her greater ability) to the group and its individual members. Her age, a topic that cannot be exhausted by psychological interpretation alone, would also seem to function as a reminder of those universal vulnerabilities that define collective obligation. In caring for her, Joe is discovering pleasure of a new kind, pleasure in caring for something genuinely distinct from his own pleasure. Theater, like government, separates us off from what we are as individuals, forces us to feel for what we are not.

In the theater group, as at the Town Hall, Joe has already been accepted before speaking a line.[43] He feels much the same comfort at work that he feels in the company of Alice. He relaxes with Alice, he says, because he feels no need to try to seduce her, no need to push himself to conquer and accomplish. In both cases he feels a valued, "first-time" experience of teamwork. At Town Hall: "We were a team of professionals, not a collection of adding-machines. . . . I was for the first time completely happy in my work" (36). At the theater: "for the first time in my life I became of my own body and voice without conceit, as instruments. Alice and I were a team" (66). This acceptance is explicitly maternal.[44] Alice is like a mother, but so is the city: "The city was mine, a loving mother" (111). Eroticism, if not eroticism of the most passionate sort, characterizes Joe's relation both to the Older Woman and to the municipality. Joe's landlady, a woman two decades older than himself and the first person from Warley he meets, combines the evasive but palpable sexuality of both: "I wanted to kiss her. Not passionately, I may add, but as I would have kissed my mother on my way to work" (105).[45] When he describes Warley, a friend comments, "'Anyone'd think you were talking about a woman and not a perfectly ordinary market town with a few mills'" (93).[46]

The special thing about Alice, Joe reflects, is that she knows the truth about his "self-pity and class-consciousness" (116), yet she doesn't blame him for it. But if this makes her a variant of the all-accepting mother, it also allows her to prefigure the state in the maternal identity (the "nanny" state) into which it was notoriously and controversially entering. Indifferent to questions of blame or fault, the Older Woman is also disinterested; Alice becomes Joe's friend at first by giving him advice on how to win over Susan. In both senses she resembles the state in its welfare mode. Hence the appropriateness of the fact that when Joe receives news of her car crash and lingering death, he is at the Town Hall, in the midst of conspicuously generous congratulations about his upcoming marriage and new employment. Indeed, Joe has just finished a monologue that would otherwise seem misplaced: "I could see the machinery of local government as it really is, appreciate its blend of efficiency and cosiness; I hear a lot of nasty things said about municipal bureaucrats these days, but if every business were run as smoothly as even the most slatternly little urban district, then Americans would come over here to learn the technique of greater productivity instead of it being the other way around" (182).

The resonance achieved by transmitting the news of Alice's death at Town Hall does not seem restricted to the contrast between his old and new salary levels. The same might be said of the scene in which Susan's father offers to make him "a rich man—a damned sight better off than you'll ever be in local government," on condition that he "never see Susan again" (174). Joe's immediate reaction is neither to accept the offer nor to protest that he loves Susan too much to think of accepting it. Instead, he says, "I'm to leave Warley too, I take it?" (175). Loyalty to the town and loyalty to Alice are strangely intermingled. Wandering through the streets in his grief after Alice's death, his mind wandering as well, he pursues a lyrical thread of association: "I think now that I was frightened because the warehouses didn't care about what had happened to Alice; but why did I hate the innocent friendly trams?" (190). The innocent friendly trams, emblems of democratically available public transport that invite contrast with the expensive private automobiles Joe obsessively notices and covets, are the perfect detail to mark "what had happened to Alice" and Joe's consequent self-loathing.

If Joe's natural good looks are what he has going for him with women, what does he have going for him with the town? The question must be asked. There would be no governmental intervention in the upward mobility story, as proposed above, if the answer were again that he owed his success to his nature alone. But he does not. Like Julien Sorel, with his uncanny ability to be bored, Joe has a remarkable self-confidence. What is truly remarkable about *Room at the Top* is that the sources of this self-confidence are presented as explicitly historical, not natural, and indeed as humble, measurable, and generalizable, shared with any number of others. Joe is already accepted, even on the day of his arrival in Warley, because he has two things going for him, and both lead directly to the state. He has a job in municipal government. And he has, very literally, money in the bank—money that confirms the government that employs him as crucial to his identity. The sources of his bank account are itemized in a strange monologue in which, working up to the question of why a girl like Susan would ever stoop to marry "a minor municipal official" (126), Joe suddenly begins to speak to himself in Who's Who–style bureaucratese.

We shall begin by examining Joseph Lampton. Born January 1921 at Dufton. Father John Lampton, occupation overseer. Educated Dufton Grammar School. Junior Clerk, Treasurer's Department, Dufton UDC, 1937. Sergeant-Observer, 1940. 1943–45, Stalag 1000, Bavaria. Present post, Senior Audit Clerk, Warley UDC. Salary, APT Two. Resources, £800, from accumulated RAF pay, gratuity, and insurance on parents. Prospects: he might be a Treasurer of Warley one day (125).

The contents of his bank account, which have allowed Joe to afford visibly better clothes than might have been expected from one in his position and in other ways too to act above it, come, first, from his army pay while in a prisoner-of-war camp and, second, from insurance money from the death of his parents in a German bombing raid. In both cases, the source is the intervention of the state, trying to compensate for the misfortunes of its citizens, especially in service to the nation. The state has singled him out, but for his sacrifice and suffering rather than for his talent or achievement. It has distinguished him according to a principle that would apply to anyone in his position. In this sense, though the results of the benefits he has received matter to him personally and he has a unique personal voice in which to say so, the irony of his adoption of impersonal bureaucratese above is canceled out by a further or higher irony. The Town Hall speaks through him, for it has in fact gotten inside him, and not necessarily for the worse.

Given Joe's determination to "enjoy all the luxuries," his decision to leave "local government" (24) may seem as inevitable as his decision to leave Alice. In an era that still suffers from postwar rationing, as we are repeatedly reminded, Joe's sensual hunger for the finer things clearly cannot be satisfied by the same state that has ordered the rationing. And working for the state leaves him especially vulnerable to gentlemanly jibes like the one he receives from Alice's husband, which "sets his teeth on edge": "You're a Town Hall wallah, aren't you?" (53). The Anglo-Indian element in the put-down (*wallah* means person connected with or defined by a particular function) is a not so subtle reminder that municipal government, like the Empire, was considered by many a secure zone of upward mobility for those not talented enough to make their way in more prestigious employment. Yet the parallel with Empire takes on a darker meaning when Joe's guilt in Alice's car-accident death echoes the sketchy, drunken story told by Joe's friend Charles of a "Wog [he] ran over in Calcutta" (162), an infraction for which he was merely fined (159). Joe is an accountant, put in charge of other people's money, and his job is ensuring accountability.[47] Yet municipal government, like Empire, seems to threaten ordinary ethical accountability, and even to sanction a kind of official irresponsibility.

The conjoined questions of proper responsibility for other people and of how much blame should fall on those who neglect it could be said to take over the novel's conclusion. In effect, the novel reaches its conclusion by splitting apart Alice and the Town Hall. It does this by means of sexual jealousy. Joe, who is responding to his self-chosen vocation "to do good to myself not others" (24), becomes irate because there have been too many others in Alice's life. He breaks up with Alice twice. The first time, the immediate issue is bohemia and respectability. Unaffected by the popular view of Alice as a Svengali, "notorious" for sleeping with younger men (178) she meets through the theater, he is outraged when he discovers that, Trilby-like, Alice has at one time worked as an artist's model. "In Dufton artists' models were thought of as tarts" (103). The second time, after he is ordered to drop Alice by Susan's father, the extra energy behind the breakup comes from the information that she has slept with Jack Wales, his rich rival for Susan and the focus of all his homosocial antago-nism.[48] Both of these seem arbitrary, excuses for a choice that has been made for other reasons. But in both cases, the problem can be expressed with analytic neutrality: to paraphrase Levi-Strauss, the problem is an overvaluation of other men. And this is something that Alice genuinely signifies. Indeed, it is something she had made their affair signify. So in rejecting Alice, it is the town that Joe is rejecting. Sexual promiscuity offers a convenient vocabulary in which democratic collectivism can be safely and inconspicuously rejected. Yet he rejects Alice in the town's name. "If I married Alice I'd be forced to leave it. You can only love a town if it loves you, and Warley would never love a co-respondent" (166).

In the novel's final lines, Joe is told "Nobody blames you," and he responds "Oh my God . . . that's the trouble" (199). The contradiction is blatant. He can only love the town if it loves him. And he can only love it if it does not love him, but instead blames him. The welfare state has become strong enough to inform Joe's passionate but somewhat confused self-condemnation. Yet its no-fault ethic and its compromise with indus-trialists like Mr. Brown also put limits on the degree of concern for others that it will ask anyone to exercise. Perhaps that is one reason why Joe does not love it quite enough. And why we don't either.

CHAPTER FIVE

The Health Visitor

DUMPY: CAROLYN STEEDMAN'S *LANDSCAPE FOR A GOOD WOMAN*

One page into her autobiographical memoir *Landscape for a Good Woman* (1986), in a short opening chapter about the death of her mother, Carolyn Steedman recalls a traumatic scene from her working-class childhood: "We both watched the dumpy retreating figure of the health visitor through the curtainless windows. The woman had said: 'This house isn't fit for a baby.' And then she stopped crying, my mother, got by, the phrase that picks up after all difficulty (it says: it's like this; it shouldn't be like this; it's unfair; I'll manage)." Steedman herself draws an angrier conclusion: "And I? I will do everything and anything until the end of my days to stop anyone ever talking to me like that woman talked to my mother."[1]

The rage that flares up here seems to have been ignited by Steedman's discovery of her place in the system of class. The health visitor (to Americans, a caseworker), a middle-class but no doubt underpaid employee of a large government bureaucracy, is a somewhat unlikely incarnation of this system. Yet it is she who first and most memorably delivers the message that others will later confirm. The family belongs to the working class, and belonging to the working class is not something to be proud of. Speaking "the disdainful language of class," she "told my mother exactly what it was she stood outside" (6). Thus it seems natural that the health visitor should be the target of Steedman's anger. If one reads closely, however—and *Landscape*'s careful but fervent prose always repays close attention—the referent of that anger becomes less obvious. One might have expected that Steedman would stand up and demand respect for the working-class identity that is here so rudely disrespected. But that is not what she does. On the contrary, her words distinguish her *from* the working class. Or at least from the working class to the extent that this class is represented by her tearful mother. According to this passage, her mother is passive and resigned, interested only in "getting by." But getting by will not be enough for Steedman herself. Moving on from her mother's tears with a haste that is almost unseemly (performing, that is, her own version of getting by), she will choose to be more active. In order not to find herself in the same situation as her mother, she will do "everything and anything"—will choose to act, that is, even at the risk that the resulting action may be hasty, unconsidered, and ethically indiscriminate, may ultimately conflict with her own sense of what is right.

The "everything and anything" she will in fact go on to do, according to the evidence of this book, mainly involves working hard at school, winning scholarships, and making a career for herself—she modestly does not tell us how brilliant a career—as a social historian. In other words, it involves climbing out of the class to which the health visitor has assigned her. And as her phrase suggests, she is aware that she or others may eventually judge this story of "embourgeoisement and state education" (20), though respectable enough, as no more ethically scrupulous than "everything and anything." She is aware, in other words, that the adjective "good" in her title marks a real question.

Landscape for a Good Woman does not display the facts of Steedman's career (which this book did much to advance) either in triumphant sequence or in much detail. The title centers the book on the goodness of only one woman, and that is her mother. But in setting her childhood self on a path leading away from her society of origin and in acknowledging, however faintly, that this departure may be a kind of betrayal, Steedman places her narrative squarely within the upward mobility genre.[2] Structurally speaking, these opening pages repeat one of the genre's most familiar scenes or touchstones. Jane Eyre's punishment for defending herself against her bully of a cousin; Pip's persecution at the hands of his Tickler-wielding sister; the drudgery of Carrie's work at the shoe factory; the murder of David Levinsky's mother by an anti-Semitic gang; the moment when Jamaica Kincaid's mother takes Lucy out of school and burns her books, or when Melanie Griffith's character in *Working Girl* is sexually assaulted by the colleague from whom she expects a chance at a serious job—in each of these moments, as in the scene with the health visitor, the protagonist's upward mobility is offered legitimation by means of a primal hurt, a set of initial circumstances so grossly oppressive and unfair that revolt against them immediately seems natural, inevitable, fully justified.

The legitimizing logic thus set in motion is not innocent. We know how easily it can be abused. Nor is it simple. The protagonist needs so strong a motive for rising in the world, one might say, because without it the reader might be tempted to refuse any initial investment of sympathy (why does he think he's so special?), or might at any rate withdraw it at the end when faced with the issue of what positive identity the protagonist will go on to assume, what loyalties she or he will put in place of those revolted against. Some conflict of loyalties, some problem of justification is announced in advance. If the motive-supplying scene distracts from this problem, in other words, it also registers its power. It reminds the reader that the grounds for sympathy with the protagonist are preemptive and necessarily shaky. That sympathy will be threatened by the new identity, values, and loyalties that result from the protagonist's self-improvement, which invites possible interpretation as a mistake, a trespass, a betrayal of someone or something.

Against this background, the righteous vehemence of Steedman's anger is suddenly hard to insulate from its hint of the unethical. On the one hand, this anger expresses her "defiance" (2), her class identification (active as well as passive) with her mother as object of class disdain. On the other hand, her anger also expresses her impulse to break away from that class, to escape her part in that disdain—even if escaping means joining the disdainers. The class ambivalence is familiar enough, I suppose, but this is something more than the garden variety. By attaching the generic label of upward mobility story to *Landscape for a Good Woman*, we remind ourselves to search for ways in which the book also seeks to resolve this anger-soaked contradiction—an extraordinary achievement even if, as Steedman says, "my inability to resolve it is part of the story" (21).

In the chapters that follow, Steedman's anger is as often directed at her mother as at the class hierarchy—often enough so that Steedman has become known for her rich and troubling articulation of daughterly hate. It's worth asking, therefore, what we are talking about when we talk about hate. The passage above gives one answer: in the person of her mother Steedman hates the working class's passive willingness to go on being mistreated. Yet the genre also suggests a different answer. The rising daughter's hatred of her mother seems to mark an anxiety about all those members of her class—here, that would include her sister as well as her mother—who through no apparent fault of their own could not and will not rise. Why not? The impulse to self-justification sends her back to her mother and sister armed with embarrassing but not uninteresting questions. Might there after all have been some secret fault on their part that would explain their failure and thus argue for the latent justice of Steedman's success? Or is there some virtue of her own? The same impulse presses her to examine how the rise happened, exactly what she has risen to become, what others did or didn't have to do with it. Did the process necessarily exclude, reject, injure her mother and sister? Or not? Is it possible that her individual escape is less individualistic or selfish, more public-spirited and defensible than it might appear?

Steedman and her mother do not always disagree. The mother too wants individual upward mobility for herself, and thus sets an interesting precedent for her daughter. And the mother too would clearly enjoy describing the health visitor as "dumpy." At least for the space of this one politically incorrect adjective, daughter and mother together can indulge a defiant sense of superiority to their local representative of the state. They can see the state, through her, as a clothed, fleshly woman—a woman who lacks ideal proportions, lacks elegance, and thus cannot stand for whatever it is in the structure of things that might generate envy or desire. Envy and desire are the keys to the mother's Tory politics. As if in compensation for her practical submission to the philosophy of getting by, she indulges envious fantasies about the rich, the beautiful, the aristocratic. The upward mobility story she has planned for herself involves not scholarships to university, but the sudden appearance of a Prince Charming to carry her off. "My mother had wanted to marry a king. . . . Mrs Simpson was no prettier than her, no more clever than her, no better than her. It wasn't fair that a king should give up his throne for her, and not for the weaver's daughter. From a traditional Labor background, my mother rejected the politics of solidarity and communality, always voted Conservative, for the left could not embody her desire for things to be *really* fair, for a full skirt that took twenty yards of cloth, for a half-timbered cottage in the country, for the prince who did not come. For my mother, the time of my childhood was the place where the fairy-tales failed" (46–47). The state, embodied by the dumpy health visitor, has no role to play in such fairy tales.

But here Steedman cannot after all agree. To her, "dumpy" cannot be the final word about the state. For it is by courtesy of the state that she is living her own fairy tale—a less showy one than her mother desired for herself, but a fairy tale nonetheless. At the time when *Landscape* was published, Steedman was already working as Reader at the University of Warwick, in other words as a state functionary, her salary supplied by the taxpayers. The scholarships she has won in order to get this far were also awarded by the state. And even before the scholarships, as Steedman hastens to remind us, her development as a child was sponsored by government-issue milk and orange juice. As was that of other children.

With the entrance of the other children, the impulse toward resolution points abruptly and somewhat surprisingly back to the state—this time not the state as the voice of class hierarchy, but on the contrary the state as a potential way to satisfy the "desire for things to be *really* fair." When Steedman worries aloud about her rise and how it distinguishes her from others who began in similar circumstances, she does so in a discussion of the postwar welfare state, acting out the same concern for its citizens' welfare that sent the health visitor to her mother's door. "It was a considerable achievement for a society to pour so much milk and so much orange juice, so many vitamins, down the throats of its children, and for the height and weight of those children to outstrip the measurements of only a decade before; and this remains an achievement in spite of the fact that the statistics of healthy and intelligent childhood were stretched along the curve of achievement, and only a few were allowed to travel through the narrow gate at the age of eleven, towards the golden city" (122).[3] One of the few who "were allowed to travel through the narrow gate . . . toward the golden city," Steedman knows it is not fair that the travelers *were* so few. Yet the unfairness to the subordinate class dangles at the end of a subordinate clause ("in spite of the fact that"). And the independent clause at the center of the sentence tells us that it *is* an achievement for society to have done so much for so many. Or, more precisely, not for "society" in the abstract to have done this, but for society in its newly and self-consciously organized political form. The repeated word *achievement* blurs her own achievement with that of the Beveridge-era state, which has helped it along while aiming (within limits) at the general welfare.

The orange juice and the milk are part of Steedman's defense of "state intervention in children's lives" in the 1950s—interventions in the lives of families as well, of course, and interventions that often took the form of health visitors at the door. As she gets toward the end of the book, Steedman appears to forget that opening scene. Such interventions were "experienced, by me at least," she writes, "as entirely beneficent." But her account of that experience is no less convincing this time through: "The calculated, dictated fairness of the ration book went on into the new decade, and we spent a lot of time after we moved from Hammersmith to Streatham Hill, picking up medicine bottles of orange juice and jars of Virol from the baby clinic for my sister. I think I would be a very different person now if orange juice and milk and dinners at school hadn't told me, in a covert way, that I had a right to exist, was worth something" (121–22). This passage and others like it return us to the health visitor scene with an inescapable feeling of paradox. How can Steedman begin in such wrath against this representative of the state's intervention in children's lives and yet inform us a hundred pages later that it is only such interventions that allowed her to feel she "had a right to exist, was worth something"?

At the contradictory heart of the book, ambivalence about Steedman's mother shades into ambivalence about the state and about the state's actions as, in effect, a parental surrogate. The state must take some of the burden, one might say, in order for Steedman to offer higher justice both to her mother and to her father. The scene of the health visitor is located very precisely, in 1951, when Carolyn was four and her little sister was a newborn baby. The precise location in time is important, for Steedman will put a second, equally traumatic and class-defining moment in the same year: a confrontation in the forest when her father was humiliated before her four-year-old eyes (for illegally picking flowers) by the forest-keeper. This second scene of class identification helps Steedman argue the limits of psychoanalysis in explaining her family history. In a working-class family, she says, the father cannot simply represent patriarchal authority. When "the father is rendered vulnerable by social relations" (72), the myths will have to be different. "What broke the relationship between mother and child in my household was indeed a representative of the law—many representatives: a health visitor, an angry forest-keeper—who demonstrated to us all the hierarchies of our illegality, the impropriety of our existence, our marginality within the social system they represented. It was not my father who acted as an agent of the law, for he too was outside it" (80).[4]

But again, Steedman cannot simply deplore or resist this traumatic transfer of authority from her parents to representatives of the law. On the side of the law is free milk and orange juice. On the side of her mother is the fairy-tale of a goose-girl who marries a king. There is only one king. Not every goose-girl will happen upon one to marry. Other girls, those who are not destined to win the hearts of marriageable monarchs, would seem to be out of luck. From the perspective of the other children, then, the law seems to make an eligible if rather minimalist proposal. It cannot raise them as high, but at least it will always be there, and it will offer them a safety-net to stop them from sinking further.[5]

I have been suggesting that the issue of other children, never fully articulated as such within Steedman's text, is nevertheless at its core. There is further evidence at the point where social landscape and individual psychoanalysis most feelingly intersect: the birth of Steedman's baby sister. As I said, both scenes of class trauma are located in 1951, the year of the sister's birth. Steedman describes this moment as something like a fall from grace, a moment when "the world went wrong" (91). She is aware that this description might well be attributed to a banal case of sibling rivalry: "I am irritated and depressed because she has come to stay" (51). But she offers a more complicated theory. Her mother got pregnant the second time, she suggests, as a strategy to win her husband (actually not her legal husband) away from the wife and family he had left behind in the north. Perhaps another child will convince him to marry her. The strategy fails; the mother is embittered by its failure; the father runs away from a suddenly hostile home. What remains is in effect a single-parent family. In that family, remains, life becomes harder.

This is the story she tells. But there is another lurking behind it. In this second story, Steedman gains a sister and loses a father. In losing her father, she loses an authority figure (though his authority is diminished), an authority figure who also loves her. She loses, let's say, her version of her mother's fairy-tale king. And in gaining a sister, she enters however unwillingly into a more democratic condition, a condition in which she can no longer be a unique object of affection but is obliged to share the available resources with someone of equal status. In other words, the monarchy is overthrown and replaced by a democracy. A democracy that looks more drab, is missing the old seductiveness, and still cannot take adequate care of everyone, but that at least supplies milk and orange juice and checks up on the health of her baby sister. In this sense, it is perhaps no coincidence that her memory of her father in the moment after the confrontation with the forest-keeper, that is, in his new state of visible vulnerability, catches him in the act of retreating, just the posture in which she chooses to remember the health visitor's "dumpy retreating figure." The new, post-fairy-tale dispensation is not populated by beings of aggressive authority. Equals more than superiors, they allow her to feel a certain contempt for the state while also forcing upon her a certain feeling of diminishment in herself. The state is no better than we are; one is almost tempted to say (prematurely, of course) that it *is* us, or is the now diminished thing we are destined to become. When the authority of the father is replaced by the authority of the state, she is shocked "to discover that I wasn't the privileged elder daughter after all" (71). But as if to compensate for this loss of privilege, both she and her baby sister—who will not rise in the world via education as Carolyn does—are now assured of more or less reliable care. The state steps into the space vacated by the not-quite-husband. Even though it pushes the father away, that is, her mother's "children as levers" (69) strategy is not an entirely losing one. Rather, it is representative of "a bargain struck between working-class women and the state, the traffic being a baby and the bargain itself freedom, autonomy, state benefits and a council house: the means of subsistence" (70).

Guaranteeing the means of subsistence to the needy is of course not a solution to the problem of social inequality, as Steedman knows well. But half a century later, when this goal is so radically contested, it is perhaps worth remembering that the institutionalizing of such guarantees was then and continues to be the closest approach to a solution that has yet been practically realized.[6] Suffering under all our accumulated cynicism about the welfare bureaucracy, we require an effort of will to reevaluate its achievement on the scale of actual and possible human enterprises, and another effort to reimagine the immense and unpredictable impact it had on the psyche of its early beneficiaries. Otherwise it will be incomprehensible that Steedman refuses to endorse the common view that "the welfare policies of the late 1940s" were "'the last and most glorious flowering of late Victorian liberal philanthropy.'" She knows this in a sense to be "historically correct," Steedman says. But this view cannot account for "the sense of self that those policies imparted. If it had been only philanthropy, would it have felt like it did?" (122). What it felt like to her, she concludes, must also be generalized to others: "within that period of time more children were provided with the goods of the earth than had any generation been before. What my mother lacked, I was given; and though vast inequalities remained between me and others of my generation, the sense that a benevolent state bestowed on me, that of my own existence and the worth of that existence—attenuated, but still there—demonstrates in some degree what a fully material culture might offer in terms of physical comfort and the structures of care and affection that it symbolizes, to all children" (122–23).[7]

Here is the logic behind the prominent and seemingly bizarre intrusion of a health visitor into a story of upward mobility. In defending what a "benevolent state" has done, and might yet do, for "all children," Steedman is also defending herself—defending, that is, her individual right to break away from her class, away from her mother, and rise in the world. This is because, first, the state has tried at the same time to help *everyone*, not just her; and second, because she herself has now become its representative—not merely in the literal sense, not merely as its employee. In the figurative and more important sense, she too has become a health visitor.

When Steedman refuses to accept the negative connotation of historical labels like "state intervention" and "charity" (122), it is in part because of what has been done for her, and in part because those same labels can now be affixed to her, because they describe what she is doing for others like her. The scene in the forest, she says, has given her "all the charity I possess" (50). As an example she immediately mentions the "little watercress girl" (51), then her own father. The two are connected as topics of her historical research, research that might be described, if the phrase were not so unbearably patronizing, as charity work.[8] Consider her obsessive interest here (and again in *Strange Dislocations*) in tracking down the eight-year-old seller of watercresses whom Henry Mayhew found on the streets of London in the winter of 1849/50 and interviewed.[9] We can think of this research as a caseworker's follow-up visit. Steedman tries to rescue this hungry, shivering, unchildlike child—not from the world's indifference, since the girl has already been discovered and remembered, but from the incomprehension of these "middle-aged men" like Mayhew and Freud "who, propelled by the compulsions of scientific inquiry, demanded stories from young women and girls" (130) but did not know how to listen for everything she herself would listen for. Specifically, Mayhew does not listen for what to the child herself is "the point of her story," namely "the financial ordering of her household, and the way in which her labor was managed and controlled by her mother" (135). Possessing nothing, receiving "the most praise and approbation" (136) at home when she shows a larger-than-usual profit on her cresses, the little girl has in effect been turned into her labor: "her labor was not an attribute, nor a possession, but herself" (136).

One might almost say, then, that Steedman rescues the girl, a girl in some ways like herself at that age, from her mother, a mother somewhat like her own mother. She tells the nineteenth-century mother, in effect, what the health visitor told hers: you are not caring for your children properly. This is nearly right, but not quite. For Steedman is aware that the girl's ordeal results from "the conditions of distress that her family experienced" (136). She wants to care for the girl properly, wants a higher, more loving justice for the little watercress seller than the girl could have received in her own lifetime. But she knows that this is not the mother's fault. Playing the historian as retrospective health visitor, prying into people's homes and telling society that it isn't fit to bring up a baby, Steedman acts out the role of the state's best self as she herself has described it acting in her own behalf: the role of caring for children—"all children"—who are not otherwise being cared for. But she is also there to say something that the health visitor did not tell her mother: that the suffering of her children is not her failure, not her fault. This is what permits her to use in her title the not entirely obvious phrase "a good woman."

It is also what permits her to think of herself as a good woman. As I've suggested, the threat of a more severe judgment has lurked between the lines of this text from its first pages: that Steedman has done "everything and anything" to avoid the contempt that left her mother in tears, that her story of "embourgeoisement and state education" is not a morally scrupulous one, but an obscure betrayal both of her mother and of all those other children, like her sister, who could not rise in the system as she did. It is an accomplishment to have conjured up this threat, which the book did not absolutely require. Many have read *Landscape* without noticing it at all. And it is an even greater accomplishment to have fashioned so relatively persuasive a response to it. Steedman makes us see the welfare state at its best as an embodiment of both sides of the contradiction: it helps her rise, but it also helps others who don't rise. As in a fairy tale, it lifts her above her former situation, defines for her a new and desirable niche. But it does so only by giving her the means of helping others like herself. Thus there can be some resolution between where she comes from and where she has gotten to. If only so as to justify its own interventionist activities, the state tells her that neither she nor the others are responsible for suffering that is systemic rather than individual, and that therefore requires organized, collective, impersonal attention. State-like attention. It reminds her that if she has received so much public assistance, and thus cannot claim that her rise is owing entirely to her own merit, the converse is also true: others should not blame their own lack of merit for their failure to rise, or (what so often follows from it) for a lack of nurture (given or received) that sets off child-welfare alarms and calls in the state's intervention. It tells her what she tells us: that under our present imperfect circumstances, it is better to have the state's intervention than not to have it, and better to be part of that intervention than to stand around waiting for a prince.

One of Steedman's explicit intentions in writing *Landscape for a Good Woman* was to offer an alternative to Richard Hoggart's "description of the plight of the 'scholarship boy' of the thirties and forties" (15). Steedman speaks on behalf of a later and less pioneering generation, a generation for which working-class novels like *Room at the Top* were already assigned texts in school (15). And she speaks on behalf of women, who for various reasons "could not be the heroines of the conventional narratives of escape" (15) that Hoggart and others told. Hoggart's somewhat idealized version of the working-class mother is "a woman who does not work" (100). Steedman brings forward her own hard-working manicurist mother, fashion-conscious, health-food serving, Tory-identified, and full of longing, in order to win acceptance for more complex feelings about child rearing and for more varieties of female desire, including envious and improper desires for goods and styles and status.[10]

But in doing so, she also offers a more subtle correction. Hoggart's idealization of mother-centered working-class domesticity has fatal consequences for the upward mobility story of both scholarship boys and scholarship girls. If this warm togetherness is the point of departure, then the narrative seems condemned from the outset to move in the direction of cool solitariness, affective emptiness, an uncomfortable failure to belong.[11] And as I suggested above, that is the only destination Hoggart can imagine for his "uprooted and anxious" protagonist. In de-idealizing the working-class mother, then, Steedman is also freeing the upward mobility story from Hoggart's before-and-after narrative of inevitable emotional decline, making it possible to imagine a more desirable and companionable endpoint. Her own modest version of that story leaves her a professional teacher working in a state bureaucracy—two distinct social principles uneasily cohabiting, one somewhat less and one somewhat more democratic. Neither could be called an organic community, but both are forms of social organization that have their own (somewhat clunky) machinery of assistance, their own (somewhat deficient) ways of reconnecting abilities with needs, one's middle-class present with one's working-class past. It's not the top, but it's not so lonely.

PERSONAL: RICHARD RODRIGUEZ'S *HUNGER OF MEMORY*

In *New Deal Modernism: American Literature and the Invention of the Welfare State*, Michael Szalay offers an explanation for why "the interventionist state" has not been very visible in American literature and now needs to be reclaimed as an object of cultural analysis (20).[12] In America, he says, the line between public and private has not been clearly drawn. During the 1930s, for example, much of what literature has to say about "the New Deal is displaced . . . onto a private insurance company" (11). If so, it might seem that the New Deal is not after all at issue. Private insurance, which is paid for individually by the insured, cannot serve as a compelling example of the public effort to offer security to those who are simply unable to pay, like children and women unemployed outside the home. Thus it deemphasizes those compensatory mechanisms, including the progressive income tax, by which wealth is redistributed away from those who have more and toward those who have less. Of course, this deemphasis on redistribution may have been necessary in order to sell the program to a skeptical public in the first place. And, according to Szalay, it set serious limits to the New Deal. Social Security, which Linda Gordon calls "the central legislation of the U.S. welfare state" (9), "provided its primary assistance almost solely to White male wage earners. Farmers, African Americans, and women were aided only indirectly by the program, despite the fact that 'welfare' as we now know it (dispensed by Aid to Families with Dependent Children) grew from a clause in the original provisions of the Social Security Administration" (21). If dependent children remain in the private sphere, on the margins of New Deal policy, then we would not expect a narrative like Steedman's to resonate very widely in the United States.

American upward mobility stories certainly offer evidence for this transatlantic difference in the relative weighting of private and public. As I argued above, Horatio Alger's not-entirely-disinterested benefactors occupy a strange middle ground between the private workings of charity characteristic of Alger's nineteenth-century lifetime and the emergent public institutions of the Progressive Era, when his books had their greatest success. And the notion of "limited liability" that these benefactors unobtrusively slip into Alger's supposed hymns to self-reliance is of course equally essential both to the modern welfare state and to the private corporation. *Billy Bathgate*'s Dutch Schultz, whose every word and gesture seems to set him against the state, has no trouble comparing his gang's benefits to those of a private insurance company: "It's better with the Dutchman than with the Prudential Life Assurance" (311).

Recent American writing in the genre of working-class autobiography also seems committed to asking from the private sphere much if not all of what Steedman asks from the state. Consider an example that, though the protagonist's mother is a heroine and a saint, otherwise comes as close to Steedman's position as any American text I've found. In *Unafraid of the Dark: A Memoir* (1998),[13] Rosemary Bray begins with an unusually explicit and eloquent tribute to the welfare state and its intervention in her life. When her mother signs up for the Aid to Dependent Children program, whose purpose was to protect children growing up without fathers, what happens to the family? Her father is pushed out of the house, where any signs of his ongoing habitation would have led to the family's disqualification. The state offers itself as a bureaucratic substitute for him. Both she and her mother welcome the exchange. "On welfare, my mother joined the ranks of unskilled women who found the state more reliable than their husbands" (22). It's not that Bray doesn't feel for her father: "Daddy joined the ranks of shadow men who walked out back doors as caseworkers came in front doors, who for a slew of reasons lost their last, tenuous grip on the hallowed patriarchal family that was never truly real for African Americans" (22). However, despite the stigma and the surveillance (which nevertheless accords her mother more independence than her husband's obsessive jealousy did), Bray clearly finds this "pact . . . with a faceless bureaucracy" (22) preferable to her father, who beats his wife, terrorizes the children, and gambles away their desperately needed income.

Near the book's conclusion, Bray reveals its inspiration: an intense need to answer back, at the moment of the Anita Hill/Clarence Thomas hearings, against Thomas's mobilization of an old-fashioned upward mobility story in his bid for public sympathy. Scapegoating his sister as a "dependent welfare queen" was the other side of his " 'bootstrap' theory of personal responsibility for success and achievement. He had done it all himself; there was no one who helped; it was his own strength of will and faith in God" (263). In telling her own quite remarkable story of upward mobility, Bray, like Steedman, is determined not to repeat this self-serving fabrication. She knows she did not rise by relying only on herself and God. "We have been poisoned by the idea . . . that nothing the government does will matter. This is a lie, and my whole life is evidence of that fact. I have been lifted up by hands both seen and unseen, both individual and governmental" (xvii). The fact remains, however, that when Bray gives credit to institutions, they are by no means all governmental. She allows for a certain confusion between public and private. "I was shaped by the welfare system," she says on the first page. The sentence then continues: " . . . and by the Catholic Church" (vii). By the book's last pages, the private sphere very nearly has the upper hand. True to the genre as I have attempted to describe it, late in the book Bray stages an effort to resolve the contradictions between her poor origins and her present success. But she does so in a role and a situation that fall somewhere between the governmental and the private: as the president of her block association in Harlem, where the fault line between her past and her present is replayed as a "class rivalry between residents of the block who owned their homes [including her and her husband] and residents who rented rooms or apartments" (223). Not only is Bray here operating as a private citizen, but the government bureaucracy is the (somewhat ambiguous) enemy: the association is trying to block the city's plan to locate a facility for AIDS patients in the neighborhood. The tension between public and private, which defines the problematic center of the upward mobility story, comes back as a troubling question with no clear answer: has the protagonist's upward mobility left her ultimately defending the interests of the few or the interests of the many? Which side is she on?

This version of the public/private dilemma will sound familiar to Americans. And yet in *Atlantic Crossings: Social Politics in a Progressive Age*, Daniel T. Rodgers shows that much the same confusion of public and private characterizes the early development of the welfare state in Europe as well as America. " 'State-centered' analyses of social politics in this period have not adequately fathomed how indistinct the line between state and society remained throughout most of Europe and the United States, how thin the apparatus of state management was, and how reliant it was on temporary and borrowed expertise" (26). What came to be called the "welfare state" was not imagined in advance as the "end goal" even by its inventors. "Like the French *solidaristes*, many of social politics' most active proponents imagined the state accomplishing its social purposes best by subsidizing the voluntary institutions of society: labor unions, cooperative associations, and mutual assistance societies of many sorts" (28).[14] The list could well include Bray's block association. Reflecting on the strange attention to the general welfare that permeates individual stories of upward mobility, we are thus encouraged to suspend hard-and-fast judgment about the institutions where an attempted synthesis of individual success and collective good may happen.

In that spirit, let us return to Bray's example of the Catholic Church. A Catholic or "private" school reappears in much the same benefactor role in Richard Rodriguez's classic *Hunger of Memory: The Education of Richard Rodriguez* (1982). Usually categorized as "ethnic" rather than as "working-class" autobiography, *Hunger of Memory* is so frequently taught to American undergraduates because it is also an uplifting if bittersweet story of accomplishment and upward mobility.[15] And this book's equivalent of Bray's father-expelling caseworkers and Steedman's dumpy health visitor—it's with a certain shock that one realizes it too includes such a scene—is provided by the Church. A delegation of nuns from Richard's Catholic school visit the Rodriguez household when Richard is five or six, leaving trauma in their wake.

Half a year into his elementary education, Richard is apparently having troubles in the classroom. His teachers "noted my silence. . . . Until one Saturday morning three nuns arrived at the house to talk to our parents. Stiffly, they sat on the blue living room sofa. . . . I overheard one voice gently wondering, 'Do your children speak only Spanish at home, Mrs. Rodriguez?' While another voice added, 'That Richard especially seems so timid and shy!' " (20). Obeying "the Church's authority" (21), the parents agree for the good of the children to speak English in their home.

For Rodriguez, as for Steedman, this intrusive visit of authoritative outsiders becomes in retrospect the moment of the fall, which is to say the moment when upward mobility begins. His parents, speaking "in broken—suddenly heartbreaking—English" (21), are humiliated, especially his father, who is no longer "the public voice of the family" (24). The "special feeling of closeness at home was diminished" (22). It is the start of Richard's Americanization, of his ambition, his success, and his betrayal. "But betrayal against whom?" (30). Against no one, it would seem. He knows that his parents chose his school, desired his English-language success. Rodriguez himself declares that this is a fortunate fall. His loss of private intimacy is compensated for by "public gain" (27): "while one suffers a diminished sense of *private* individuality by becoming assimilated into public society, such assimilation makes possible the achievement of *public* individuality" (26). In short, the visiting nuns were right. Perhaps such visits should be mandatory for all Mexican American or Spanish-speaking families. Then his own painful but successful transition from private to public might be universalized. The pain is necessary—that is the point of Rodriguez's well-known and (especially to his fellow Mexican Americans) willfully scandalous positions against bilingual education and affirmative action, positions that for years dominated academic discussion of him. If his politics is who he is, then one might say that Rodriguez has become one of the nuns, much as Steedman ends up enacting the role of health visitor.

But *is* his politics who he is? Recent writing on Rodriguez, especially criticism attentive to the homosexuality that he announced in *Days of Obligation* (1992) and that can now be read back into *Hunger of Memory*, has experimented with pulling them apart.[16] Underlining the parallel between his upward mobility story and Carolyn Steedman's is another way of posing the same question. If each ultimately identifies with the intrusive visitors who bring a more public law into the privacy of the family, and yet if the political upshot of these two identifications is so very different—Steedman ends up arguing for state intervention, Rodriguez against—then what difference does the formal similarity of the two upward mobility stories make? Does the generic urge to resolution reveal anything about Rodriguez that is not already crystal clear in the public positions he has espoused?

Here, as so often, the upward mobility story gets murkiest and most interesting at the points when it wrestles with the self-accusation of betrayal. As we saw, Rodriguez blurs the line between public and private.

By his definition, the nuns would be no less public than the health visitor. There is no reason why the Church should not take over the state's responsibility for education. He says of the nuns (the emphasis is his) that "they provided excellent *public* schooling" (79). The italics seem to be added in order to displace the public/private line, taking it away from the source of funding and applying it to the division between English and Spanish. The most obvious thing his use of the word *public* excludes is his Mexican-ness. It must be his Mexican-ness, then, that he feels has been betrayed by his successful transition to public identity. And just as Steedman asks the state, whose representative has inflicted the wound of class, to do what can be done to heal that wound, so Rodriguez asks the Church, which has lured him away from his Mexican identity, to represent a resolution between what he has become and what he has abandoned. This explains something that needs explaining: why this short book should devote a full chapter to the Church, and why that chapter immediately follows Rodriguez's decision to abandon his dissertation and what seems like a promising university career.

Like Steedman, Rodriguez has gotten his start via scholarships. And like Steedman, he finds himself in dialogue with Richard Hoggart's account of the "scholarship boy." But Hoggart's effect on Rodriguez is to make him decide to drop out. "For the first time I realized that there were other students like me, and so I was able to frame the meaning of my academic success, its consequent price—the loss" (46). He credits Hoggart with great insight into the incongruity of the home and the classroom. "Here is a child who cannot forget that his academic success distances him from a life he loved, even from his own memory of himself" (48). "He cannot afford to admire his parents" (49). Rodriguez ends his attempt to read his life through Hoggart at the end of Hoggart's own account, when the scholarship boy suddenly becomes nostalgic for the membership he has lost. This is because, Rodriguez observes, the scholarship boy is "unable to feel easy, a part of the community of academics" (69). As we have already observed, Hoggart allows for little or no satisfaction at the end of the road to upward mobility. And it is a premonition of this final emptiness that decides Rodriguez to step off the academic ladder. "After only two or three months in the reading room of the British Museum, it became clear that I had joined a lonely community" (69). The new society is real, and he doesn't worry about his ability to fit in. But it is too restricted: "Who besides my dissertation director and a few faculty members, would ever read what I wrote?" (70). Is his dissertation "more than an act of social withdrawal?" (70). For Hoggart and for himself, he declares, no resolution is possible: "The scholarship boy does not straddle, cannot reconcile, the two great opposing cultures of his life" (66).[17]

The next chapter is about the Church. For the Church seems to promise just that reconciliation of opposites, of Mexican privacy and American publicness, that "the community of academics" was unable to deliver. "When all else was different for me (a scholarship boy) between the two worlds of my life, the Church provided an essential link" (82). "It mediated between my private and public lives" (96). It does so by making room for his Mexican identity: "I was *un católico* before I was a Catholic" (81). In other words, the Church does precisely what Rodriguez does not want the state to do: it offers a public space for his private (ethnic) identity. But what kind of space? The chapter goes on to show what the real difference is between the two forms or degrees of publicness embodied in the church and the state. For him, as for Steedman, the state refuses to treat his parents with the respect they deserve. His mother worked "for the California state government in numbered civil service positions secured by examinations. The old ambition of her youth was rekindled." She gets a job in "something called an 'anti-poverty agency.'" Then disaster strikes. "One morning there was a letter to be sent to a Washington Cabinet officer. On the dictating tape, a voice referred to urban guerrillas. My mother typed (the wrong word, correctly): 'gorillas.' The mistake horrified the anti-poverty bureaucrats who shortly after arranged to have her returned to her previous position. She would go no further" (54).[18] So much for anti-poverty agencies and the bureaucrats who run them. The Church, on the other hand, shows proper respect for those left behind. "Of all the institutions in their lives, only the Catholic Church has seemed aware of the fact that my mother and father are thinkers—persons aware of the experience of their lives" (90).

On the other hand, respect for those left behind comes at a stiff price: it means they must *stay* behind. Their advancement would threaten the grounds of their respect. "I realize that I am a Catholic . . . when I listen skeptically to a political thinker describe with enthusiasm a scheme for lasting political change" (102). Lasting political change means change like his own, but shared with others. The resolution offered Rodriguez by the Church allows him not to share. Being a Catholic means his background will be respected—in this sense there is a synthesis of his origin with his destination—but it also means that those who have the same background will be kept away from the benefits of "lasting political change," benefits like those he himself now enjoys. The Church is open to all, but his success is not. The door to transformation clangs shut behind him. All of which makes a perverse case, for us though not for him, in favor of that governmental disrespect that begins Steedman's story with such brutality but then goes on to lead it toward change for others as well as for Steedman.

An outflowing of sentiment toward the immobile also informs Rodriguez's treatment of sexual identity, a theme in Hoggart that Rodriguez's long commentary omits to mention. Hoggart describes how the scholarship boy "tends to be closer to the women of the house than to the men. . . . The man and the boy's brothers are outside, in the world of men; the boy sits in the women's world" (245). Though estranged from both parents, he is thus more estranged from his father.[19] Another consequence is that "his sexual growth is perhaps delayed" (247). Rodriguez, not pausing for parallels, expresses his own "suspicion that my education was making me effeminate" (127) immediately after his discussion of his Catholicism, in a chapter ostensibly devoted to skin color. But the chapter has at least as much to do with his sexuality. He judges himself effeminate by measuring himself "against some shadowy, mythical Mexican laborer—dark like me, yet very different" (127). The group to which these dark laborers belong is called "*los pobres*," and his consciousness of poverty is associated with the birth of desire: "I'd see the Mexican gardeners. I was unwilling to admit the attraction of their lives. I tried to deny it by looking away. But what was denied became strongly desired" (126). It does not seem to be their "lives" so much as their bodies that unwillingly attract him and that he looks away from. He does however try out their way of life. Offered a summer construction job, he describes his reaction as follows: "Desire uncoiled within me" (131). This desire, which could declare its name only a decade later, reenacts the logic he has ascribed to the Church. In order for him to "come face to face with *los pobres*" (139), in order for them to remain objects of desire, the poor must stay poor: "I would not become like them. They were different from me" (136). His desire to have them seems of a piece with his desire not to be them. What he likes libidinally and respects religiously is a poverty he has no interest in changing and certainly does not want to fall into.[20]

Rodriguez's unspoken identification with the visiting delegation of nuns does not however stop with religious reverence or sexual desire (which overlap interestingly in the discussion of Catholicism). *Hunger of Memory* ends with a different effort to resolve his contradictory loyalties. It locates in his final choice of profession a way of justifying the disrespect and betrayal that his accounts of sexuality and religion try to cover up or resolve too painlessly. Rodriguez was always a Catholic; the new thing he climbs off the scholarship-boy ladder in order to become is a writer. And his attitude comes closest to the disrespect he associates with the state when he talks not about his Catholicism but about his writing.

Writing is attractive because it seems to offer another mode of resolution. "If, because of my schooling, I had grown culturally separated from my parents, my education had finally given me a way of speaking and caring about that fact" (72). In an attempt to mediate between the broad opposites of public and private, fame and intimacy, he comes up with the new term "personal": "I sensed for the very first time some possibility of fellowship between a reader and a writer, a communication, never *intimate* like that I heard spoken words at home convey, but one nonetheless *personal*" (60). Having left one sort of fellowship behind, can he enter into another via writing—something like the fellowship he seems to have felt when he discovered Hoggart? And what sort of fellowship would "personal" writing create? The personal seems to differ from the intimate in that it maintains a proper distance. It does not divulge everything, or even everything of interest to others, but only what is of *legitimate* interest to others. It draws a line, in other words, but it also assumes (this is a larger step) that there exists a zone of material, neither entirely private nor entirely public, that readers have as legitimate an interest in hearing as the writer has in divulging. This notion of a reader/writer fellowship built around the reader's legitimate interest (the writer's can be taken for granted) is reminiscent of certain theories of modern governmentality, including Christopher Lasch's model of the therapeutic society. By means of the personal, Rodriguez seems to be imagining the writer either as a therapist or as someone impelled (as Will is legally impelled in *Good Will Hunting*) to undergo therapy, in either case one who braves embarrassment in order to satisfy the public's intrusive but nonetheless legitimate interest in the troubled domain of the personal.

At any rate, it is precisely this analogy that Rodriguez sees his mother rejecting. She disapproves of psychiatry, and in doing so she disapproves by proxy (she will later do so explicitly) of the public avowal of personal and familial experience that Rodriguez as a writer will make his bread and butter: "'You mean that people tell a psychiatrist about their personal lives?' Even as I begin to respond, I realize that she cannot imagine ever doing such a thing. She shakes her head sadly, bending over the ironing board to inspect a shirt with the tip of the iron she holds in her hand" (183). For her, there is no difference between the personal and the intimate. And her refusal to be reconciled means that Rodriguez is blocked in his effort to see writing as doing the work of reconciliation. The final chapter begins, "I am writing about those very things my mother has asked me not to reveal" (175). His most explicit statements retract this hope for writing as resolution. "But I do not give voice to my parents by writing about their lives. I distinguish myself from them by writing about the life we once shared" (186).

This is clearly true, but true in a sense Rodriguez does not fully intend. He distinguishes himself from his parents by becoming a commercially successful writer, and he becomes a commercially successful writer not by his verbal competence alone (though he has plenty of that), but rather by having a story to tell and sell. The story he has to tell is the story of his separation from his parents. What sells is the pathos of his and their loss of a common intimacy. If he were to be convinced that there had *been* no loss, perhaps he could not sell his work or make it as a writer.[21] So the cruel clarity of his alternatives (them or me) is somewhat self-serving. The cruelty flatters Rodriguez by turning his upward mobility story into a story of heroic self-reliance. But it also obscures a more difficult and elusive hypothesis. This is the double possibility, first, that Rodriguez can "give voice" to his parents in spite of what their own voices say, and second, that he can do so in the very act of distinguishing himself from them, doing the "personal" writing that they deplore.

There is of course a better case to be made for "personal" writing than Rodriguez himself is prepared to make. He is unprepared to make this case, it seems, because he is unwilling to reveal the secret of his homosexuality. His parents' commitment to privacy is a commitment to keeping him in the closet. Their resistance to speaking about matters that are "intimate" becomes something "personal" (in more than one sense of the word) because it keeps him from joining together in public with others like him. Though he will not say so, this means that Rodriguez would be right to speak publicly about his sexuality. To speak on the level of the "personal" would be, precisely, the basis for a new fellowship. And for the same reason, he is right to be speaking here about his and his parents' Mexican-ness. There is more than an analogy between the two minority identities thus in play. To be gay is to exist in public; it is to assume an identity fashioned for public use, no less genuine but certainly more advantageous and desired than the private, secret identity it superseded. But if so, if there is so clear a collective benefit to the emergence of this public identity, then the same would seem to hold for the Mexican American, Latino, or Chicano identity available to the Rodriguez family. The cliché is worth repeating: here the personal is the political, at least in the sense that diversity of representation is. Rodriguez offers his parents a means and a space of representation that many others do desire, and rightly, even if they themselves don't.

Rodriguez's decision to be a writer is only confirmed after a second dropping-out moment. After the discussion of skin color and sexuality, in a chapter entitled "Profession," he tells us that he went back to finish his dissertation after all, tried out the job market, was offered a slew of top jobs, and finally decided to refuse them all. His reason is that the jobs were offered to him only because he was a "minority student." This government-invented category of identity, essential to the policy of affirmative action and the allocation of government funds to higher education, sustains the idea that "the scholar" is and can remain "united with his people" (157). Whether because it lessens the pathos of his rise or reduces the credit he can take for it, Rodriguez declares this idea an intolerable illusion. Rather than allow his identity to be made into a public matter by the state, he will choose to be a writer. The implication is that in this important sense, he is choosing to be a private person, and that as a private person he will deserve all the rewards he did not feel he deserved as representative of a minority.

One might object that he did deserve these rewards in the first place—that receiving affirmative-action scholarships does not detract from his merit. But the deeper fallacy here is to believe that it's possible to escape the political contexts by which merit is always defined. Rodriguez seems to believe, and he is in good company on this point, that as a writer—in other words, by selling his writings to publishers—he can cease to be a representative of a minority. But he provides a great deal of evidence that he cannot. If only because of the expectations his readers bring to him, the way audiences look at the skin color and cheekbones of the "guest speaker," he continues to perform the work of representation, however unwillingly. This point is also general. We cannot assume, as Rodriguez seems to, that the writer's sale of his writing to publishers and editors is free from political interference in a way that his sale of his teaching and research to a university would not be. Neither market is free.

This is not to say that one always sells out. Selling is not necessarily selling out any more than acting in the interests of the state is. The particulars of each sale must always be inquired into. The question is not whether one is giving "them" what "they" want, but what it *is* that they want and whether it is good for them to get it. It is no doubt humiliating for Rodriguez to know that he is "much in demand," as he says, because of his opposition to state action on behalf of minorities, because like Clarence Thomas he can be used to undercut the voices of others who belong to the same minority. But there ought to be some solace in knowing that the demand for him to be a representative of that minority is not solely a demand for these particular opinions. Market demand can indeed be a vehicle of public expression, as the market's apologists never tire of claiming, but it performs this function by aligning itself with, not separating itself from, the interests of the state and the various constituencies that do battle over it. The legitimacy of the state depends on its ability to elicit and integrate voices of its Mexican American citizens and residents. Rodriguez's parents, who recognize no distinction between the intimate and the personal, thereby reject both their son's work as a writer and the work of political representation more generally. In disrespecting that desire, representing them against their will, overcoming their resistance to "personal" speech, he is acting on behalf of the democratic process. In spite of himself, he is doing the work of the state, which always wanted him to be "united with his people" (157). In this sense, the betrayal is legitimate.

Chapter 4 of Rodriguez's most recent book, *Brown: The Last Discovery of America* (2002), entitled "Poor Richard," is a further reflection on upward mobility that comes shockingly and gratifyingly close to agreeing with the argument I've just made.[22] The chapter segues from his childhood identification with Benjamin Franklin to his less admiring fascination with another "federal figure" (81), President Richard Nixon. Nixon too was a scholarship boy: "I won my share of scholarships, and of speaking and debating prizes in school, not because I was smarter but because I worked longer and harder than some of my more gifted colleagues" (84). But there's a price to pay for having to make it on hard work. Nixon's nervousness, his "sweat rings and dried lips" are a reminder of the embarrassment with which Rodriguez too, another poor Richard, will have to wear the black suit of ambition. They remind him of what he would like if possible to escape. What he seeks is the secret of "how not to be a scholarship boy" (92), the "sprezzatura," "naturalness," "artless grace" (84) of Kennedy, the rich man's son. And these seem unobtainable. Yet they have been obtained, Rodriguez goes on, and by another federal figure. "Lyndon Johnson came from a past as humble as Nixon's, as humble as Franklin's, as humble as Lawrence's, as humble as my own. Johnson the populist, Johnson the signer of civil rights legislation, Johnson the militarist, Johnson would not have shared my embarrassment" (86). Why not? Because, as the list of epithets suggests, "Johnson believed in the power of legislation to change history" (87). Johnson takes over "the American novel," the story of self-invention, and "rescue[s]" it, by turning it into a story of state policy. "The Negro Civil Rights movement became, during Johnson's administration, the great American novel" (91). There's no question that Rodriguez retains more than a little of his old exasperation at state interventions that intervene in his identity: "After all that Richard Nixon had written about how hard work wins the day in America, finally it was Nixon who arranged for me to bypass the old rules. Through the agency of affirmative action, akin to those pivotal narrative devices in Victorian fictions, I had, suddenly, a powerful father in America, like Old Man Kennedy. I had, in short, found a way to cheat" (95).[23] Rodriguez calls this cheating, but he also gives us reason to disagree with him. He himself has said, after Nixon perspired during the Nixon/Kennedy debates and was thus perceived to have lost, that "the game is fixed" (88). How do you compete with a natural aristocracy, unembarrassed and unperspiring? The rules will have to be changed. And the government is of course the only entity that can change them. What is even more telling, however, is that governmental agency seems the one reliable antiperspirant. Only Johnson, whom Rodriguez describes as his "Victorian benefactor" (98), can escape Nixon's sweat rings and embarrassment—can make upward mobility seem natural and legitimate.

Help: Tillie Olsen's "I Stand Here Ironing" and Alan Sillitoe's "The Loneliness of the Long-Distance Runner"

In Richard Hoggart's portrait of working-class domesticity, the aspiring son does his schoolwork on one corner of the living room table while "[o]n the other side Mother is ironing" (244). Richard Rodriguez describes his mother ironing at the moment when she feels most resistant to what he is doing as a writer. Tillie Olsen's "I Stand Here Ironing" (1953–54), a hauntingly teachable short story about motherhood as working-class experience, again offers this image of a mother's routine, repetitive, unpaid labor, labor of upkeep rather than invention or construction, in order to throw into relief the break with that routine by an upwardly mobile child.[24] But the two are not frozen in a binary opposition. Once again, child and mother are points in a triangular constellation whose third term, less visible from the usual critical perspectives, is the state.

Though it is narrated from the mother's rather than the child's point of view, that is, the story also resembles the texts by Steedman and Rodriguez in a by now familiar sense. At its center is intervention in the life of the family by an official outsider, an annoyingly intrusive messenger from the public world who comes offering "help." Indeed, the entire story could be described as an anticipated interview with a caseworker. Someone from the school—perhaps a guidance counselor or school psychologist, we are not told exactly—has called the mother, described her daughter Emily as "a youngster who needs help" (11), asked her to "come in" and talk. Everything that follows is a reflection on this call and a possible rehearsal for what she would say, how she would explain. What could have led to this ominous need for help?

The answers begin with Emily's birth into poverty, then the father's abandonment and the mother's single parenting. "It was the pre-relief, pre-WPA world of the depression" (12). The institutions of the welfare state didn't exist yet. Still, the semipublic charitable institutions that do interfere with their lives are close and recognizable forerunners of the welfare state, which was in fact emerging as such in the course of Emily's childhood. And in responding to that interference the narrator expresses an attitude that might also have been expressed by Steedman's or Rodriguez's mother. Public institutions are perhaps not the prime cause of their difficulties, but they have made things worse rather than better. Emily, having lost weight after a bout of the measles, is sent away. "They persuaded me at the clinic to send her away to a convalescent home in the country where 'she can have the kind of food and care you can't manage for her. . . .' They still send children to that place. I see pictures on the society page of sleek young women planning affairs to raise money for it" (15–16). The place is "handsome" (16), but a nightmare of icily impersonal institutionalization. Children are not allowed to keep their letters from loved ones, and visiting parents are kept separated from their children as if by "an invisible wall 'Not To Be Contaminated by Parental Germs or Physical Affection'" (16). The daughter says, "'They don't like you to love anybody here'" (16). "It took eight months to get her released home, and only the fact that she gained back so little of her seven lost pounds convinced the social worker" (17). Is there any reason, we ask ourselves, why this new social worker should be any more sympathetic than the last one?

At "that huge school" (20) from which the telephone call has come, things do not improve for Emily: "she was one, she was lost. She was a drop" (20). And then she wins first prize in the school amateur show. "The control, the command, the convulsing and deadly clowning, the spell, then the roaring, stamping audience, unwilling to let this rare and precious laughter out of their lives" (21). This is the moment of discovered talent that permits us to describe "I Stand Here Ironing" as a miniature upward mobility story, even though (like Steedman's) it is centered on the mother rather than the daughter. And here the upward mobility, promised though not yet achieved, seems set against the grim institutional surroundings of convalescent home and school. The mother's final speech is an act of defiance aimed at all those institutions that she takes her unnamed interlocutor to represent. No, she will not "come in." "I will never total it all. I will never come in to say: She was a child seldom smiled at. Her father left me before she was a year old. I had to work her first six years. . . . She is a child of her age, of depression of war, of fear" (22–23). After giving us convincing evidence of how callous the bureaucratic machinery can be, she refuses to offer her assistance to its representative. The story requested by the state is told, but not to the caseworker or psychologist or guidance counselor. The mother delivers to us, the readers, the truth about Emily that she cannot or will not deliver to the official whose interest in "helping" has provoked this monologue.

Asked to take sides between the mother and the state, we do not seem to have any real choice. The mother is a winningly modest and self-aware narrator, while the institutions of the state have not shown themselves to be good parental surrogates. The state, it seems, is the domain of loveless, depersonalized abstraction. The mother's perspective seems to be its opposite and antidote. But there is a problem with this first-level reading. The problem is that the mother refuses to take her own side.

It's almost impossible to read "I Stand Here Ironing" without pausing over its final words, the mother's declaration that she wishes her daughter to see herself as "more than this dress on the ironing board, helpless before the iron." This famous and faintly chilling sentence obliges us to identify the mother herself as the product and vehicle of all those hostile forces (the Depression, the war, and so on) that have put the daughter in need of help and now conspire to ensure that "all that is in her will not bloom." Of course, this is just what the narrator has been consciously arguing: even mothering cannot be protected from historical circumstance, which forces its way into the tenderness of familial intimacy.[25] Like her daughter, the mother too has been fashioned by history, has come to embody the history that fashioned her. She too is helpless, she tells us—helpless before herself. But this helpless historicality also threatens to escape from her conscious control. Consider the sentence that follows the news of the daughter's sudden and unexpected success on the stage: "'Mother, I did it. I won, I won; they gave me first prize; they clapped and clapped and wouldn't let me go.'" The mother's reaction is too fast for self-censorship: "Now suddenly she was Somebody and as imprisoned in her difference as she had been in anonymity." There is not so much as a comma to mark a decent pause after mother notices that daughter has become "Somebody," that this is a big break, that Emily has gone from problem child to budding star. She does not savor for more than an instant, and we are not allowed to do so either, the sweetness of the daughter's achievement and whatever it may promise. With perverse eagerness, the mother rushes to replace the sweetness with more imprisonment, to pull her daughter down to earth or simply to pull her down. She concludes that "probably little will come of" her daughter's talent.

There is a reason why the phrase "wouldn't let me go" might set off this discouraging and badly timed fit of motherly edification. Letting her go is precisely the mistake the mother has made, by her own account, when Emily was sick and she was urged to send her away to the convalescent home.[26] Reproaching herself for the nightmarish results, she might well hear a reproach in these words. *They* wouldn't let me go, but *you* did. Reproachful or not, however, the words clearly signal a transfer of the parental function from mother to audience. And to all appearances, for Emily the transfer is a happy one. The audience's enthusiasm for her acting not only contrasts with the mother's gloom, prophesying the success in the world outside the family that her mother is so quick to doubt. It also marks—like Rodriguez's relation to his readers—her entry into a kind of fellowship. Though the outcome remains uncertain, her future success is here redefined not as lonely individualism, but as an alternative social bond.

As the example of Rodriguez indicates, there is less of an abyss than one might have expected between audience or market demand, on the one hand, and the institutional voice of the state, on the other. It should not be a surprise, then, that despite all that has been said here against bureaucratic school and anonymous convalescent home, despite the mother's refusal of the requested official interview, this transfer of the parental function into the public domain clearly includes (like Steed-man's) a willingness to accept the state's interference.[27] Indeed, the mother invites that interference. Grammatically speaking, the famous "helpless before the iron" phrase is the object of an imperative: "Only help her to know—help make it so there is cause for her to know—that she is more than this dress on the ironing board, helpless before the iron." The imperative is addressed, of course, to the same unnamed interlocutor to whom the entire story is addressed: the health visitor. She is the one who has provoked the mother into speech by announcing that the daughter is someone who "needs help." And it is her help, or the help of the state, that the mother appeals to in this last sentence. When the word "help" reappears, as it does three times in the final paragraph, the mother has come to stand behind the imperative: she too is saying "help!" The key to her daughter's individual future, she concedes, the factor that can lead her to feel that she is not "helpless" after all, is the state's intervention.

For only the state, one might have added, can respond to the quiet hesitation that precedes this imperative: "help her to know—help make it so there is cause for her to know." It's not enough for her to know it, there must also be *cause* for her to know it. In other words, *just* cause, based on a proper understanding of how Emily and her talents and ambitions fit into a larger society composed of other people and *their* talents and ambitions. Her knowledge must not only express an individual's blind self-confidence, however badly out of tune with the threatening aspects of the social world that will test her. Her confidence must correspond to the real circumstances in which that testing will happen. No amount of individual confidence can pull this off. But Emily would be the wrong person to inform of this limit on her possibilities. The state, on the other hand, is the proper recipient of the mother's imperative. Only the state is in a position to add just cause to Emily's self-confidence, for only the state (if only it would listen to mothers like our narrator) might be capable of "mak[ing] it so there is cause," improving and balancing the life chances both for Emily and for other children.

The mother's reconciliation with the state is motivated, of course. She addresses the state not because she naively thinks it is the designated friend of working people like herself, but so as to lighten the excruciating burden of responsibility for her daughter's welfare, which would be too heavy for her to bear alone. Already a secret sharer in that responsibility, if only via Emily's school, the state that is now offering its help is the most plausible candidate for the job of sharing that responsibility. Even the welfare state at its best of course devotes much of its energy to such Keynes-ian market-control policies as making war and putting people in prison. It cannot and should not be protected from the feelings that are naturally elicited by military Keynesianism and what has come to be called the prison-industrial complex, not to speak of its other activities. Needless to say, we can never allow ourselves to forget any of these. And yet we also cannot forget that, for the same people who are deeply suspicious of them, the state is an abstract solution to a personal problem of hyperresponsibility.[28] And this abstraction is not a simple error. It is better understood as an appeal for the state to remake itself, or to be remade, so as to offer properly collective solutions to problems that are not always recognized as collective. If this appeal is not held open, the least that can be expected is a further privatization of solutions. The complicity of Foucaultian anti-statism with Republican free-market enthusiasm for privatization should give pause even to those who are most likely to be skeptical of expanding state surveillance and intervention.

I have remarked on the irony that hyperresponsibility or self-reliance, which is so often identified as the ideology of upward mobility, turns out on the contrary to be the problem that narratives of upward mobility attempt to resolve. Here too, in a story that's distinctive for revealing how the responsibility for child-rearing spreads out into society and into history, the narrator in effect declares that even her deliberately historical account has been too self-reliant. The very concern for her daughter's future that makes her blame herself also provokes her to put a limit to the self-blame, which makes her so negative and thus risks cutting her daughter off from the support and encouragement she needs. Hence the about-face in which she calls for the help of the very authority she has seemed to want to defy.

The cost of not performing this critique of self-reliance is illustrated by Alan Sillitoe's "The Loneliness of the Long-Distance Runner," a somewhat unlikely English analogue that like "I Stand Here Ironing" dates from the 1950s.[29] Here the working-class attitude toward the new institutions of the welfare state is still more defiant, and predictably so, for the setting is a prisonlike institution for juvenile offenders, or reform school— the English term is Borstal—where the narrator is serving a sentence for burglary. Doing time in prison does not necessarily entail taking the state as one's primary enemy. But this is just the vocabulary used by Smith, Sillitoe's everyman protagonist and narrator. What the Borstal has taught him is "who my enemies are" (16), namely those who run it and more generally the criminal justice system He himself is an "Out-law," and his enemies are the "In-Laws" (10), those who do not know that a class war is going on and that the other side is represented by the state. In the end, however, the story suggests that this out-law/in-law division of the world may after all be deluded and self-destructive.

As with "I Stand Here Ironing," 'The Loneliness of the Long-Distance Runner" is written as a monologue whose wonderfully unstudied, somewhat Holden Caulfield–esque voice is clearly meant to contrast favorably with the empty-headed euphemisms and moralisms of the bureaucrats. Again, as with Olsen's Emily, the young man has an extraordinary talent—here, long-distance running—that serves the purposes of the institution while also promising him a better future: "He might take up running in a sort of professional way when he gets out" (39). And again, at the heart of the story is an unwanted intrusion by representatives of the state who say they only want to help.

The climax of this monologue is not Smith's decision to stop short of the finish line and let someone else win the All-England Cup. That dramatic gesture of disaffection has been foretold well in advance (41), at the moment before the starting gun goes off. Though the end of the story is keyed to the big race, its climax is the story of his father's death from cancer. As he runs, Smith sees "my bloody dad behind each grass-blade in my barmy runner mind" (48). Just before the end, he describes how he found his father's body, and especially "the Out-law death my dad died" (50). The predeath scene offers another staging of the health visit, another confrontation with authorities who are there, though we are encouraged to doubt it, for the good of the family. It is a heroic scene to him because his father, who knows he is dying, treats them as the enemy, "telling the doctors to scat from the house when they wanted him to finish up in hospital (like a bleeding guinea-pig, he raved at them). He got up in bed to throw them out and even followed them down the stairs in his shirt though he was no more than skin and stick. They tried to tell him he'd want some drugs but he didn't fall for it, and only took the pain-killer that mam and I got from a herb-seller in the next street. It's not til now that I know what guts he had, and when I went into the room that morning . . ." (50). This is the memory that sustains him as he refuses to win, refuses what he has been told may be a path to upward mobility: "By God I'll stick this out like my dad stuck out his pain and kicked them doctors down the stairs; if he had guts for that then I've got guts for this and here I stay waiting" (51).

He's got to lose the race, it seems, in order to be loyal to his father's memory. But what if, as seems plausible enough, his father was wrong to kick the doctors down the stairs, refuse the painkillers, and rely instead on what could be obtained from the herb-seller in the next street? As if this did not give pause in itself, Sillitoe provides more reason for skepticism. In these same final pages he speaks of "the rotten life mam led him ever since I can remember, knocking-on with different men even when he was alive and fit and she not caring whether he knew it or not, and most of the time he wasn't so blind as she thought and cursed and roared and threatened to punch her tab, and I had to stand up to stop him even though I knew she deserved it. What a life for all of us" (49). Before this, we have heard about the six children watching the new television, bought with the "insurance and benefits" (20) from the father's death, "while mam was with some fancy-man upstairs on the new bed she'd ordered" (21). But we need not hear so much in order to feel convinced that there has been a major displacement of anger, both in the father and in the son, away from its real causes inside (and outside) the family and onto the representatives of the state, even in their arguably most innocuous form of doctors bearing painkillers. Family solidarity has thus been preserved, but at the expense of extreme political incoherence.

One name for this incoherence is individualism. In order not to blame his mother, he will blame no one but himself, and accordingly give credit to no one but himself. More precisely, the only blame he will indulge will be aimed at those who are insufficiently individualistic. He complains about the bureaucrats who say "We" rather than "I" (32) As far as he is concerned, he tells us, "the loneliness of the long-distance runner running across country" was "the only honesty and realness there was in the world" (43). His philosophy is to be "a long-distance runner, crossing country all on my own" (52). It's him running alone through and against the world.[30] This unrepentant self-reliance is especially striking in someone who claims, at least intermittently, to be fighting a class war. "I know who my enemies are" (16), he says. But he doesn't seem to. The one skirmish we see in his class war is fought against the local baker whose shop he burglarizes. His only conscious antagonism is against belonging as such. Hence the final gesture of withholding any satisfaction from the Borstal that thinks he belongs to or represents it, even if he has to hurt himself in order to do so. It's worth it if he can stop the "governor" or warden from being able to say, " 'My Borstal gets that cup' " (49).

Strangely enough, however, the warden is the one person he anticipates with pleasure having as a reader for what he has written. On the last page, he tells us: "I'd like to see the governor's face when he reads this, if he does, which I don't suppose he will" (54). Like Tillie Olsen, Sillitoe has his self-reliant protagonist address himself to a bureaucrat, though across an abyss of uncertainty that may or may not ever be bridged. And this uncertainty has the feel of a question in which this text is seriously and centrally interested. *Could* the governor actually read these pages? Though the protagonist does not end up reversing himself and appealing to the state for help, as Olsen's narrator does—his individualism goes much too deep for that—he tells us enough so that we can see he is wrong to consider such an appeal out of the question. He is sure, he says, that if the warden were to read his words, they would be incomprehensible to him. One sentence before suddenly recounting the kicking of the doctors downstairs, the warden's uncomprehending response is again what he foresees: "I'll show him what honesty means if it's the last thing I do," he says, "though I'm sure he'll never understand because if he and all them like him did it'd mean they'd be on my side which is impossible" (51). It's as if his sense of that impossibility produces the health visitor mistake, the self-reliant individualism that takes doctors making house calls as its symbol of the enemy. And yet as readers we have good reason to know that being "on his side" is not after all impossible. Even those of us who do not especially like the Borstal warden as a category will often be "like him" at least in the sense of being closer to In-laws than Out-laws. So if we *can* understand the narrator, or at least feel more than a passing tug of sympathy for his worldview, then we are also proving him wrong—wrong about governors, perhaps, but certainly about health visitors and about his determination never to rely on anyone but himself.

"I HATE LAWYERS. I JUST WORK FOR THEM": *ERIN BROCKOVICH*

In *Under the Cover of Kindness: The Invention of Social Work*, Leslie Margolin opens with an anecdote in which a five-year-old autistic boy wanders away from his rural Iowa home. The boy is picked up and brought to a police station by a passing motorist. A social worker is sent to investigate. As a result, though the child was ordinarily well cared for, the mother is cited for child neglect and her name placed "for ten years on a state-run child abuse registry, sharing space with those who torture, molest, and kill children. Also, she is not allowed to adopt a child, be a foster parent, or work in a child-care business."[31] This is not "an example of bureaucracy gone berserk" (2), the author says, but rather of the normal way in which "social work produces trust, conviction, ways of seeing things" (6). "My goal is to show that we always have social work at the same time as—and precisely because—we have the belief that it is 'doing good,' and that the more intense the belief in social work's essential goodness, the more immune it is to criticism, and the less clients are able to resist its ministrations" (6–7). The book is a brief on behalf of the clients and their right to keep these authorized intruders out of their homes, to resist having their personal lives scrutinized, judged, and classified.

Margolin presents this argument as controversial. It may well be. But in the humanities, at least, it represents something closer to received opinion. The powerful interdisciplinary influence of Foucault (much cited by Margolin) has helped produce or reaffirm a generalized antistatism that dictates the meaning of "doing good" every bit as pervasively as the governmental and professional language Margolin analyzes, though the two languages are of course at cross-purposes. Academic argument after academic argument builds itself around Margolin's own counterassumption: one is doing good if one is showing the insidious intentions and effects of the putatively benevolent representatives of the state and the professions, and thereby protecting the rest of us against them. Thus for example Typhoid Mary is resurrected as a modern heroine thanks to her stubborn resistance to surveillance and regulation by the emergent authorities of public health, which remorselessly tracked her down by following the trail of those she infected.[32] Anyone who thinks that protecting those she infected and would have gone on to infect was a real and legitimate motive for the public health authorities risks being considered politically naive. As things stand, the father who throws out the doctors in Sillitoe's story could count on being greeted with little if any skepticism as to the virtues of his political analysis. We too, like Sillitoe's narrator-son, have come to see ourselves as loyally fighting the good fight by obstructing the designs of the In-laws, especially those that seem most well intentioned.

There is of course always something to be said in favor of this fight. Margolin makes the excellent point, for example, that while social workers tend to align themselves theoretically with large, systemic reform, their actual effect as a profession is too often a pathologizing of individuals: "social workers attempt to change individuals and families, while social reformers such as Jane Addams aim to change institutions and culture" (4). On the other hand, it is unclear that one can accomplish any sort of large, systemic reform *without* working through individuals and families. To do so, however, one has to overcome considerable resistance—resistance to systemic reform as much as resistance to finding oneself subject to unflattering diagnosis. The cause of systemic reform (which also demands a certain amount of unflattering diagnosis) is not an argument for acquiescing in the need to defend the sphere of privacy against public intrusion (as in Margolin's example) or in the attitudes of extreme self-reliance (as in Sillitoe's) on which resistance to intrusion is based.

As one would expect, upward mobility stories are a genre in which this resistance, and the subset of self-reliance in particular, are much on display. What has been more unexpected, a discovery in which I obviously take a certain pleasure, is how powerfully the genre manages to contest both attitudes, even at its apparently most light-hearted and uplifting. It's as a lighthearted and uplifting specimen of the genre that I want to say a few words in conclusion about Steven Soderbergh's popular and not extravagantly highbrow film *Erin Brockovich* (2000). A crowd-pleasing upward mobility story starring Julia Roberts, who so successfully revived the Cinderella formula in *Pretty Woman* and here reminds us of it more than once, *Erin Brockovich* does little to invite special critical attention. Yet what has been argued thus far will make its interest for me plain enough. The title character *is* the health visitor. Indeed, she is the health visitor as protagonist of her own upward mobility story.

Like other courtroom dramas about a lone lawyer taking on a corporate giant, *Erin Brockovich* makes the obligatory reference to David and Goliath—or as Erin puts it, "David and whatsisname." But this is not a story about a heroically small individual. On the contrary, individualism is the problem it has to solve. Once Erin has figured out that the law firm has a case against the now notorious Pacific Gas and Electric, much of her screen time is spent getting the inhabitants of Hinckley to sign on to it. Intruding in the private lives of ordinary people, she has to prove herself by conquering their reluctance to get involved, house by house. She knocks at their doors and, if she can get past the door, tells them the unwelcome news about why their health is so bad. They have been allowing their children to wash and swim in water that was contaminated by Pacific Gas and Electric. There is a collective historical reason for the horrible diseases by which each of their families has been individually ravaged. And there is something collective that they can do about it, the suit against the utility that her boss is bringing.

The usual walls of privacy and individual responsibility are not easily breached. She cannot merely tell them, like other health visitors, that she is doing this for their own good. But Erin has a special talent, an ability to intrude into families *in the right way,* in the personal style of a single parent who has children rather than professional credentials. Asked whether she is a lawyer, she responds, "Hell, no. I hate lawyers. I just work for them." Hating lawyers is what allows her to be successful in her work, since the people of Hinckley, like the population at large, are suspicious of lawyers and of everything lawyers represent. The intrusion of the law must be humanized by someone who is, as she says, "great with people." But she does, as she says, work *for* lawyers, and this in more than one sense. Her hatred of lawyers, her experience as a single parent, are placed in the service of an impersonal professional expertise that many find repugnant. It is only this professional expertise, backed by the laws of the country, that can correctly diagnose the misfortunes of Hinckley and force the guilty parties to assume their responsibility. If Erin is more personable than the suits around her, in other words, the work she does is not accomplished in the name of the personal. On the contrary, she can succeed only if she can get the people of Hinckley to accept a distant collective cause that is invisible to any of them as individuals, but made available to them as a product of professional expertise. (Late in the case, after 634 plaintiffs have signed on, we see the same principle again: all of Erin's personality is needed in order to get the plaintiffs to take a chance on a legal judgment arrived at *without a jury*—in other words, with minimal leverage for personal sentiment.) She has to induce them to stop thinking in terms of personal, individual responsibility—precisely the terms that keep intruders like her at bay.

The crucial break in the case, and the moment that reveals the secret of her success, comes when she is approached by the second Hinckley couple, a couple that has suffered through five miscarriages and now has suddenly made the connection to Erin's talk of contaminated water. The woman says, "I figured it was something I did. Like when I smoked marijuana or took birth control pills." Here is the familiar pathological hyper-responsibility at work, ravaging self-respect in the name of self-reliance. And the antidote Erin brings, though disguised by her personal charm, is the ideology of the welfare state. She tells them it's not their fault. Responsibility is shared and systemic. As the woman herself translates what she has learned from Erin's crusade: "maybe it *wasn't* just me."

In short, it's not by means of self-reliance, but on the contrary by helping solve the *problem* of self-reliance, that she both achieves and justifies her own upward mobility. Without her work of mediation, enlisting legality-mistrusting people in a legal project, the suit could not have succeeded, and she could not have won her own personal victory, which is just as sweet if one sees it as resulting in a good job with respect and good benefits rather than paying undue attention to the $2 million bonus. She has risen in the world by doing good in the world.

This does not make her a direct representative of the state. Working for lawyers, she is a direct representative of their professional expertise, which is licensed by the state but not identical with it. It would be fair to call her an *indirect* representative of the state, however, in the sense that she melodramatically confronts professionals with their common citizenship: "By the way we had that water brought in special for you folks. It's from a well in Hinckley." And in the sense that something resembling justice can be done here, the corporation can be made to pay up, only because expertise is backed up by the force of common citizenship articulated (however imperfectly) by the law. Once again, the line between public and private is less distinct than for Steedman. But is there any doubt about how public-spirited and un-Cinderella-like the outcome is? We need no more legible sign of concern for the public welfare than defending the right to clean water. The film's emphasis on rising by doing good makes one wonder whether, like its foregrounding of a single mother who does not keep close watch over her language or her sexuality, this example of how we tell upward mobility stories now represents a change, or on the contrary an open tribute to a buried truth about the genre.

CHAPTER SIX

On the Persistence of Anger
in the Institutions of Caring

ANGER

Anger, Philip Fisher writes in *The Vehement Passions*, "in its legitimate form has its source in the feeling and in the perception of injustice" (175).[1] Fisher resuscitates this Aristotelian account of anger in order to redeem the concept from its sad fate in "our therapeutic, post-Freudian culture" (172). In Aristotle's view, feeling too little anger is no less of a problem than feeling too much. "The in-irascible man," the one who "does not feel anger when he should" (173), has fallen away from Aristotle's ideal of virtue. Our "therapeutic, post-Freudian culture" is of course very attentive to anger, but it is not, Fisher argues, respectful of it. On the contrary, it counts the prevention or eradication of anger as itself a virtue. Its "keenest interest lies in controlling anger or understanding the roots of anger, or learning how displacement has concealed from us the actual target of our visible anger, which is often in modern culture imagined to be about something else, often some experience long ago in childhood" (172). The culprit Fisher mentions is "modern culture," but it is hard not to infer that for Fisher, as for Christopher Lasch (whom he does not cite), the blame for diluting and delegitimating anger is to be shared with the therapeutic institutions of the welfare state.[2]

The welfare state conceived as part of an anger-management system made an appearance in the last chapter. This conception, characteristic of works written in or about the mid-twentieth century, returns in Kazuo Ishiguro's hauntingly beautiful novel *Never Let Me Go* (2005), and the continuity is intriguing. The moments Ishiguro is writing about (the late 1990s) and from (the early twenty-first century) seem at first glance to belong to a period that is very different from the 1950s and 1960s. In the last quarter of the twentieth century, the welfare state came under sustained assault by the right-wing parties of Margaret Thatcher and Ronald Reagan, thereby inaugurating what Malcolm Bradbury calls "the age of Sado-Monetarism."[3] The return of Labour under Tony Blair restored little of what had been cut from a wide variety of services. The so-called welfare reform passed by Bill Clinton and the Democrats in 1994 effectively usurped the Republican platform, eliminating large numbers of people from the rolls.[4] State policy seemed to have arrived at a bipartisan transatlantic antistatism so broadly popular that in the United States even September 11, 2001, with its surveillance hysteria and spectacular outburst of military Keynesianism, could not seriously disturb it. As a character remarks in David Lodge's *Nice Work* (1988), "You and I, Robyn, grew up in a period when the state was smart: state schools, state universities, state-subsidized arts, state welfare, state medicine—these were things progressive, energetic people believed in. It isn't like that any more."[5]

The new distrust of state intervention on the part of "progressive, energetic people," which as I've said helped provoke me to write this book, can be illustrated from among the protagonists of Pat Barker's novels. In both *Border Crossing* (2001) and *Double Vision* (2003), the plot could be said to center on the failure of the welfare state. Before *Border Crossing* begins, a child psychologist has performed his official functions in the case of a child who murdered an old woman. The psychologist is persecuted and almost destroyed when his patient comes back and insinuates himself into his life, having been imprisoned, supposedly rehabilitated, and then set free.[6] The novel opens with an act of rescue performed by a variant of the "health visitor." The question it poses is whether rescue—the premise of the welfare state, and of the upward mobility story as well—is possible or worthwhile. It becomes clear that from the perspective of the child, now grown to young adulthood, the pertinent plot is that of the upward mobility story, his own, and our psychologist/protagonist is to be classified as another in the long line of mentor/benefactors—again, from the child's perspective, a morally ambiguous one. In retelling this story from the benefactor's perspective, Barker casts considerable doubt both on the welfare state's ability to rehabilitate those in its care and on the upward mobility story that, as she confirms, always depended for its legitimacy, directly or indirectly, on the transformative power of rescue and rehabilitation.

In *Border Crossing* an old woman is murdered. In *Double Vision* an older woman is threatened with violence. Here too the target seems to be the very principle of the mentor/ benefactor as we have seen it, figuring a possible passage from object to subject of the "providential" state. Again the threat comes from a child murderer who has been locked up, treated, and then liberated. Thanks to the efforts of a progressive and energetic vicar who knows his past and is trying to help him rebuild his life, this character lands a job as assistant to the sculptor, Kate, who is our center of consciousness.[7] Soon Kate finds the strange but attractive young man wearing her work clothes, imitating her movements with the chisel, getting inside her head. Meanwhile we discover through Stephen, a writer and the novel's other center of consciousness, that this former prisoner is also a budding novelist whose stories, often about "female helplessness" and aggression against it, "kept slipping into sympathy with the predatory behavior they attempted to analyze" (137). One such story, whose plot is recounted, tells of an official representative of the welfare state, an art teacher in a prison, who is attracted to one of the prisoners and as a result is eventually murdered by him. Another, called "The Odd Job Man," tells a story very like the story we are reading, about a widow and the menacing younger man she hires. The suggestion is that this is a society in which progressive energetic people, hopeful that their intervention can make a difference, are willing to bend the rules in order to help someone. Officially or unofficially, they occupy a position in which they *can* hire and help. And it is that privileged position that is at stake. The charming perhaps-artist who receives the assistance, whose artistry signifies both deprivation and self-making, then repays them with physical or psychological violence. The violence seems to be motivated in part by a desire to become like them, or occupy a similar position. It is not inconceivable that this desire could eventually be satisfied; the elements of the upward mobility story are in place, waiting to be activated. And yet from the benefactor's perspective, which the reader is obliged to inhabit, the assistance rendered to the violent young man can hardly be described as anything but a terrible mistake.

Specifying the moral of Barker's stories in greater detail would be tricky. In the name of what particular naivete do these well-intentioned liberals put themselves and their loved ones at risk? Is it the refusal to acknowledge how much evil is out there? How irredeemable that evil is? How much or how little of the evil is properly their own responsibility? Or simply how feeble their own redemptive capacity is in comparison with the evil, wherever it came from? The question of origins cannot be judged irrelevant. One persuasive premise of liberal guilt is that the same system that produced the liberals' comforts also produced the discomfort and aggression of the less privileged. Barker neither acknowledges nor rejects this premise; she merely sidesteps it. It's as if at a certain point a new brand or level of logic clicked in, a logic of emergency and survival. OK, perhaps I should not enjoy the privileges I enjoy. But when I am threatened, questions of social justice disappear. My first obligation is to defend myself. In both *Border Crossing* and *Double Vision* there is an odd moment in which the protagonist suddenly panics, for what appears to be no adequate reason, and is overwhelmed with a fear of drowning. Each seems to be a moment in which "society" is abruptly reduced to a faceless quasinatural force threatening to suck you down, take your life. All that matters, therefore, is self-preservation.[8]

Politically speaking, the successful delegitimation of the interventionist state clearly marks an epoch. A great deal of anger was mobilized. Some of it took the politically polyvalent and mildly paradoxical form of anger against an antianger state—this is one possible reading of Fisher's tone above. Some constituencies performed the fusion that sociologist Richard Sennett discovered in Boston in the 1970s: a collapsing of the distinction between the recipients of welfare assistance and the professionals (social workers, guidance counselors, therapists, and so on) who provide that assistance, thereby of course securing employment in the system for themselves. Interviewing white working-class families, Sennett says, he noticed a "peculiar turn of phrase," "the use of the word 'them' as equally applicable to poor blacks and to liberal, middle-class professionals like teachers and social workers. The usage confounds race and class, marking 'them' as a single invasive threat" (12).[9] Needless to say, the money saved by cutting services and "excising supervisory fat" (186) did not flow back into these threatened communities. In its direct political effects, the social self-image of lean, mean autonomy led to an ever-widening gap between rich and poor. But these facts did not alter the period's political shape.

One might assume that the upward mobility genre would be reshaped accordingly. No doubt there are some versions that follow this political curve, offering up protagonists (CEOs, for instance) who succeed by being leanly and meanly autonomous. But what seems to me most worth remarking about the genre, seen against the recent political background of successful anti-welfare-state agitation, is its tendency to generate examples that hold out against the tide. As I have suggested, Sennett's menacing compound image of blacks and professionals, the employed and unemployed melded together as "unproductive," is by no means a simple error. It registers a genuine collusion. Without this collusion, the modern upward mobility story could not exist. Becoming a "liberal, middle-class professional" in a "helping" profession, the moderate, socially responsible, less-than-sensational endpoint of these stories, is possible only because there are "poor blacks" and others who are dependent on the assistance these middle-class professionals, white and black, are trained to provide. It is on these terms that the self-interest of the upwardly mobile stakes its claim to be compatible with the common good. The achievement of the genre in its most recent embodiments has been to acknowledge this reciprocal dependence, even while trying to look beyond it, and to do so without losing itself in the malicious cynicism that the insight seems to demand.

To put this another way, anger against the welfare state may well mark an epoch, but it does not dictate a new way for the upward mobility story to organize its emotions, nor does it define a new period in that genre's history. The generation of the Angry Young Men and women discussed above, including Sillitoe, Osborne, and Olsen, was often as angry at the "smart" state as anyone since. And yet as we have seen, these authors express the welfare state's promise as well as its threat. They show us, among other things, the grounds on which "progressive, energetic people" based their belief.

Consider novels satirizing the university, a subgenre which flourished in the 1950s and after. James English, following Malcolm Bradbury, A. S. Byatt, and others, describes British academic novels of this period as "texts of the welfare state" (132).[10] This seems right, and in a profound sense. The Education Act of 1944 (universal free schooling based on the eleven-plus examination) and the dramatic democratizing of higher education that followed, made possible by the intense experience of national solidarity in World War II, were part of "a rapidly enlarging system of government benefits and entitlements to provide a social safety net of unprecedented breadth." As a result, English concludes, "[at] no time in British history has education occupied such a privileged place in political discourse, or carried such a burden of societal hopes and expectations" (129–30).[11] These hopes and expectations are visible, of course, in the familiar novelistic forms of rebelliousness and disillusionment. Rebellion and disillusion are inevitable from the moment when the welfare state, symbolized first and foremost by the university, becomes the privileged mediator of postwar upward mobility. The welfare state can thus be blamed for the protagonist's betrayal of his or her community of origin, a betrayal that, as we have seen, is always a more or less salient component of the upward mobility story. Much postwar satire of the university asks therefore to be interpreted as an expression of anger both about the welfare state and about upward mobility itself.

Yet the anger in these novels also works on behalf of upward mobility and on behalf of the welfare state. In Malcolm Bradbury's *The History Man*, the Marxist doctrine of "historical inevitability" (26) that is satirized has as its shadow parallel a different "progressive" version of history: the upward mobility of its protagonists. Barbara and especially Howard Kirk, who begin in "the grimmer, tighter north, in respectable upper-working class cum lower-middle class backgrounds" (18),[12] rise in the world along with increased funding for higher education. How does Bradbury feel about these conjoined versions of progress? Though a commitment to grim northern respectability certainly informs his satire, he seems unable or unwilling to impose a corrective "decline" upon either the private ascent or the democratization of public resources that makes it possible. Like other satirists, Bradbury sees the university as a haven for pretentious political extremists. But the "gleeful skewering of radical chic" trumpeted by the Penguin cover is not an accident of authorial political orientation or a mere marketing strategy. The left-wing convictions of the sociologist antihero are organic to the trajectory of the "scholarship boy" (18). However sincerely Howard may hold these convictions, they also follow a logic that works behind his back, legitimizing his upward mobility by suggesting that his rise, enabled by public expenditure as well as personal effort, returns its value to the public—that it belongs not to Kirk alone, but to all of those who have been, like him, disadvantaged by birth. The anger seems excessive, unsympathetic, and even inexplicable. But it redounds to his moral credit.

Barbara Kirk calls her husband "a radical poseur" who has "substituted trends for morals and commitments . . . there's nothing in you that really feels or trusts, no character" (32). In doing so, however, she is merely repeating charges of insincerity and inauthenticity that have been made about the upwardly mobile scholarship boy since Richard Hoggart's founding analysis and that inevitably cluster around any successful self-transformation.[13] The real questions at issue are, first, whether the university will be allowed to serve as a site for self-transformation, and second, whether the progressive (though hardly revolutionary) ideology of the welfare state will be allowed to legitimize the university's role by pointing toward an ultimate democratic redistribution of educational benefits.

With a little interpretive latitude, Barbara Kirk's list of charges against her sexually predatory husband might be rewritten as a mission statement of the modern university. Enjoying the mind's freedom to shake loose from the firm bedrock of given "character," taking a critical distance from what one habitually "feels and trusts," and exploring new modes of being and feeling are all openly declared pedagogical goals. These are much the same values J. M. Coetzee's David Lurie articulates shortly before he is accused of sexual harassment—"He is all for double lives, triple lives, lives lived in compartments" (6).[14] They are also the values Bradbury himself puts in the mouth of his sexually needy surrogate in *Rates of Exchange*: "He travels, he thinks, for strangeness, disorientation, multiplication and variation of the self" (25).[15] If the academic novel makes this legitimizing case to the public, then it would seem to do so, ambivalently at best, in the lexicon of extramarital and/or unconventional sexuality. From this perspective, one might say that sex, which figured in H. G. Wells and Philip Larkin primarily as a distraction from scholarship, comes later in the century to stand for the true if necessarily unofficial meaning of higher education. The wild beginning-of-term parties in *The History Man*, designed so as to facilitate adventurous social and sexual mingling among nonpartners, would thus be a figure for the new university itself, conceived as a site of deliberate social experimentation, or at any rate for new disciplines like sociology. The reader is told nothing of the motives behind the sociologist Howard Kirk's cold, systematic, somewhat impersonal promiscuity, but others understand his and the novel's other seductions as a response to "need" rather than desire (185), and even (however ironically) as a form of therapy. "Another Miss Phee, getting the help," his colleague Miss Callendar says as she surrenders to him (212). Couplings like these among students and colleagues, open to the scrutiny of others and continuous with the analytic discourse of the classroom as well as the rescue discourse of the welfare state, might almost be considered official exercises.

As an institution representing the new, statutorily egalitarian opportunities of the welfare state, the university has also been exemplary for its self-conscious gender politics, or at any rate for being a workplace in which men and women are expected, however idealistically, to mix with uncharacteristic freedom and equality. This is no doubt one large structural reason why, beginning with *Lucky Jim* and continuing through imitations like Howard Jacobson's *Coming from Behind* (1983), masculinist backlash against feminism, homosexuality, and "political correctness" is so much in evidence.[16] Ambivalence about the welfare state takes the form of ambivalence about the new sexual equalities and freedoms, expressing itself in a familiar blend of satire and disavowed vicarious enjoyment.

On the other hand, the welfare state can also be taken as doing what we have seen it do in earlier chapters: legitimizing the upward mobility story by extending its benefits to others. As I've suggested, this is certainly a reason why Howard Kirk's anger, a motive that clearly transcends mere careerism and is indeed visibly self-destructive, pushes him to confront, provoke, keep up the rebellious pressure even on people and institutions that have proven themselves friendly to him. And it is a reason why, alongside the rebellion, the "societal hopes and expectations" that define the project of the welfare state remain vigorously alive within the academic novel, however unconsciously. The collision between (old) scholarly standards and the (new, more universal) right to employment is one instance— as it happens, an important one for Kingsley Amis's *Lucky Jim*. Consider the key dialogue between Jim and Gore-Urquhart, who is about to become his benefactor, just before Jim's drunken antilecture: "You're ambitious?" "No. I've done badly here since I got the job. This lecture might help to save me from getting the sack" (219).[17] Keeping his job is the only thing that Dixon seems to stand up for. Amis may prefer the semifeudal patronage of the Good Rich Man, but in besting the posh Welch family, Jim acts out the more democratic principles of the welfare state, which has now become a patron, if an impersonal, institutional one.[18] What's wrong with Mrs. Welch can be seen "most clearly, really, in her attitude towards the welfare state [. . . .] She argues, you see, that if people have everything done for them . . ." (81—ellipses in original). It seems significant that in the novel's climax, a comic chase scene, Christine is driven off to the railway station in Welch's car and Jim is obliged to give chase by means of a local bus. The bus, of course, stops to pick up and deposit other passengers. No matter what your personal hurry, no one must be left behind: this is the morality of public transport. And Amis quietly vindicates this morality, for in the end Jim gets the girl when—if only thanks to Welch's criminally incompetent driving—the bus wins the race.

In the United States, where higher education is of course more separable (though never completely so) from the funds and authority of the state, the university could not become a representative state institution in quite the same way. And yet the mediating relation to upward mobility and thus the core ambivalence are very similar. A recent issue of the *Hedgehog Review* entitled "What's the University For?" declares a truth that is universally acknowledged: that "a university education has become more integral to individual success in our society than ever before" (5).[19] Among the various ideas of the university, the one that is probably uppermost in the minds of prospective students and their parents is, as Gerald Graff has remarked, "the vulgar utility of culture as a means of upward mobility."[20] This means that the upwardly mobile are likely to feel both love for the university and anger at the university. It is in terms of this structural ambivalence that sociologist Neil Smelser explains some recent critiques of the university: "The collegiate experience is culturally defined as an avenue for *social mobility*" (49). To provide such an avenue, however, is to "pull students away from the cultural values and attitudes of their family, their social class, and their community" (48). The result is "ambivalence toward culture of origin and culture of invitation" (49). In the name of identity and diversity, this ambivalence can express itself in an attack on such university traditions as their "meritocratic criteria—that is, universalistic standards of judgment" (38).[21]

As in the UK, the university becomes a target of anger because it is a site of conflict. And as in the UK, stories about this so-called culture of invitation ("destination" seems preferable, since it avoids the misleading hint that someone has actually issued an invitation) will try to resolve this conflict as best they can by reconsidering such "universalistic standards of judgment" as the common good. If the university cannot be confused with the state, it nonetheless resembles other institutions, both public and private, that also depend on the claim to represent the universal or general welfare. And it is by pushing and pulling on this claim that the upward mobility stories set in these institutions distinguish themselves most radically from simple wish fulfilment. In *Brothers and Keepers*, John Edgar Wideman asks how he got ahead, making a career as a university teacher, while his brother was serving a life term for murder. In *Parallel Time*, Brent Staples asks how he got ahead, landing a job with the *New York Times*, while his brother sold drugs and was murdered. Both of these are angry books, and some of the anger is aimed at the university and the *New York Times*, institutional destinations that, whatever their differences, play much the same structural role in the upward mobility story.

Both books, as we will see, come closest to answering their questions when they turn to the explicit help of the welfare state.[22]

Despite the delegitimation of the welfare state, then, today's "progressive, energetic people" seem to experience some of the same motives for anger as their predecessors: a desire to reject the help offered them, to escape their own entanglement within a less-than-ideal system of official restitutions and rewards, to express a loyalty to the culture of origin by somehow forcing the benefits of upward mobility to be shared. They too are ambivalent about an upward mobility that is often both state-assisted (via scholarships, arts subsidies, and so on) and by the same token state-defined. In more than one sense, that is, they are representatives not of autonomy but of dependence, or interdependence. Troubled, critical, and self-critical, they remain insiders, angry both despite and because of their commitment to the institutions that have helped raise them up. Readers will be willing to take this historical continuity, I hope, as a source of comfort. It suggests that the seemingly triumphant delegitimation of the state is less than complete—that popular belief in democratically mandated state intervention has not disappeared, nor has belief in the possibility and desirability of shaping an individual life as part of that collective project (which is indeed what Lodge's Robyn will decide about her own life.). Even where anger is concerned, credit can still be given for genuine good intentions. As Richard Sennett testifies: "Only the paranoid could believe that the welfare state *aimed* . . . at pacifying those it helped" (178). Sometimes, though not always, bureaucratic anger fuels the commitment of those who continue to participate, however ambivalently, in the welfare state's appointed mission to lighten the load of existing injustice.

Sennett, who will be discussed at greater length below in company with fellow sociologists Paul Willis and Pierre Bourdieu, offers an illustration. In *Respect in a World of Inequality* (2003), he writes: "I grew up in the welfare system, then escaped from it by virtue of my talents. I hadn't lost respect for those I'd left behind, but my sense of self-worth lay in the way I'd left them behind. So I was hardly a neutral observer." Failing to be a neutral observer either of the welfare system or of the sense of self-worth derived from escaping it, Sennett could easily pass for an exception among sociologists, or even a renegade. But his prestige among his colleagues, along with the strange public salience of his life history—two things he shares with Bourdieu and Willis—suggest a different possibility: that although both Sennett's talent and his upward mobility story are exceptional, his story asserts a general principle about "making it," both in sociology and in other official "caring" institutions that, like sociology, work in parallel with the milieu of his childhood. Sennett has arrived at an official position where it is his duty to study, more or less angrily, the social injustice that made him angry. He has climbed out of that milieu in part by writing about it, and writing about it in turn has allowed him to do something about it. His upward mobility story suggests that one can rise by caring, and can care while being angry.

Caring: Kazuo Ishiguro's Never Let Me Go

In the first sentences of Ishiguro's *Never Let Me Go*, we discover that its protagonist is another health visitor, another officially appointed benefactor without money. The self-description she gives is "carer."

> I'm Kathy H. I'm thirty one years old, and I've been a carer now for over eleven years. That sounds long enough, I know, but actually they want me to go on for another eight months, until the end of this year. That'll make it almost exactly twelve years. Now I know my being a carer so long isn't necessarily because they think I'm fantastic at what I do. There are some really good carers who've been told to stop after just two or three years. And I can think of one carer at least who went on for all of fourteen years despite being a complete waste of space. So I'm not trying to boast. But I do know for a fact that they've been pleased with my work. (3)[23]

If the word "carer" seems a bit mysterious, it's because the congenial everyday verb has been absorbed into an official-sounding occupational category. Like health visitor, which performs the same bureaucratic swearing-in on visiting, carer exudes a slight chill, and that chill—milder no doubt in the UK, where both terms are in use, but not totally absent even there—is what the novel is most obviously about. The society that invented the "carer," not our own, turns out to harbor a sinister semisecret. In this dystopian England of the late 1990s, colonies of children are being cloned—that's why Kathy is Kathy H., with no family name. They are raised in isolation from normal children. Once they reach adulthood, their vital organs are harvested, one by one, and used in the treatment of other people's diseases. Each operation is called a "donation." Before these cloned children become "donors," most of them spend some time as carers, health visitors who move around the country tending pre- and postop to those who are making donations. Donors sometimes "complete," or die, after the first or second donation, and almost inevitably by the fourth. When Kathy says she will remain a carer "until the end of this year," we do not yet understand that she is announcing, with a lack of complaint that will later come to seem noteworthy, the beginning of the organ donations that will lead more or less speedily to her death. Her cheerful patter about how long she has been doing this job and how much her superiors appreciate her work is thus encircled by an immense moral obscenity.

Kathy's thoughts are preoccupied not with her imminent end, but with her professional success. In dispatching that success down the track toward a nightmarish terminus, Ishiguro would seem to be querying both the institution of the welfare state and the ideology of upward mobility. He also clearly assumes—conveniently, for the purposes of the present argument—that the two have become intimately connected. Kathy's professional ambitions are set within a bureaucracy that, while explicitly described neither as public nor as private, resembles the welfare state both in its rationale and in its total penetration of the private lives of those in its care. For those in its care, who are also those who do much of the caring, this bureaucracy defines a possible path of modest professional advancement. The modesty of the advancement, defined by the transformation of the object (the one cared for) into the subject (the one who does the caring), is also a welfare-state theme, touched on above, that *Never Let Me Go* helpfully recapitulates. The glaring difference here is of course the absolute, biological blockage of advancement. Seen from the perspective of the cloned children, what's wrong with upward mobility stories is that they are not going to come true. One of the teachers or "guardians," Miss Lucy, explains this to her students in a sudden fit of frankness:

> "You've been told, but none of you really understand, and I dare say, some people are quite happy to leave it that way. But I'm not. If you're going to have decent lives, then you've got to know, and know properly. None of you will be going to America, and none of you will be film stars. And none of you will be working in supermarkets as I heard some of you planning the other day. Your lives are set out for you. You'll become adults, then before you're old, before you're even middle-aged, you'll start to donate your vital organs. That's what each of you was created to do. You're not like the actors you watch on your videos, you're not even like me." (73)

The phrase "not even like me" announces the closing off of that second-best, subfantasy option, imitating and becoming a benefactor without money, on which the modern upward mobility story has been so crucially dependent.

In extrapolating from our own society, Ishiguro's science-fiction premise also of course sends us back to it. Reading Miss Lucy's speech, it is hard not to speculate about intended comparisons to upward mobility in the present. Here and now, in the absence of segregated clones or a system of obligatory organ removal masquerading as voluntary "donation," it is almost equally certain that the futures the vast majority of children dream of will not be realized.[24] The organ-donation gulag, tucked away from public view and yet not kept fully secret, has its obvious real-world counterpart in what we call class. Doesn't class divide just as effectively, allowing some of us to expect a reasonable return on our career investments while deviously ensuring that little will come of any expectations the rest may have? What difference does it make that in our society class origin does not define an official identity, a box to be checked on the census form, grounds for compulsory segregation during childhood? We too have schools that resemble prisons and prisons where almost everyone seems to be from the same background. There is pervasive censorship in the cloned children's "progressive" school, as we can see when Miss Lucy defies it, and yet—this is one of the more striking ironies of the science fiction premise—the expectationless in the twenty-first century USA are probably told *less* of the truth about what will turn out to be their destiny than they are in Ishiguro's brave new world. Ishiguro obliges us to wonder whether the freedom on which his uncloned readers pride themselves is anything more than a similarly managed ignorance of what in all probability awaits them, even if the hope and (one can almost say) the happiness that ignorance sometimes brings with it may be hard to give up. How much does it matter that in the novel the split between those who have a future and those who don't results from the biological facts of one's birth, which result in turn from a deliberate decision by the authorities, while in our society it is an effect without originary legislation or identity, with no "they" visibly making the decisions, an outcome that can merely be predicted with high statistical reliability?

As the proper frame for this high-tech revival of quasifeudal hierarchy, Ishiguro delivers an inspired piece of genre modification. He takes the bland, squeaky-clean idiom of the middle-class boarding school novel, with its beguilingly motivational assumption that the world is just and that effort will eventually be rewarded, and infuses it with a dark, late-twentieth-century punk or slacker vision of "no future."[25] The narrative choice is familiar from his previous novels. We look at the world through the eyes of a character of limited consciousness, immersed in concerns and anxieties that one cannot confidently call trivial, who prefers not to contemplate the Big Picture. What kind of system does her routine belong to? Where is the seemingly endless file of workdays leading? We ourselves do not look any ultimate questions in the face, but we watch as the character looks away from them, and are thus made to feel the force both of these questions and of our own resistance to them.

The technique assumes, justifiably I think, that at some point we will ask, defensively: who *does* want to contemplate the Big Picture? Who can afford to? Even as we recoil from Ishiguro's premise, its existential force jolts us into sudden sympathy with Kathy. Like her, and like the butler of *Remains of the Day* and the pianist of *The Unconsoled*, I depend for my daily dose of contentment on a blinkering of awareness that I myself in my better moments would find outrageous and shameful. If the novel is trying to be the cause or occasion of such moments, as seems plausible, *Never Let Me Go* paradoxically does so by going deep into the partly existential desire that sustains the upward mobility story, the desire that keeps me identifying with the uncloned, who do or at least may have a future. It goes so deep as to make the reader wonder which side Ishiguro is on. And which side we are on. Isn't it plausible for me to assert my conviction that after all I am not a statistic, that what holds statistically or generally need not turn out to hold for me in particular, that in any case I must act as if I didn't know what will happen, as indeed in a sense I don't? Such reasoning seems by turns logically flawless, socially dishonest, and practically unavoidable. The intensity of primal pain may vary, but the principle comes close to what we heard in Carolyn Steedman's wonderfully honest outburst: "And I? I will do everything and anything until the end of my days to stop anyone ever talking to me like that woman talked to my mother." "Everything and anything": the rules are suspended. The absolute peremptoriness of the practical—the responsibility to pay the rent, put food on the table, keep up the home, avoid humiliation—can be seen as a sort of state of exception, a falling back on irreducible individual sovereignty that precedes and overrides the ideology of collective justice.

Collective justice can provisionally reassert its authority only if we can be seduced into contemplating, coldly and impersonally, the absurd panorama that results as endless crowds of us, unique individuals every one, try to assert our boundless sovereignty and pack ourselves into the cramped space of a minute statistical possibility. This is one hypothesis about what the upward mobility story at its best accomplishes. In what is less a negative critique than a riff on the genre's established repertory of images, Ishiguro suggests again that my logic of individual freedom, irrefutable as it seems, involves literally trying to get away with murder. As if by extension of Brent Staples's autopsy-table image, here upward mobility means turning your head away so as not to see that someone else's organs are being excised, and excised in order that your own life can go merrily forward. The reader's only apparent alternative in *Never Let Me Go* is to identify with the carer/donors, who speak the middle class's own optimistic, system-trusting language and yet embody the reality of the exploited, a collectivity of sheep that do not seem to have realized (to refer to an authority cited in the preface) their lives consist mainly of standing around waiting to be eaten. It is necessary to add, however, that this vision of upward mobility could also be taken as a backhanded argument in favor of sheep learning to fly, whatever the odds—in other words, as a case for arousing rather than rejecting social aspiration, if aspiration can be seen as including the impulse to change the system. In the same mildly perverse spirit, we might see Ishiguro as teaching that I must *try* to think of myself as a statistic, if only so as not to join the millions in thinking of myself as an improbable individual exception to the statistical rule. And we might see this lesson as undercutting his seemingly absolute skepticism toward the welfare state. These interpretive options, however inconclusive, are reinforced by the ambiguities into which the novel plunges as it tries to pursue its more overt argument.

If Ishiguro is urging us to perceive the horror that floats just beyond the horizon of our daily routine, he seems more directly concerned with the question of what makes action against it almost unthinkable. In this novel, the primary answer to that question seems to be the welfare state, whose quintessential activity is caring. Caring gives a grateful semblance of meaning and legitimacy to the stopgap efforts of every day. How can it not be right to care? Why is it that Miss Lucy's revolutionary truth-telling speech to the students makes no apparent difference? "[T]here was surprisingly little discussion about what she'd said. If it did come up, people tended to say: 'Well, so what? We already knew that' " (74). At one point the characters drive to the coast in order to stand and gaze at a stranded boat, a mere symbol rather than an actual means of escape. The closest they get to challenging the rules by which they live and die is the heartbreaking myth—exposed as such in the novel's climactic scene—that it is possible to win "deferral" of one's donations on the basis of one's artwork, which is sometimes taken away without explanation by the headmistress of the school. (The irony, exquisitely compressed into this theology of provisional salvation, is that the school fails to recognize the children's genuine creativity, which expresses itself not in the artwork itself but rather in this myth-making about the ability of artwork to transform their lives.)[26] As an explanation of the headmistress's actions, the myth that their "best work" is preserved in her "Gallery" is also an explanation of how the children can avoid knowledge of "[w]hat's going to happen to us one day. The donations, and all that" (27). They need to believe that the merit of what they are doing will be rewarded, if only by being recognized, and this entails a belief in the fundamental rightness of the authorities doing the recognizing and rewarding. This belief is already in evidence when Kathy introduces herself on the first page. Canny as she is about the existence of unfairness in the system—she alludes to cases in which the competent have been told to stop, or die, while the incompetent have been kept on—Kathy does not talk as if "they," representing the system, are the people who have decided she will turn donor and die. "They" appear as those who are "pleased with [her] work." To question what they have proclaimed to be her future would mean also questioning what they feel about the value of her work, and thus her entire life narrative.

The ultimate sanction of this obstinate, almost suicidal clinging to the value of one's work is clarified in a late dialogue between Kathy and Tommy. Tommy becomes Kathy's lover only when she finally becomes his carer, although they have loved and cared for each other for many years without acknowledging it. He says to her: "I mean, don't you get tired of being a carer? All the rest of us, we became donors ages ago. You've been doing it for years."

> I shrugged. "I don't mind. Anyway, it's important that there are good carers. And I'm a good carer."
> "But is it really that important? Okay, it's really nice to have a good carer. But in the end, is it really so important? The donors will all donate, just the same, and then they'll complete."
> "Of course it's important. A good carer makes a big difference to what a donor's life's actually like." (258)[27]

Here the ideology of the welfare state colludes with the ideology of upward mobility, lending its authority to the socially respectable form that (as I have argued) upward mobility has little by little come to assume. As in *The Unconsoled*, which this passage strongly recalls, the excuse for an excessive devotion to one's work (or a devotion that others will see as excessive) is the belief that the work is socially valuable, that it makes a positive difference to others as well as to oneself, that it responds to a genuine need. Caring means you can win credit and advantage for yourself without "trying to boast" or to get ahead of the others, that is, while innocently carrying out a service for the benefit of the social whole. The work may be self-destructive; as Tommy says, "all this rushing about you do. All this getting exhausted and being by yourself. I've been watching you. It's wearing you out." But it can lay claim to representing a synthesis of individual merit and the collective welfare.

Without leaning too hard on the pertinent biographical facts—Ishiguro is married to a former social worker, and they met during the year he spent doing social work himself—it seems plausible to read some of his signature effects as attempts to hold up and examine, at the level of the individual sentence, a welfare-state vision of life, a vision centered on that bittersweet compromise between social justice and the injustice enforced by capitalist competition. Nothing could be more characteristic of his style, for example, than the syntax of "muddling through." "The recovery rooms are small, but they're well-designed and comfortable" (16). Here a mild concession to suffering (small rooms) receives, as if by a miraculously swift response from the appropriate department, instant compensation—yet compensation that is also trivial. Kathy's brisk efficiency leaves no space for surprise at the fact that there *are* recovery rooms, that recovery rooms exist in the first place only because of "donations," that the existence of donations and recovery rooms signals a suffering that is beyond any possible compensation. The sentence structure seems engineered to guarantee that the best will always be made of a bad situation, with no acknowledgment that the situation will always be bad because the same system has also begotten it. The same is true of course of the initial passage, which sets Kathy's ingratiating consciousness that the reward system is unfair against her breathtaking *un*consciousness of the much greater unfairness that underlies it. She cheers us up, as she cheers herself up, with evidence of minor compensations, improvements, or advantages within what might otherwise be seen as an irredeemable disaster. Thus she makes her own peace with the inevitable, eventually deciding that it is "right": "though I'll miss being a carer, it feels just about right to be finishing at last come the end of the year" (4). And she takes pride in her professional ability to spread the same message around her, inducing others to make peace with their own fate: "My donors have always tended to do much better than expected. Their recovery times have been impressive, and hardly any of them have been classified as 'agitated,' even before the fourth donation" (3). It might seem that Ishiguro has been reading Perry Anderson's metanarrative of the birth of the welfare state out of working-class compromise. Blank and bureaucratic, cravenly accepting of monstrously limited expectations, dedicated to suppressing all "agitation" at the deep injustice that underlies the system as a whole: this is the voice of the welfare state much as Anderson understands it.[28]

The action of keeping donors from being "classified as 'agitated,' even before the fourth donation," a rephrasing of Philip Fisher's point about the fate of anger in modern culture, throws a harsh light on the legitimacy Kathy claims for her labors. Yet I ask you to reconsider how this account of what carers do fits into the first and longest of the novel's three parts. Like Stevens in *The Remains of the Day*, Kathy does not want to recognize that hers is a sort of love story—a rivalrous triangle in which her best friend Ruth pairs off with the passive Tommy, who might have seemed better suited to Kathy, until the time of the donations has begun, when Kathy briefly inherits the little that is left of him. On reflection, however, the focus of these hundred-odd pages seems too significant in its own right to be considered a mere diversion from the love triangle. The issue here is Tommy's anger: his fits, when he is teased or not chosen for a team, and how he overcomes his feelings, learning to fit in better with those around him. Both the problem and the resolution seem to leap right off the brightly lit shelf devoted to young adult fiction. But given this novel's macabre framework, they make more sense if considered as an example of welfare-state ideology—for the purposes of the present argument, a familiar example. Kathy tells Tommy that he's "happier these days" (21). He knows what she means: "You're talking about me not . . . getting so angry" (21). The secret of how he has stopped getting so angry is revealed as a conversation with Miss Lucy about his artwork. His other teachers have judged his artwork unsatisfactory. Miss Lucy tells him something we have heard over and over in the course of this book: that this is not his fault: "What she said was that if I didn't want to be creative, if I really didn't feel like it, that was perfectly all right. Nothing wrong with it, she said" (22). "I realized she was right, that it wasn't my fault. Okay, I hadn't handled it well. But deep down, it wasn't my fault. That's what made the difference" (26). Both the advice and its effect—less anger or "agitation," therefore more happiness—are again perfectly in keeping with the critical view of the welfare state that permeates so much of the novel. The welfare state, so the moral would go, is the institution that bribes us with minor restitutions and supplements so as to divert us from deep and systematic injustice, which is to say from our legitimate causes for anger.

This seems unambiguous enough. But thinking about "it's not your fault" as a slogan both of the welfare state and of upward mobility, I find myself suspecting that this version of "it's not your fault" is more ambiguous than it appears—something one might also have deduced from the place of "war guilt" in Ishiguro's fiction. In *Good Will Hunting*, the welfare state's "no fault" philosophy seems committed both to getting rid of Will's anger and to liberating his aspiration, which the anger has blocked. In order to alleviate Tommy's sense of unworthiness and make him happier, Miss Lucy's version of this therapeutic wisdom seems at first glance more willing to shut the aspiration down along with the anger. Yet Miss Lucy is the same teacher who rebels against the reigning policy (by telling the children the truth) and soon after disappears from the school. The "no fault" advice likewise is taken, at least by Kathy, as the expression of a revolt against the school's common sense, not a repetition of it. Kathy is normally a reliable representative of that common sense, and she dismisses Miss Lucy's words as "just rubbish" (22). When Tommy replays the conversation for her again—"It was wrong for anyone, whether they were students or guardians, to punish him for it, or put pressure on him in any way. It simply wasn't his fault" (25)— again Kathy can't believe anything so subversive was sincerely meant. "She wasn't having you on, was she?" (25).[29] This advice must be understood to contradict the principles of the school. One can see why. In eliminating fault it also eliminates merit, hence aspiration. The school encourages the children's aspirations to excel, and children cannot be expected to demonstrate their excellence if they don't think that failure to do so will be taken as their own fault. In her revolt, Miss Lucy is of course implying that it makes no sense to encourage these futureless children to think in terms of merit and reward. She knows the habits of aspiration inculcated by the school are intended merely to distract the students from the dark truth of the impending donations.

Yet her straightforward logic leads to a devious conclusion. For if her articulation of the "no fault" philosophy is a way of soothing Tommy's anger, it simultaneously asks to be construed as a way of adapting his feelings to the terrible truth of his situation—which is of course something very much worth being angry about. Getting rid of anger by getting rid of merit leads circuitously but logically back again to anger.

One of the things Tommy himself doesn't know how to interpret in his conversation with Miss Lucy is the place of anger in it. "When she said all this, she was shaking . . . With rage. I could see her. She was furious. . . . I don't know who she was angry with. But she was angry all right" (26). Getting rid of anger, Tommy's anger, is what the scene supposedly accomplishes. But rather than vanishing, anger is displaced to Miss Lucy herself. If for the moment at least Miss Lucy is the representative of the welfare state, as she seems to be, then the welfare state would seem to be something quite different from a therapeutic agency that preserves the system by cushioning its worst blows and dispelling violent anger from it. In the very act of delivering its most characteristic message, Miss Lucy reveals the welfare state as a bearer of anger.

At the very end of the novel the meaning of that anger is confirmed— confirmed as an Aristotelian "perception of injustice." Tommy and Kathy, now donor and carer, find the address of the retired head of their old school, which has since been closed down (though the organ donation program has not), and they confront her with the question of deferrals. They learn that deferral was a myth. On the drive back, Tommy runs off into an open field and expresses the feelings appropriate to this lesson. Seeing "Tommy's figure raging, shouting, flinging his fists and kicking out" (250), Kathy is inspired to propose to him, a few moments later, an interpretation she has developed of his childhood behavior. Her idea is "maybe the reason you used to get like that was because at some level you always *knew*" (252). Tommy hesitates; he still wants to think it was only him. But finally he agrees. Maybe he did know. If so, then Miss Lucy seems to have failed in the mission of eliminating Tommy's anger—or on the contrary maybe she has succeeded in maintaining it. (That untamed anger is perhaps why we never see Tommy as a carer, only as a donor, and indeed as a donor who in Kathy's view identifies a bit too strongly with his fellow donors.) Miss Lucy's advice to him that his conduct in school was "not [his] fault" was not "conservative" but politically correct, if that phrase can be cleansed of recent associations: it confirmed that what his anger expressed (as in so many stories of juvenile delinquency) was a precocious knowledge of a blocked future, knowledge of a general social injustice.

About aspiration, as about anger, Miss Lucy can advise Tommy properly only by contradicting herself. Contradiction is inherent in the situation she is trying to address. Of course she wants Tommy to aspire. But in order to aspire, he must inhabit a system that makes aspiration reasonable. He doesn't. Instead of delivering a coherent message, therefore, she acts out the incoherence around her by taking back what she has said. Just before departing from the school and the plot, at the end of part 1, she changes her mind about whether Tommy's artistic failures are his fault. As Tommy puts it: "And she said no, I wasn't all right. My art was rubbish, and it was partly her fault for telling me what she had" (99). The recantation could well signify no more than her own resignation to the inevitable: if there is no way out for Tommy, then better to leave him in a state of self-delusive aspiration, even if he therefore blames himself for failures that are not his fault. Yet the recantation also implies that fault, which goes with aspiration, belongs not on Tommy but on the system that she herself represents. This is included in her message: "it was partly her fault for telling me what she had." Just as anger was displaced from Tommy to Miss Lucy in the previous scene, so here fault passes from the passive object to the active subject of the welfare state. This passage has various consequences. If the representative of the welfare state can be angry and at fault, then it is much easier to imagine working within the welfare state—being "like me"—as a potential terminus for the upwardly mobile juvenile offender of talent. It becomes possible to hypothesize such a thing as angry aspiration, a goal that would require maintaining rather than eliminating the anger that seems to block the passage upward. The system itself might be imagined as capable of seeing legitimate merit in those who aspire to change it—to change decisions about which aspiration is and isn't legitimate, what merit there is in caring and who deserves it, whether society should be divided into donors and those who benefit from their organs.

The implication of this line of thinking is that Miss Lucy was also exaggerating when she told the children that they are "not even like [her]." In a sense, they are. They are about to enter into training to be carers. But our understanding of caring, the generic work of the welfare state, has clearly been expanded by the anger against the system expressed in Miss Lucy's supposedly anger-managing "no fault" speech. Perhaps that occupational category has even been expanded far enough so as to become a goal of angry aspiration. As Kathy works with donors, Miss Lucy works with donors-to-be. As Kathy works to keep her donors from being "classified as 'agitated,' even before the fourth donation," Miss Lucy works on Tommy's anger. They both work "on" Tommy. And they both care for him in more than one sense of the word. The parallel in their caring gets even more intriguing when one notices that both of them end up telling him his art is "rubbish."

Miss Lucy's declaration has just been quoted. Kathy's comes in one of the novel's strangest moments, its one instance of a type of scene for which Ishiguro has become famous: a scene of inexplicable cruelty between people who love each other. (For fans of Ishiguro, I imagine this as the real payoff of my argument.) Ruth, whose earlier acts of casual cruelty have seemed explicable enough, suddenly tells Tommy that when he dreams of getting his pictures of imaginary animals into the Gallery, he is making a fool of himself—not because Gallery and deferrals are merely mythic, but because his pictures are no good. She says that she and Kathy have talked about it and that Kathy agrees with her: "Kathy here finds your animals a complete hoot" (178). This is a barefaced lie. Kathy knows she has to say so, but she doesn't. How can she be so cruel, even by omission, to the one person she has always loved? Is it simply the fatality of human nature that stops people from ever seizing the happiness offered them, as critics like Louis Menand have exasperatedly suggested about similar scenes in *The Unconsoled*? (I specify, sounding as I do so all too much like that novel's narrator: the dead hamster and manual-flinging scenes.)[30] On reflection, Kathy's cruelty might after all make sense if it is taken as her sole and unique expression of anger. Behind her gesture would be an anger like that of Tommy and Miss Lucy, an anger that is inevitably misplaced or self-contradictory, but also inevitable—in brief, her one moment of genuine if oblique response to the horror of the system that she ordinarily will not acknowledge. "Something in me just gave up. A voice went: 'All right, let him think the absolute worst. Let him think it, let him think it' " (179). This is ambiguous in a more than trivial sense. Does Kathy want him to think the absolute worst about *her*? Or does she want him to think the worst about himself? The latter, which seems more likely, would exactly duplicate the logic of Miss Lucy's recantation: telling him his art is rubbish. But since she has not expressed this opinion of his drawings earlier, it seems more likely still that she is drawing your-art-is-rubbish into a larger judgment about things in general: let him think the absolute worst about his own situation, about what awaits them all, about everything. In short, either of the two likeliest interpretations would suggest that cruelty is almost indistinguishable from caring. True caring (love) would necessarily have cruelty in it. And in this it would have something in common with the official caring of the carer.[31]

The point is especially worth emphasizing because Ishiguro has so often seemed to be interested in making only the most banal and uncontroversial sorts of moral statement, on the order of "cruelty is bad." Cruelty *is* bad. But here at least it also seems to be part of a more expansive political vision, one that allows us to consider caring, and the welfare state, as projects that do not merely aim at willful delusion. It seems worth speculating as to whether similar scenes of intimate cruelty in Ishiguro might also register, if only partially and distortedly, the pressures of moral responsibility to the long term and the far away.

As the reader comes to the end of this novel, the job of caring that Kathy speaks about with such enthusiasm on the first page will not have come to seem a dazzling employment opportunity. Yet it will have accumulated a certain number of interesting surprises. One is anger against the system in which it is forced to work. Another is the two-way communication between work and love, extremes of personal affect and impersonal affectless supervision that are of course already present in the term. Ishiguro seems eager to separate caring in the professional and nonprofessional senses.[32] Perhaps the purest expression of love in the novel is when Tommy, knowing his impending donation is likely to be his last, sends Kathy away, saying he doesn't want her anymore as his carer: "I don't want to be that way in front of you" (257). At the same time, it can hardly be a coincidence that the relationship of carer and donor is also Ishiguro's only published account of what might be termed successful, reciprocated love—love marred by dependence perhaps, but love nonetheless. (*The White Countess* would now have to count as another.) This love is cool and dispassionate, at least as Kathy presents it; it is based on what might look like an excess of understanding. It doesn't feel very triumphant, and it's certainly not immortal. The horror of imminent mortality in the form of the donations explains perhaps why there is so little passion and so much ambivalence about "accepting" the other—for example, why even Kathy, who by character is accepting almost to a fault, is betrayed into her silent acquiescence in Ruth's (and Miss Lucy's) harsh judgment that Tommy's art is rubbish. Both Ruth and Miss Lucy are angry. Kathy has seemed to be the opposite. But it's only by being angry with Tommy that she can hold open the possibility of an aspiration for him.

Rising in Sociology: Pierre Bourdieu, Paul Willis, and Richard Sennett

A recent French documentary about Pierre Bourdieu is entitled "La Sociologie est un sport de combat," or sociology is a martial art.[33] Bourdieu, who pronounces this line in the film, clearly knew whereof he spoke. When he died in January 2002, he was widely considered France's best-known sociologist, its most influential intellectual, and one of its angriest men. In an autobiographical fragment published within days of his death (now available in book form as *Esquisse pour une auto-analyse* [2004]), Bourdieu recalled the "stubborn rage" (123) engendered in him by his experience of boarding school and the mockery he suffered there.[34] The fragment's unauthorized publication set off a noisy public dispute that returned again and again to his personal combativeness. Even his defenders conceded that he was a "choleric genius" (or spirit) (génie colérique) (Michel Onfray) and begged sympathy for "the frailties of a sociologist of combat" (les fragilités d'un sociologue du combat) (Philippe Corcuff).[35] In the eyes of his philosopher friend Jacques Bouveresse, the serene politeness of the Establishment, which Bourdieu had manifestly failed to acquire, was merely the sign of its immense, taken-for-granted privileges, and it was just those privileges that Bourdieu had spent his life in justified fury against. Others pointed out that Bourdieu had picked fights with everyone, including some who were no more privileged than he was.[36] And climbing to the pinnacle of the French academic world, the prestigious Collège de France, might be thought to disqualify him from presenting himself as an eternal and uncompromising rebel.

What made this self-presentation so irresistible a target was Bourdieu's calm certainty, repeated in book after book, that scholarship boys from lowly provincial backgrounds will invariably sell their souls to the institutions that elevate them and that claims to rebelliousness will just as invariably turn out to be empty, disconnected from any real-world stakes, unconscious but self-interested moves in a prescribed game. At one point in the film a young woman passing by recognizes Bourdieu and tells him, smiling, that his books have changed her life: "I thought I was free, but I wasn't." Bourdieu no doubt winced at this abridgment of his thought, but the filmmakers, despite their unambiguously friendly intentions, did not see fit to cut it. It is not quite a travesty. In the decades of research he and his collaborators devoted to the scientific laboratory, literary and artistic career-making, musical taste, family photography, leisure-time athletics, and above all the apparatus of education, the constant refrain is that social status continues to be transmitted faithfully from generation to generation. There is less freedom out there than we think. Domains like art and science, which appear to be free of the political and economic constraints operating elsewhere, are in fact structured by an aggressive competition for symbolic capital that is neither open nor equitable. In one way or another things are arranged so that rewards end up in the hands of those who started out at the top of the social hierarchy. Bourdieu's work discovers the law that he himself broke by producing that work: that social origins deviously reproduce themselves.

However oblivious Bourdieu may be to the contrary force of his own example, much credit is due him for the labor of showing that on the whole social origins *do* reproduce themselves—a simple indignant premise that sent him off to explore a fascinating variety of archives, outside and inside the school. In *Homo Academicus*, for example, Bourdieu discusses student files from an elite girls' high school that conveniently recorded, next to remarks about the student's progress, the parent's profession. He points out a flagrant correlation between the educational level of the parents—what Bourdieu calls their cultural capital—and the talents attributed to the children. Students of petit-bourgeois origins (the poor have already been eliminated) tend to receive adjectives like clumsy, insipid, servile, awkward, and simplistic. At the other end of the social scale, the daughters of surgeons and professors are described in terms of mastery, subtlety, cultivation, and ease. *Reproduction in Education, Society, and Culture* (1970), cowritten with Jean-Claude Passeron (who was responsible for the French translation of Hoggart's *The Uses of Literacy*), examines the genre of the written examination and how it tends to be judged, exposing class assumptions that drag heavily on a vocabulary of teacherly evaluation supposed to be neutral and objective. Addressing topics as far-flung as the language of obituaries and the meanings of the "don't know" answer on political surveys, Bourdieu distinguished himself from other French thinkers of his generation by his openness to empirical testing and falsifiability. Like those thinkers, he was extremely skeptical about the structures of formal democracy, which for him functioned so as to whitewash the hereditary transmission of privileges, allowing the success of some and the failure of the rest to appear as an innocent selection according to merit. Again like the cohort with whom he so often quarreled, Bourdieu made a backhanded but powerful case for the significance of culture. So deeply unjust a system, he suggested, could not persist without the constant legitimation it receives from the cultural meanings we seize and cling to. The system's definitive constraint comes from the domain in which we think we are most free. Finally and paradoxically, he too seemed to imply that if there was any freedom in so determined a system, it would be found in those doing the work he himself was doing. The sociologist, even when working for the state, remained a sort of implicit hero.

Unsurprisingly, this brand of heroism tended to replace others. Consider his account of the events of May 1968. Like most of Bourdieu's analyses, this one emphasizes dynamics within a local field—here, the university—at the expense of larger political issues or movements, and it expresses skepticism about any meaningful links between the two. A sizable proportion of the most active protesters, he notes, were students and young faculty members in new disciplines like sociology (for men) and psychology (for women). The reason is that, unlike professional schools and the traditional humanities, these young, fragile disciplines could not satisfy the expectations of further employment they had succeeded in inciting. Many of those thus frustrated were students from the dominant class whose educational achievement did not correspond to their social origin, and who would otherwise have been excluded from the system. The key actors in the protest are "all those who have not managed to obtain social recognition of and reward for their inherited cultural capital." At the center of the protest, in other words, is a failure of just the scheme of class reproduction Bourdieu had elsewhere laid out. What was happening in the world outside the university was almost irrelevant. Outreach to nonstudents was a strategic goal of the movement, and it was furthered by the student experience of "downclassing." But for Bourdieu left-wing politics is about nothing more than outreach. Those who are subordinate *within* the field of power, a subset of the powerful, declare their solidarity with those who are subordinate in the social field as a whole, the truly powerless. The relatively minor complaints of some intellectuals lead them to declare their solidarity with, say, the proletariat, who have altogether more serious problems. Only in this indirect fashion do movements for revolution and reform come into being. The protesters are not victims, absolutely speaking; they are merely trying to negotiate a better position for themselves among other intellectuals. Those who are truly dominated initiate nothing. The depth of Bourdieu's cynicism appears in an afterthought: alliances like those between students and workers have more chance of working, he says, "if the partners . . . have less opportunity to enter into direct interaction, to see and speak to each other."

Exposing the prodigious tenacity of the class system, rocklike beneath the surface flux and onrush of change, and exposing the devious means by which its stability has been disguised, thereby preserving the appearance of equal opportunity, are accomplishments entirely worthy of the honors Bourdieu has received. Yet Bourdieu's view of society has made it hard to conceive that there would be anything *but* stability, while also leaving it anomalous that accomplishments like his—representing after all a sort of change, a demonstration of freedom—would be so honored. Tempted by the glaring contradiction between life and work, critics have thus been able to use the theory to discredit its author: "accuser of glory and honor, he is avid for glory and honor . . . disdainful of the system of education, he has submitted himself to the greatness of the School, and so on ad infinitum," as an annoyed Bourdieu paraphrases in *Esquisse*. Jealousy and resentment, the motives he suspects, can never be discounted. But it would be more interesting and more generous, to the critics as well as to Bourdieu, to use the life to amend the theory. Perry Anderson has compared Bourdieu to Raymond Williams, another scholarship boy who turned into a social critic—and, however reluctantly, into a kind of social success.[37] Surely there are further conclusions to be drawn from such stories—from the lesson of Monty Python's Four Yorkshiremen, once again, that lowly origins can themselves serve as a perverse but effective sort of cultural capital. Shouldn't such lessons provoke a revised view of the system that gives out the rewards and the possible place of anger within it? The embarrassment of social criticism reaching its ironic consummation in social success, whether despite or because of the critic's anger, seems a phenomenon important and widespread enough to call for theoretical amendments.

Like the smiling passerby in the film, Bourdieu invites the question of what difference it makes to *know* one is not free. Can living in the self-consciousness of unfreedom become a kind of freedom? What has her life been like since absorbing this lesson from Bourdieu? The closest Bourdieu comes to an answer is when, rather than discussing himself, he discusses his discipline. *Science of Science and Reflexivity* (2001), an annotated version of his final course of lectures at the Collège de France, the last book Bourdieu published during his lifetime and in part a palimpsestic look back at his career, expresses his pride at having given birth to a "reflexive" version of sociology.[38] Reflexivity exempts sociology from the seemingly universal guilt of reproducing the general struggle for symbolic capital. It makes the discipline the presumed site of society's own self-consciousness. As such, sociology appears as the desired endpoint of a collective upward mobility story that both overlaps with Bourdieu's own and, crucially, gives meaning to it. When he started out in the field in the 1950s, he says, "sociology, and to a lesser extent anthropology, were minor, even despised disciplines" (96). Like photography, sociological analysis is something everyone thinks he can do. Bourdieu will prove that sociology and the sociologist are superior to the common crowd by showing, for example, that the amateur photographer's freedom to improvise is only apparent: "there is nothing more regulated and conventional than photographic practice and amateur photographs" (7). Thus the two underdogs, individual and discipline, begin their conjoined and magical rise, vanquishing dragons at every step. Bourdieu's teacher, Raymond Aron, Sartre's estranged friend and political enemy, is the one who "transported into sociology the total ambitions of Sartrean-style philosophy" (99). But it is Bourdieu himself, we are given to understand, who realized those ambitions by entering into interdisciplinary battle. His ungenerous analyses of the careers of Sartre and Heidegger give a fair sample of the method. Bourdieu professes to feel no hostility at all to "the French philosophers who achieved fame in the 1970s" (104). But he accuses them of achieving success by trying to destroy (while mimicking) the rival social sciences. True or not, this accusation recalls Bourdieu's own tactic of borrowing the language of philosophy and anthropology in order to seize as much of their authority as possible. The projection is almost blind enough to be charming.

Projection is again the unavoidable diagnosis when Bourdieu comes to the book's main theme, the careers of natural scientists—a characteristic and gripping unit of analysis that often makes Bourdieu more readable than his somewhat off-putting titles might suggest. He tries to take a distance from what he calls "a naively Machiavellian view of scientists' strategies," according to which "the symbolic actions they perform in order to win recognition for their 'fictions' are at the same time influence-seeking and power-seeking strategies through which they pursue their own glorification" (28–29). But when he goes on to describe the scientific world as "a universe of competition for the 'monopoly of the legitimate handling' of scientific goods" (45), it's hard to see how his view differs. On what grounds can he justify, for example, his scorn for Bruno Latour? In *Les microbes: Guerre et paix* (1984—translated into English as *The Pasteurization of France*), Latour uses the muddle of a Russian defeat of Napoleon's army, as described by Tolstoy, by way of analogy for how Louis Pasteur actually arrived at the defeat of anthrax. As the battle analogy suggests, Latour believes the victory was real, however unplanned and unheroic. Something was really discovered about how nature works, or how it can be manipulated; anthrax, like Napoleon, was really beaten. This is no doubt why, as Ian Hacking notes, Latour's 1979 book on the "social construction" of scientific fact in Jonas Salk's laboratory could be prefaced with a "bemused but admiring" tribute from Jonas Salk. When Bourdieu accuses Latour of ignoring the "purely scientific" side, he is himself ignoring their common premises—in particular, their epistemologically untroubled respect for the reality of nature. Tellingly, what these two moderate constructionists don't share is Bourdieu's investment in "society" as the agent doing the constructing. Uncommitted to any one discipline, Latour favours unpredictable sociotechnological hybrids, agents that straddle the nature/society divide. The comparison makes Bourdieu look like a mere apologist for sociology, itself now a well-established discipline by comparison with what is only starting to be known as "science studies." If science were as self-regulating as Bourdieu suggests, it would hardly need the strenuous sociological oversight that he demands for it in the next lecture. Here as elsewhere he is ready to forget a great deal in order to assert the right of social science to sit in judgment upon all rival branches of knowledge, including the natural sciences and philosophy.

It is hard not to sympathize with Bourdieu's conflicting desires to defend sociology's claim to be a genuine science, on the one hand, while also liberating it (via reflexivity) from unselfconscious positivism and thus accrediting, on the other, its distrustful surveillance of science, its guardianship of the common social good. What he is trying to account for is in effect the mystery of his own life, the paradox of the rebel who has arrived at a situation of power. Or more precisely, a rebel who, even though he is now in power, *remains* a rebel.

The paradox of a site that might serve, as he says of the Collège, as "the home of the consecrated heretics" seems to guide many of his brushes with self-contradiction, as when he writes in *Science of Science and Reflexivity* that there are "two ways" in which existing "systems of selection (such as elite schools) favor great scientific careers" (12). The first is "by designating those whom they select as remarkable"—the implication being that those selected could be anyone, genuinely talented or not. The second is "by conferring a particular competence." This formulation takes away with the one hand what it has given with the other. Is competence an objective set of skills that some will be better than others at acquiring? If so then the "great scientific career" would seem less arbitrary, more like an objectively verifiable achievement, and it might even reflect a preexisting talent.[39] The equivocation also seems to express Bourdieu's unwillingness either to confirm or deny the possibility of a career that, like his own, might be seen as genuinely meaningful, a site of collective as well as individual achievement. On other occasions, however, he seems conveniently if not quite convincingly certain that such an achievement is possible only for a sociologist like himself.

In *Esquisse pour une auto-analyse*, Bourdieu is open about the formative effect of his boarding school experience on his subsequent sociological career and in particular his paradigm of society as a site of ferocious competition. As he recounts it, his experience is much more brutal than the teasing of Tommy in *Never Let Me Go*. For all the extremity of that novel's dystopian premise, Ishiguro's Hailsham is a model of polite refinement by comparison. What is not so clear is the relation between the torments of the young Bourdieu and his later perception of injustice. Is he, like Oliver Twist asking for more, a victim who stands up to the authorities and demands what he and his fellows deserve? What is the connection, if any, between his anger then and the sociologist he was later to become?[40]

What the reader sees at first, in the autobiographical section of *Esquisse*, is a war of all against all. There is general misery and oppression among the students, but there are no coherent sides. Bourdieu himself occupies no special position—unless a particular position is subtly implied by the memory of him "secretly washing his handkerchiefs" (118). Why did the washing of the handkerchiefs have to be hidden? Would it have been taken as a sign of refinement, of social superiority? This hint is left undeveloped, at least initially. The premise seems to be that the children, here undifferentiated, are all like animals, struggling against each other with fists and cunning for a place at the table—struggling, "in short, to survive" (119). Recapitulating a familiar narrative of general social development, Bourdieu also hints that the children found themselves locked in a vendetta-like cycle of endless revenge whose origins have become irrelevant (121). But little by little his own origins force themselves into the picture. He says he could not explain his misery to his parents because "I seemed privileged to them" (121). The idea that he might seem privileged to others as well, that his privilege might have to vie with his familial handicap as a contradictory explanation of his anger, is again raised only to be instantly abandoned.

His parents blame his "bad conduct" (121). He admits the question of his "character" is one that (like Tommy at the end of *Never Let Me Go*) he cannot quite discount. The admission does him credit: his "character," presumably formed at home before his schooldays, by the same token also precedes sociology and thus threatens to escape the field of interpretation that sociology claims. In this autobiographical sequence, sociology will assert its rights only gradually and gropingly. Searching for the key to his suffering, Bourdieu next speaks of his solitude. The closest he comes to trying to explain that personal, particular solitude, which cannot be accounted for by such universally shared causes of suffering as sadistic monitors, is an analogy. He says his solitude at school resembles what he later experienced in the army, among his "illiterate" fellow soldiers, when he "preached" (his word) against their mission to "pacify" Algeria. The likeness suggests, without quite asserting, (1) that he was more principled than his fellow students in his revolt against the school authorities while (2) he was also, not being "illiterate," more devoted to his studies. Of these two somewhat dissonant hypotheses as to why he feels cut off from his fellow students (or why they feel cut off from him), he has more to say about the second. As he presents them, the other *internes* resemble the "miserable fucking louts" from whom the protagonist disdainfully rises in *Billy Bathgate* or (closer to Bourdieu) the oafish seminarists of *The Red and the Black*. They only talk about girls and rugby, they plagiarize their homework, and so on. The teachers, by a pleasant and surprising contrast, offer Bourdieu a world of "affectionate sweetness" (125). The mockery of his peasant origins comes not from either of these groups, as one might have expected, but only from the *externes*, students who do not live at the school—and who would therefore seem to be innocent of the unmentionable nighttime horrors to which Bourdieu alludes. The *externes*, as he presents them, are of a higher social background. They do things like writing poems and playing the violin, and in Bourdieu's account they seem to suffer for this reason from "a sort of class racism" (125). The phrase "class racism" pops up, however, at the precise point where Bourdieu suddenly stops speaking about their suffering and begins instead to speak about his own, which is imposed for example by one of their number, who mocks him for his peasant accent. This is the theme

Bourdieu stresses: the righteous anger of one unjustly mocked by a supposed social superior.

But the injustice in the picture he has drawn is anything but simple. It is immediately and irrevocably complicated by the fact that, as he admits, he is "a bit disgusted" by the macho antiintellectualism of his fellow *internes* and in danger from them because of his "school success and the suspicious docility" assumed to go with it. To be fair, Bourdieu admits eventually—at some cost to the posture of rebelliousness with which he has begun—that his docility was real. If he is "always in a state of revolt approaching delinquence" (123), he is also "always ready to trust and abandon the struggle" (123). He says that he is caught between two sets of "irreconcilable values" (127). What he cannot seem to say outright is how much the anger suffusing his memories of school is not after all his response to those who looked down at him with class scorn. He cannot admit to the anger directed at him by those who looked up at him from below as he rose away from them, angry themselves at this traitor to their culture, at the "eagerness and submission of the good student, thirsty for knowledge and recognition" (128), who has given in to the rules of the game. The closest he comes to acknowledging this familiar theme of the upward mobility narrative is when he concedes, in somewhat tortured syntax, the presence in himself of "that form of self-hatred that the horror of the petit-bourgeois opportunism of certain of my colleagues was for me" (130).

It is within these same autobiographical pages of the *Esquisse* that Bourdieu underlines what has perhaps been the moral of his story all along: this is how he has become such a successful sociologist. It's the experience of boarding school, with its solitude and rage, he says, to which he owes his unique ability to "communicate, despite differences of all sorts and without having to force myself in the least, forgetting both my age and my status . . . with the young *beur* of *The Weight of the World* and his buddy, immediately seeing their 'disarmed' side, beyond their appearance of intractable closedness" (123–24). Readers of this powerful section of *The Weight of the World* will immediately notice how, though his "youthful offender" subjects seem to come straight out of *Esquisse*, the sort of sympathetic dialogue he engages with them has no place in the social world of the boarding school, at least as he depicts it. It is only when he has become a credentialed sociologist that Bourdieu knows how to speak to these so-called failures. It is in sociology that Bourdieu's anger comes into its own, makes a proper home for itself, finds a proper set of objects. My point is not that Bourdieu is in bad faith when he bases his success on his subjects' failure or when he declares that his story explains how he acquired "the deep sense of revolt, which has never left me, against the educational system" (110). The revolt is real. But the revolt belongs as much to the educational system as it does to him. That's why it is shared with so many others, whether or not they too had traumatic boarding-school years.

The "personal" problem of Bourdieu's theory, so to speak, is its unwillingness to share the revolt with others. His vision of society is arguably determined by what it represses. By keeping out of sight the *internes'* anger at him, Bourdieu authorizes himself to be their representative, the vehicle rather than the butt of their rage. He borrows from them, of course, a generous endowment of what he refuses to see as cultural capital—the quantity frequently referred to as "victimization." In order to cash in on this victimization, however, he must make sociology stand alone among the disciplines and institutions of the state, allow it to be the only truly subversive site in a crowd of ineligible institutions meant only for traitors and complacent time-servers. Except for sociology, which is the ladder Bourdieu himself has climbed, all other educational ladders must lead to an endpoint of blockage or co-optation, disappointment or illusion. Outside the constitutive anger of sociology, upward mobility must remain an error. For if it were not an error, if there were nothing special and redemptive about sociology, then he would have broken faith with his fellow *internes*; he would no longer be a fellow victim; he himself would deserve their anger. Shutting his classmates up, he also allows them the last and authoritative word. The question is whether this is really *their* word or only his own. In light of Bourdieu's story, does the authority of his fellow students naturally and properly come to support his antimobility position? Or is it possible on the contrary that, in some sense and to some extent, what is true about sociology is also true about the endpoint of other trajectories?

The classic sociological account of Bourdieu's angry schoolfellows is Paul Willis's *Learning to Labor: How Working Class Kids Get Working Class Jobs* (1977).[41] According to Willis, the refusal of the working class to compete in the struggle for credentials at school is perfectly logical: "A few can make it. The class can never follow. It is through a good number trying, however, that the class structure is legitimated. The middle class enjoys its privileges not by virtue of inheritance or birth, but by virtue of an apparently proven greater competence and merit. The refusal to compete, implicit in the counter-school culture, is therefore in this sense a radical act: it refuses to collude in its own educational suppression" (128). Anger against someone who would choose to defy this logic and forge ahead on his own, like a youthful English Bourdieu, thus seems perfectly coherent, a means of policing class solidarity.

The immediate problem with this otherwise plausible argument is the twist Willis has put in his subtitle: "How Working Class Kids Get Working Class Jobs." On the very page where he quotes Bourdieu, he draws a very different conclusion: anger against the school and against those fellow students who choose to strive for its credentials and rewards—the so-called ear-'oles—is precisely what keeps working-class kids in their place at the bottom of the class hierarchy. Though this belligerent refusal to compete may be "radical" in the sense that it offers the working-class students subjective confirmation of their identity, all it accomplishes objectively is to channel them into just those working-class jobs that the system needs them to take. And it does so all the more effectively because it allows them to think that this is their own choice, a free choice, even a proud choice. If upward mobility is, as is endlessly repeated, an ideological trick of the system, the same would therefore have to be said about the rejection of upward mobility. And if, as this familiar paranoid-style argument goes, anger against the system is actually part of the system, indeed the very principle without which the system could not work, then this would be a strong incentive to consider the perverse but in fact dialectically necessary possibility that some *less* angry position might turn out to be *more* effective, though perhaps effective in some other way.[42] I allude to the welfare state's characteristically cooler mixture of anger and caring.

Ideally, of course, it is the class system itself, as Willis says, that should be subverted. "To the *individual* working class person mobility is this society may mean something. Some working class individuals do 'make it' and any particular individual may hope to be one of them. To the class or group at its own proper level, however, mobility means nothing at all. The only true mobility at this level would be the destruction of the whole class society" (128). The only true or proper solution to this dilemma is revolutionary politics. But revolutionary politics, it must be said, is a lot to ask. There is a problem judging any individual life by the standard of a collective enterprise that, in this time and place, remains hypothetical, the abstract beckoning of a logic and a desire rather than the imperative to join a process that is clearly and massively under way. In the prolonged prerevolutionary interim—an interim that can be used to absolve many sins, but that can't be escaped on those grounds alone—the demands of self-sovereignty, however unjustifiable in ultimate terms, cannot be ignored. In Ishiguro's seductive meantime, we have only uneasy compromises. And in the meantime, therefore, Willis has no right to say that "to the class," as opposed to the individual, "mobility means nothing at all." For his own life offers just such a compromise: a case of individual mobility that, if it means anything, *does* mean something to the class left behind. Just as Bourdieu's does.

Even in the fragmentary and parsimonious form that Willis and Bourdieu give to their autobiographical materials, the two lives have a great deal in common. In a 2001 interview, Willis tells a story in which, as for Bourdieu, upward mobility is first and foremost someone else's story.

Specifically it is his father's. Bourdieu describes his father as a "poor little municipal employee" (petit fonctionnaire pauvre) (*Esquisse*, 110). The father was clearly not prosperous, but neither was he any longer the peasant he had been; he was employed in an official capacity. Willis's father too has risen, and he too has come to serve, at least for a time, as a state employee. "[M]y cultural background was working-class, perhaps petit-bourgeois. My father was a carpenter who became a 'general fore-man' and went on to work for the local authority as a building inspector. He then developed his own small property business" (389).[43] It cannot be a coincidence that both sons will end up working for the state and that each will identify that work, directly or indirectly, as a compromise between the desire "to make an economic success of his life" (389), as Willis says of his father, and the desire to remain loyal to his community of origin. Having assumed some of the burden of these contradictory desires, both fathers blunt their force, embodying the possibility of a provisional resolution. Willis says, in an ironically but tellingly moral-ized locution, that the push for him to go to Cambridge was "my father's fault!" (391).[44] "So what's my background? A very particular version of upward aspiration: a classic Hoggartian 'scholarship boy' story of being selected through a grammar school system to go into a good, privileged education. I was in fact the only boy ever from my grammar school then to go on to Cambridge" (390). The only thing that's even potentially "particular" about this story is the full support he receives from his fa-ther, which seems to protect him at least partially from the charge of betrayal. His interviewers ask him, immediately after the "scholarship boy" story: "Did that make you, in the language you describe as em-ployed by 'the lads' in *Learning to Labor*, an 'ear-'ole'?" Willis gives no evidence that it did. He does however go on at some length about how playing rugby ingratiated him both with the teachers and with the stu-dents, the display of rugged masculinity keeping him from being labeled an "ear-'ole," suck-up or sellout. Again, this is much the same story Bourdieu tells, right down to the redemptive rugby.[45]

Willis's building-inspector father, like Bourdieu's *fonctionnaire*, antici-pates what amounts to a state-centered narrative and a state-centered telos. For the son, first, there is the father-surrogacy of the Birmingham Centre, a new institution that is universally seen as subversive, much as Bourdieu sees the emergent discipline of sociology. There are radical men-tors like Stuart Hall and Richard Hoggart. Hoggart, founder of the Centre and Willis's tutor during his first year, seems a bit less radical, yet he tells Willis: "Immerse yourself in the destructive element" (394). Whether as a result of their mentorship or as a self-invented solution to the contradic-tions of his story, Willis comes up with a distinctive scholarly approach, seen even at the Centre as controversial, which recalls the policy of Ishiguro's Hailsham: he celebrates the "creativity" of the working-class lads (399). And it is this "accidental drop into anthropological methods [which] relieved me, as I see it, almost entirely of colonial bad faith and guilt" (403). Anthropological method gives form to his loyalty to the community of origin, thereby solving the "guilt" problem. By this means, he can bring forward those he has left behind, allowing them to speak through him. Or, to be more precise, he can allow them to address the interlocutor that they must address in order to improve their lot: the state.[46] The interview leaves no doubt that the state is indeed the intended addressee. "I thought I was helping the 'people' to formulate their position in order to make demands on the local state" (403). The journal he helped found in those years, he says, aimed "to reorient the local state to the needs and problems of youth, rather than what has predominated since, which is to use the state to reform youth as more useable and low priced labor power for internationalized capitalist labor markets" (403). He insists this is the future, foreseeing "a whole new role, or much extended regular role, for the state" in forming "a whole terrain of experience" for young people (404). He insists that the involvement of the state and its agents in this terrain—technology, communication, information, and so on—is *inevitable* (405). He underlines the possibility for "liberating dimensions of a new governance" involving "feelings from below" (405). "Don't forget that state sectors are still hugely important—45 pence in every pound spent in this country is spent by the state" (406). The state pays for him, and in doing so also makes it possible for those "feelings from below" to be expressed, weighed, and perhaps integrated into a new sort of governance.

In *Learning to Labor* Willis shows a special interest in the category of "state agents," in particular those counselors and therapists who offer working-class students career guidance. But he himself does not figure there as a state agent who might accomplish anything of value. The word *merit* always comes weighted down by the adjective *spurious* (128). There seems no way that his work as a state agent, or for that matter a book like *Learning to Labor*, might possess an unencumbered or more genuine sort of merit. In his definitive account of resistance to upward mobility, in other words, Willis modestly omits himself—omits the autobiographical details out of which, a quarter of a century later, he allows us to fashion an alternative and more desirable model of upward mobility.

In *Respect in a World of Inequality* (2003),[47] a book intended to be "about welfare" (xv) but also about the upward curve of his own life and about the connection between the two, Richard Sennett gives a sympathetic summary of *Learning to Labor*. Willis, he says, "showed how young working-class adolescents held themselves back from progress in school for fear of standing out, 'getting above themselves,' losing ties to their friends if they went too far, losing touch with their communities" (97). Sennett, who as he says "grew up in the welfare system, then escaped from it by virtue of my talents" (xvi), did not hold himself back, but he speaks knowingly of the neighborhood's anger against those who embody the system's inequalities, whether as welfare providers or as lucky escapees. In a section called "The Ones Left Behind" (32), he tells an anecdote, referred to above, in which he was asked to serve as a "role model" to a group of poor young people from his old Chicago neighborhood. He shared the podium, he says, with a young Puerto Rican doctor from the same neighborhood who "spoke with an evangelist's fervor about self-improvement" (33). The doctor, a born-again Christian, tells a heckler, "You are not a victim! Strive!" (34). The audience response to the doctor's upward mobility story is at first angrily vocal, then it subsides into "a sullen, hostile silence" (35). Sennett interprets the anger as a rejection of the implicit message that upward mobility stories so often transmit: "if I could do it, why can't you?" (34). To the one left behind, someone else's success story signifies that "something must be wrong with me" (77). It's my fault. To the extent that it is not simply "about welfare," the question of Sennett's book, as of so many of the works dealt with above, is how to tell an upward mobility story that will not invite this response.

Dissatisfied with what he actually said to his audience on that occasion, Sennett concludes that "I should have spoken about the history of my hand" (37)—that is, about the injury that cut short his promising career as a musician. But since he went on to make a spectacular career as a sociologist, it's not clear that a display of his early bout with adversity would have avoided "invidious comparison" or improved on the obliviousness of the doctor's sermon on self-improvement. The rhetorical challenge for which the occasion stands is after all no small thing: how can respect be compatible with a world of inequality? Can the one who has risen narrow the gap between these two terms, bolster his audience's self-respect, subdue the angry effects of inequality—and even perhaps take a shot at diminishing the cause, inequality itself?

Sennett tries to do so not by telling the story of how he himself rose, but by attacking popular attitudes toward welfare. "Welfare clients often complain of being treated without respect" (xv). Why? Sennett gives several different answers. One is that "modern society lacks positive expressions of respect and recognition by others" (xv). This diagnosis seems a bit too encouraging. If disrespect is merely the result of a lexical lack, then surely people of goodwill ought to be able to put their heads together and come up with some catchy "positive expressions." Yet there are metaphorical signs that things may not be so easy. "Respect," Sennett writes, "costs nothing" (3). Is there really no price to pay? Or is respect, like other forms of status, a zero-sum game, so that more for you means less for me? According to Sennett, thinking of respect in zero-sum terms is a mistake (46). In other words, respect can and must be disengaged from the quantification of economic inequality. It seems to follow, then, that in Sennett's view inequality itself can remain in place without fatally hindering the growth of respect for those at the bottom of the economic ladder. In the book's closing pages, Sennett confesses his belief that inequality *will* remain: "In the welfare state, the nub of the problem we face is how the strong can practice respect toward those destined to remain weak" (263). "Destined to remain": these words are briskly and obnoxiously complacent. It's hard to imagine them spoken from that podium in Chicago, or how the audience would have responded if they had been. Is it mere coincidence that the bottom of the ladder is where disrespect is most strongly felt? The notion of cost-free respect seems an effort to avoid paying the real and burdensome costs of trying to change the conditions of economic inequality, which are indeed zero-sum, and as such arguably make up the objective template out of which the zero-sum structure of subjective respect arises.[48] And yet this in all its nakedness is the deal struck by the welfare state.

It is perhaps an unconscious acknowledgment of how binding that deal is (in more than one sense) that prods Sennett, having treated "respect in a world of inequality" as if we were miraculously free to reimagine and reinvent it, to experiment with a set of terms that on the contrary make the problem seem so ideologically constrained as to be almost beyond solution. The keywords of this more taxing formulation are *dependence* and *autonomy*. Sennett says we need to stop thinking "dependency is shameful" (102). "The dignity of dependence never appeared to liberalism a worthy political project" (125). The clear implication is that dependence can and should be treated with dignity. Then Sennett goes on to say that people need to be respected in and for their autonomy, something that has not yet happened. "From its origins . . . the British founders of the modern welfare state knew they had a problem in treating clients as human beings in need yet respecting their autonomy" (174). The question that seems to be begged here is whether recipients of welfare are indeed autonomous or not. Can they be at once autonomous and dependent? If not, can others be asked to respect them for an autonomy they don't actually possess, that is merely polite or wishful? In other words, Sennett seems to be suggesting that dependence can be accorded dignity only when it is really autonomy, which is to say when it is not dependence at all. "The provision of autonomy within dependency was the great bureaucratic dilemma faced by the social-democratic creators of the welfare state" (176). Having laid out this dilemma, Sennett briefly switches his ground, saying that for the clients, "passivity, not dependency, was the issue" (176). Dependency might indeed contradict autonomy, but dependence need not be irreconcilable with *activity*, which makes a lesser demand. A page later, however, we are back to the dilemma of dependency and autonomy. "What kind of institution could allow them . . . to participate in the conditions of their own dependency? How can they experience both support and autonomy? It's a riddle I hardly know how to solve" (177).

As in the cases of Bourdieu and Willis, it is difficult to avoid the conclusion that the political-intellectual riddle rhymes with an autobiographical one, the riddle of Sennett's own personal trajectory. And its solution, to the extent that it has one, seems again to lie in what is proposed about the role of sociologist, that branch of the welfare state's "social project" by which the trajectory was shaped. "What kind of institution" is sociology? Sennett does not address this question directly, but one of his impulses is to want to claim considerable autonomy for it, and through it for himself. "The experience of ability I've called craftwork" (98) is the best solution he can imagine, Sennett says, to "invidious comparison." If sociology is a craft, then it can be distinguished from "mastery over others" (83) and can be credited with an enviable degree of autonomy.[49] "Craftwork certainly does not banish invidious comparison to the work of others; it does refocus a person's energies, however, to getting an act right in itself, for oneself. The craftsman can sustain his or her self-respect in an unequal world" (99). But even if it were possible to distinguish a pure mastery over nature (craft) that did not simultaneously represent direct or indirect mastery over other people, this asocial formulation seems an especially unlikely one for sociology.

Alan Ryan, in a review of *Respect in a World of Inequality*, notes the book's failure to "uncover one unequivocal concept of respect," a failure to offer a "novel moral philosophy of mutual respect" or "a blueprint for a welfare state about which we could all feel morally comfortable" (31).[50] The book has too little to say, Ryan points out, about the simple mean-spiritedness of the American welfare system. Most important, however, it avoids recognizing the contradiction between the ideal of the hard-working, self-supporting individual, which continues to define what is deserving of respect, and the welfare system, which implies "a readiness to take without giving, or a passivity that is at odds with the idea of making something of ourselves. It implies a character nobody would want" (31). Perhaps Sennett, like the born-again Puerto Rican doctor, remains too enamored of self-reliance, the idea or ideal of "making something of ourselves."

And yet if we consider the "character" of the sociologist as bodied forth by Sennett's narrative, what we think of is not the "ideal of the hard-working, self-supporting individual." Rather than working at his desk or actively combing the streets or archives, we see Sennett in the act of listening to people. In that sense he too is prepared, one might say, "to take without giving." Rather than self-reliant action, he offers a repeated image of a certain professionally distinctive "passivity." Having grown up, as he says, in the welfare system, he conveys an image of the sociologist that distinctly echoes this "character nobody would want." One might argue that it is this regenerated and refined profile of the welfare recipient that he makes his reader want.

The character of the sociologist as Sennett presents it carries visible reminders of an older tradition of theatrical performance and self-display, which Sennett has argued elsewhere are threatened elements of the public sphere.[51] But what is more striking about the sociologist's publicness is the simple repeated gesture of showing up or turning up, being seen among others, persisting in one's social being. In *The Corrosion of Character: The Personal Consequences of Work in the New Capitalism* (1998), Sennett sees the new "flexible" capitalism as corroding character because it corrodes loyalty—that is, the social attachments on which character is based. The slogan he offers is a distinctively temporal one: the loss of the long term. In the general frenzy of risk-taking, job-hopping, and geographical displacement, he says, there is no longer anyone there to serve as "a long-term witness to another person's life" (21). For Sennett publicness is less spatial than temporal: its key is the long term. It is precisely the supplying of this missing (long) term that Sennett could be said to act out in his role as sociologist.

He claims no special merit for this. On the contrary, the encounter that defines this task and thus begins the book is entirely and self-deprecatingly accidental. At an airport, he meets the son of someone he had interviewed and written about twenty-five years earlier in *The Hidden Injuries of Class* (1972). The father was an immigrant and a janitor. The son is a successful executive who has fulfilled his father's "American dream of upward mobility for the children" (17). Yet the son feels his life is out of control, not least because his own children are. "The objective example he could set, his upward mobility, is something they take for granted, a history that belongs to a past not their own, a story which is over" (21). To them, his upward mobility is someone else's story. In other words, the long term has been lost. Or would be lost, except for the intervention of the sociologist. The narrative continuity that everyone in all three generations seems to need can be provided, it seems, only by the providential outsider who does what society itself seems unable to do. The sociologist bears "witness to another person's life." Sennett uses the word *career* in "the old English sense," meaning something "durable and sustained" (147). The definition is weighted more to temporality than (as is traditional) to the privileged, class-specific curve of middle-class work. Thus he can argue that a quarter of a century ago careers were available even to the extremely unprivileged;

his example is again the immigrant janitor interviewed for *The Hidden Injuries of Class*.[52] And for all the son's success, Sennett implies that the sustained and durable career may be less available to him than to his father, whose commitment was to the long term. To the extent that story-telling can maintain the long term, it is therefore the sociologist-as-witness who now does the work of large-scale temporal maintenance. The sociologist's career is based, narratively speaking at least, on the capacity to give careers to others.

Along with "craft," the other conception of work discussed here to which sociology might be assimilated is "public service."[53] Sociology might be considered public service in any one of a number of senses. It might be feared, for example, that the use of narrative to provide careers is public service in only in the most weakened and abstract sense. For those who have lost "control" over their lives, how much control does mere narrative restore? Sennett's references to "life narratives" (165–66) sometimes have a Durkheimian feel, as if he assumed an urgent and universal need for order as such and thus celebrated "service" to an institution—any institution, whatever its goals and values—on the politically neutral grounds that experience must at all costs be organized, anomie must at all costs be overcome.[54] To certain constituencies, the idea of anger-management on the cheap, guaranteeing a socially stabilizing minimum of respect without threatening the economic inequality that generates the disrespect and the anger, might seem like an extremely useful disciplinary project, one well worth keeping adequately funded. To others, nothing short of direct action to eliminate or at least reduce inequality would validate sociology's claim to public service.[55] What counts as public service, like what counts as individual merit, is open to the imagination, but the imagination as constrained by ongoing struggle in the field of public opinion, which is to say the field of politics. What after all is "usefulness" to the public? The question is political in the sense that it crosses the border of economic calculation, demanding a decision that cannot be reached by numbers alone. Criteria like productivity and profitability cannot decide it any better. For better or worse, the "ethos of public service" (200) is not incompatible with profit, however incompatible it may be with profit in the short term.[56] The definition of public usefulness will often be the site of a struggle between short term and long term.

How useful, for example, is caring? How much does the public care about it? One of the many ironies of so-called welfare reform has been that people kicked out of the welfare system and into the paid workforce will often end up caring for others, and will be paid very little to do so. "The work available to former welfare clients," Sennett observes, "is usually low-skill service labor in flexible businesses: work in fast-food restaurants, or as contract-term guards, or as temporary hospital aides"

(188–89).[57] The figure of the temporary hospital aide, a poignant echo of Ishiguro's Kathy, is a reminder that our system, too, makes it impossible for the gainfully employed carer to care adequately for her own loved ones or, in the long run, for herself. In the long run, as Keynes famously declared, we are all dead. Before we are dead, however, we will, if we are lucky enough, require to be cared for, perhaps by a temporary hospital aide. Whether this existential realization can be translated into a public will to care for those who are not yet at the end of their lives, as well as those who are, is of course an unanswered political question. In the messy meantime, Sennett's circular vision of able and disabled, giver and receiver, carer and cared for, is not the worst possible case for sociology as public service or for his own rise within it as a form of angry but respectful caring.

"A concern with respect in the character-based sense may be inimical to an effective welfare state," Alan Ryan speculates; "emphasis on respect can undermine the support for a welfare state" (34). Though the burden of Sennett's argument of course demands the warmth of respect, the book also has a chilly undercurrent that seems to factor in Ryan's objection. Sennett describes at one point how his mother, a social worker as well as a writer, wrote an unpublished story in which the protagonist, also a social worker, "dreads one night making a home visit to a welfare mother the next day, hating her role as 'the investigator'" (19). His mother also deals with her dread of condescension by acting like a professional: "As a professional, my mother kept that feeling of involvement locked up; hers was no passionate embrace of the oppressed, she was precise and calm in her work, firmly marking out human distances" (19). "To make compassion work, perhaps it was necessary to defuse sentiment, to deal coolly with others. Crossing the boundary of inequality might require reserve on the part of the stronger person making the passage; reserve would acknowledge the difficulty, distance could make a signal of respect, if a peculiar one" (20). Something like the coolness I have pointed out between upwardly mobile protagonist and mentor, this legacy—in this case, interestingly, from the sociologist's mother rather than the father—looks like a caution against trying to solve at the level of emotion a dilemma whose solution clearly demands larger, institutional changes. And yet as we have seen, such emotions are the very stuff of political change. And these emotions seem to make themselves most accessible, or accessible in the least life-threatening way, in works of fiction, where we have found them explored. It would seem that the imagination's struggle for the public good, in space and in time, must happen in institutions and in narrative simultaneously.

Coda: Anger, Caring, and Merit

In *Parallel Time* (1994), journalist Brent Staples says he is frequently asked to "explain my existence": "Why was I successful, law-abiding, and literate, when others of my kind filled the jails and the morgues and the homeless shelters? . . . Usually I answered by talking about my encounter with Sparrow [his high school mentor] during my final days of high school. How I'd met him at a place where I'd never seen him before and would never see him again. How Sparrow had wedged me into college, even though I'd been a mediocre student and hadn't taken the college boards. How Chance had worked mightily in my favor" (259–60).[58] He likes this benefactor story in part, he says, because other people do not. "People preferred a story about an individual who triumphs over all through force of character. The least charitable of these people cited me as proof that the American dream was alive and well—if only those shiftless bastards in the slums would reach for it." Sparrow's mentorship is called in as a corrective when people impose the "American dream" story on his brother's murder: "My 'escape' from the ghetto was being marshaled as evidence against him" (260).

Yet there is another principle of mentorship to which Staples is less eager to acknowledge his debt, though it too undermines the "force of character" doctrine. Before returning, in the final pages of the book, to the details of the murder and the burial, Staples ends the parallel story of his own rise by recounting two job interviews. At the first, with the *Washington Post* magazine, he shows his anger and loses the job. "Yes, I am linked to the ghetto by pain and despair. Here's a freshly murdered brother to prove it. Is that real enough for you?" (260). At the second interview, with the *New York Times*, he cuts himself short when his anger begins to rise, and he gets the job. The implication is that a job, a place in the system, is acquired only by sacrificing or suppressing one's anger against the system. The system has no room for anger. Upward mobility is betrayal of your anger, betrayal of everything in you that refuses and contests the system.

But this is not the whole story. What has made him so angry, Staples suggests, is "what I'd come to call the Real Negro questions. He wanted to know if I was a Faux, Chevy Chase, Maryland, Negro or an authentic nigger who grew up poor in the ghetto besieged by crime and violence. White people preferred the latter, on the theory that blacks from the ghetto were the real thing. Newspaper editors preferred them on the theory that they made better emissaries to the ghetto. . . . I was blind with rage. Here was this motherfucking son of privilege rummaging my life for racial bona fides. I hated him. I'd have spat blood in his face if I could" (259–60). It's hard not to feel that at least some of this anger, understandable as it is, is also self-directed. For if Staples fears that others are using his brother's death to shore up their belief in the American dream, he must also fear that he himself is getting some benefit from it. His book is itself a kind of job interview, a rummaging in his own life for racial bona fides, proof (offered to readers who are also, comparatively speaking, sons and daughters of privilege) that he is indeed "an authentic nigger who grew up poor in the ghetto besieged by crime and violence." His presumed motives for saying all this to us cannot be so different from his motives for saying it at a job interview. He wants the job, and he wants to be read. We have to credit him with knowing, in other words, that the motives of those listening to him are not as simple as he pretends they are. In each case, both the exotic information and the anger that so naturally accompanies it are *desired* by his interlocutors, and they are willing to pay accordingly. Perhaps anger against the system cannot be too blatant or out of control, but it is a socially valued quantity, a form of cultural capital, a means not merely of losing a job but of getting a job. Not something to be hidden away but (with due decorum) to be displayed. If we can assume that the editors, irritating and patronizing as they seem to be, are moved not by tokenism or sensationalism, but simply by a sense of responsibility to deal as knowledgeably as possible with the hard facts of African American life, then we could also conclude that in their eyes, as in ours, Staples's anger is a kind of summation of what he has learned. In this sense I think it's fair to say that his anger is part of his merit, and is acknowledged as such.

This would be to suggest that there is an unsuspectedly close relation between professional credentials and popular credibility, or what we sometimes call street cred. I don't imagine that most of us would have trouble thinking of anger at the state of the world, or emotions like anger, as part of our intellectual equipment, helping us do our work and do it well. Resistance to thinking of anger as part of our *credentials* will arise because we want to think of such emotions as personal, not as items that an impersonal bureaucratic institution like a newspaper or a university could systematically recognize or demand. I'm not sure I'm ready myself to imagine filling out a promotion form in which there would be a box to check or a paragraph to write or outside letters to confirm the degree of my anger. And yet the thought experiment is worth performing. If at present we all lack sufficient faith in the institutions we inhabit to make such a procedure bureaucratically imaginable, it may be that something like this institutional leap of faith is what a renewed idea of the university, and the welfare state, would require.

For this argument is of course not just about the university. Nor is it just about anger. It is also about other institutions and other emotions—about prisons, say, and about the official emotions they express: both society's anger at criminals and, simultaneously, that amalgam of solicitude and cruelty that I have labeled "caring." Considering his brother's life sentence, John Edgar Wideman's book *Brothers and Keepers* ends on a surprising note of uplift. A federally funded program has enabled the prison to offer Community College courses. Robby Wideman has earned a degree, and he delivers a speech to the other inmates: "I give this speech in hopes that my example will help my fellow prisoners to strive for their own self-attainment. I hope that they can look at me and say, 'Well, if he can do it with no guarantee that he will ever have the chance to pursue all of his goals, then why can't I?'" (240). The good news is followed swiftly by bad. "The Community College program of which I am graduating from here has been cut off completely, leaving some students stuck with only a few courses to take to receive their Associate Degrees but no way to get them" (241). Wideman has warned us: "The program that allowed him to work for a degree has been canceled. He was the first and last graduate" (239).[59]

Wideman has worried aloud about the shape of his narrative and its lack of an "apotheosis" (194). Robby's graduation speech and the simultaneous news of his program's defunding are something less than such an apotheosis. Yet this moment comes as close as anything else to socializing and justifying John Edgar's own rise through the university system, which has been at issue throughout his description of his brother's fall, by tying the two back together. The society to which John Edgar has attached himself imprisons people like Robby, and perhaps must do so, if not with such brutal finality. At its best, however, it also recognizes its own responsibility in producing the crimes it punishes, and thus—pending more drastic changes—tries to give them back some of the hope that it has taken away. The margin between imprisonment and imprisonment with hope may seem too slight to care about. Yet this slight margin, bland and budgetary, marked off here by the space between a degree program funded and not funded, is where the work, skill, effort, dedication of people like John Edgar Wideman can "make a difference," as the saying goes, and make one now. Neither rags nor riches, and yet fully as fragile as the dream of riches itself, the federally funded prison degree program is nevertheless what allows John Edgar to say that "Prison had changed my brother, not broken him" (195). It is neither an unrealistic nor an uninspiring figure for upward mobility in our time.

The Luck of Birth and the International Division of Labor

On the last page of *Never Let Me Go*, Kathy describes a landscape she has stopped to contemplate while driving in the country soon after Tommy's death.

> I found I was standing before acres of ploughed earth. There was a fence keeping me from stepping into the field, with two lines of barbed wire, and I could see how this fence and the cluster of two or three trees above me were the only things breaking the wind for miles. All along the fence, especially along the lower line of wire, all sorts of rubbish had caught and tangled. It was like the debris you get on a sea-shore: the wind must have carried some of it for miles and miles before finally coming up against these trees and these two lines of wire. [. . .] That was the only time, as I stood there, looking at that strange rubbish, feeling the wind coming across those empty fields, that I started to imag-ine just a little fantasy thing, because this was Norfolk after all, and it was only a couple of weeks since I'd lost him. I was thinking about the rubbish, the flapping plastic in the branches, the shore-line of odd stuff caught along the fencing, and I half-closed my eyes and imagined this was the spot where everything I'd ever lost since my childhood had washed up, and I was now standing here in front of it, and if I waited long enough, a tiny figure would appear on the horizon across the field, and gradually get larger until I'd see it was Tommy. (263).

Placed as it is, the "rubbish" caught in the barbed wire fence has the force of a poetic summation. Picking up the novel's talk of artwork as rubbish, it suggests the futility of all those creative efforts and aspirations. According to the children's myth, their art was supposed to reveal their inmost selves. If so, then the flapping plastic caught in the wire becomes an image of what they really are—or what they have tried so hard to believe they aren't. After investigating the woman she suspects of being her "possible" or genetic mother, Ruth says bitterly that she was wrong to follow a white-collar employee working in a modern office: "If you want to do it properly, then you look in the gutter. You look in rubbish bins" (152).

At the same time, the barbed wire recalls the wire fence around the school. That fence has symbolized the children's special status, and it continues to do so even once it is no longer necessary, once they have internalized their lessons and left school, headed without further prodding toward the donations. In this sense, the barbed wire also stands for those teachers or guardians who helped them learn those lessons—helped them learn to subdue their own agitation in order to help others subdue theirs. If Kathy sees herself and her fellows as rubbish, she can also see herself and her fellow carers as wires in a fence, catching the rubbish (now representing others *like* herself) as it's flung across the countryside by the force of the wind. This momentary, meaningless catching thus becomes a bleak and final figure for caring. It suggests that Tommy was right to ask whether in the end caring really accomplishes anything. The barbed wire can hardly be said to do the rubbish any good.[1]

The present book, like Ishiguro's, might well choose to end on this image of wires and rubbish. For whatever has been said here about the hidden virtues of the upward mobility story, the welfare state (one of whose characteristic duties is the efficient and dependable collection of rubbish), and the caring that links them together, there are of course horrors lurking over its horizon, and this conclusion offers a last chance to come clean about them. The most obvious limitations of the argument are geographical. Ishiguro's rubbish-driving wind need not be imagined as blowing across the Channel or the North Sea in order for us to consider, for example, the story's hitherto excluded international dimension. The narrative negotiations between upward mobility and the common good I have been discussing have rarely exceeded the scale of the nation-state. This is because what I've called welfare, however niggardly, has by and large been restricted to people within the state's borders. It is only within those borders that the "good" has been recognized, however tentatively, as "common." The state's treatment of those outside its borders has tended on the contrary to oscillate between the poles of indifference and violent aggression. It is arguable, though by no means firmly established, that both upward mobility and the welfare state have managed to exist, in countries with more or less developed welfare systems, only by taking advantage of the violence that Bismarck's Germany, the European colonial powers in their colonial phase, and the neocolonialism of the United States have been in the habit of meting out to countries that have no such systems. Empire offered both direct outlets for upward mobility and indirect sources of funding for what were to become welfare institutions. The socioeconomic thickening of the concept of citizenship intended to lead toward what Marshall called "social citizenship" was rarely if ever intended for anyone but fellow citizens.[2] Noncitizens, more radically excluded from the metropolitan upward mobility story than the domestic brothers and sisters left behind, might thus be expected to disturb the story's composure and cast some shadow on its claims.

Take for example the claims of Debra Dickerson's memoir *An American Story* (2000).[3] These rest on its heroine's genuinely heroic overcoming of racial and gender adversity, but they do so within a strictly and perilously American frame. Adding to the rich evidence of her own life, Dickerson illustrates the nonexistence of the proverbial level playing field by means of an anecdote about an African-American schoolkid who can't understand why he didn't get credit for the answer "cup and table"; he has never encountered the expression "cup and saucer" because he has never met anyone who interposed anything between the table and the cup. State intervention to remedy the inequalities of birth has been and remains necessary. In Dickerson's own case, the state is directly involved in the mentor/benefactor function, and in Dickerson's view it fulfills that function satisfactorily. Outside her view, however, her case also allows us to understand that in creating possibilities for some of its citizens, the state may be increasing the inequality between citizens and noncitizens, or indeed doing something worse than that. Dickerson expresses equal gratitude toward the two institutions that helped raise her up: the university and the United States Air Force. She does not seem troubled by what others might see as an incongruity of goals between the two institutions. Writing before 2001 and the latest fit of neoimperial violence from the air, Dickerson need not take personal responsibility for, say, the bombing of Afghanistan or Iraq and the deaths of tens of thousands of their citizens, most of them noncombatants. But she was in uniform during the first Gulf War, and even if she had not been, the meaning of her personal upward mobility would have to include the possibility that the military skills she has worked so hard to obtain would be used and would have consequences for others, especially foreigners, if and when they were. Dickerson is by no means devoid of political consciousness. While in the Air Force she speaks of herself as "a hard-core leftist" (201). She frets "over my own role in history" (208). She makes "mental lists of places I had to refuse to go, missions I couldn't in good conscience support" (208). Yet when she is waiting to be posted to Ankara to do military intelligence during the buildup to the First Gulf War, all she can think about is the unpleasant fact that she is being sexualized. "The Air Force was a wonderful place for black people. . . . The Air Force wasn't such a wonderful place for women" (211). She explains: "Even though every GI understood that this was a war about cheap oil, paid for with the suffering of long-oppressed Iraqis, politics went out the window for me once we were at war. I may have serious bones to pick with my country, but it's still mine" (225). Here a surge of patriotism coincides conveniently with upward mobility's demand for strategic moral blindness, especially outside the nation's borders. Dickerson's narrative of her time in Turkey ends not in a pause for reflection but in careerist infighting. She herself is the only victim of a bureaucratic struggle with her replacement over who will "[steal] whatever glory might be in store during a wartime, front-line posting" (225). She returns again and again to the problems of a woman in a man's world, but *An American Story* makes no further reference to the aims and actions of American air power as concerns the "long-oppressed Iraqis."

When upward mobility goes wrong, this is how. Founded on an initial injustice or deprivation, the genre always risks allowing the screen to be filled by the challenges to be overcome and the joy of overcoming them. For Dickerson, there is room for nothing else. She writes as if she could be proud of her own accomplishments without any allusion to those of the organization in which she rises—say, the Highway of Death, littered with bodies and burned-out vehicles wantonly destroyed as they tried to flee back the way they had come. She rejects any further information about the Air Force's victims, victims who, though foreign, clamor to be recognized as metaphorical versions of her own initial state.[4]

Tempted as it is by self-enclosure and self-satisfaction, however, the genre has an answer to this temptation, at least when it goes right. As I've been suggesting, "upward mobility" can be justly juxtaposed to "the common good," despite appearances, to the extent that the story finds some means of reaching back to indicate that some of the benefits of mobility are to be shared. Most typically it does this by associating the endpoint of its protagonists with the redistributive mentor/benefactor role that others have played in their own stories. This logic has been supported, I've argued, by the rise of welfare state institutions and the profound shift in moral sensibility that is both a cause and an effect of that rise. The moral sensibility that insists on an enlarged sense of the common good has not been caught in the wires at the nation's frontier. Indeed, it could not be. Thus, though the institutions of the welfare state, beaten back even at home, largely have been stopped at the border, there is some real question as to whether the nation in fact continues to set severe and even absolute limits to the logic of upward mobility. In conclusion, I will try to push this question a bit further.

In saying that welfare state institutions "largely" stop at the nation's borders, I am of course suggesting that some institutions do not. As an example, take those public services that are encountered by the African emigrant protagonist of Caryl Phillips's *A Distant Shore* when he arrives, destitute, in Great Britain: "I told her that I had no money, but she laughed and told me that the vouchers were a form of money. She informed me that there was a method whereby a person might exchange them for food or other supplies. Incredibly enough, this did not mark the conclusion of her glad tidings. She told me that a local council would pay for my board and lodgings (247–48). Or consider the official welcome provided by Canada to Algerian political refugees in Lorraine Adams's *Harbor*:[5] "When she had completed the paperwork that gave him a date for an asylum hearing, she told him it was a formality. All Algerians in Canada were granted 'immediate and unconditional and indefinite residency because of the grave human-rights crisis that existed in their homeland.' She also said her shift was ending, and she wanted to help him by driving him to the train station so that he could get to Montreal, where there was a sizable Algerian community, not to mention a national welfare system that would make it possible for him to 'get his bearings and recover from the trauma he had suffered' " (150). When he gets to Montreal, "the government dole" turns out to be "better than anyone could hope to have in Algeria" (154).

Neither of these novels could be accurately described as an upward mobility story. Each migrant protagonist—the word *protagonist* is not quite exact, as both novels have other characters who are no less central—ends badly. One is tempted to suggest that these migration stories end badly for the same reason that there has been less life these days in the conventions of upward mobility: because the enormous inequality of resources between rich nations and poor nations weighs so heavily on the collective consciousness or collective conscience, even in the metropolitan center. For better or worse, however, there is no lack of recent upward mobility stories. "Coming to America" novels like Bharati Mukherjee's *Jasmine*, Jamaica Kincaid's *Lucy*, and Julia Alvarez's *How the Garcia Girls Lost Their Accents* could be said to reinvent the genre on a transnational scale, though sometimes (as in the Alvarez novel) they do so by passing off an upper-class story of lateral mobility—that is, the acculturation of the same class within a different language and culture—as if it were a more strenuous story of class mobility. And even in the darker portrayals of the Third World migrant in the metropolis offered by Phillips and Adams, upward mobility conventions are visible and, within limits, active and significant. In the passages above, for example, note that each of the welcoming voices is female. Both novels display an ambiguously eroticized Older Woman who acts as mediator, assisting a social metamorphosis for the protagonist that, though finally frustrated, carries the reader through a good deal of the novel. *Harbor* makes the eroticism explicit, while *A Distant Shore* echoes the displaced mode of *Great Expectations*. Washed up on the cold English coast, starving and in rags, its hero encounters a young girl who brings him food. This version of the life-saving and life-defining Pip-Magwitch encounter leads to arrest and the (false) accusation of rape. There is also a replay of Pip's relation to Miss Havisham—another romance, again truncated, between a younger man with aspirations and a lonely, retired Englishwoman who is driven to something like madness.[6] In another variant on the donor-acquisition scene, the protagonist gets to know this woman, who will in a sense rescue him and in a sense be rescued by him, when she is waiting at a bus stop and he gives her a lift in his car. Public transport is trumped, one might say in the allegorical mode, by the luxury of a private vehicle. Yet as we saw above, public services in this novel are shown as generously extending to noncitizens, and they are not negligible. In the end, the British state seems less racist, and less divided as to whether the African refugee protagonist belongs in Britain, than many of the British are.

Intriguingly, the protagonist might be said to repay the state by speaking in its voice, or giving it a voice. Solomon speaks with the abstract correctness of the nonnative who has learned standard English from books. About Mike, the Irish truck driver who is another in the succession of benefactors, he says, almost comically: "I knew that this drinking could not be beneficial to his health" (254).[7] This sentence is not colloquial in the same way that the state is not colloquial. Its tone might suit the health visitors of chapter 5, or for that matter almost any of this book's long line of official inspectors: the inspector from Paris who sets off the plot of *The Red and the Black*, the Federal Crime Commission inspectors in *On the Waterfront*, the fire inspector Dutch Schultz murders in *Billy Bathgate*, or Paul Willis's building inspector father. (Even Jodie Foster's Clarice Starling is a sort of health visitor, finding the right house at last.) Foregoing the comfortable but exclusive intimacies of the already-known and taken-for-granted, Solomon's words sound dry, unnatural, impersonal. But the novel might be said to offer them official approval of a sort when Mike is killed by a drunk driver—by drinking, that is, though not by his own. The plot here is moved by the impersonal logic of the state, which is less concerned with who did it and to whom than by the abstract cause: alcohol. This is the logic, I'm suggesting, that we hear in the strange abstraction of Solomon's voice: the kindness of strangers, reversibly identified with kindness *to* strangers, that speaks for a system that is sometimes better than the people on whose behalf it operates.[8]

If, as it seems, the Third World migrant or refugee can now serve as an exemplary subject of the transnational upward mobility story, it's because the Third World situation offers two promising approaches to the dilemma around which the genre at its most serious is constituted.[9] The political disaster that forces the migrant to seek refuge abroad dispenses him or her from anything but minimal loyalty to the society of origin. Any society from which one must flee in order not to be killed has already lost much of its hold over the protagonist's sentiments. In *A Distant Shore*, for example, the protagonist's family has been murdered, caught up in a familiar and seemingly unavoidable sort of ethno-tribal chaos. He too would have been murdered had he stayed. There is no side worth fighting for, nothing worth returning to. "His every movement would appear to be an attempt to erase a past that he no longer wishes to be reminded of" (237).

Here global history is enlisted to support what every young protagonist of upward mobility feels: life at home is unlivable. The risk that this geopolitical version of initial deprivation will turn into gross, uncritical flattery of the society of destination is of course always high. Bharati Mukherjee's *Jasmine* arguably succumbs to this risk. Yet even in *Jasmine*, as I've argued elsewhere, the protagonist's rise is subtly linked to violence against the receiving society.[10] And even if the benefits received by the upwardly mobile protagonist seem to be freely offered rather than forcibly seized, they can come to seem evidence of leveling between the two societies, hence a sort of blow struck against the superiority or hegemony of the metropolis, or part of a general impulse to redistribute the world's goods in favor of the have-nots. In this sense and to this extent, the migrant's rise resolves the genre's constitutive paradox: how anyone can move up into the society of destination while simultaneously doing something to pull that society down.

Gayatri Spivak has famously warned against allowing the narrative of "eurocentric economic migration" to provide a norm for our current sense of globality, against "theories, however subtly argued, that support the idea that upward class mobility—mimicry and masquerade—is unmediated resistance" (xii).[11] The warning is necessary, given the sorts of self-legitimizing and self-aggrandizing impulses that the upward mobility story reveals. I have mined these impulses for what seemed most valuable in their anger and perceptions of injustice, assuming as I went that there is an important distinction between "unmediated resistance" and the sorts of mediation this book has put in relief: to be specific, the compromises of the welfare state. But the question of how the welfare state looks in international perspective demands to be posed more than once, and in more than one way. Spivak tends to remind her readers that, as Samir Amin and Immanuel Wallerstein have long maintained, the existence of the welfare state in the North is the definitive sign of systematic inequality between North and South.[12] Thus even if there is, as I've suggested, a hidden egalitarianism in the upward mobility story, it could still be true that the price of egalitarianism at home is imperialism or neoimperialism abroad.

Spivak's impatience with egalitarianism at home helps explain why she takes little pleasure in Jane Eyre's displacement of Bertha Mason, even though Bertha Mason is apparently of a higher class. Being on the privileged side of the class line means less than being on the unprivileged side of the colonial line, the line that Spivak usually calls "the international division of labor." The term is worth pausing over. It is a very potent one. Any identity conferred by the domestic division of labor (class identity) is dissolved, or at least trumped and reshaped, by the identity conferred by the *international* division of labor (crudely, colonial identity). For we must remember that the division of labor between nations and regions is not merely the same division at a larger scale. On the contrary, it is a replacement and counterterm, one that shakes the orthodox, internalist, undifferentiated notion of class identity to its very foundations.[13] One is tempted to count Spivak's references to the international division of labor among her Marxist, economistic, or anticulturalist moments. But by the criteria of orthodox Marxism they could also be described as *anticlass* moments.[14] The phrase "international division of labor" appears in the essay "Can the Subaltern Speak?" (indeed, it appears in the sentence in which this famous question is posed) when Spivak is chastising Deleuze and Foucault, caught forever in the embarrassment of their Maoist-sympathizing youth, for displaying excessive reverence for the knowing subaltern.[15] "This statement [Deleuze's "genuflection" to "the workers' struggle"] ignores the international division of labor, a gesture that often marks poststructuralist political theory" (250). Excess of loyalty to *class* is not among the usual charges brought against poststructuralism. This charge only makes sense if we recall that the struggles to which Deleuze and Foucault are referring are conducted by *European* workers. Spivak is saying, with appropriate circumspection, that the class position occupied by workers in the metropolis is ambiguous. As partial beneficiaries of the core/periphery divide, a divide of which they cannot be easily or fully aware, they are not *simply* workers.

Spivak is even more circumspect in drawing out another corollary of the international division of labor. She seems unwilling to admit except in a very guarded mode, while warning against its dangers, that if the international division of labor takes some political representativeness away from the working-class European, it also *bestows* some political representativeness upon the middle-class non-European. It is only the core/periphery disparity dictated by the international division of labor that gives the middle-class postcolonial any right at all to speak for fellow nationals, a right that a more orthodox Marxism, seeing in such a figure only another member of the bourgeoisie, would be strongly motivated to deny her. This is a large point. It explains why Spivak must so persistently return to the story of the "eurocentric economic migrant," the story of upward mobility and the vexed question of who else, if anyone, is carried along or represented in that upward mobility. By blurring class identities, the international division of labor makes upward mobility genuinely interesting. To be more precise, it suggests the possibility that upward mobility stories may not after all be built on the absolute necessity of betraying and sacrificing some Bertha Mason or some representative of Third World indigeneity.

Spivak rejects the idea that she and her fellow diasporic intellectuals can be considered not guilty but lucky. But it is a half-hearted rejection.

"Postcolonial persons from formerly colonized countries are able to communicate to each other (and to metropolitans), to exchange, to establish sociality, because we have had access to the so-called culture of imperialism. Shall we then assign to that culture a measure of 'moral luck'? I think there can be no doubt that the answer is 'no.' This impossible no to a structure that one critiques and yet inhabits intimately is the deconstructive position, of which postcoloniality is a historical case" (191). Rather than a paralyzingly purist or theological anguish in the face of the capital O Other, I prefer to think of deconstructive ethics as just this acknowledgment of dirty hands that can never be cleaned. Upward mobility stories as well are about inhabiting, intimately and dirty-handedly, a structure that one also critiques, being unable to say a simple "no" to "moral luck."[16] Like the more dramatic distances of transnational geography, they too offer a historical context for deconstructive ethics.

Bernard Williams, whose essay on moral luck Spivak cites several times, is like her a critic of Kantian ethics, and his insistence that people make moral choices amid "elements which are essential to the outcome but lie outside their control" (48), elements however that will go on to constitute who they are (this is what makes luck moral), could pass with nonexperts as a version of the deconstructive position. (The relation between Williams and Spivak would be worth a longer discussion.)[17] And, oddly enough, what to make, ethically speaking, of a "success story" is also the question Williams addresses in working out his theory of moral luck. His example is the painter Gauguin. Daniel Statman, Williams's editor, sums up the example as follows: "Gauguin, a creative artist, abandoned his wife and children to live a life in which, so he supposed, he could pursue his art. He believed that only be going alone to Tahiti, turning away from his obligations to his family, could he realize his gifts as a painter. Now, according to Williams, whether this choice can be justified depends primarily on Gauguin's *success*. If he failed, it would become clear that he had no basis for thinking that he was justified in acting as he did. But, argues Williams, 'whether he will succeed cannot, in the nature of the case, be foreseen.' . . . Therefore, at the time of the choice, Gauguin had to rely on factors that were beyond his control. Obviously one's will, strong as it might be, is not sufficient to make one a great artist. Much more is needed, in particular talent and inspiration. Hence the justification of Gauguin's decision depends on factors that are a matter of luck."[18]

In the preface to *A Critique of Postcolonial Reason*, Spivak describes the argument of its *Jane Eyre* chapter as a "lesson" in how *not* to present "the ethics of alterity as a politics of identity." "Today," she goes on, she "would have added" Jamaica Kincaid's *Lucy* to this argument, for *Lucy* claims "the right/responsibility of loving, denied to the subject that wishes to choose agency from victimage" (x).[19] Lucy's success story is just the sort of migration narrative about which Spivak is elsewhere quite severe. The people Lucy is learning to love are largely white representatives of the metropolitan world for which she has abandoned Antigua. Speaking a bit crudely, one might translate this rejection of victimage in favor of loving as a positive embrace by the "eurocentric economic migrant" of her upward mobility story, an embrace in which Kincaid and Spivak now seem to join.

When Lucy thinks about the meaning of her migration, like Bernard Williams she too thinks of the example of Gauguin. She thinks of

> some paintings by a man, a French man, who had gone halfway around the world and had painted pictures of the people he found living there. He had been a banker living a comfortable life with his wife and children, but that did not make him happy; eventually he left them and went to the opposite part of the world, where he was happier. I don't know if Mariah meant me to, but I identified with the yearnings of this man; I understood finding the place where you were born an unbearable prison and wanting something completely different from what you are familiar with, knowing it represents a haven." (95)[20]

One page after this passage, which occurs in a chapter called "Cold Heart," Lucy is taken to a party in a bohemian setting where she will almost immediately feel both comfortable and sexually excited. The guests are artists, or as she says, "in the position" of artists, "a position that allowed for irresponsibility," like that of "the man whose paintings hung in the museum that I liked to visit" (98). She likes the host, and she describes her feeling as follows: "This is usually the moment when people say they fall in love, but I did not fall in love. Being in such a state was not something I longed for. . . . the question of being in love was not one I wanted to settle then; what I wanted was to be alone in a room with him and naked" (100).

With or without Lucy's references to *Jane Eyre*, we can perhaps think of the bohemian host as her St. John Rivers—a Rivers in a story without a Rochester. In other words, *Lucy* is another Cinderella story without Prince Charming. If Rochester is the reward for Jane's personal effort and merit, this alternative bond between the powerful and the subaltern embodies, rather, the "irresponsibility" and impersonality of luck, which is to say the irresponsibility and impersonality of society itself in its most democratically open mode, flaunting those elements beyond the protagonist's control that do not express her although they help determine success or failure. The move is from one form of responsibility, the tight individualism of work ethic and self-reliance, to another, which acknowledges almost infinite social interdependence and in the eyes of self-reliance will thus look like happy-go-lucky irresponsibility. (That's why artists, like the ethnic underclass, are forever being asked why they don't go out and get a job.) The libidinal extension of Lucy's identification with Gauguin, this bohemian scene leads out of romantic passion and into a cooler, more collective sort of feeling, feeling diluted by an uncontrollable democratic reference to other scenes and other people. As Lucy puts it elsewhere, "I said goodbye to Hugh, though he did not know it. . . . As I kissed [him], my tongue reaching to caress the roof of his mouth, I thought of all the other tongues I had held in my mouth in this way" (82).

In a more recent reading of *Lucy*, Spivak quotes this chilly passage as a symptom of "withdrawal from affective connectives" (339).[21] Lucy thinks, falsely for Spivak, that emotional withdrawal is a solution to hating and loving both her mother and her white mistress—in brief, a solution to the diasporic dilemma that Spivak explains as "enter[ing] the conquering class at the expense of someone she knows" (348). By reformulating this as the question of whether the subaltern can love, and by pointing it toward eventual if still postponed resolution in "access to the subjectship of loving" (352), it seems to me that Spivak has gestured toward something like my own argument: toward the linkage of upward mobility to the cooler, less satisfying brand of love, still compromised by hierarchy and injustice, that is historically embodied in the welfare state.

More might be said here about Lucy's (and Kincaid's) brothers, whose favoring by the mother is offered as the rationale for Lucy's upward mobility narrative but who also come to figure, like so many other siblings, those who are left behind by the upward mobility story and who must be somehow factored in again in order for it to achieve resolution. *My Brother*, published in 1997, continues the same wrestling with love and responsibility across the international division of labor that divides her family. At its center is the absence from Antigua of adequate health services for AIDS sufferers. Thus Kincaid, ferrying medicine to her brother from Vermont and thereby prolonging his life, reargues the meaning of her upward mobility story by becoming a First World/Third World go-between. The example is perhaps enough so as to indicate at least that the issue is alive, in Kincaid's novels and elsewhere.

If you, reader, are a fellow academic, as seems likely, then "soul making" will perhaps seem to you like a description of our common work as well as Jane Eyre's: that is, the teaching of culture to those who must be assumed to lack it, or subject-formation in the domain of civil society cathected as social mission. I've been trying to establish that soul making in this sense is part of the history that has brought us the welfare state, which must be seen as an adventurous and incomplete project—not a collection of empty administrative mechanisms, but a rechanneling of risky and ethically unpredictable desires, erotic and otherwise, that challenges all our skills in the analysis of narrative and metaphor. In the era of so-called welfare reform, among other indignities, this struggle for common sense is obviously ongoing. It is also worthy of our efforts, despite the reasonable fear that it will only help consolidate the international division of labor. In his book *Mirages and Miracles*, Alain Lipietz concludes that "the classical theory that imperialism reproduces dependency and an International Division of Labor with a center-periphery division between the manufacturing and primary sectors is both realistic and contingent" (67).[22] It is realistic because this is what really happened at a given historical moment. It is contingent because "it is true only of one period" (68); it is not a "*logic*" (68) that can be permanently generalized, but "one of 'History's chance discoveries' " (68). Lipietz illustrates this openness to chance (a theme on which Spivak and Bernard Williams would presumably agree) with the example of "peripheral Fordism," the brief but telling appearance on the other side of the international division of labor of what I have been calling the welfare state. More recent history, with its shift of global resources in the direction of East and South Asia, suggests that he may be right. One pertinent piece of evidence among many is Wang Hui's influential critique of deregulation in China, which despite its complaints about the forms of continuing state intrusion speaks up in the name of state-sponsored "safety-net" guarantees.[23] If developed welfare states have in fact been able to resist the supposedly inexorable pressure of globalization, as Duane Swank argues, then political resistance ought to be at least conceivable at less favored sites as well.[24] Other signs include the reemergence of "the commons" as a concept suddenly reinvigorated by the counterglobalization movement, on the one hand, and by the Internet, on the other. A set of political demands for the restraint and regulation of global capital and a technology that is increasingly normalizing notions of open access and unpaid cooperation on a planetary scale may not make self-evident political partners. But each might well excite those same fears about the corrosion of character that we've repeatedly heard expressed about the welfare state. Wild optimism would be uncalled for. But it seems reasonable at least to hope that what welfare's opponents fear may well come to pass. People in large numbers may begin thinking in terms of entitlements not based on paid employment. Social justice may be imagined as irreducible to the rewards of the work ethic. It is of course only if these fears and hopes are realized planetarily that the dilemma that brought the upward mobility story into being and that continues to sustain its latest transnational forms—the zero-sum necessity according to which a postcolonial migrant's upward mobility can only happen at the expense of someone at home whom she might know—can be definitively laid to rest.

Notes

PREFACE
SOMEONE ELSE'S LIFE

1. The "Four Yorkshiremen" Sketch, Monty Python's Flying Circus—from *Live at City Centre* (New York: Arista Records, 1997 [1976]).
2. The *Times* series has been reprinted as *Class Matters*, by the correspondents of the *New York Times*, introduction by Bill Keller (New York: Henry Holt/Times Books, 2005); *PMLA* 115:1 (January 2000), Special Topic: "Rereading Class," edited by Cora Kaplan. In the field of textbooks, see Paul Lauter and Ann Fitzgerald, eds., *Literature, Class, and Culture: An Anthology* (New York: Longman, 2001).
3. Walter Benn Michaels, "The Neoliberal Imagination," *N+1* 3 (Fall 2005), 69–76.
4. See for example Clare Brant and Yun Lee Too, *Rethinking Sexual Harassment* (London: Pluto Press, 1994); Jane Gallop, *Feminist Accused of Sexual Harassment* (Durham, NC: Duke University Press, 1997); Susan Baur, *The Intimate Hour: Love and Sex in Psychotherapy* (Boston: Houghton Mifflin, 1997); James R. Kincaid, *Erotic Innocence: The Culture of Child Molesting* (Durham, NC: Duke University Press, 1998); and Anson Shupe, William A. Stacey, and Susan E. Darnell, eds., *Bad Pastors: Clergy Misconduct in Modern America* (New York: New York University Press, 2000).
5. Karen Moncrieff's film *Blue Car* (2003) is a brilliant addition to the genre.
6. Isabel Wilkerson, "Angela Whitiker's Climb: Up From the Projects, a Journey Never Easy, Never Over," *New York Times*, June 12, 2005, A1, 22–24.
7. Steven Greenhouse, "Crossing the Border into the Middle Class" and "Local 226, 'the Culinary,' Makes Las Vegas the Land of the Living Wage," *New York Times*, June 3, 2004, A22.
8. Junot Diaz, *Drown* (New York: Riverhead, 1996).

INTRODUCTION
THE FAIRY GODMOTHER

1. Thomas Harris, *The Silence of the Lambs* (New York: St. Martin's, 1988), 25.
2. Elizabeth Young, "*The Silence of the Lambs* and the Flaying of Feminist Theory," *Camera Obscura* 27 (September 1991), 5–35. See also Adrienne Donald, "Working for Oneself: Labor and Love in *The Silence of the Lambs*," *Michigan Quarterly Review* 31:3 (1992), 347–60; and Judith Halberstam, "Skinflick: Posthuman Gender in Jonathan Demme's *The Silence of the Lambs*," *Camera Obscura* 27 (September 1991), 37–52.
3. In the novel, Chilton insists (to Lecter) on an erotic interpretation of Starling's relationship to Crawford: "Jack Crawford and his fluff. They'll get together

openly after his wife dies. He'll dress younger and take up some sport they can enjoy together. They've been intimate ever since Bella Crawford got sick, they're certainly not fooling anybody about that. They'll get their promotions and they won't think about you once a year. Crawford probably wants to come up personally at the end and tell you what *you're* getting." (176).

4. Eve Kosofsky Sedgwick, "Tales of the Avunculate: *The Importance of Being Earnest*," in *Tendencies* (Durham, NC: Duke University Press, 1993), 52–72.

5. "Behavioral Science"—the first two words of the novel—could be seen to align *Silence of the Lambs* against Freud and sexualized psychology. In "MacKinnon's Dog," Mandy Merck exposes some of the consequences of such a position for feminism (talk delivered at Rutgers University, Spring 1993). However, as Slavoj Zizek notes, the same point might also be made about Freud's own interpretation of the dream of Irma's injection: "the meaning of the dream," Zizek writes, "is obviously neither of a sexual nature (it rather concerns professional ethics) nor unconscious (the failure of Irma's treatment was troubling Freud day and night)." Slavoj Zizek, *The Sublime Object of Ideology* (London: Verso, 1989), 12. As usual, there is nothing to stop an orthodox Freudian from dismissing such materials as mere screen memories.

6. Lecter has no more reason to require a story of sexuality from Starling than he has to want from her what he has already in effect predicted, the professional motive of "advancement." Indeed, with this scene she may even be giving him what *he* really wants; advancement, to use his term again, could certainly be seen as what he *wants* her to want, since it's only her desire for advancement that will give him a hold over her, will eroticize his own otherwise ineligible position.

7. I develop this argument at greater length in "Murder and Mentorship: Advancement in *The Silence of the Lambs*," *UTS Review* 1:1 (August 1995), 30–49 and *boundary 2* 23:1 (Spring 1996), 71–90. The portions of that essay used here have been revised.

8. I am inspired here by Étienne Balibar, *Masses, Classes, Ideas: Studies on Politics and Philosophy before and after Marx*, trans. James Swenson (New York and London: Routledge, 1994). 87–174.

9. On the role of racism in arousing and channeling majoritarian anger against welfare, even when American public opinion does not favor cuts to government funding for housing, day care, job training, and other programs, see Martin Gilens, *Why Americans Hate Welfare: Race, Media, and the Politics of Antipoverty Policy* (Chicago and London: University of Chicago Press, 1999). On the enormous human cost of the abolition of Aid to Families with Dependent Children, see for example Nina Bernstein, "Studies Dispute Two Assumptions about Welfare Overhaul," *New York Times*, December 12, 2000, A18.

10. It is perhaps worth saying that a more satisfactory version of collective advancement—let's call it socialism—would occupy precisely the same empty, utterly unimaginable position in the film that is occupied by the only true or logical solution to the slaughter of the lambs problem, in Starling's presentation of it: namely, universal vegetarianism.

11. This ambiguity is arguably present in even the narrow definition, which includes (1) "state provision of social services" to individuals and families in need, "basically social security, health, social welfare, education and training, and hous-

ing," but also (2) "state regulation of private activities . . . which directly alter the immediate conditions of life of individuals and groups," which would include social legislation and consumer protection. Ian Gough, *The Political Economy of the Welfare State* (London: Macmillan, 1979), 4–5.

12. Alice Kessler-Harris, *In Pursuit of Equity: Women, Men, and the Quest for Economic Citizenship in 20th-Century America* (Oxford: Oxford University Press, 2001). Even in the Depression and even among members of the organized labor movement, as Kessler-Harris shows, the masculinist ideal of independence and self-help went so deep as to induce the AFL to help defeat a bill that would have shortened the work-week, but would have done so under the authority of a new federal bureaucracy. See also Theda Skocpol's *Protecting Soldiers and Mothers: The Political Origins of Social Policy in the United States* (Cambridge and London: Harvard University Press, 1992), which salvages from the critique of the top-down "paternalist welfare state" the more desirable historical precedent of a "maternalist welfare state, with female-dominated public agencies implementing regulations and benefits for the good of women and their children" (2). "The new governmental functions," Skocpol writes, "were normatively justified as a universalization of mother love" (522).

13. Étienne Balibar, *Nous, citoyens d'Europe? Les frontières, l'État, le peuple* (Paris: La Découverte, 2001), chap. 12.

14. On the welfare state as a means of regulating the capitalist labor market, see for example Frances Fox Piven and Richard A. Cloward, *Regulating the Poor: The Functions of Public Welfare* (New York: Vintage, 1971) and Ian Gough, *The Political Economy of the Welfare State* (London: Macmillan, 1979). My own position coincides with that of the editor of the series in which the latter book appeared, Peter Leonard: "the welfare state can be envisaged *both* as functional to the needs of capitalist development *and* as the result of the political struggles of the organized working class" (editor's introduction, ix). On the "pressure from below" thesis, see also Alexander Hicks, *Social Democracy and Welfare Capitalism: A Century of Income Security Politics* (Ithaca and London: Cornell University Press, 1999), which argues that "labor organizations and their politics built the welfare state by exploiting—sometimes quite fortuitously, sometimes most deliberately—the political opportunities offered to them" (x).

15. Fredric Jameson, "Five Theses on Actually Existing Marxism," *Monthly Review* 47 (April 1996), 1–10.

16. As Christine Stansell observes, Thomas's "story of growing up black was structured as a rags-to-riches tale of rising from obscure and humble origins to high places by dint of application and hard work. Less noticed was the story of growing up male," Stansell says, meaning that "uplift" and "mission" come from escaping "the downward pull of his mother's poverty" (258). These "Algeresque claims to providential fortune" (258), based on "leaving women behind" (259), were of a piece with the position taking that had first given Thomas national prominence, his denunciation of African American dependence on the welfare system. Speaking of his sister, Emma Mae Martin, he declared, "She gets mad when the mailman is late with her welfare check. . . . That's how dependent she is. What's worse is that now her kids feel entitled to the check, too. They have no motivation for doing better or for getting out of that situation" (260–61). In real-

ity, Martin was working two minimum-wage jobs while taking care of her three children; she went on welfare only for one four-and-a-half-year period when the aunt who raised her had a stroke and Martin quit her paying jobs in order to care for her. Christine Stansell, "White Feminists and Black Realities: The Politics of Authenticity." Toni Morrison, ed., *Race-ing Justice, En-gendering Power: Essays on Anita Hill, Clarence Thomas, and the Construction of Social Reality* (New York: Pantheon, 1992), 251–68.

17. I will come back to the more familiar case of the younger woman and the older man, as in *Silence* and *Jane Eyre*.

18. René Girard, *Deceit, Desire, and the Novel: Self and Other in Literary Structure*, trans. Yvonne Freccero (Baltimore: Johns Hopkins University Press, 1965), 138.

19. I owe this insight to Fredric Jameson's brilliant analysis of "the donor" in Vladimir Propp's *Morphology of the Folktale*, which is discussed below.

20. Michael McKeon, *The Origins of the English Novel, 1600–1740* (Baltimore: Johns Hopkins University Press, 1987), chap. 6.

21. Hannah Arendt, *Rahel Varnhagen: The Life of a Jewess*, ed. Liliane Weissberg, trans. Richard Wilson and Clara Winston (Baltimore: Johns Hopkins University Press, 1997).

22. John Richetti, *The English Novel in History, 1700–1780* (New York and London: Routledge 1999). On the other hand, "John Brewer has argued that England in the eighteenth century developed the most efficiently administered bureaucratic apparatus in Europe, the nation emerging in a period of nearly continuous warfare with France and its allies from 1689 to 1783 as 'a fiscal-miliary state' " (6). Still, this coexists with strong "patronage and kinship" bonds (7). Richetti quotes Giddens from *The Nation State and Violence* (Berkeley: University of California Press, 1985), 21.

23. David Lloyd and Paul Thomas, *Culture and the State* (New York and London: Routledge, 1998).

24. Sean McCann, *Gumshoe America: Hard-Boiled Crime Fiction and the Rise and Fall of New Deal Liberalism* (Durham, NC: Duke University Press, 2000); Michael Szalay, *New Deal Modernism: American Literature and the Invention of the Welfare State* (Durham, NC: Duke University Press, 2000). Each strikes a useful balance (different in the two cases) between critical and redemptive attitudes toward the New Deal context. For an analogue in the area of British Victorian fiction, see Lauren M. E. Goodlad, *Victorian Literature and the Victorian State: Character and Governance in a Liberal Society* (Baltimore: Johns Hopkins University Press, 2003).

25. Norman Barry, *Welfare* (Minneapolis: University of Minnesota Press, 1990). Barry himself traces the concept of the welfare state back to Tom Paine's *The Rights of Man* (viii). I take this as sufficient authorization for going back to Rousseau, theorist of the modern state, and the fiction he directly inspired.

26. For a nuanced position on class, see Wai Chee Dimock and Michael T. Gilmore, eds., *Rethinking Class: Literary Studies and Social Formations* (New York: Columbia University Press, 1994).

27. Daniel T. Rodgers, *Atlantic Crossings: Social Politics in a Progressive Age* (Cambridge: Harvard University Press, 1998).

CHAPTER ONE
EROTIC PATRONAGE: ROUSSEAU, CONSTANT, BALZAC, STENDHAL

1. Mary McCarthy, *The Groves of Academe* (New York: New American Library, 1951, 1952), 71–72

2. Jean-Jacques Rousseau, *Les Confessions I*, ed., Michel Launay, (Paris: Flammarion, 1968); Jean-Jacques Rousseau, *The Confessions*, trans. J. M. Cohen (Harmondsworth: Penguin, 1953).

3. An earlier version of this section appeared as "Cerebral Love: Rousseau, the Novel, and the State," *Annals of Scholarship* 14:3 and 15:1 (2003), 123–27.

4. Nicole Fermon, *Domesticating Passions: Rousseau, Woman, and Nation* (Hanover: Wesleyan University Press, 1997).

5. After the death of Claude Anet, with whom Rousseau initially shared the affections of Madame de Warens, Rousseau was asked to do the same with another of her younger live-in lovers, whom he was also asked to address as "brother." The exposure of the surrogate son to something like surrogate sibling rivalry offers more evidence that sexual "sharing" opens directly onto Rousseau's mature theory of democracy. The significance of sharing-with-siblings to the upward mobility story is developed further at various points below.

6. The French here has "froids et tristes" (231), "peu sensuelle" (235) "tempérament de glace" (237), "possédé par un autre homme" (233) and "elle n'a connu qu'un seul vrai plaisir au monde; c'était d'en faire à ceux qu'elle aimait" (237).

7. Leo Damrosch notes that "the nature and significance of this newly sexual relationship has attracted endless commentary, all of it hampered by the fact that we have no evidence except what Rousseau himself has given us. Accordingly, it has become something of a Rorschach picture onto which critics have been free to project their own values." My own reading is no exception. Leo Damrosch, *Jean-Jacques Rousseau: Restless Genius* (Boston and New York: Houghton Mifflin, 2005), 114.

8. Linda M. G. Zerilli, *Signifying Woman: Culture and Chaos in Rousseau, Burke, and Mill* (Ithaca: Cornell University Press, 1994). This opposition between the mother substitute and the modern or big-city woman offers a handy way into Stendhal's *The Red and the Black*.

9. Joan B. Landes, *Women and the Public Sphere in the Age of the French Revolution* (Ithaca: Cornell University Press, 1988).

10. For a parallel interpretation, see Jean Starobinski, *Jean-Jacques Rousseau: Transparency and Obstruction*, trans. Arthur Goldhamer (Chicago: University of Chicago Press, 1988 [1971]). Jean-Jacques's arrival at Madame de Warens's home "begins a period in his life marked by a return of transparency" (129).

11. Bonnie Honig, *Democracy and the Foreigner* (Princeton: Princeton University Press, 2001), 20.

12. Jean-Jacques Rousseau, *On the Social Contract*, trans. Donald A. Cress (Indianapolis: Hackett, 1987), book II, chap. 7, 164, quoted in Honig, *Democracy and the Foreigner*, 20.

13. Robert Castel, *Les Métamorphoses de la question sociale: Une chronique du salariat* (Paris: Fayard, 1995).

14. John Osborne, *Look Back in Anger* (London and New York: Penguin, 1957), 71.

15. André Maurois, *Prometheus: The Life of Balzac* (New York: Harper and Row, 1966), 96.

16. (speaking of 1825 in Paris, 114).

17. Invoking Rousseau's *Confessions*, Balzac called Madame de Berny "maman" (Maurois, *Prometheus*, 95).

18. Honoré de Balzac, *Lost Illusions*, trans. Herbert J. Hunt (London: Penguin, 1971).

19. See for example Dennis Wood, *Benjamin Constant: A Biography* (London and New York: Routledge, 1993); and J. Christopher Herold, *Mistress to an Age: A Life of Madame de Stael* (New York: Grove Press, 1958).

20. *Adolphe* is not strictly speaking an upward mobility story; the hero's father is a government minister. But the stakes in his love affair with Ellénore are the career he will or will not make for himself, the use he will nor will not make of talents we are led to understand are considerable. Her disinterestedness is in direct conflict with his self-interest, self-interest expressed in the Napoleonic field of "la carrière ouverte aux talents."

21. Benjamin Constant, *Adolphe*, préface Marcel Arland, édition Alfred Roulin (Paris: Gallimard, 1957/58); *Adolphe*, trans. Carl Wildman (Indianapolis: Bobbs-Merrill, 1948).

22. Laurie Langbauer, *Women and Romance: The Consolations of Gender in the English Novel* (Ithaca: Cornell University Press, 1990).

23. Margaret Cohen, *The Sentimental Education of the Novel* (Princeton: Princeton University Press, 1999), 66.

24. Tzvetan Todorov, *Benjamin Constant: La passion democratique* (Paris: Hachette, 1997), 33–37.

25. Todorov, *Constant*, 65 ff. See also Benjamin Constant, *Political Writings*, ed. Biancamaria Fontana (Cambridge: Cambridge University Press, 1988), for example the section of "The Spirit of Conquest" in which Constant examines military conquest based "on self-interest alone" (56–59).

26. Biancamaria Fontana, *Benjamin Constant and the Post-Revolutionary Mind* (New Haven: Yale University Press, 1991), 135. On Constant's specific commitment to disinterestedness, see also Paul Benichou, *The Consecration of the Writer, 1750–1830*, trans. Mark K. Jensen (Lincoln: University of Nebraska Press, 1999), 160–61.

27. It is the conflictual meaning of citizenship, a paralyzing conflict between individual freedom and responsibility to others, that Cohen, drawing on Margaret Waller, finds in *Adolphe*—in Waller's phrase, "the double bind of liberalism" (40–46). Margaret Waller, *The Male Malady: Fictions of Impotence in the French Romantic Novel* (New Brunswick, NJ: Rutgers University Press, 1993), 94.

28. Auerbach ends his chapter with Flaubert, in whom (despite Flaubert's own contempt for Stendhal) it is hard not to see another version of Stendhal's contemptuous and "aristocratic loftiness" toward the society around him. Indeed, contempt permeates Flaubert's distinct, not to say bizarre, contribution to the upward mobility genre, *Sentimental Education*.

29. Another example, from *Illusions Perdues* (1837–43), is the Cénacle: a sort of Bohemian alternative community or all-male family that sets an absolute standard. The novel speaks of "the serenity of countenance peculiar to young people still innocent of grave transgressions who have not stooped to any of those cowardly compromises which are wrested from men by poverty impatiently supported, the desire to succeed at all cost and the facile complacency with which all men of letters accept or pardon acts of treachery. What makes these friendships indissoluble and doubles their charm is a feeling not found in love—the feeling of certainty. These young people were sure of one another: the enemy of one became the enemy of all; they would have sacrificed their most urgent interests in obedience to the sacred solidarity which united their hearts. One and all were incapable of treachery" (220–21). Note the same "fixed star" principle that Balzac attributes to the Older Woman. "This community of feeling and interests lasted for twenty years without any clash of misunderstandings" (221).

30. The same might be said of adultery, a sentimental theme that is treated with more searching irony by the male realists. As Cohen says, adultery is given moral dignity in sentimental fiction without being celebrated for its transgressiveness (37). One might add that sentimental adultery is not just an assertion of personal freedom to choose one's partner, but an unofficial reimagining of the social bond, a miniature and unofficial collectivity, another version of the collective welfare. And again the same would hold, despite modifications, in realism.

31. See Sharon Marcus, "The Profession of the Author: Abstraction, Advertising, and *Jane Eyre*," *PMLA* 215 (1995): 206–19. Even this loophole was too wide for Henry Fielding, who felt obliged to rewrite Richardson's virtuous and upwardly mobile Pamela as Shamela, a calculating hypocrite.

32. Leo Braudy, *The Frenzy of Renown: Fame and Its History* (New York: Oxford University Press, 1986), 568. Braudy is talking about the paradox whereby the leader who wins a following is the one who never looks back, who has a "lack of interest in playing to an audience" (568).

33. "The odd thing is that if happiness is as indeterminate a notion as he suggests elsewhere—and as he suggests rightly elsewhere, for the Kantian notion of happiness has been detached from any notion of socially established ends and the satisfaction to be gained from achieving them—he can scarcely be consistent here in introducing happiness as the reward of virtue which though unsought, being indeed the reward of virtue only if it is unsought, is that without which the whole enterprise of morality would scarcely make sense." Alasdair MacIntyre, *A Short History of Ethics* (New York: Macmillan, 1966), 196.

34. Stefan Collini, "The Culture of Altruism: Selfishness and the Decay of Motive," in Collini, *Public Moralists: Political Thought and Intellectual Life in Britain 1850–1930* (Oxford: Clarendon, 1991).

35. Albert O. Hirschman, *The Passions and the Interests: Political Arguments for Capitalism before Its Triumph* (Princeton: Princeton University Press, 1977). Before declining into "material advantage," Hirschman writes, interest was not merely material, but "comprised the totality of human aspirations," suggesting "an element of reflection and calculation with respect to the manner in which [one's] aspirations were to be pursued" (32). In *Keywords*, Raymond Williams notes the way an objective relation (investment, legal share) takes over the subjec-

tive dimension (power to attract attention): "our most general word for attraction and involvement [developed] from a formal objective term in property and finance" Raymond Williams, *Keywords: A Vocabulary of Culture and Society* (London: Fontana, 1976), 144.

36. "les affections domestiques remplacent les grands intérêts publiques" (my translation). *Principes*, 1806, book, 7, 433; quoted in Todorov, *Constant*, 47. Benjamin Constant, *Principles of Politics Applicable to All Government*, ed. Etienne Hofmann, trans. Dennis O'Keeffe (Indianapolis: Liberty Fund, 2003).

37. Todorov, *Constant*, 94.

38. Erich Auerbach, *Mimesis*; Stendhal, *Le Rouge et le noir*, ed. Roger Nimier (Paris: Gallimard, 1958); *The Red and the Black*, ed. and trans Catherine Slater (Oxford and New York: Oxford University Press, 1991).

39. I've changed the translation from "historism."

40. In *The Red and the Black*, it seems clear that Julien's rise does not result directly from his conscious, deliberate acts, acts he likens to a military campaign. As D. A. Miller writes, "Brilliance and hard work don't move him from Verrières to Besançon—only the fear of scandal that his affair with Madame de Rênal has put into her husband, who wants to get him out of town in a socially plausible fashion. Similarly, it is not his academic success at the seminary that procures him his appointment as secretary to the marquis de la Mole; simply, the Abbé Pirard accepts a benefice in Paris and decides to rescue Julien along with himself. Even Julien's title and commission do not result directly from his schemes of advancement, but from the unforeseen pregnancy of Mathilde, who now wants to marry him. It is always as though the direct channels established for a linear progression from one stage to another were being deliberately ignored." D. A. Miller, *Narrative*, in Harold Bloom, *Stendhal* (New York: Chelsea House, 1989), 142.

41. As Georg Lukacs noticed, there is something bizarre about the republican Stendhal's admiration for Mathilde. "Balzac has never created so positive a type of romantic monarchist youth as Stendhal's Mathilde de la Mole. Mathilde de la Mole is a sincere convinced monarchist who is passionately devoted to romantic monarchist ideals and who despises her own class because it lacks the devoted and passionate faith which burns in her own soul. She prefers the plebeian Julien Sorel, the passionate Jacobin and Napoleon-admirer, to the men of her own station" Georg Lukacs, *Studies in European Realism* (New York: Grosset and Dunlap, 1964), 79; Bloom, *Stendahl*, 44.

42. Guy Chaussinaud-Nogaret, *The French Nobility in the Eighteenth Century: From Feudalism to Enlightenment*, trans. William Doyle (Cambridge: Cambridge University Press, 1985). Girard makes much the same point about the overlap in class worldviews: "The aristocracy is trying to prove to the Others that it has 'earned' its privileges; that is why it borrows its code of ethics from the class which is competing for those same privileges. Mediated by its bourgeois audience, the nobility copies the bourgeoisie without even realizing it" (123).

43. René Girard, *Mensonge romantique et vérité romanesque*; [Bloom, *Stendhal*, 73].

44. Carrie's talent, sometimes indistinguishable from her looks, is presented at other times as a matter of attitude. Consider the laugh she gets onstage with "I am yours truly" (Dreiser, *Sister Carrie*, 340), introducing herself when no response

was called for—yet responding only by not in fact introducing herself at all, by her gracious acceptance of not having a "self" to introduce. She has none of what Samuel Smiles and Horatio Alger would call "character." In another vocabulary, she is all "other-directedness." Her dependence on others makes her a representative of interdependence in general, not just consumer capitalism.

45. Patricia Highsmith, *The Talented Mr. Ripley* (New York: Vintage, 1992), 8.

46. Everett Knight, *A Theory of the Classical Novel* (London: Routledge and Kegan Paul, 1969), 69: "in the classical novel *no change of identity ever occurs*." Knight excepts Stendhal from this harsh but stimulating judgment.

47. It might seem that it's Rastignac's respect for the principle of kinship, expressed in his shock and horror at the treatment of Père Goriot, that wins her admiration by its contrast with the hard-heartedness of her lover. But the lover is not representative of the rule of kinship. And he wins more ground by coming to the defense of Madame de Beauséant against the malicious gossip of her friend. By the end of the conversation about the disowning of Goriot by his daughters, she has forgotten Rastignac is even there. When Rastignac explains, " 'Père Goriot is sublime!' " we are told that she "did not hear" Honoré de Balzac, *Le Père Goriot*, ed. Philippe Berthier (Paris: Flammârion, 1995), Honoré de Balzac, *Père Goriot*, trans. A. J. Krailscheimer (Oxford: Oxford University Press, 1991). (71).

48. Vautrin has said that what women really love is ambition (94).

49. Compare with a parallel moment in *Illusions Perdues*: "His love for her was mingled with ambition. He was in love and he wanted to rise. . . . Lucien felt that his calculation was motivated by a noble sentiment, his friendship for David" (60, 61).

50. As Anne Gillain suggests, there may be a displacement here of her own suppressed ambitions. (Private communication)

51. "Je vis dans une sphère plus élevée que celles des autres hommes" (196).

52. Fredric Jameson, *The Prison-House of Language: A Critical Account of Structuralism and Russian Formalism* (Princeton: Princeton University Press, 1972).

53. The logic of fairy tales tells us that we might just be rewarded for helping those in need, who may turn out to have supernatural powers. The logic of the novel tells us the same.

54. Victor Brombert, *The Romantic Prison: The French Tradition* (Princeton: Princeton University Press, 1978).

55. Baldick has "gave a new turn to."

56. A romantic link will be made via the inspector's visit between Julien's mentor and his lover: between Father Chélan's caring for the poor and Madame de Rênal's caring for the poor.

57. Later, when he is secretary to Monsieur de la Mole, he uses his power to ask for a change.

58. Robert Tombs, *France, 1814–1914* (London and New York: Longman, 1996), 176.

59. Note a resemblance to the film *Dead Man Walking*, which makes a perverse and surely unintended case in favor of the death penalty. Would the protagonist have confessed and made his peace if he had not faced execution?

60. On Rousseau's pervasive influence on Stendhal, see for example Dennis Porter, *Rousseau's Legacy: Emergence and Eclipse of the Writer in France* (New York: Oxford University Press, 1995), chap. 2; and Raymond Trousson, *Stendhal et Rousseau: Continuités et ruptures* (Köln: DME Verlag, 1986). "Tout se passe comme si Stendhal utilisait volontièrement le mythe rousseauiste, mais en le désacralisant: ramener la scène de l'empyrée sur la terre, c'est éconduire l'idéalisme chimérique de Rousseau" (Trousson, 124).

61. "On se moque de moi" (134, 414). The theme of triangular desire that Girard has discussed, among others, and that works so well for Julien in winning Mathilde's love, grants enormous power to Others. It also works on Madame de Rênal, when she thinks he loves either the portrait she burns, or Elisa.

62. Stendhal, *Lucien Leuwen* (Paris: PML, 1995); Stendhal, *Lucien Leuwen*, trans. Louise Varèse (New York: New Directions, 1950). Text references refer to part and page.

63. We know that Lucien is vulnerable to it, because while weighing what it would mean to have inspired such a self-sacrificing love, Lucien looks not like the hero of a novel but like "un banquier qui pèse la convenance d'une spéculation" ("a banker who is weighing the suitability of a speculation") (595).

64. Indeed, he thinks of the prisoners twice in this scene. It's possible that the repetition would have been corrected had Stendhal been able to put the novel in finished form.

65. D. A. Miller, "Love Plots and Love of Plots in *Lucien Leuwen*," Bloom, *Stendhal* (New York: Chelsea House, 1989). See also Marc Redfield: "The more banally sordid kind of upward mobility that drew Hegel's irony is for similar reasons an essential ambiguity within *Bildung*, which, though it manifests the universal disinterestedness of aesthetic culture . . . always remains exposed to its seeming opposite, philistinism—and more generally, in complex and far-reaching ways, to the commodity form and the ruses of capital." Marc Redfield, *Phantom Formations: Aesthetic Ideology and the Bildungsroman* (Ithaca and London: Cornell University Press, 1996), 53.

66. Helen Small, *Love's Madness: Medicine, the Novel and Female Insanity, 1800–1865* (Oxford: Oxford University Press, 1996),

67. These quotations are taken from Janice Carlisle, "A Critical History of *Great Expectations*," in Janice Carlisle, ed., *Charles Dickens, Great Expectations* (Boston and New York: Bedford/St Martin's, 1996), 450.

68. Franco Moretti, *The Way of the World: The Bildungsroman in European Culture* (London: Verso, 1987), 200. The dynamic element of the British bildungsroman, Moretti argues, cannot come either from its protagonist, who is insipidly normal, nor from its society, which is too stable and thoroughly classified. Instead, it comes from the "the Other," the villain who "stands for social mobility" (200) in a world that does not acknowledge it. It is only by virtue of these monstrous others that "narrative becomes possible" (201). The formula for narrative is "a monster *inside* an unyielding system" (201).

69. George Orwell, "Charles Dickens," in *A Collection of Essays* (New York: Harcourt Brace Jovanovich, 1946), 48–104.

70. Nuala O'Faolain, *Are You Somebody? The Life and Times of Nuala O'Faolain* (London: Hodder and Stoughton, 1996).

71. This thought might make it easier for O'Faolain to find some further satis-faction in the role of benign witch, which seems most of the time to leave her cold.

CHAPTER TWO
HOW TO BE A BENEFACTOR WITHOUT ANY MONEY

1. George Gissing, *New Grub Street* (Harmondsworth: Penguin, 1968 [1891]), 35.

2. John Edgar Wideman, *Brothers and Keepers* (New York: Vintage, 1984), 4.

3. Brent Staples, *Parallel Time: Growing Up in Black and White* (New York: Avon, 1994), 3.

4. Charles Dickens, *Great Expectations*, ed. Janice Carlisle (Boston and New York: Bedford Books, 1996 [1861]), 23–24. These lines might be read, in other words, as an allegory of the Young Man from the Provinces in relation to his Family. They actualize the notion that the provinces are, as the metaphor has it, "dead." Here death *is* the provinces.

5. The insight that "aggression" is a disguised version of Pip's "ambition" (660) was formulated in Julian Moynahan's classic essay, "The Hero's Guilt: The Case of *Great Expectations*," originally published in 1960 and reprinted in Charles Dickens, *Great Expectations*, ed. Edgar Rosenberg (New York: Norton, 1999), 654–63. Pip's symbolic guilt in the murder of his sister is of course also pertinent here.

6. Norman Podhoretz, *Making It* (New York: Random House, 1967), 25.

7. Richard Rodriguez, *Hunger of Memory: An Autobiography* (New York: Bantam: 1982), 5.

8. Richard Hoggart, *The Uses of Literacy: Aspects of Working Class Life with Special Reference to Publications and Entertainments* (Harmondsworth: Penguin in association with Chatto and Windus, 1957).

9. For an interesting reinterpretation of the nineteenth-century novel's orphan motif, see Catherine Gallagher and Stephen Greenblatt, *Practicing New Histori-cism* (Chicago and London: University of Chicago Press, 2000), chap. 6.

10. As for example in Jerome Buckley, *Season of Youth: The Bildungsroman from Dickens to Golding* (Cambridge: Harvard University Press, 1974); and Franco Moretti, *The Way of the World: The Bildungsroman in European Culture*, trans. Albert Sbragia (London: Verso, 2000).

11. Upward mobility stories differ from the *bildungsroman* in that, as the term implies, they posit an initial social status for the protagonist that is lower than the final one, whereas the *bildungsroman* may well involve a lateral move, neither rising nor falling in the social hierarchy. Otherwise the two categories will often overlap.

12. Stephen Edgell, "Class and Social Mobility" in *Class* (London: Routledge, 1993), 83–102. For a fascinating comparative study of the immense literature on social mobility in France and the United States, see Charles-Henry Cuin, *Les Sociologues et la mobilité sociale* (Paris: PUF, 1993).

13. Michael Denning, *Mechanic Accents: Dime Novels and Working-Class Culture in America* (London: Verso, 1987).

14. Richard Hoggart, *The Uses of Literacy* (Harmondsworth: Penguin in association with Chatto and Windus, 1958), 250.

15. Honoré de Balzac, *Père Goriot*, trans. A. J. Krailsheimer (Oxford: Oxford University Press, 1991), 124. Honoré de Balzac, *Le Père Goriot*, ed. Philippe Berthier (Paris: GF-Flammarion, 1995), 171–72.

16. Carlo Ginsburg, "Killing a Chinese Mandarin: The Moral Implications of Distance," *Critical Inquiry* 21 (Autumn 1994), 46–60, 55. In a similar passage in *Modeste Mignon*, noted by Ginsburg, Balzac comes even closer to Gissing by again setting the image of violence at a distance against the normality of breakfast: "In India the English are killing thousands of men as good as we are . . . but you have had coffee for breakfast all the same?" (55).

17. Alasdair MacIntyre, *After Virtue: A Study in Moral Theory*, 2d ed. (Notre Dame: University of Notre Dame Press, 1984), 23.

18. For an alternative reading, see D. A. Miller, "Body Bildung and Textual Liberation," in Denis Hollier, ed., *A New History of French Literature* (Cambridge: Harvard University Press, 1989), 681–87. According to Miller, the central factor in the success story of Rastignac and of Balzac himself is "Vautrin's homoerotic admiration (said to make Rastignac tremble 'in every member')" for Rastignac's seductive "good looks," his *beauté* (681). Or rather, the central factor in that success story is the *sacrifice* of Vautrin. In Miller's version, Rastignac can only succeed in Parisian society by sacrificing the bodily pleasures that Vautrin obscurely promises. "The price of success under Balzac's patriarchal capitalism is a rigorous ascesis."

19. Theodore Dreiser, *Sister Carrie*, introduction by E. L. Doctorow (New York: Bantam, 1958 [1900]), 392–94. The irony is that though Balzac himself evades moral judgment, he seems to stand in here for the judgment that Dreiser himself refuses to supply. Passing the buck in this way seems to be another of the uses of literariness.

20. The parallel here would be Hurstwood's strong sympathy for the striking transport workers, which does not prevent him from signing up as a scab.

21. Craig Calhoun, *Critical Social Theory: Culture, History, and the Challenge of Difference* (Oxford: Blackwell, 1995).

22. Pierre Bourdieu, *Homo Academicus*, trans. Peter Collier (Stanford, CA: Stanford University Press, 1988). Translator's note: 291 n. 31.

23. Bourdieu: "those whom I call 'oblates,' and who, consigned from childhood to the school institution (they are often children of the lower or middle classes or sons of teachers) are totally dedicated to it" (xxiv).

24. It is perhaps a mere coincidence, given the fit between this position and the upward mobility documentary *Hoop Dreams*, that the critique of this position by Craig Calhoun in *Critical Social Theory* takes up the example of basketball. "Bourdieu's account of the habitus," Calhoun writes, includes "tacit knowledge, even embodied in modes of action that agents are unable to bring to linguistic consciousness, like basketball players able to perform hook shots better than describe them" (149). As Calhoun points out, the concept of the habitus as rich but inarticulate knowledge or skill does not allow for correct and successful calculations on the part of those who possess it. Such knowledge or skill might involve, he says, implicitly continuing the racialized example of the basketball player, "a

more complex strategy—achieving success in one field which seems relatively open while minimizing investment in another—say school—which seems closed, while half-consciously or even unconsciously engaging in strategies for achieving a sense of personal autonomy or perhaps escaping the ghetto and gaining a better standard of living" (129–30).

25. Gayatri Chakravorty Spivak, "Three Women's Texts and a Critique of Imperialism," *Critical Inquiry* 12 (Autumn 1985), 243–61.

26. Susan Fraiman, *Unbecoming Women: British Women Writers and the Novel of Development* (New York: Columbia University Press, 1993).

27. The same critical attitude that downplays Ames also identifies Carrie with the empty formlessness of consumer capitalism; her triumph in this view is its triumph. Note, however, that Carrie's emptiness is also consistent with Ames's own advice to her. Note too the overlap, here as elsewhere, between consumer capitalism and the welfare state.

28. Horatio Alger, Jr, *Ragged Dick and Struggling Upward*, ed. Carl Bode (New York: Viking Penguin, 1985), 214.

29. John Cawelti, *Apostles of the Self-Made Man* (Chicago: University of Chicago Press, 1965), 109. "Alger's heroes are well aware of their indebtedness to these patrons," Cawelti adds, "and modestly make no pretense of success through their own efforts" (109).

30. Jeffrey Louis Decker, *Made in America: Self-Styled Succees from Horatio Alger to Oprah Winfrey* (Minneapolis: University of Minnesota Press, 1997), 2.

31. Amy Schrager Lang suggests that Alger was specifically avoiding any representation of the industrial working class and the conflicts—distinct of course from those between "rich" and "poor"—that followed its emergence. Amy Schrager Lang, *The Syntax of Class: Writing Inequality in Nineteenth-Century America* (Princeton: Princeton University Press, 2003), 104–16.

32. In mid-March 1866, Alger left Brewster, where he had been Unitarian minister for a little over a year, when he was accused of engaging in sexual acts with boys from his congregation. His father, also a minister, interceded in his behalf with the American Unitarian Association; it was agreed that there would be no public charges if Alger promised never to seek to reenter the ministry. Horatio Alger, Sr., wrote to the Unitarians on March 22: "His future, at the best, will be darkly shaded." Quoted in Gary Scharnhorst with Jack Bales, *The Lost Life of Horatio Alger, Jr.* (Bloomington: Indiana University Press, 1985), 2.

33. According to Scharnhorst, the competitor had stolen an editor from Allen's journal, *Student and Schoolmate*; as Scharnhorst puts it, "He retaliated by raiding their fall catalog for a plot" (81). On the other hand, the theme of the young hero's "patronage by benevolent adults" (83), missing from *Ned Nevins*, was added by Alger. And according to Scharnhorst, this was "by far the most significant innovation" Alger made (83).

34. Alger, *Ragged Dick and Struggling Upward*, 5. Dick's street sassiness is clearly borrowed from Dickens's Sam Weller and the Artful Dodger.

35. Michael Moon, " 'The Gentle Boy from the Dangerous Classes': Pederasty, Domesticity, and Capitalism in Horatio Alger," *Representations* 19 (Summer 1987), 87–110.

36. The following argument draws on sections of my "Celeb-Reliance: Intellectuals, Celebrity, and Upward Mobility," *Postmodern Culture* 9:2 (February 1999).

37. Were Alger's sustained and well-documented philanthropic efforts only the legitimate margin of a lifetime of illicit erotic activities? Did this life remain secret only because these boys, unlike the children of his congregation, conveniently had no parents to suspect or complain? These are not unreasonable questions, but evidence is lacking.

38. Alger's references to "patronage" reinforce this sense of its reversibility (the object of patronage becoming a patron in turn) or rather democratic accessibility. He repeatedly uses the term in the sense of "buy from," a sense in which merely choosing where you spend the money for your daily necessities of food and clothing makes you a patron.

39. Nancy Fraser compares two models of the welfare state, each of them better than what we in the United States have now, and yet each of them also seriously flawed in its consequences for women. The "Universal Breadwinner" model aims to "make women more like men are now." The "Caregiver Parity" model leaves men and women "pretty much unchanged, while aiming to make women's difference costless. A third possibility," she says, "is to *induce men to become more like most women are now*, namely, people who do primary carework" (60). "What would such a welfare state look like? . . . all jobs would be designed for workers who are caregivers, too; all would have a shorter workweek than full-time jobs have now; and all would have the support of employment-enabling services. Unlike Universal Breadwinner, however, employees would not be assumed to shift all carework to social services. . . . Some would be performed in households by relatives and friends, but such households would not necessarily be heterosexual nuclear families" (61). Aside from the missing "services," this description resembles the all-male surrogate family of Alger's Dick, Fosdick, and Mark. Nancy Fraser, *Justice Interruptus: Critical Reflections on the "Post-Socialist" Condition* (New York: Routledge, 1997).

40. Robert H. Bremner, *From the Depths: The Discovery of Poverty in the United States* (New York: New York University Press, 1956), 70.

41. Another indication of Alger's commitment to the regulation of capitalism emerges from a contrast with Benjamin Franklin. While Franklin suggests the need for an aspiring young man to be critical of *everyone*, including his employer, Alger's heroes are never self-serving in a way that even suggests criticism of the employer, let alone a conflict of interests between them (Cawelti, *Apostles of the Self-Made Man*, 119).

42. David Montgomery, *Beyond Equality: Labor and the Radical Republicans, 1862–1872* (New York: Random House, 1967), 8. See my "Telescopic Philanthropy: Professionalism and Responsibility in *Bleak House*," in Homi Bhabha, ed., *Nation and Narration* (London: Methuen, 1990), 213–30, reprinted in Jeremy Tambling, ed., *Bleak House: Contemporary Critical Essays* (London: Macmillan, 1998), 139–62, for further discussion of the political ambiguity of limited liability.

43. Alan Trachtenberg, *The Incorporation of America: Culture and Society in the Gilded Age* (New York: Hill and Wang, 1982), 106–7. Along with Emerson,

Horatio Alger was one of Henry Ford's favorite authors (132). But rather than simply the parallel "Henry Ford as Alger hero—simple mechanic to industrial giant" (132), we can think of Alger as part of Ford*ism*, and think of Fordism, as Warren Susman does, as belonging to a radical tradition of political thinking. Warren I. Susman, *Culture as History: The Transformation of American Society in the Twentieth Century* (New York: Pantheon, 1984).

44. I am grateful to the two teachers who inspired reflection on the great-expectations-to-lost-illusions trajectory: Harry Levin and Donald Fanger.

45. Robin Gilmour, "The Pursuit of Gentility," in *The Idea of the Gentleman in the Victorian Novel* (London: Allen and Unwin, 1981); page numbers are from the reprint in Charles Dickens, *Great Expectations*, Norton Critical Edition, ed. Edgar Rosenberg (New York: Norton, 1999). An example is Humphry House, for whom "Pip's 'acquired' culture . . . came to little more than accent, table manners, and clothes" (from *The Dickens World*, reprinted in Rosenberg, 575).

46. Sharon Marcus, *Apartment Stories: City and Home in Nineteenth-Century Paris and London* (Berkeley: University of California Press, 1999).

47. This point has been made by Franco Moretti. "Whereas in France, or in Dostoevsky," Moretti writes, "[the middle class] identifies itself with *mobility*, even to the point of transgression or crime, in England it is the champion of the opposite values: security, stability, transparency" (200). Moretti laments the deep conservatism of the English *bildungsroman*, in which there is no mobility, and not even members of the middle class are allowed to become anything they weren't already. Franco Moretti, *The Way of the World: The Bildungsroman in European Culture* (London: Verso, 1987).

48. On pigs and pig-keeping, see Kate Soper, *What Is Nature? Culture, Politics, and the Non-Human* (Oxford: Blackwell, 1995).

49. For the old question of "just what progress has been made," see K. J. Fielding, "The Critical Autonomy of *Great Expectations*," *Review of English Literature* 2 (1961): 75–88; quoted in Janice Carlisle "A Critical History" in Carlisle ed., p. 460. The usual answers are in terms of Christian ideals of love and forgiveness, spiritual freedom, individualist self-expression and Foucaultian self-oppression.

50. One of the many failings of the recent film version of *Great Expectations* is not to have perceived this. The relationship with Magwitch (Robert De Niro) is cursory, and the relationship with Estella (Gwynith Paltrow) cannot bear the burden of the plot.

51. George Eliot, *Daniel Deronda*, ed. Barbara Hardy (Harmondsworth: Penguin, 1967 [1876]).

52. The preceding three paragraphs draw on, while revising, my essay "Death and Vocation: Narrativizing Narrative Theory," *PMLA* 107:1 (Jan. 1992), 38–50.

53. Orlick's room in the porter's lodge at Miss Havisham's house, when he works there, is described as follows: "In its small proportions, it was not unlike the kind of place usually assigned to a gate-porter in Paris. Certain keys were hanging on the wall, to which he now added the gate key; and his patchwork-covered bed was in a little division or recess. The whole had a slovenly confined and sleepy look, like a cage for a human doormouse" (223). Orlick, a figure for Pip without the expectations, ironically is the one who brings the dreaded French

fad of apartment house living to London, which had refused it so adamantly that
the terms "comfort" and "at home" were used in English by French writers resisting Paris's trend toward multifamily dwellings.

54. Consider also the nightmarish inn where Pip has tea with Estella on her
arrival in London. First they are shown by waiter to a "black hole" with "somebody's pattens." "On my objecting to this retreat, he showed us into another
room with a dinner-table for thirty, and in the grate a scorched leaf of a copy-
book under a bushel of coal-dust. . . . I was, and I am, sensible that the air of this
chamber, in its strong combination of stable with soup-stock, might have led one
to infer that the coaching department was not doing well, and that the enterprising
proprietor was boiling down the horses for the refreshment department. Yet the
room was all in all to me, Estella being in it" (251, chap. 33).

55. Susan Walsh, "Bodies of Capital: *Great Expectations* and the Climacteric
Economy," *Victorian Studies* 37:1 (1993), 73–98; reprinted in Rosenberg, *Great
Expectations*, 709–20. Of course Miss Havisham also keeps Jaggers well em-
ployed, keeps Estella educated and well dressed, and even gives a job to Orlick.
Her money is hardly idle. Thanks to an anonymous reviewer for this observation.

56. I am grateful to Jonathan Arac for making the connection.

57. One endpoint of this logic of indirect and seemingly unintended consequences will become clear if we consider how it has been anticipated in Balzac's
Père Goriot. Goriot has of course sacrificed his fortune to the happiness of his
socially ambitious daughters, one of whom, Delphine, becomes Rastignac's lover.
As Goriot is dying, he is tended only by Rastignac and his medical student friend
Bianchon. Delphine finds excuses not to come to his bedside, nor does she show
up at the cemetery when her father is buried. There is no need to underline the
moral about what Restoration Paris has done to the sacred ties of kinship. What
may need to be underlined, however, is a logic that is so faint as to be almost
imperceptible. In surrendering his money to his daughters, Goriot does end up
paying, if the word is not too crude, for the care that he receives at the end of his
life and for his funeral. For as Delphine's lover, Rastignac too benefits from the
money given to her. While thinking only of his family, Goriot inadvertently does
what "social insurance" will one day go on to do. He participates in a scheme of
what the French call "prévoyance." The care he receives in his last illness and the
cost of burying him, to put this as coldly as possible, come from or are supported
by money he has paid out, little by little, while he was healthy and thinking of
other things entirely.

58. D. A. Miller, *The Novel and the Police* (Berkeley: University of California
Press, 1988).

59. Tony Bennett, "The Multiplication of Culture's Utility," *Critical Inquiry*
21:4 (Summer 1995), 865.

60. Mary Poovey, *Making a Social Body: British Cultural Formation, 1830–
1864* (Chicago and London: University of Chicago Press, 1995).

61. Carolyn Steedman, *Landscape for a Good Woman: A Story of Two Lives*
(London: Virago, 1986). See chapter 5 below.

62. Mary Poovey, *Uneven Developments: The Ideological Work of Gender in
Mid-Victorian England* (Chicago: University of Chicago Press, 1988).

CHAPTER THREE
"IT'S NOT YOUR FAULT": THERAPY AND IRRESPONSIBILITY FROM DREISER TO
DOCTOROW

1. D. A. Miller, "Discipline in Different Voices: Bureaucracy, Police, Family, and *Bleak House*," *Representations* 1 (February 1983), 59–89. I quote it from D. A. Miller, *The Novel and the Police* (Berkeley: University of California Press, 1988), 58–106.

2. Miller speaks of "a social order whose totalizing power circulates all the more easily for being pulverized" (xiii).

3. I'm not sure that Miller himself can claim to avoid this sort of scapegoating. He announces in the preface that his goal is "to redress the 'positive' achievement of nineteenth-century fiction" (xii). This rectification is also an accusation, and it could certainly be seen as attributing to a part of society—fiction—responsibility that by Miller's own lights would seem better attributed to the social system as a whole. Perhaps one has no choice but to accuse, always a bit arbitrarily and erroneously.

4. Judith Butler picks up the connection between prison and upward mobility when she discusses Foucault in the first chapter of *Gender Trouble*.

5. Luther H. Martin, Huck Gutman, and Patrick H. Hutton, eds., *Technologies of the Self: A Seminar with Michel Foucault* (Amherst: University of Massachusetts Press/London: Tavistock, 1988). "According to Foucault, his project on the self was suggested by a reading of Christopher Lasch's *The Culture of Narcissism: American Life in an Age of Diminishing Expectations* (New York: Norton, 1979). Foucault understood Lasch's description of disillusionment with the modern world and a subsequent turning within to be similar to the situation of the Roman Empire" (4).

6. Note too the constraint on "critical judgment" or rather the zero-sum relation between generalizing irresponsibility and limit to critique. I'm not suggesting that either Foucault or Miller, in their own deep suspicions toward bureaucratic state institutions, intended to echo or offer support to Lasch's crude and nostalgic individualism. (Some of their enthusiastic readers may have done so, but that's another matter.) And for my own part, I want to acknowledge some ambivalence about the therapeutic sensibility and its seemingly limitless willingness to encroach upon the domain of personal responsibility.

7. Note the parallel with *Little Dorrit*, Dickens's original title for which was "Nobody's Fault" and which also centers on a problematic of will.

8. What's really utopian about this—more so than the genius, maybe—is the suggestion of the existence of a working-class solidarity strong enough to hold an individual back from seizing all the chances that life seems to offer.

9. Christopher Lasch, *The Revolt of the Elites and the Betrayal of Democracy* (New York: Norton, 1995). For a useful corrective that enables Lasch's insights to be recoded in a less tragic vein, see James Livingston, *Pragmatism and the Political Economy of Cultural Revolution, 1850–1940* (Chapel Hill: University of North Carolina Press, 1994). See also Philip Rieff, *The Triumph of the Therapeutic* (New York: Harper, 1966).

10. Perhaps the opposition has already broken down, for Inspector Bucket of the Detective Police is also a humor-producing bureaucrat.

11. See my "Telescopic Philanthropy: Professionalism and Responsibility in *Bleak House*," in Homi Bhabha, ed., *Nation and Narration* (London: Methuen, 1990), 213–30; reprinted in Jeremy Tambling, ed., *Bleak House: Contemporary Critical Essays* (London: Macmillan, 1998), 139–62.

12. Michel Foucault, "Social Security" in Lawrence D. Kritzman, ed., *Michel Foucault: Politics, Philosophy, Culture: Interviews and Other Writings 1977–1984*, trans. Alan Sheridan and others (New York and London: Routledge, 1988), 160. The original title was "A Finite Security System Confronting an Infinite Demand." Thanks to Alan Keenan for the reference.

13. See for example Andrew Barry, Thomas Osborne, and Nikolas Rose, *Foucault and Political Reason: Liberalism, Neo-Liberalism, and Rationalities of Government* (Chicago: University of Chicago Press, 1996); and Jack Z. Bratich, Jeremy Packer, and Cameron McCarthy, eds., *Foucault, Cultural Studies, and Governmentality* (Albany: State University of New York Press, 2003). For arguments about Foucault and the welfare state that anticipate my own in several points, see Lauren M. E. Goodlad, "Beyond the Panopticon: Victorian Britain and the Critical Imagination," *PMLA* 118:3 (May 2003), 539–56; and Simon Joyce, "Victorian Continuities: Early British Sociology and the Welfare of the State," in Amanda Anderson and Joseph Valente, eds. *Disciplinarity at the Fin de Siècle* (Princeton: Princeton University Press, 2002), 261–80.

14. Ann Oakley and A. Susan Williams, eds., *The Politics of the Welfare State* (London: University College London Press, 1994), 13.

15. Will's desire for his wealthy Harvard girlfriend (played by Minnie Driver) is the easiest way to naturalize and justify the break with his buddies, though they buy him the car in which he makes his escape and, through the Ben Affleck figure, reassure him that his mobility is what they want for him. But even his escape is mediated through the therapist; it is McBride's story of leaving his World Series ticket with his friends in order to "see about a girl," the woman he eventually married, that echoes through the ending. In other words, the therapist is more than a transitional object. He is the film's central model of an alternative social bonding, a representative of the sort of person we have to imagine Will able to become, and of the sort of life work that would enable him to satisfy his conflicting loyalties and not merely succumb to the beckoning upper class and Minnie Driver's millions.

16. V. S. Naipaul, *The Mystic Masseur* (New York: Vintage, 1957), 119.

17. Hanif Kureishi, *The Buddha of Suburbia* (New York: Penguin, 1991).

18. Michael B. Katz, *In the Shadow of the Poorhouse: A Social History of Welfare in America* (New York: Basic, 1986/1996). Katz defines "welfare capitalism" more narrowly as the initiative of progressive businesses. "Unable to solve all their labor market problems by themselves, they joined with labor and academic reformer-experts to support social insurance legislation: workmen's compensation, unemployment insurance, and pensions" (186). Derek Fraser argues that the broader definition is supported by a comparative international perspective. Derek Fraser, *The Evolution of the British Welfare State: A History of Social Policy since*

the Industrial Revolution, 3rd ed. (Basingstoke: Palgrave Macmillan, 2003 [1973/ 1984]), xxxii.

19. In his book *Situatedness*, David Simpson discusses the "critical expansion of the category of mitigating or extenuating circumstances and diminished responsibilities in the minds of contemporary juries" (65), an expansion exemplified by the so-called Twinkie Defense: fast food made me do it. Going back to Jeremy Bentham, whose iconic usage by Foucault has recently been contested by Frances Ferguson, Simpson sees the history of modernity as a movement in the direction of personal irresponsibility—one sense in which Bentham and Foucault are after all on the same page. Like the limited liability corporation and the bankruptcy laws, two important instances, and for that matter like "no fault" insurance as well, this "no fault" movement has arguably been more convenient for risk-taking capitalist entrepreneurs than it has for the rest of us. But as Simpson also says, recent excesses of irresponsibility like the Twinkie Defense are in part results of the withdrawal of the state from its previous responsibilities. "The retreat on the part of juries from attributing strict responsibility . . . may also reflect a sense that we are, as individuals, being increasingly deprived of the social and economic support systems whose existence would alone justify stringent demands of personal responsibility by a general agreement that we really might all be starting from the same place in life. If government does nothing (or less and less) for our collective well-being and self-maintenance, why should we fault each other for not meeting its standards for abiding by the law?" (64).

20. E. L. Doctorow, Introduction to Theodore Dreiser, *Sister Carrie* (New York: Bantam, 1982), vi.

21. Theodore Dreiser, *The Financier*, afterword by Larzer Ziff (New York: New American Library, 1967). Chapter numbers are given in parenthesis.

22. Alex Pitofsky, "Dreiser's *The Financier* and the Horatio Alger Myth," *Twentieth-Century Literature* 44:3 (Fall 1998), 276–90.

23. On the Older Woman as a figure of motherly forgiveness, and in that sense for the "it's not your fault" position, see for example John Braine's *Room At the Top* (1957). The protagonist is told, after he has announced his engagement to a young heiress and his (older) lover has killed herself, "Nobody blames you" (199). He replies, "That's the trouble." The older woman—in the film version, played unforgettably by Simone Signoret—is a kind of therapist for him, giving him much-needed confidence and disinterestedly helping him succeed with the younger, wealthier woman he has set his sights on.

24. Walter Benn Michaels, *The Gold Standard and the Logic of Naturalism: American Literature at the Turn of the Century* (Berkeley: University of California Press, 1987), 61.

25. In *Dreiser and Veblen: Saboteurs of the Status Quo*, Claire Eby shows that Dreiser is at best weakly and intermittently committed to the valuing of utilitarian "industry" over a no-holds-barred "business." Eby takes Veblen's "yardsticks" of "serviceability, productivity, and usefulness to the entire community" (76) and his preference for the engineer over the financier (77) and demonstrates that they have little if any hold over Dreiser, whose value as a cultural critic, she concludes, comes solely from his refusal of self-denial and other aspects of conventional mo-

rality. Clare Virginia Eby, *Dreiser and Veblen: Saboteurs of the Status Quo* (Columbia: University of Missouri Press, 1998).

26. Gifts seem different in this sense from speculations, which are based on debt that must be repaid, as Cowperwood discovers when he is indicted.

27. Ralph Waldo Emerson, "Gifts," in *Emerson's Essays* (New York: Crowell, 1926), 376.

28. See John Frow, "Gift and Commodity," in *Time and Commodity Culture: Essays in Cultural Theory and Postmodernity* (Oxford: Clarendon Press, 1997), 102–217; and Bruno Karsenti, *Marcel Mauss: Le fait social total* (Paris: Presses Universitaires de France, 1994).

29. One might describe this as a (misplaced) deconstructionism, locally and opportunistically applied in the service of an ultimately antideconstructive determinism.

30. Frank is described as possessing a natural "magnetism," an ability to inspire confidence in others. This ability is clearly of much usefulness both in his erotic life and in his business life. (In this sense it reinforces the intuition that the two go together.) In both, it can be translated as an ability to receive more loyalty from others than one is obliged to give them—that is, to benefit from a loyalty surplus that can be exchanged for its equivalent in money. Or an ability to inspire loyalty in others above and beyond the limits of their own self-interest.

31. Martin J. Sklar, *The Corporate Reconstruction of American Capitalism, 1890–1916: The Market, the Law, and Politics* (Cambridge: Cambridge University Press, 1988). See also James Livingston, "How To Succeed in Business History without Really Trying: Remarks on Martin J. Sklar's *Corporate Reconstruction of American Capitalism*," *Business and Economic History*, 2d ser., 21 (1992), 30–35. On the reworking of merit within what he calls the "welfare-corporate state," see Roberto Mangabeira Unger, *Knowledge and Politics* (New York: Free Press, 1975, 1984), chap. 4.

32. Note that the corporation is not yet the characteristic business organization in *The Financier*.

33. Howard Horwitz, *By the Law of Nature: Form and Value in Nineteenth-Century America* (New York and Oxford: Oxford University Press, 1991).

34. *New York Times*, November 23, 1986, sec. 3:5, quoted in Horwitz, *By the Law of Nature*, 190.

35. Of course, there is no level playing field even in prison: Cowperwood's advantages on the outside translate directly into privileges in prison.

36. It's worth noting that, along with Yerkes, Andrew Carnegie was part of the composite that went into Cowperwood's character: see James M Hutchisson, "The Revision of Theodore Dreiser's *Financier*," *Journal of Modern Literature* 20:2 (Winter 1996), 199–213.

37. James Mackay, *Allen Pinkerton: The First Private Eye* (New York: John Wiley and Sons, 1996). The strike on the New York streetcars in *Sister Carrie*, where the down-and-out Hurstwood offers himself as a scab and is driven away from the streetcar by union sympathizers, might be seen as an imaginative synthesis between the role the Pinkertons played in the Homestead strike and the more ethically ambiguous role they play in *The Financier*, where streetcars stand

for the dynamically expanding aspect of the city that Cowperwood most desires to possess.

38. On the characteristically American overlap between public and private agencies in the development of the welfare state, see Daniel T. Rodgers, *Atlantic Crossings: Social Politics in a Progressive Age* (Cambridge: Harvard University Press, 1998).

39. Here I am drawing again on the theory of triangulated desire developed by René Girard in *Deceit, Desire, and the Novel: Self and Other in Literary Structure*, trans. Yvonne Freccero (Baltimore: Johns Hopkins University Press, 1965).

40. Michael Denning, *The Cultural Front: The Laboring of American Culture in the Twentieth Century* (London: Verso, 1996). An alternative genre concept that has the advantage of recognizing the existence of interclass movement is Renny Christopher's "narratives of unhappy upward mobility." Renny Christopher, "Rags to Riches to Suicide: Unhappy Narratives of Upward Mobility; *Martin Eden, Bread Givers, Delia's Song*, and *Hunger of Memory*," *College Literature* 29:4 (Fall 2002), 79–108. Christopher argues that "to rest happy with upward mobility, one must completely stamp out one's previous, working-class self" (80).

41. Budd Schulberg, *What Makes Sammy Run?* (New York: Random House, 1990 [1941]). Despite subsequent changes in Schulberg's politics, this is much the same speech about us all being part of each other that Eva Marie Saint makes to Marlon Brando in *On the Waterfront*, which Schulberg wrote.

42. Of course, the choice of Al as narrator relies on him sustaining an "interest" in Sammy, but Al's interest is much more than a narrative convenience. It's also out of control—and being out of control is what makes this novel so much more than an anti-Hollywood satire or screed.

43. On Sheik: "he was the enemy slave brought home behind the conqueror's chariot. He was the measuring stick that was always at Sammy's elbow to remind him of his rise" (233). "Word has gotten around that Sheik was an ex-mobster and soon, with Hollywood's talent for self-dramatization, Sheik had become a famous gunman, in fact, Capone's right-hand man" (236).

44. This could of course be seen as effective political rhetoric: positive heroes put the message across less well than the lukewarm and the unconverted.

45. Neal Gabler, *An Empire of Their Own: How the Jews Invented Hollywood* (New York: Doubleday Anchor, 1988), 334–35.

46. *On the Waterfront* again pits upward mobility rhetoric against labor solidarity in the speech by the gangster Johnny Friendly (Lee J. Cobb) about how he came to control the local: "When I was sixteen, I had to beg for work in the hold. I didn't work my way up out of there for nuthin'. . . . You know, takin' over this local took a little doin'. There's some pretty rough fellas in the way."

47. The state prefers not to tamper much with the free market, and on the free market Sammy can use the power of his name, however obtained, to market what he himself has not created. This is what capitalism does. The law, largely adapted to capitalism, takes such behavior as perfectly normal and legal. The principle involved is that which Michaels applied to Dreiser's Cowperwood: the fact that Sammy has created nothing, just derived speculative profit from the creations of others, means paradoxically that he is guilty of nothing. Under finance capitalism, where profit derives from so many complex, interlocking, uncontrollable factors,

the fact that as an individual one has created nothing is not a scandal; it means that one is in perfect harmony with the system. Property has been divorced from labor.

48. As the film's first viewers were well aware, this was a more complex gesture at the time, when the argument that "testifying" and thus breaking with loyalty to fellow workers (in the name of higher loyalty) was right also referred to McCarthy and testifying to the House Un-American Activities Committee.

49. The other side of the coin would be that the state will intervene only when pushed to do so by the labor movement. This is more or less what Elizabeth Sanders argues about the immediate prehistory of the New Deal. Answering the instrumentalist argument of Gabriel Kolko and his followers "that Progressive Era state expansion reflected almost exclusively the interests of large capitalists" (2), Sanders tries to give "credit" to the "public-policy achievements" of farmers and workers pushing from below. "My argument is that the dynamic stimulus for Populist and Progressive Era state expansion was the periphery agrarians' drive to establish public control over a rampaging capitalism. The periphery generated the bulk of reform agenda and furnished the foot soldiers that saw reform through the legislature. It did so because the political economy of the late-nineteenth- and early-twentieth-century periphery was innately antagonistic to the designs of core industrial and financial capitalism and had no effective means with which to fight it than the capture and expansion of state power" (4). The paradox here is that the farmers and workers didn't like or want state power: "social forces profoundly hostile to bureaucracy nevertheless instigated the creation of a bureaucratic state" (6). The New Deal itself exacerbated this paradox. "With the decline of indigenous organization for both farmers and workers in the 1920s and the shift of policy initiative definitely to the executive branch, neither farmers nor workers were able to dictate terms in national politics. When the economic crisis of the 1930s arrived, the stage was set for state actors and public-service-oriented intellectuals to propose and *impose* a program that offered to do a lot *for* farmers and workers, according to the interpretation of their interests developed *within* the state, but to grant them little autonomy from national administrative control" (416–17). Elizabeth Sanders, *Roots of Reform: Farmers, Workers, and the American State, 1877–1917* (Chicago and London: University of Chicago Press, 1999).

50. As I have said, the assumption here and throughout is that the New Deal, in America and in Europe, was at least partially a response to pressure from below. On early responses of the British working class to welfare policies, see Henry Pelling, *Popular Politics and Society in Late Victorian Britain* (London: Macmillan 1968), "The Working Class and the Origins of the Welfare State," 1–18; and especially Pat Thane, "The Working Class and State 'Welfare' in Britain, 1880–1914," *Historical Journal* 27:4 (1984), 877–900, for a balanced assessment of Pelling's theses. Thane suggests that while as Pelling argues many union leaders feared the influence of the state and called for labor movement self-reliance, "rank-and-file spinners, experiencing low pay, poor housing and no dramatic gains from years of trade union organization, were unimpressed by such high-minded abstractions and were more willing to place their faith in action by the

state or local authority than in hypothetical long-term gains by the trade union movement" (886).

51. This section first appeared as foreword to Michelle Tokarczyk, *E. L. Doctorow's Skeptical Commitment* (New York: Peter Lang, 2000), xi–xvii

52. E. L. Doctorow, *Loon Lake* (New York: Bantam, 1980), 1.

53. The question of how Joe connects with Bennett is worth considering as one in the long series of donor-acquisition scenes. He shows Bennett a disrespectful pride in which Bennett perhaps recognizes the same callousness that permits him to run his system. "You're brash enough" (125). But why should the mentor have a "heart . . . for spunky derelict kids" (183)?

54. E. L. Doctorow, *Billy Bathgate* (New York: Penguin, 1989).

55. F. Scott Fitzgerald, *The Great Gatsby* (New York: Scribner's, 1953).

56. Fredric Jameson's suggestion is that the paradigm of the Mafia is ordinary business: "When indeed we reflect on an organized conspiracy against the public, one which reaches into every corner of our daily lives and our political structures to exercise a wanton ecocidal and genocidal violence at the behest of distant decison-makers and in the name of an abstract conception of profit—surely it is not about the Mafia, but rather about American business itself that we are thinking, American capitalism in its most systematized and computerized, dehumanized, 'multinational' and corporate form. What kind of crime, said Brecht, is the robbing of a bank, compared to the founding of a bank?" (145). Fredric Jameson, "Reification and Utopia in Mass Culture," *Social Text* 1 (1978), 130–148

57. Rarely does he speak, on the contrary, of "this sordid profession" (388).

58. "I had come into his life when it had begun not to function in his interest, all I had ever seen him do was defend himself" (420). Billy describes his own arrival as "the beginning of the end" for Schultz (420).

59. I have been inspired here by Jameson's suggestion that, although "crime" has been substituted "for big business, as the strategic displacement of all the rage generated by the American system" (146), the crime family also has a utopian function: "the family itself [is] seen as a figure of collectivity and as the object of a Utopian longing" (146). "Thus the tightly knit bonds of the Mafia family (in both senses), the protective security of the (god)father with his omnipresent authority, offers a contemporary pretext for a Utopian fantasy which can no longer express itself through such outmoded paradigms and stereotypes as the image of the now extinct American small town" (147).

60. There is otherwise little room for "bad sex" here. When Billy and Drew have sex, her eyes go flat "as if her mind had collapsed, as if time had turned in her and she had passed back into infancy and reverted through birth into nothingness, and for an instant they were no longer eyes, for an instant they were about to be eyes, the eyes of soullessness" (325–26). The passage invites juxtaposition with what Gayatri Spivak calls soul making.

61. Something allegorical might also be made of another donor-acquisition scene: Billy is accepted into the gang when he brings a paper bag filled with cupcakes to their door. Schultz, in the middle of a temper tantrum, absently picks up a cupcake, bites into it, and is pacified (80). See chapter 5 for the paradigm of the Home Visit.

CHAPTER FOUR
A PORTRAIT OF THE ARTIST AS A RENTIER

1. Portions of this chapter appear in somewhat different form in my "A Portrait of the Artist as a Social Climber" in Franco Moretti, ed., *The Novel*, vol. 2, *Forms and Themes* (Princeton University Press, 2006), 409–35.

2. H. G. Wells, *Kipps: The Story of a Simple Soul*, ed. Peter Vansittart (London: J. M. Dent, 1993 [1905]).

3. On the künstlerroman see Herbert Marcuse, *Der Deutsche Künstlerroman* (Frankfurt: Suhrkamp, 1978).

4. It is by no means sure that Masterman's speech reflects Wells's own misogyny. Wells may be caricaturing one of Gissing's well-known and eccentric positions.

5. See Francis Mulhern, *The Moment of "Scrutiny"* (London: New Left Books/ Verso, 1979).

6. One may disagree with the particulars of this case and still maintain that it is legitimate and even indispensable to make some case of this kind. In a democracy, narratives of public legitimation are how the game of politics is played, and by players of very different kinds, labor unions as well as academic professionals.

7. George Gissing, *Born in Exile*, ed. David Grylls (London: J. M. Dent, 1993 [1892]).

8. Miles Franklin, *My Brilliant Career* (Sydney: A&R Classics/HarperCollins, 1973 [1901]).

9. See for example Elizabeth Wilson, *Bohemians: The Glamorous Outcasts* (New Brunswick, NJ: Rutgers University Press, 2000).

10. Pierre Bourdieu, *The Rules of Art: Genesis and Structure of the Literary Field*, trans. Susan Emanuel (Stanford, CA: Stanford University Press, 1995).

11. The mentor personifies what bohemia spatializes. Hence the two often overlap, as in the character of Masterman. Upwardly mobile himself in spite of his admonition against it, Masterman is located, structurally speaking, midway between the upper-class fiancée, on the one hand, and the lower-class sweetheart, on the other—another woman who must reject upward mobility absolutely in order to be classified as virtuous. Masterman shares with the fiancée his pride in his education, and he shares with the sweetheart his rejection of upward mobility. The convention by which marriage indicates a definitive choice of values would omit this mediation between the two sets of values. But it is precisely the mediation, rather than one set or the other, that the novel comes closest to choosing. In this sense we would have to understand Masterman's name as neither announcing a Nietzschean Übermensch nor taking the part of the masters against the men, but rather as suggesting that Masterman is both master *and* man, or something that is not quite the one nor quite the other.

12. George Du Maurier, *Trilby* (Harmondsworth: Penguin, 1994 [1894]. See also Daniel Pick, *Svengali's Web: The Alien Enchanter in Modern Culture* (New Haven: Yale University Press, 2000).

13. Gaston Leroux, *The Essential Phantom of the Opera*, ed. Leonard Wolf (New York: Plume, 1996 [1910]).

14. One thinks of the ending of *Jane Eyre*, in which the novel's last words are given to St. John Rivers, another mentor figure whom neither the reader nor the heroine prefers in marriage, and yet who presides over her social self-fashioning in ways that a mere husband seemingly cannot. On the female Gothic tradition, in which the fairy godmother and Prince Charming are the same figure, the two combining to form a beast or ogre who is perhaps susceptible of redemption, see for example Tania Modleski, *Loving With a Vengeance: Mass-Produced Fantasies for Women* (New York: Methuen, 1982), chap. 3; and Bonnie Honig, *Democracy and the Foreigner* (Princeton: Princeton University Press, 2001), 109–20. When she wrote *Rebecca*, an offspring of *Jane Eyre* and a classic of the genre, Daphne Du Maurier was much more charmed by her own version of her grandfather's Svengali, an older and (here) richer man who is asked to play the parts of conventional husband and sinister mentor at the same time. And she wrote more into her lowly heroine's magical ascension than a simple acquiescence in or enjoyment of a place at the top of the social hierarchy. After the events of the novel are past, the heroine sees an allegory of them in a dream about Manderley, the house that she won by her efforts but that then burned down: "I saw that the garden had obeyed the jungle law, even as the woods had done. The rhododendrons stood fifty feet high, twisted and entwined with bracken, and they had entered into alien marriage with a host of nameless shrubs, poor, bastard things that clung with about their roots as though conscious of their spurious origin. A lilac had mated with a copper beech." (2). The "alien marriage" among the flora is of course her own. The devastation she sees is the democratic result, seemingly unwilled by her, of the mating between Manderley and her own "spurious origin."

15. This is a reasonably close parallel to the ending of *Great Expectations*, as discussed above.

16. George Gissing, *Born in Exile*, ed. David Grylls (London: Dent, 1993 [1892]).

17. The lower-middle-class Gissing himself was repeatedly entangled with working-class women. This is not the only sense in which his own life—that of the successful but principled author of *New Grub Street* rather than either of the writers it represents, one successful and the other principled—cannot be figured within his fiction.

18. Perry Anderson, *English Questions* (London: Verso, 1992). See also Martin J. Wiener, *English Culture and the Decline of the Industrial Spirit, 1850–1980* (Cambridge: Cambridge University Press, 1981).

19. Gregory Elliott suggests that in order to preserve the exceptionality of the English case, Anderson later shifts away from aristocratic hegemony, putting more emphasis on the United Kingdom's advantages and disadvantages as historical first-comer to capitalism. Gregory Elliott, *Perry Anderson: The Merciless Laboratory of History* (Minneapolis: University of Minnesota Press, 1998). It's also arguable that Anderson's sense of expectations disappointed is more acute at home than abroad.

20. Giovanni Verga, *Mastro Don Gesualdo*, trans. D. H. Lawrence (Sawtry: Dedalus, 1984 [1888]).

21. Sándor Márai, *Embers*, trans. Carol Brown Janeway (New York: Knopf, 2001 [1942]).

22. Hannah Arendt, *Rahel Varnhagen: The Life of a Jewess*, ed. Liliane Weissberg, trans. Richard and Clara Winston (Baltimore: Johns Hopkins University Press, 1997 [1957]); Judith N. Shklar, "Hannah Arendt as Pariah," in *Political Thought and Political Thinkers*, ed. Stanley Hoffmann, foreword by George Kateb (Chicago: University of Chicago Press, 1998), 362–75. Thanks to Ross Posnock for the reference.

23. One benefit of this perspective goes to literary history. If identifications like this are a large and representative fact about the social placement of the writer, then it is clear why there can be no simple linear history of the upward mobility story. One never arrives at that hypothetical point where the narrative perspective shifts from a predominantly negative to a predominantly positive view of the aspiring protagonist—unless perhaps when the story is recast as tragedy, as in *Jude the Obscure*. Much can no doubt be inferred from upward mobility stories about changes in who runs society, but the result of this inference would have to be a complicated figure in which Raymond Williams's useful categories of dominant, residual, and emergent would be hard to distinguish from one another. This is in part because, as I noted above, Masterman's aristocratic critique of social climbing is also a disguised means of social climbing—intended, by definition, for non-aristocrats. So the writer's aristocratic identification does not entail a simple rejection of upward mobility, nor a simple embrace, even a wishful one, of everything the aristocracy stands for.

24. W. G. Rogers, *When This You See Remember Me: Gertrude Stein in Person* (1948), quoted in Janet Malcolm, "Gertrude Stein's War: The Years in Occupied France," *New Yorker*, June 2, 2003, 59–81, 64.

25. Charles Dickens, *Bleak House*, ed. Nicole Bradbury (London: Penguin, 1996).

26. Rachel Bowlby, *Just Looking: Consumer Culture in Dreiser, Gissing, and Zola* (New York: Methuen, 1985); Raymond Williams, *The Country and the City* (London: Paladin, 1975), 270; Christina Lupton and Tilman Reitz, "*New Grub Street*'s Self-Consciousness," in Martin H. Ryle and Jenny Bourne Taylor, eds., *George Gissing: Voices of the Unclassed* (London: Ashgate, 2005), 133–44.

27. Debates over the Poor Law in the 1890s provide a possible context for Gissing's sense of larger demands, as yet unrecognized and unmet. Peter Wood writes: "Demands for better treatment of such deserving groups as children and the sick were being expanded to include the aged and some of the unemployed" (3). Why not, then, the unemployed or underemployed artist? Peter Wood, *Poverty and Workhouse in Victorian Britain* (Stroud: Alan Sutton, 1991).

28. Indeed, even his writing does so. It makes its own most obvious compromise with realism by remaining within the limits of "decency," refusing any sexual "vulgarity." Finally, however, as if giving up on the difference between Reardon and his friend, Gissing transfers to the latter the former's need for Amy's love, and it is that need that ultimately kills Biffen, not his poverty. Realism, like art for art's sake, is a bohemian position, Bourdieu suggests, in the sense that both define themselves by a demand for autonomy from bourgeois society. But Biffen's

"solution" to the problem of writing and the marketplace is not Bohemian, for it makes little or no allowance for sexual desire.

29. George Bernard Shaw, *Pygmalion: A Romance in Five Acts* (Harmondsworth: Penguin, 1914).

30. James T. Kloppenberg, *Uncertain Victory: Social Democracy and Progressivism in European and American Social Thought, 1870–1920* (New York: Oxford University Press, 1986), 253 and 475 n. 22. See also Walter Lippmann: "a minimum standard of life below which no human being can fall is the most elementary duty of the democratic state" (*Drift and Mastery*, 254, quoted in Kloppenberg, *Uncertain Victory*, 356).

31. What prevents this resolution from being anything more than utopian, aside from the historical fact that state funding of the arts and the welfare state in general were not yet a palpable part of ordinary English life, is once again an exclusive and seemingly nonnegotiable erotic fixation on the genteel, upper-class woman, the woman with money behind her. The same obstacle precludes happiness for Marian, whose planned marriage to Milvain became possible only because of an inheritance and is allowed to collapse because of another piece of offstage financial misfortune. Once Reardon is out of the picture, Milvain will instead marry Amy, whose inheritance is intact.

32. Shaw's mother, Lucinda Elizabeth Gurley, knew something about Trilby-style bohemianism. Not having the privilege of an independent income and having married a man with "only a small pension," she decided, perhaps for that reason, to make a career for herself in music. Her teacher "was a slight, dark man, crippled in childhood by an accident to his foot," known as G. J. Lee, who was unable to sing himself but was "tremendously ambitious and must have been something of an opportunist" (31–32). Shaw described him as having "mesmeric vitality and force" (31). Even before the Shaws moved into one Dublin house with Lee and rumors began (indignantly denied by Shaw) that Lee and Mrs. Shaw were lovers, Shaw said that Lee had supplanted his father as the dominant factor in the household. In this Bohemian household, Lee played the part, in Shaw's words, of a "damaged Svengali" (40). Lee got Shaw his start in London theater. Vincent Wall, *Bernard Shaw: Pygmalion to Many Players* (Ann Arbor: University of Michigan Press, 1973).

33. There is obviously no absolute taboo on long-term pairing up. Look what happens to Clarice Starling and Hannibal Lecter in *Hannibal*, sequel to *Silence of the Lambs*. Thomas Harris, *Hannibal* (New York: Delacorte, 1999).

34. Shaw described *Pygmalion* as one of his "shameless potboilers." Quoted in Robert Brustein, *The Theater of Revolt* (Boston: Little, Brown, 1964), 211.

35. Anderson, "The Figures of Descent," in *English Questions*.

36. Thompson responded to Anderson in a piece the following year entitled "The Peculiarities of the English" (1965). He scored some points at the expense of Anderson's implied standard of "healthy" (that is, French) development and the teleology of revolution; he noted the dissuasive force of Communism abroad as an image deterring Marxism at home; and he made a strong case that, cultural style aside, it was indeed the middle class rather than aristocracy that has been running the show in Britain. About the role of the Empire and finance capital, however, Thompson leaves the field to Anderson: "[I]n a metropolitan imperialist

country even the politics of the Left must be, on occasion, that damnable art of the possible." Thus "the overthrow of imperialism has generally been, not the first item on the agenda, but a little lower down—among the other business" (68–69). One can always judge the achievements of the working class by the criterion of revolution, of course, and by that criterion they will always be safely open to criticism. The risk of applying so high a criterion and/or straying too far from the actual path history has taken is that of missing out on the sites where something has been done, and is still being done, to further goals that, like revolution, belong both to the working class and to humanity in general.

37. Here maturity has migrated from a quality of the working class itself to a quality of the viewer who values the concessions the working class has forced out of the state, and perhaps of the state itself to the extent that it has made these concessions. E. P. Thompson, *The Poverty of Theory and Other Essays* (London: Merlin, 1978).

38. An example is when Dolittle refuses an extra five pounds.

39. Gareth Griffith, *Socialism and Superior Brains: The Political Thought of Bernard Shaw* (London and New York: Routledge, 19933), 73.

40. As actual performances underlined, the love question remains titillatingly open. And if, after all, Higgins has fallen in love with Eliza, more would be suggested than another eccentric brought back to normality. His love for Eliza would throw into doubt the maternal-financial vector of desire I just described. And that would be of a great deal of interest. When Higgins says, "I like you like this" in their final dialogue, it is because Eliza has just said she "can do without [him]" (138). Which she clearly can. He then goes on: "Five minutes ago you were like a millstone round my neck. Now youre a tower of strength. . . . You and I and Pickering will be three old bachelors instead of only two men and a silly girl" (138). If this vision of shared and transgendered bacherlorhood is an expression of love, as it may be, the suggestion would be that Higgins has come to love in Liza an independence of character that doesn't need the backing of an independent income. Which would be to say that such a thing is possible. If so, this would mean that Higgins's pedagogy has performed a much larger feat than merely passing off a flower girl at a garden party as a duchess. That was a matter of imitation, a brief theatrical interlude. To beat the power of money and to make it last, and to do so while working only in the medium of words, creating a character that will be genuinely self-sustaining without in fact being sustained economically in the way that such characters are—that would be a real miracle. The play ends with the open question of Higgins's feelings for Eliza because only those feelings can test the existence of a genuinely new character: hers, and also his. Can Higgins, who loves his mother's independence in the double sense, now love someone who is like her but without the corresponding financial resources? Can he love the work he actually does—let's call it literacy—as opposed to an ideal of "the best art of [the] time" that stands unattainably high above it and makes it seem inessential— let's call it literature? Can he admit that he too is a Svengali—that is, that he is himself part of the process of upward mobility that he makes possible for another?

41. Luc Gillemin, *John Osborne, Vituperative Artist: A Reading of His Life and Work* (New York and London: Routledge, 2002).

42. *Room at the Top* (Boston: Houghton Mifflin, 1957) is something of a compendium of upward mobility motifs from Stendhal on. He has already "felt like a murderer" (156) long before Alice dies. Like Julien, for example, Joe leaves behind his first great love, then is given a renewed idyll with her after her young rival is already on the scene, thus underlining the contrast between them. The novel is one of the few great English versions of the French narrative—which is one reason why the casting of the French actress Simone Signoret in the older woman role in the film (1959) was so brilliant.

43. Theater performs the same upward mobility function in Hollywood classics like *All about Eve*. Here theater also means calculation, the "maneuvering" he does with Susan: "I was maneuvering for position all the time, noting the effect of each word; and it seemed to devalue everything I said" (64). This depresses him (65). But he suddenly finds himself doing better as an actor in his role as Alice's stage lover.

44. "When Alice came to sit beside me the sense of pleasure increased. I felt reassured too, protected, like a child. I could tell her everything and be sure she'd understand" (65). "I didn't feel any necessity to make love to her, and consequently had no fear of rejection" (43).

45. Older women are also an interest elsewhere in the novel. His best friend Charles writes from London: "so far I've been unable to find one of the rich old sugar-mammies with whom, I'd been given to understand, the place abounded" (147).

46. Compare with the love-for-the-town motif in Dreiser's *The Financier*. Nearly all the women he desires are in fact identified with the town. "I raised myself on my elbow and looked down at Warley in the valley below. I could see it all: the Town Hall with the baskets of flowers above the entrance, the boats on the river [. . .] I loved it all, right down to the red-brick front of the Christadelphian reading room and the posters outside the Coliseum and Royal cinemas, I couldn't leave it" (166). In this passage it is Susan who comes to embody the town, with his desire to "force the town into granting me the ultimate intimacy" shading a page later into what amounts to a rape.

47. In relation to the theme of other people's money, note that he catches a subordinate stealing petty cash and gives him the money to make it up (170).

48. The familiar homosocial aspect of upward mobility, here emerging between him and Jack Wales, is much stronger in the novel than the film. Alice has slept with Wales. He would have to be friends with Wales, or at least give up his hatred, in order to break free of his desire for Susan, an imitative desire that comes directly out of competition with Wales. Note that he pretends to be Jack Wales when with Mavis after Alice's death.

CHAPTER FIVE
THE HEALTH VISITOR

1. Carolyn Steedman, *Landscape for a Good Woman: A Story of Two Lives* (London: Virago, 1986), 2. On early working-class resentment of health visitors, see Pat Thane, "The Working Class and State 'Welfare' in Britain, 1880–1914,"

Historical Journal 27:4 (1984), 877–900: "There was resentment of the newly-appointed health visitors at the turn of the century for inspecting working-class homes and child-rearing practices, and too often offering well-meaning advice which was simply inappropriate to the lives of the underpaid in miserable homes. . . . Above all, individuals resented the unwillingness of 'reformers' to treat working people with the respect and good fellowship of equals" (893–94). A colliery weighman named Hobson is quoted as saying, "People dislike that sort of interference because it's applied to one class and not another" (894).

2. On Steedman and social mobility see Rita Felski, "Nothing to Declare: Identity, Shame, and the Lower Middle Class," *PMLA* 115 (January 2000), 33–45.

3. The so-called eleven-plus was a selective examination that determined which children would go to grammar schools or private schools, and which would remain in less privileged state schools, in the process often driving a wedge between children of the same families. The exam still exists, though much diminished in sociopolitical influence. The word *stretched* here seems to include some suggestion of torture, as if being examined were also being stretched on the rack—true to the social facts of how many were excluded by the eleven-plus exams, if not to Steedman's psychological experience of them. In this sense, what the state gives with one hand, it takes back with the other. Note too how the male teacher, who intervenes on the subject of her failing eyesight, doubles as both health visitor and examiner. She thinks he is being kind, but adds: "I preserved the voice so that I might later hear the disapproval in it. I think they must have used the eleven plus and the amount of blackboard work it involved as a lever [with her mother], because I got a pair of glasses before the exam" (45). I owe both insights to Helen Small of Pembroke College, University of Oxford. The relevant passage of the Education (Provision of Meals) Act, 1906 can be found in Maurice Bruce, ed., *The Rise of the Welfare State: English Social Policy, 1601–1971* (London: World University/Weidenfeld and Nicolson, 1973), 130.

4. Freud's famous discussion in *The Interpretation of Dreams* of the scene in which his father's hat was knocked into the gutter by a Gentile suggests that, far from being the counterexample Steedman suggests, the father's humiliation by higher social powers may count as a sort of founding fact of psychoanalysis. Even without belonging to the working class, the father cannot simply be identified with patriarchy.

5. The point of the welfare state was of course not to facilitate rising, but to prevent sinking. As James Kloppenberg puts it, the Webbs' "national minimum" scheme, introduced in 1897, "wanted the government to provide a floor of services, a national minimum standard beneath which no one would be allowed to sink in the areas of work, housing, health, and education" (253).

6. More might be said about the intimate connection between the mother's philosophy of "getting by" and what Perry Anderson calls "corporatism" or (with a bow to Hegel) "proletarian positivity"—the self-defensive density of a working-class culture that survives all too well, in part by virtue of welfare institutions, but at the cost of any radical ambitions for self-transforming social change. This connection would target both the mother's Prince Charming fantasies and her

welfare state realities, that is, her implicit choice of the welfare state as substitute for her disappointing and then absent husband. It would also target Steedman, Anderson, and myself to the extent that we are all state functionaries. Perry Anderson, *English Questions* (London: Verso, 1992), 36.

7. What might seem a confusion here between the symbolic and the material should I think be interpreted as the revelation of how disproportionately large a psychic benefit can be produced even by social programs that do not achieve anything like real material equality. Similarly, the U.S. formula "equality of opportunity," for whose British equivalent Steedman may seem to be showing excessive enthusiasm, could be said to aim much farther, and to deserve better, than the actual results of the programs it has inspired.

8. The historian who, as charitable rescuer of the past, tries to dislodge what E. P. Thompson called "the enormous condescension of posterity" can never escape either from self-interest or from some degree of condescension toward those rescued. Generalized from the historian to other figures who serve or represent the welfare state, the historical inescapability of condescension is one of the premises of this book.

9. See Carolyn Steedman, *Strange Dislocations: Childhood and the Idea of Human Interiority, 1780–1930* (Cambridge: Harvard University Press, 1995), chap. 7.

10. Steedman discovers after her mother's death that her mother has left behind substantial savings of £40,000, money she had apparently been saving in order to buy a house. This discovery has a complex effect on Steedman's story as we have been led to understand it. With the money her father continued to provide plus her mother's salary and some help from the state, they had enough to accumulate a respectable surplus. This means that to some extent the deprivation of her childhood was artificial. While they were hardly prosperous, doing without resulted from aspiration rather than from simple necessity. The model for the dream of purchasing a private home is middle-class: delayed gratification. Thus what the health visitor said to her mother has to be revalued. It was in part her mother's choice that rendered their home "not fit for a baby." The fault, if there is a fault, is shared out between the class system and her choice as an individual.

11. The possibility remains, of course, though Hoggart does not avail himself of it, that the isolation of the scholarship-boy misfit would be the midpoint rather than the endpoint of the narrative, which would go on to some other, perhaps more satisfying, conclusion.

12. As mentioned above, arguments like the one I've been making here, proposing that the development of the welfare state has played an obscure and underappreciated role in literary texts that seem to be about something quite different, have recently surfaced in two excellent books: Sean McCann's *Gumshoe America: Hard-Boiled Crime Fiction and the Rise and Fall of New Deal Liberalism* (Durham, NC: Duke University Press, 2000); and Michael Szalay, *New Deal Modernism: American Literature and the Invention of the Welfare State* (Durham, NC: Duke University Press, 2000).

13. Rosemary L. Bray, *Unafraid of the Dark: A Memoir* (New York: Doubleday, 1998).

14. Daniel T. Rodgers, *Atlantic Crossings: Social Politics in a Progressive Age* (Cambridge: Harvard University Press, 1998).

15. This labeling is perhaps justified by the fact that Rodriguez's family might be described as middle class, though it hovers in the lower range of that category.

16. Richard Rodriguez, *Hunger of Memory: The Education of Richard Rodriguez: An Autobiography* (Boston: Bantam, 1983); Richard Rodriguez, *Days of Obligation: An Argument with My Mexican Father* (New York: Viking, 1992). For critical reevaluation, see for example Randy A. Rodríguez, "Richard Rodriguez Reconsidered: Queering the Sissy (Ethnic) Subject," *TSLL (Texas Studies in Literature and Language)* 40:4 (Winter 1998), 396–423; Henry Staten, "Ethnic Authenticity, Class, and Autobiography: The Case of *Hunger of Memory*," *PMLA* 113:1 (January 1998), 103–16; and the dissertations of Sandra Soto (University of Texas at Austin) and Aureliano Maria De Soto, "Chicana/o Intellectuals: Politics, Polemics, and Paradigms," Ph.D. thesis in History of Consciousness (University of California at Santa Cruz, 2000).

17. It's worth observing that Hoggart (citing F.R. Leavis) describes what the scholarship boy is lacking as "poise" (241). Poise, or balance, could be seen as the organicism of class identity, either that of the upper class or of the working class, wishfully reestablished at a higher level. Or, alternatively, it could be what the state is supposed to represent.

18. Note that the mother's fatal error takes place in transcribing a Spanish word.

19. Rodriguez says at one point that his story "is not a version of Sammy Glick's" (4). But loss of authority by the immigrant father is exactly what Budd Schulberg says about "what makes Sammy run."

20. Rodriguez's homosexuality is also possibly important here as a private sign of irreconcilable difference with one's family and one's community, an unspoken reason accounting for the otherwise mysterious impossibility of ever going back or indeed remaining loyal. On the other hand, *Days of Obligation* suggests that here, too, betrayal is his mode. Rodriguez claims the expertise of the insider in order to sell back to outsiders their own harshest stereotypes about the gay community of San Francisco.

21. There is also a different and perhaps contradictory logic: the story of the loss is an affirmation that he still possesses the identity that he claims has been lost, and without which he would have nothing to sell. In other words, one might still argue that it is the identity rather than the loss that is his commodity.

22. Richard Rodriguez, *Brown: The Last Discovery of America* (New York: Penguin, 2002).

23. "In college, because of Lyndon Johnson, I became a 'minority student'" (94). But this was a transformation in which Nixon concurred. It was under "Nixon's administration that I became brown. A government document of dulling prose, Statistical Directive 15, would redefine America as an idea in five colors" (94).

24. Tillie Olsen, *Tell Me a Riddle*, introduction by Cora Kaplan (London: Virago, 1980 [1960]). A sign of its pedagogical ubiquitousness: the story is richly though not brilliantly represented as an essay topic in online archives selling term papers.

25. This is something that's not always recognized in the profusion of "writing back" exercises in which the same events are told from the daughter's perspective.

26. Reasons for guilt here might include the personal experiences of the mid-1930s that Olsen was drawing on in the story, though of course not reproducing exactly. There was a time when she herself had to send her daughter away not merely because she was poor but because she was trying get started as a writer.

27. It seems significant, then, that Emily's "let me go" phrase is attributed to the official interlocutor: "You spoke of her rare gift for comedy on the stage that rouses a laughter out of the audience so dear they applaud and do not want to let her go" (14).

28. To balance the picture here, it's worth remembering that responsibility is not merely the mantra of the welfare reformers, who in 1996 gave to the eviscera-tion of the Aid to Families with Dependent Children program the apt name of the Personal Responsibility and Work Opportunity Act. If it is used to strong-arm lower-income groups in the direction of an economic self-sufficiency they are kept back from ever achieving, it is also an explicit goal of official therapists. "In the therapeutic register," as Sanford F. Schram notes, "the notion of personal respon-sibility implies owning up to bad personal habits and disciplining oneself to avoid them" (32). See Schram, "Where the Welfare Queen Resides: The Subtext of Per-sonal Responsibility," in his *After Welfare: The Culture of Postindustrial Social Policy* (New York and London: New York University Press, 2000).

29. Alan Sillitoe, *The Loneliness of the Long-Distance Runner* (Harmonds-worth: Plume/Penguin, 1959).

30. Peter Hitchcock defends the political coherence of Smith's individualism in the following terms: "Although his battle is often intensely private, especially with the warden of the institution, the staging of this political position is overde-termined by a collective subjectivity which Smith speaks as 'us.' In any event, the triumph of his own battle, in deliberately losing the cross-country race, is a de-ferred victory in the individual and collective sense, for Smith knows, as we should, that coming to political consciousness is not in itself the act of overcoming 'them,' but a prelude to such an act. This realization defines Smith's loneliness" (102). Peter Hitchcock, *Working-Class Fiction in Theory and Practice: A Reading of Alan Sillitoe* (Ann Arbor: UMI Research Press, 1989).

31. Leslie Margolin, *Under the Cover of Kindness: The Invention of Social Work*, Foreword by Eileen Gambrill (Charlottesville and London: University Press of Virginia, 1997), 1.

32. The example is inspired by Priscilla Wald., "Cultures and Carriers: 'Ty-phoid Mary' and the Science of Social Control," *Social Text* 52/53 (December 1997), 181–214.

CHAPTER SIX
ON THE PERSISTENCE OF ANGER IN THE INSTITUTIONS OF CARING

1. Philip Fisher, *The Vehement Passions* (Princeton: Princeton University Press, 2002). "Anger is the necessary bridge between a purely internal account of the passions and an interest in action, because it is with anger that the aroused state in the soul or spirit has the most immediate links to the physical acts of our fists or our body in the outer world" (172).

2. For Aristotle, Fisher explains, anger could and should be felt on behalf on injuries done to "those close to us, our friends, family members, and certain others" (174). Today, Fisher says, the emotion is more egocentric; one is more likely to feel anger on one's own behalf. But there has also been an extension in the range of those who, if injured, become legitimate causes of anger. Indeed, it is distinctive of modernity that anger should be felt on behalf of "strangers" or "others" (174). The threat to proper anger depends of course on the scale and nature of the social unit; it is one aspect of a more general process by which personal, intimate feeling adapts to the impersonality of a social space in which there must be concern for strangers. Care for strangers of course could define the welfare state, but it also would have to include noncitizens. This helps explain Sianne Ngai's impulse to treat feelings like envy that lack anger's "cultural recognition as a valid mode of publicly recognizing or responding to social disparities" Sianne Ngai, *Ugly Feelings* (Cambridge: Harvard University Press, 2005), 128. Ngai's position, useful as contrast to Fisher, is that "in the transnational stage of capitalism that defines our contemporary moment, our emotions no longer link up as securely as they once did with the models of social action and transformation theorized by Aristotle, Thomas Hobbes, and others under the signs of relatively unambiguous emotions like anger and fear" (5).

3. Malcolm Bradbury, *Rates of Exchange* (London: Picador, 1983), 21.

4. On the human consequences of "welfare reform," see for example Jason DeParle, *American Dream: Three Women, Ten Kids, and a Nation's Drive to End Welfare* (New York: Viking, 2004).

5. David Lodge, *Nice Work* (London: Secker and Warburg, 1988).

6. Pat Barker, *Border Crossing* (New York: Farrar Straus and Giroux, 2001).

7. Pat Barker, *Double Vision* (New York: Farrar Straus and Giroux, 2003).

8. There is perhaps an echo here, at a much higher level of cultural sophistication, of the Reagan-era film allegories of *Alien* and *Predator*, where the socially representative "team" is little by little reduced, in the face of pure threatening alienness, to one lone survivor, forced to fend for him- or herself alone: *homo economicus* extricated from the encumbrances of both the corporation and the welfare state.

9. Richard Sennett, *Respect in a World of Inequality* (New York: Norton, 2003).

10. James F. English, *Comic Transactions: Literature, Humor, and the Politics of Community in Twentieth-Century Britain* (Ithaca: Cornell University Press, 1994). D. J. Taylor notes in *After the War: The Novel and English Society since 1945* (London: Chatto and Windus, 1993) that A. S. Byatt's character Frederica in *Still Life* (1985) "is able knowledgeably to place Jim's antics as part of what was known as 'the limited revolt of the intellectuals against the welfare state'" (68). Taylor says neither he nor Byatt would agree with this sociological placement, but a page later he does not disagree with Malcolm Bradbury's assessment that his own fiction belongs within "a report on the new England of the welfare state" (69).

11. This section draws on my essay "What the Porter Saw: On the Academic Novel," in James F. English, ed., *A Concise Companion to Contemporary British Fiction* (Oxford: Blackwell, 2006), 248–66.

12. Malcolm Bradbury, *The History Man* (London: Picador, 2000).

13. Richard Hoggart, *The Uses of Literacy* (Harmondsworth: Penguin, 1959).

14. J. M. Coetzee, *Disgrace* (New York: Viking, 1999).

15. Malcolm Bradbury, *Rates of Exchange* (London: Picador, 1983).

16. Howard Jacobson, *Coming from Behind* (London: Chatto and Windus, 1983). Attempting to synthesize the regular guy perspective of *Lucky Jim* with the alienated Jewish figure of Philip Roth's *Portnoy's Complaint*, Jacobson seems to insist more than is strictly necessary on his hero's heterosexuality, or his heroic refusal to be politically correct about homosexuality. The climax of the novel, a sort of conversational jousting for the prize of a job at Cambridge and a version of Jim Dixon's antilecture, allows the hero to substitute a sexual for a scholarly triumph.

17. Christine likes the odious Bertrand, however, because of his ambition (144), precisely the quality that Jim is lacking.

18. English notes that in Amis and the academic novel in general a bottom-up working-class hostility to "dissident 'middle-class subculture'" (149) mixes with top-down aristocratic disdain, thereby blurring any clear class politics. But the welfare state too involved a blurring of class politics. Kingsley Amis, *Lucky Jim* (London: Gollancz, 1955).

19. Introduction, *Hedgehog Review* 2:3 (Fall 2000).

20. Gerald Graff, Foreword to Jerry Herron, *Universities and the Myth of Cultural Decline* (Detroit: Wayne State University Press, 1988),10, 9–19.

21. Neil J. Smelser, "The Politics of Ambivalence: Diversity in the Research Universities," in Jonathan R. Cole, Elinor G. Barber, and Stephen R. Graubard, eds., *The Research University in a Time of Discontent* (Baltimore and London: Johns Hopkins University Press, 1994), 37–53.

22. Consider for example Ellis Cose's *The Rage of a Privileged Class* (1993). Cose presents the rage of the African American middle class as if its sole cause were the persistence of racism. The complaints of the African American middle class about racism are clearly well founded. But they don't account for the full richness and complexity of the anger, which is clearly and deeply infused with guilt, ambivalence about their own success and the institutions that made it possible, loyalty to those who have not risen. Ellis Cose, *The Rage of a Privileged Class* (New York: Harper, 1993).

23. Kazuo Ishiguro, *Never Let Me Go* (London: Faber and Faber, 2005).

24. Of course, this could always be the fault of the dreams themselves, as suggested by "film stars." The clause "working in supermarkets" seems added in order to head off that interpretation; in our world, the supermarket is a sort of class-neutral site, by no means impossible as a goal of eventual employment, though it might be especially attractive to the cloned kids, who are not allowed outside the grounds to shop.

25. A usefully synoptic discussion of how the styles and stages of working-class youth subculture relate to the ideology of upward mobility can be found in Dick Hebdige, *Subculture: The Meaning of Style* (London: Methuen, 1979). Hebdige cites for example Phil Cohen's argument that the skinhead style was "'a metastatement about the whole process of social mobility' produced by the systematic exaggeration of those elements within mod style which were self-evi-

dently proletarian" (55). See Phil Cohen, "Sub-cultural Conflict and Working Class Community," Working Papers in Cultural Studies, 2, University of Birmingham (1972). Hebdige: "The music papers were filled with the familiar success stories describing the route from rags to rags and riches—of punk musicians flying to America, of bank clerks become magazine editors or record producers, of harassed seamstresses turned overnight into successful business women" (99). The effect was ambiguous, as Hebdige says: the impression of "limitless upward mobility" thus given "reinforced the image of the open society which the very presence of the punk subculture—with its rhetorical emphasis on unemployment, high-rise living and narrow options—had originally contradicted" (99).

26. Note the ethnographic effect of getting us to read with the eyes of this subculture, like the wonderful moment when Tommy catches Kathy speed-reading pornographic magazines and suddenly realizes why; she's looking only at the faces, searching for a match with her genetic "mother."

27. The passage continues, linking her up with Ryder: "But all this rushing about you do. All this getting exhausted and being by yourself. I've been watching you. It's wearing you out. You must do, Kath, you must sometimes wish they'd tell you you can stop." Kathy's own self-description is even more reminiscent of The Unconsoled's Ryder: "Then there's the solitude. You grow up surrounded by crowds of people, that's all you've ever known, and suddenly you're a carer. You spend hour after hour, on your own, driving across the country, centre to centre, sleeping in overnights, no one to talk to about your worries, no one to have a laugh with. . . . You're always in a rush, or else you're too exhausted to have a proper conversation. Soon enough, the long hours, the traveling, the broken sleep have all crept into your being and become part of you" (189).

28. Ishiguro seems not to want to present this system as either exclusively private or exclusively public, the sole result of the profit motive or of government bureaucracy. The point seems to be that it doesn't much matter. The "they" is not seen as divided in this way, though it's divided in other ways—ways discovered to be so trivial, as one expects to find that a hint of division will reveal someone's full revolt and each time is disappointed to see the divisions are only *within* the horror.

29. Elsewhere in this novel Ishiguro alludes to earnest movements of dissenting opinion—for example, opponents of the "progressive" school where Kathy, Tommy, and Ruth go—that take themselves seriously, and are so taken, yet clearly miss the point entirely. Indeed, this is another of his signature effects. So we cannot assume that "It simply wasn't his fault" represents an ideological position to reckon with.

30. Louis Menand, "Anxious in Dreamland," *New York Times Book Review*, October 15, 1995, 7; see also James Wood, "The Human Difference," *New Republic*, May 16, 2005.

31. It would perhaps be possible to read Kathy's gesture differently: as an act of solidarity with Ruth. Taking the erotic element away from their triangle—and it's so weak that it would hardly be missed—Ruth would seem to stand for Tommy's opposite: creative, successful, competitive, and aspiring (it is her "possible" and the attendant image of work in a modern office that represent aspiration for

the children). Unlike Kathy, she believes in fault: Ruth has said "it's his own fault. If he learned to keep his cool, they'd leave him alone" (9).

32. Perhaps the purest expression of love in the novel is when Tommy, knowing his impending donation is likely to be his last, sends Kathy away, saying he doesn't want her anymore as his carer: "I don't want to be that way in front of you" (257).

33. *La sociologie est un sport de combat*, produced by C-P Productions and VF Films, (Brooklyn, NY: First Run/Icarus Films, 2001). Part of this section first appeared in slightly different form in the *The London Review of Books*, to which I am grateful for permission to reprint.

34. Pierre Bourdieu, *Esquisse pour une auto-analyse* (Paris: Raisons d'Agir, 2004).

35. Michel Onfray, *Célébration du génie colérique: Tombeau de Pierre Bourdieu* (Paris: Galilée, 2002); Philippe Corcuff, *Bourdieu autrement: Fragilités d'un sociologue du combat* (Paris: Textuel, 2003).

36. Jacques Bouveresse, *Bourdieu, savant et politique* (Marseille: Agone, 2004).

37. Perry Anderson, "Union Sucrée," *London Review of Books*, September 23, 2004, 15, 10–16. This discussion does not appear in Anderson's *Spectrum: From Right to Left in the World of Ideas* (London: Verso, 2005).

38. Pierre Bourdieu, *Science of Science and Reflexivity*, trans Richard Nice (Cambridge: Polity and University of Chicago Press, 2004). "The history that I shall relate here is not inspired by the concern to aggrandize the person who delivers it" (9). If he hadn't pointed that out, one might have misunderstood entirely. The palimpsestic quality, with comments that had been added to the lectures later printed in smaller type, is frequently an opportunity to score another point at the expense of "my critics" or to muse on accomplishments of his own in the area under discussion which he had inadvertently omitted to mention. "When one is young—this is elementary sociology of science—other things being equal, one has less capital, and also less competence, and so, almost by definition, one is inclined to put oneself forward in opposition to the established figures, and therefore look critically at their work" (13). He does not apply this model when he uses an interposed section to regret and rebuke the apostasy of a former student like Karin Knorr-Cetina, who unlike the young challenger of his model, first cited her mentor Bourdieu "very positively" (36), and only little by little arrived at a "critique" that shows "a very high degree of incomprehension" (37). The unconscious comedy of these score-settling moments is not quite dispelled by the knowledge that this was, after all, a last course of lectures. It is strange that in such moments Bourdieu ignores what might be called the "sucking-up" model of professional success, with which he is most associated: "the tendency of the 'scholarship boy' towards awestruck hyperidentification with the educational system" (91).

39. In Bourdieu's style, oxymoronic phrases like "regulated improvisation" and "unconscious strategy" habitually try to have it both ways. The "habitus," his term for an individual's largely unconscious knowledge of his or her context, is both structured (from without) and structuring (enabling the individual to improvise actions that may change the context). Fair enough, and one of sociology's more intriguing ripostes to *homo economicus*. But Bourdieu goes on to boast that

the concept transcends the oppositions that everyone else remains stuck within: objective versus subjective, practical versus theoretical, and so on. If overcoming oppositions required nothing more than coining a term and quarreling more or less violently with proponents of each opposing side, there would be less doubt as to Bourdieu's right to count it among his achievements.

40. In Tommy's case, as we saw, the mentor/benefactor Miss Lucy appears as a Bourdieu-like figure, spending her time in power, however limited, trying to be a rebel. In his studies of education, Bourdieu is reluctant to allow this possibility to the role of teacher.

41. Paul Willis, *Learning to Labor: How Working Class Kids Get Working Class Jobs* (New York: Columbia University Press, 1981 [1977]).

42. The idea that emotions that seem to represent disaffection are really means of making the system work also appears in Paolo Virno (in Ngai's account): "the classic 'sentiments of disenchantment' that once marked positions of radical alienation from the system of wage labor—anxiety, distraction, and cynicism—are now perversely integrated, from the factory to the office, into contemporary capitalist production itself: 'Fears of particular dangers, if only virtual ones, haunt the workday like a mood that cannot be escaped. This fear, however, is transformed into *an operational requirement*, a special tool of the trade. Insecurity about one's place during periodic innovation, fear of losing recently gained privileges, and anxiety over being "left behind" translate into flexibility, adaptability, and a readiness to reconfigure oneself.' Here we see how capitalism's classic affects of disaffection (and thus of potential social conflict and political antagonism) are neatly reabsorbed by the wage system and reconfigured into professional ideals. Nothing could be further from Fredric Jameson's more widely known thesis about the 'waning' of negative affect" (4) Ngai, *Ugly Feelings*.

43. David Mills and Robert Gibb, " 'Centre' and Periphery—An Interview with Paul Willis," *Cultural Anthropology* 16:3 (2001), 388–414.

44. The constitutive hesitation in both cases between working class and petit bourgeois invites comparison with Carolyn Steedman. "My immediate group was classic working-class, grammar-school selected, upwardly-aspirant, many of whom I still know" Carolyn Steedman, *Landscape for a Good Woman* (London Virago, 1986), 393.

45. School sports work better than school itself to disguise the inequalities waiting on the other side, for unlike educational achievement, athletic achievement cannot be correlated with the social rank of the parents. For Willis and Bourdieu, as for Ishiguro's Tommy and John Updike's Rabbit Angstrom, glory on the school playing field sets itself apart from the glories that will or more likely will not follow in the real world.

46. The risk that his work will be seen as a betrayal never quite goes away: "You take from trust-like and reciprocal relations something which is then one-sidedly and academically 'marketized' as public, exchangeable: ripped out of local use for a particular kind of exchange value. You take it off and cash it in the academy, such as *Learning to Labor*" (413).

47. Richard Sennett, *Respect in a World of Inequality* (New York: Norton, 2003).

48. One might argue that Sennett sees "no denouement" (221) to the welfare state story only because there is one denouement that, even indefinitely postponed, he is unwilling to envisage: an end to inequality. If so, this is no doubt in part because his commitment to sociology, the field where he has accumulated his personal merit, impels him to insist that "society," sociology's object of knowledge, is distinct from material interests, the currency in which equality and inequality are measured. Sennett makes this argument explicit in his introduction to Richard Sennett and Jonathan Cobb, *The Hidden Injuries of Class* (New York: Vintage, 1972), where he defends the aphorism "Man does not live by bread alone" and warns that "a politics of working-class revolt based principally on material deprivation" will mislead us into "conservative enemy territory" (7). His autonomy depends on the discipline's autonomy, and the discipline's autonomy requires that the social should remain irreducible to the economic.

49. Sennett is highly critical of "the dream of autonomous work" in Sennett and Cobb, *The Hidden Injuries of Class*, 239. Yet only the assumption that there exists such a thing as economic autonomy can explain Sennett's description of "the act which is at the heart of any welfare system" as "making a gift" (*Respect*, 137). If he believed in "mutual dependence" as seriously as he has frequently said (for example, in *The Corrosion of Character*), his undoubtedly sincere and passionate defense of the welfare system against the charge of parasitism would make of welfare not a gift but a right.

50. Alan Ryan, "Call Me Mister," *The New York Review of Books* February 27, 2003, 31–34.

51. Richard Sennett, *The Fall of Public Man On the Social Psychology of Capitalism* (New York: Vintage, 1976).

52. Richard Sennett, *The Corrosion of Character: The Personal Consequences of Work in the New Capitalism* (New York: Norton, 1998).

53. Unlike "craft," public service obviously does include other people. Yet it is not implausibly altruistic. Self-interest and the desire for autonomy need not disguise themselves as something else; Sennett argues against "the error of believing that doing good necessarily entails self-sacrifice" (*The Corrosion of Character*, 202–3).

54. The narrative of Ishiguro's Kathy would make an interesting case to investigate in these terms.

55. The careers the sociologist provides for others are not pecuniarily equal to the career he has made for himself—though some, like that of the executive in *The Corrosion of Character*, may well be more rather than less lucrative. When the career is caring, inequality does not necessarily shrink or disappear.

56. Like the recipients of welfare, and for that matter like all the "caring" professions and their clients, sociologists are liable to the accusation of being "unproductive." But if they were seen as unproductive, then the same would have to be said about the whole service sector, private as well as public, no matter how profitable that sector may be.

57. Jason DeParle gives the example of a single mother on welfare, Angie, who becomes a helper in a nursing home and takes pride and pleasure in her job even though it does not bring the sort of stability it's supposed to—more than a bit like Ishiguro's Kathy.

58. Brent Staples, *Parallel Time: Growing Up in Black and White* (New York: Avon, 1994), 3.

59. John Edgar Wideman, *Brothers and Keepers* (New York: Vintage, 1984). The brothers agree that "most avenues of success had been blocked or blown" (169). The one exception Robby mentions is another federally funded project, a public service job educating those for whom there is no level playing field. Before he takes the drug route, Robby "was working at a center for retarded kids. Best job I ever had. . . . I liked the kids and the kids liked me" (136–37). The recipient of welfare remains a "character no one would want." In Robby's words: "We supposed to die. Take our little welfare checks and be quiet and die. That ain't news to nobody. It's what's happening every day in Homewood" (132). For Robby, at least, the word *welfare* does not seem to invoke the experience of providing state services, just the experience of receiving them.

CONCLUSION
THE LUCK OF BIRTH AND THE INTERNATIONAL DIVISION OF LABOR

1. This desolate image of caring is perhaps a distant and disappointed echo of Holden Caulfield's titular field-dream of meaningfulness in *The Catcher in the Rye*. Ishiguro, *Never Let Me Go*.

2. T. H. Marshall and Tom Bottomore, *Citizenship and Social Class* (London: Pluto Press, 1991). I discuss Disraeli's case for imperialism in terms of upward mobility in " 'The East Is a Career': Edward Said and the Logics of Professionalism," in Michael Sprinker, ed., *Edward Said: A Critical Reader* (London: Basil Blackwell, 1992), 48–73. Nicholas Dames argues "that the bureaucratized colonial governance of the mid-to-late nineteenth century provides British culture with its first image of the careerist" (271) in "Trollope and the Career: Vocational Trajectories and the Management of Ambition," *Victorian Studies* (Winter 2003), 247–78.

3. Debra Dickerson, *An American Story* (New York: Pantheon, 2000).

4. For Dickerson's powerful version of the "brother left behind" motif, see "Who Shot Johnny?" in Ian Frazier, ed., *The Best American Essays, 1997* (Boston: Houghton Mifflin, 1997), 46–50.

5. Caryl Phillips, *A Distant Shore* (New York: Knopf, 2003); Lorraine Adams, *Harbor* (New York: Knopf, 2004).

6. *A Distant Shore* ends in an asylum, and one could easily read it therefore as accusing the official institutions of public health and welfare in much the style of Gilman's "The Yellow Wallpaper." "They say they're protecting us. In here, time doesn't matter. At night they allow me to leave the windows open and I watch the shadows of the trees making strange shapes against my wall. I know this is not Weston. Or Stoneleigh. There is no viaduct in the distance. My heart remains a desert, but I tried. I had a feeling that Solomon understood me. This is not my home, and until they accept this, then I will be as purposefully silent as a bird in flight" (277). Dorothy never liked Stoneleigh, and she discovers after the racist reception of Solomon that she doesn't like Weston either. These are places that have not treated her well as a woman, or as an aging woman. They are home, yet

have for this reason become strange even before the discovery of racism. So the state institution that is not her home is where she waits, as if waiting for the bus, for a different public space to emerge that would be more like a genuine home.

7. Note that in giving Solomon a lift, Mike sets the benefactor pattern by which Solomon will later give Dorothy a lift.

8. The disjunction between the chronology of the events and the order in which they are narrated, which puts Solomon's murder early, well before his rescue, seems intended to balance the emphasis, allowing for a less ironic insistence on how the helping gets done and a more positive sense of its value. This way of having the cake of upward mobility while eating it too invites comparison with Junot Diaz's *Drown*, which as I've noted rearranges its anti–upward mobility materials so as to give seemingly anomalous prominence to the father's triumphant coming-to-America narrative.

9. In *Democracy and the Foreigner* Bonnie Honig suggests, commenting on the popularity of naturalization photos in newspapers, that Americans appear to need their commitment to their political system affirmed by noncitizens because that commitment has become so weak among citizens themselves. It's worth asking whether the same has happened to upward mobility stories.

10. "Upward Mobility in the Postcolonial Era: Kincaid, Mukherjee, and the Cosmopolitan Au Pair," *Modernism/Modernity* 1:2 (1994), 133–51. Reprinted in Bruce Robbins, *Feeling Global: Internationalism in Distress* (New York: New York University Press, 1999).

11. The phrase "upward mobility" figures with a strange prominence in Spivak's arguments. On the same page, she claims, unlike other critics of metropolitan postcolonialism, "a productive acknowledgment of complicity" (xii). "Feminism within the social relations and institutions of the metropolis has something like a relationship with the fight for individualism in the upwardly class-mobile bourgeois cultural politics of the European nineteenth century" (148). Within the arena of "tertiary education in literature, the upwardly mobile exmarginal, *justifiably* searching for validation, can help commodify marginality" (170). She also describes "the mainstream project of Western feminism" as one that "both continues and displaces the battle over the right to individualism between women and men in situations of upward class mobility" (282). This section has appeared in slightly different form as "Soul Making: Gayatri Spivak on Upward Mobility," *Cultural Studies* 17:1 (2003), 16–26.

12. Samir Amin, who seems to be Spivak's main source, argues in *Class and Nation* (New York: Monthly Review Press, 1980) that there has been a "social-democratic alliance" between the metropolitan bourgeoisie, the affluent metropolitan working class (cut off from unprivileged minorities, women, etc.), and the satellite/comprador bourgeoisie at the periphery.

13. On page 69 of *A Critique*, Spivak begins a footnote of almost a page and a half explaining that the international division of labor does not reflect, cannot be derived from, is not a mere extension of, the social division of labor of which Marx spoke. When Balibar describes "the term 'proletariat' [as] only connot[ing] the 'transitional' nature of the working class," Spivak takes his description as "the moment where the Marxian text transgresses its own protocols—so far as Balibar is our guide—so that it can be turned around and let the subaltern (who is not

coterminus with the proletarian) enter in the colonial phase, and today make room for the globe-girdling nationalist-under-erasure Southern (rather than only the Eurocentric migrant) subject who would dislocate Economic Citizenship by constant interruption" (69n). Gayatri Chakravorty Spivak, *A Critique of Postcolonial Reason: Toward a History of the Vanishing Present* (Cambridge: Harvard University Press, 1999).

14. This is indeed the purpose for which the concept of the international division of labor was introduced. In addition to the modified dependency theory of Amin, who uses the phrase consistently, see Immanuel Wallerstein, "Class Conflict in the Capitalist World-Economy" in Etienne Balibar and Immanuel Wallerstein, *Race Nation Class: Ambiguous Identities* (London: Verso, 1991), 115–24: "At a certain level of expansion of income and 'rights,' the 'proletarian' becomes in reality a 'bourgeois,' *living off the surplus-value of others*, and the most immediate effect of this is on class consciousness" (122). Robert Brenner charges that Wallerstein equates "capitalism with a trade-based division of labor" (38), thereby imitating not Marx but Adam Smith. The key to this "neo-Smithian Marxism" is its subsumption of "class relations within the broader . . . development of a trade-based division of labor" (39). "The dynamic of development clearly resides in trade, not in . . . class relations" (56). Robert Brenner, "The Origins of Capitalist Development: a Critique of Neo-Smithian Marxism," *New Left Review* 104 (July—August 1977), 25–92.

15. The title question "can the subaltern speak?" is in fact asked with regard to the challenge to speech posed most unambiguously not by "discourse" but by the international division of labor. The sentence comes at the end of the essay, and it begins, "On the other side of the international division of labor from socialized capital, inside *and* outside the circuit of the epistemic violence of imperialist law and education supplementing an earlier economic text, *can the subaltern speak?*" (269).

16. It's in the context of luck that one might return to the difficult area of existential self-obligation raised in the previous chapter apropos of Ishiguro's *Never Let Me Go*.

17. Bernard Williams, "Moral Luck," in Daniel Statman, ed., *Moral Luck* (Albany: State University of New York Press, 1993).

18. Williams says this about Gauguin (37ff): "in such a situation the only thing that will justify his choice will be success itself. If he fails . . . then he did the wrong thing" (38). But this doesn't mean he can justify himself *to others* (38). "Even if he succeeds, he will not thereby acquire a right that they accept what he has to say: if he fails, he will not even have anything to say" (38). "Granted that Gauguin offended a certain conception of the ethical in abandoning his family," David Statman writes, "it is still far from certain that we would like to condemn him for that when taking into account his great success as a painter. Gauguin encourages us to put a limit to the 'imperialist' character of ethical concerns, which seek to invade the whole practical realm" (9). As Statman notes, Thomas Nagel objects that "if success does not permit Gauguin to justify himself to others, but still determines his most basic feelings, that shows only that his most basic feelings need not be moral" (8). In other words, the desire to be a successful painter is simply not moral. To which Williams responds, in a postscript, that the force of

the example for him was precisely that it did make a moral claim. "I took the case of artistic activity because the products of that activity, not least in a 'romantic' or bohemian form, are things that people concerned about the ethical . . . often take to be valuable" (Statman, 255). This is of course very close to the question that those of us who live off literature, art, culture must ask ourselves, and that Spivak has specialized in helping us ask: is there something ethically "valuable" in our own "artistic activity" that offsets or changes our sense of privilege and betrayal?

19. *Jane Eyre* is the contrasting term, standing for the implication of imperialism in the story of metropolitan subject-formation and upward mobility—specifically, "progressive" or transgressive subject formation, since the key example is feminism.

20. Jamaica Kincaid, *Lucy* (New York: Farrar Straus Giroux, 1990). Compare: "Gauguin might have been a man who was not at all interested in the claims on him, and simply preferred to live another life, and from that life, and perhaps from that preference, his best paintings came." This is Williams speaking (37), but to my ear at least, it might have been Kincaid.

21. Gayatri Chakravorty Spivak, "Thinking Cultural Questions in 'Pure' Literary Terms," in Paul Gilroy, Lawrence Grossberg, and Angela McRobbie, eds., *Without Guarantees: In Honor of Stuart Hall* (London: Verso, 2000), 335–57.

22. Alain Lipietz, *Mirages and Miracles: The Crises of Global Fordism*, trans. David Macey (London: Verso, 1987). Empirically, there is no doubt that the international division of labor exists. All you have to do is compare income or life expectancy figures for Sweden and Sierra Leone. On the conceptual level, however, this way of naming global injustice remains open to question. See also Alfredo C. Robles, Jr., *French Theories of Regulation and Conceptions of the International Division of Labour* (London: St. Martin's Press, 1994).

23. Wang Hui, *China's New Order: Society, Politics, and Economy in Transition*, ed. Theodore Huters (Cambridge: Harvard University Press, 2003).

24. Duane Swank, *Global Capital, Political Institutions, and Policy Change in Developed Welfare States* (Cambridge: Cambridge University Press, 2002).

Index

achievement: in Braine, 156; in Dreiser, 100; in Ishiguro, 200; in Rodriguez, 170; in Staples, 197; in Steedman, 162; in Stendhal, 31; Thomas on, xvi, 169; in upward mobility stories, 34; in Wideman, 197–198. *See also* advancement; reward; rise; success

Adams, Lorraine, *Harbor,* 21, 236

advancement: in Balzac, 11; in Dickens, 11; in Harris, 1, 2, 3, 4, 5, 6, 7, 8; in O'Faolain, 53; in Stendhal, 46, 48. *See also* achievement; rise; success

affirmative action, in Rodriguez, 176, 177, 178

African Americans, 58, 74, 168, 169, 193, 229, 230, 234, 279n22

Alger, Horatio, 67–73, 80, 81, 88, 93, 103, 168; and Dickens, 75; and Doctorow, 118; and Dreiser, 98; *Ragged Dick,* 38, 68–69, 70–71, 75, 100; *Struggling Upward,* 67, 68

All About Eve (film), 52, 273n43

Allen, Joseph, 68

Allen, Woody, *Bullets over Broadway,* 12

Althusser, Louis, 6

Alvarez, Julia, *How the Garcia Girls Lost Their Accents,* 236

ambition: in Amis, 196; in Balzac, 12, 31, 39, 40, 60; in Dickens, 12, 50, 51; in Doctorow, 120; in Dreiser, 98; in G. Du Maurier, 134; in Gissing, 55; in Harris, 4, 8; in Ishiguro, 200; in Márai, 138–139; and older woman, 12; in Olsen, 182; in Rodriguez, 171, 178; in Stendhal, 43, 46–47, 48, 50; in upward mobility stories, xiii

Amin, Samir, 238

Amis, Kingsley, *Lucky Jim,* 196–197

ancien régime, 35, 37

Ancients and Moderns debate, 33

Anderson, Perry, 141, 146–147, 150, 151, 205, 213, 274n6; "The Figures of Descent," 141–142; "Origins of the Present Crisis," 137–138, 147–148

anger: of Bourdieu, 210–211, 217, 218, 219; at class system, 21; in *Good Will Hunting,* 206; in Ishiguro, 206, 208, 210; and Sennett, 227; in Sillitoe, 185; in Staples, 229–230; in Steedman, 158, 160; in upward mobility stories, xiii; and welfare state, 20, 190, 192–194, 206, 220; Willis on, 219, 220

Angry Young Men, 152, 193

Arendt, Hannah, *Rahel Varnhagen,* 13, 16, 52, 139, 140

aristocracy: Anderson on, 141, 142, 147, 149; in Arendt, 140; in Balzac, 40; in Gissing, 140, 143; and literary criticism, 131; in Márai, 138, 140; and noble foundling motif, 36; and patron, 17; in Rodriguez, 178; in Shaw, 149, 151; in Steedman, 161, 163; in Stendhal, 34–35, 36, 37–38, 40, 47, 48; in Wells, 140; and writer, 19

Aron, Raymond, 214

art: and bohemia, 132, 140; Bourdieu on, 133; in Franklin, 135; in G. Du Maurier, 133, 134; in Gissing, 145; and independence, 133; in Ishiguro, 232; in upward mobility stories, 19–20; in Wells, 136

artist: in Dickens, 140, 141; in Doctorow, 126; in Franklin, 131; in upward mobility stories, 128. *See also* writer

aspiration: in Harris, 3, 6; in Ishiguro, 206–207, 208

Auerbach, Erich, 17, 37, 40, 250n28; *Mimesis,* 34–35, 36

autonomy, 198; and bohemia, 132; in Brontë, 64; in Constant, 29; Foucault on, 92; Sennett on, 193, 224–225; and state, 14; in Steedman, 164. *See also* independence

Balibar, Étienne, 9, 285n13

Balzac, Honoré de, 18, 22, 25, 26; and de Berny, 26; and Dickens, 76; and Dreiser, 61, 62, 65, 256n19; and Gissing, 256n16; *Le Lys dans la vallée,* 26; *Les Illusions Perdues,* 26–27, 132, 251n29,